Revised Edition

The Handbook of
MORTGAGE BANKING

Trends,
Opportunities
and Strategies

Jess Lederman, Editor

PROBUS PUBLISHING COMPANY
Chicago, Illinois
Cambridge, England

ISBN 1-55738-494-0

Printed in the United States of America

BB

CTV/BJS

1 2 3 4 5 6 7 8 9 0

For the men and women of the mortgage banking industry—from the smallest retail shop to the nationwide wholesaler—you make it happen

Table of Contents

Section I:
The Mortgage Banking Industry

Chapter 1

Chapter 2

Chapter 3

Section II:
Programs for Mortgage Origination:
Meeting the Need for Mortgage Finance

Section III
Opportunities in the Secondary Market

Section IV
Developments in Mortgage Loan Servicing

Section V:
Shaping Mortgage Banking Operations for Success

Contributing Authors

Arthur B. Axelson
Pepper, Hamilton & Scheetz

David Barkley
Freddie Mac

Mary Bruce Batte
Mortgage Dynamics, Inc.

Jan Beaven
Symmetrix, Inc.

Richard Bryan
Freddie Mac

Jeffery F. Butler
Countrywide Funding Corp.

Coopers & Lybrand Risk Analysis Group
Coopers & Lybrand

Jack Daly
Pratt • Daly Corporation

Frank Demarais
Fannie Mae

Douglas D. Foster
Alliance Mortgage Company

Clay S. Green
Coldwell Banker Residential Mortgage Services

Stephen Z. Hoff
Hamilton, Carter, Smith & Co.

John J. Jacobs IV
BancPlus Mortgage Corporation

Don M. "Dusty" Lashbrook
Maryland National Mortgage Corporation

Jess Lederman
Author and Private Investor

John E. Lott
Mortgage Dynamics, Inc.

Rick L. McGuire
Inland Mortgage Corporation

John F. Macke
Inland Mortgage Corporation

John P. McMurray
BancPlus Mortgage Corporation

Cam Melchiorre
Commonwealth Mortgage Assurance Company

Patricia A. Mikel
PMI Mortgage Insurance Co.

D. William Mulcahy
Mortgage Flex Systems Inc.

Fred Portner
Symmetrix, Inc.

Warren A. Raybould
Freddie Mac

Howard Schneider
Freelance Writer

Anthony W. Schweiger
*Consultant to Mortgage Banking Financial Services
and other businesses*

Gary S. Smuckler
Pepper, Hamilton & Scheetz

Gordon Steinbach
Mortgage Guaranty Insurance Company

Hunter W. Wolcott
*Reserve Financial Management Corp.
RF/Spectrum Decision Science Corp.*

Preface

Since the first edition of this book appeared in 1987, the mortgage banking industry has been almost completely transformed. In the fall of 1982 I began working with some of the most talented mortgage professionals in the country to create a completely revised version. Our goal was to look back and analyze the experiences of the late 1980s and early 1990s and draw conclusions that mortgage bankers can use to successfully compete in the years ahead.

Thanks to the outstanding efforts of its expert authors, *The Handbook of Mortgage Banking: Trends, Opportunities and Strategies* includes 23 entirely new chapters and offers a wealth of information to industry participants, from newcomers to seasoned professionals.

Chapters 1-6 present a broad perspective of the strategic, legal, and economic dynamics of the mortgage banking industry.

Chapters 7-10 discuss both traditional and innovative origination strategies, as well as issues in production management and automation.

Chapters 11-15 describe the current state-of-the-art and science of secondary marketing and hedging interest rate risk, including a full description of Fannie Mae and Freddie Mac programs.

Chapters 16-18 explore several aspects of mortage loan servicing, and cover cost factors, purchase and sale, and valuation.

Chapters 19-25 provide a comprehensive overview of mortgage banking operations, including automation, new technological developments, warehousing, underwriting, and loss minimization techniques.

Many thanks must be given to each of the contributing authors for the time and energy they took from their hectic schedules to produce a significant contribution to the existing body of literature on mortgage finance. A special thanks also to Janet Reilley Hewitt, editor of *Mortgage Banking* magazine, and Warren Lasko and Lynn Powell of the MBA, whose help was invaluable.

Jess Lederman

I
The Mortgage Banking Industry

Chapter 1

LESSONS LEARNED: AN OVERVIEW OF THE MORTGAGE BANKING INDUSTRY, 1980–1993

Jess Lederman
Author and Private Investor

When I first entered the world of mortgage finance in 1980, it didn't take very long to master the tools of the trade. Thirty year fixed rate mortgages were the norm. Mortgage bankers had only recently begun venturing beyond government lending into conventional production, and jumbo lending was essayed only by a daring few. Because of the rapid home price appreciation experienced during the late 1970s, 'credit risk' was considered an oxymoron. In fact, the mortgage insurance company I worked for was embarassed to report a 5 percent loss ratio for the previous year, and several executives wished for just a few more loans to go bad so that our clients would better appreciate the value of our service. The typical mortgage banker was a small, independent, retail originator that packaged FHA/VA loans into Ginnie Maes, or sold whole loans to thrifts. Pricing was based on a twelve year prepay assumption, and cash flow yield was only a glint in Dexter Senft's eye. The Fannie Mae MBS did not yet exist, while private mortgage-backed issues were rarer than sightings of Elvis. Because interest rates had been on a steady uptrend for years, pipeline fallout and negative convexity were merely academic concepts. Servicing traded infrequently, and when it did, valuation was simple: it was worth one percent. I produced my first financial forecast with a pencil, a hand held calculator and a large green accounting pad. Later that year, when we bought a personal computer and I transferred my numbers to a Visicalc spread-sheet, that was high-tech state of the art.

How times have changed!

The 1980s: A Decade of Transition

In retrospect, the 1980s was a transitionary decade, a time of unprece-dented challenges, of experimentation and consolidation. The smartest and toughest players learned quickly and adapted to the new environ-ment, while the rest were casualties who shrunk or sold out or simply closed up shop. The first great challenge was the high level of interest rates that all but shut down origination volume. Creative lenders took advantage of liberalized lending regulations, and the result was a vast expansion in the menu of mortgage products, including over two hun-dred types of adjustable rate mortgages (it took several years for the industry to decide between "ARM" and "AML" as the preferred acro-nym) and a sometimes bewildering profusion of graduated payment, growing equity, shared equity, wrap, and second mortgage loans. I remember long debates with colleagues about which of these loans would survive. As so often happens, the wishes of consumers and investors were diametrically opposed: investors demanded loans that would adjust immediately to market, while consumers sought out loans that looked as fixed as possible—only with lower interest rates. For a long while, mortgage bankers despaired as thrifts dominated the origi-nation market with teaser rate ARMs (loans with starting rates well below the fully indexed accrual rate); getting a whole loan standby to sell such ARMs to a thrift investor was often the difference between sitting on the sidelines or being a player on the street.

The marketplace eventually winnowed the product menu down to a manageable few choices, and the lower interest rates of the later 1980s brought back the popularity of fixed rate loans. The competitive-ness of mortgage bankers was enhanced not only by the return of a fixed rate environment, but also by two other factors that dramatically changed the industry: the demise of the thrifts, and the rise to domi-nance of the MBS.

The thrift industry was at once a blessing and a bane: while thrift investors were a primary outlet for whole loan product, thrift origina-tors were frequently unbeatable competitors. But the same short-sighted impulse that led thrifts to aggressively market teaser rate ARMS (some of which actually had lifetime caps below the prevailing level of fixed rates!) led to a multitude of other dubious business decisions that sealed their fate. Fortunately, at the same time that thrifts were diminishing in importance as investors, the MBS was coming into its own. By the late 1980s, even ARMs and jumbo loans were being packaged into generic MBS and resold through Wall Street to a wide variety of institutional investors, many of whom would never dream of investing in whole loan product. Early fears that the thrift investor base could never be replaced proved groundless: MBS are distributed internationally, at prices that translate into competitive rates on the street. These developments helped mortgage bankers, because the industry excels at competing on a level playing field, in a market rate environment.

By mid decade it had become painfully clear that the lax underwriting standards and some of the more dubious new products (such as the 95 LTV negatively amortizing GPM, aka "the loan that ate Texas") of the early 1980s were producing catastrophic results. Lenders had blithely passed on risks to mortgage insurers, and mortgage insurers had become so dominated by their sales and marketing departments that few even bothered to employ actuaries. As losses mounted, insurers had to move fast, and action—sometimes draconian—often preceded analysis. One of the great debates of the mid 80s was whether payment shock or equity erosion was the more significant contributor to default risk; eventually it became clear that equity is the single most important determinant of credit risk. As underwriting ratios were tightened and LTV limits were cut back, many lenders complained bitterly that they were being punished unfairly for the "other guy's" sins. Gradually, however, insurers analyzed the delinquency and default experience of millions of loans and arrived at sensible standards that protect the interests of borrowers, lenders, insurers, and investors.

Just as the early 1980s were dominated by the effects of high interest rates, the second half of the decade was strongly colored by declining interest rates. This had several profound effects. Origination and refinance volume soared, and this opened up many profit opportunities for mortgage bankers—as long as they weren't overwhelmed as volume poured into back offices that were often understaffed as a result of layoffs during the lean years. But there was a dark side to these years as well. Old fashioned secondary marketing officers, who had often been hired for their skill at cultivating thrift investors, were ill prepared to deal with the volatility in both interest rates and pipeline fallout ratios. The new secondary marketing manager had to be adept at analyzing pipeline behavior and using the full array of futures, forwards, and options to hedge interest rate and fallout risk. The MBS market felt the effects of the refinance boom as well, as outstanding pass-through issues experienced the full meaning of negative convexity (price compression above par), and MBS-Treasury yield spreads soared. But the outcome of this experience was ultimately very positive: a profusion of new products that have increased the investor base for mortgage loans and helped to dampen the volatility of every mortgage banker's bottom line.

The 1990s and Beyond

The stresses and strains of the 1980s led to an unprecedented shakeout among mortgage lenders, and the number of players today is far smaller than only a few years ago. While the cost of entry into loan origination continues to be low, the financial resources necessary to compete and succeed as a full service mortgage banker have increased several fold. As a result, the industry is increasingly dominated by the largest players, behemoths with servicing portfolios of $30 billion or more who often obtain a considerable portion of their volume from wholesale, rather than retail production. Although there will always be a profitable niche for small originators, that niche may well be in mortgage *brokerage*, and the outlook for the medium-sized mortgage banking firm that services its own loans is much less certain.

A number of the largest mortgage bankers grew very quickly in the past several years through bulk purchases of servicing portfolios. The secondary market for mortgage loan servicing has grown twelve fold in the past ten years, far outpacing the growth in origination volume. The valuation of servicing, which was still in its infancy as recently as the mid 1980s, is now as sophisticated as the analysis of MBS. In the early 1990s, the demise of the thrifts, combined with new bank capital requirements, put enormous pressure on the servicing market, and a resulting mismatch between buyers and sellers led to required yields that sometimes exceeded 20 percent. In a perfect example of how the market tends to return to equilibrium, these yields attracted new investors into the mortgage banking business, helping to offset the loss of thrift capital. By 1993, prices for mortgage servicing were heading back toward their old highs.

Perhaps the single most important factor affecting mortgage banking in the 1990s has been—and will continue to be—advancements in technology. The mortgage banking operations in the 1980s were generally paper intensive, time consuming, costly, and error prone. Thanks to technological developments such as electronic data interchange, artificial intelligence, imaging, and optical character recognition, mortgage bankers will be able to operate faster, cheaper, and with higher quality than ever before.

Technology is affecting every aspect of the business, often in several ways. For example, automated origination systems not only reduce costs, but also open up entire new origination channels, such as computerized loan origination networks (CLOs). Automated expert systems will handle routine underwriting, freeing up underwriters to focus on the most difficult loans. State of the art technology is helping mortgage bankers to analyze and manage pipeline risk, which will stabilize earnings and attract more capital into the business. Technology is reducing servicing costs, maximizing loan workout opportunities and minimizing foreclosure losses. Not every technical innovation will prove fruitful, but it is safe to say that the leading mortgage bankers of the year 2000 will be using new technologies undreamed of today.

The Secret of Success

A few months into my first job I was invited to attend the company's national sales conference, where an outside consultant—a famous inspirational speaker—was going to be giving a lecture to the salesforce entitled "The Secret of Success." What a break! I wasn't going to have to discover the secret by trial and error over many long years, I was going to find out right away. When the great day arrived I showed up an hour early to get a front row seat and sat there, pencil poised, ready to take notes.

I still have my notes from that lecture. They consist of three words:

JUST SHOW UP.

(Well, there was an advanced version of this lecture where two additional words were added: **ON TIME.**)

At first I was pretty disillusioned by this lecture. What kind of recipe for success is 'just show up'? I wanted my money back! But over the years, the more I thought about it (and the more sales calls I made) the more I appreciated the consultant's remarks. The best secrets of success, whether in sales or anything else, *are* simple. People are always looking for complicated ways to get ahead, but that's not usually the way things work.

During the 1980s, a lot of us had a very simple secret indeed:

JUST SURVIVE.

It took a lot of patience to follow this rule. When thrifts were offering teaser rate ARMs, the temptation to compete by gambling on rates or relaxing underwriting standards was awfully high. But when the smoke cleared, the mortgage bankers who kept their heads down and played for the long haul came out on top.

In the 1990s, I think we can expand the rules just a bit. Here are my revised secrets of success, good to the year 2000 or $25 billion in origination volume, whichever comes first:

Learn the Lessons of the Past

Mortgage bankers who have entered the business after the mid 1980s are unfamiliar with what it takes to compete in a high interest rate environment. We have a natural tendency to assume that current conditions will continue in perpetuity, but that of course is not the case. Rates will one day return to unaffordable levels, and it is important that we remember what worked and what didn't work in the early 1980s. Similarly, it is not hard to imagine a young mortgage banking executive in the year 2000, who has never gone through a period of high defaults or volatile interest rates. If we don't learn from history, we are doomed to repeat it.

Analyze the Risks of the Present

As we learned in the 1980s, if you want to succeed, the first thing is to survive. The environment for mortage bankers is still filled with risks. Every innovation usually introduces new risks. For example, the drive to streamline the origination process with limited documentation loans was well intentioned, but the introduction of certain lax 'no income check' underwriting programs in the late 1980s produced severe losses on defaulted loans. The popular strategy of emphasizing growth and diversification can often lead to unanticipated management problems and higher, rather than lower costs. New legal and regulatory risks abound. And the very pace of change poses the risk that your competitors will find a way to take away your client base. The most successful mortgage bankers of the year 2000 will undoubtedly have adopted a meaningful strategic planning process that places a high priority on identifying and planning for risks.

Master the Tools of the Trade

Not every new tool makes sense for every mortgage banker. But if you don't take advantage of the latest products, marketing strategies, and technological developments that might benefit your business, you may not only have given up a potential competitive advantage—you may find yourself at a marked competitive *disadvantage*. Or out of business entirely.

Identify the Opportunities of the Future

If you've learned the lessons of the past, survived by avoiding the risks of the present, and mastered the tools of the trade, you are poised for success. All that remains is to remember that the markets are in a constant state of flux. The winners of tomorrow tend to be companies that are always looking forward, anticipating new market developments and their client's changing needs.

I wish you the best of luck!

Chapter 2

STRATEGIC OVERVIEW OF MORTGAGE BANKING

John E. Lott,
Senior Consultant
Mortgage Dynamics, Inc.

INTRODUCTION

For most of its history, the mortgage banking business was comprised of a relatively small number of independent firms who filled the role of intermediary between borrowers and permanent mortgage investors. The major part of their activity concentrated on residential loan origination, and most of that consisted of FHA and VA loan production. Savings and loan associations dominated most of the conventional residential market and there were few sources of mortgage capital besides the traditional mortgage investors such as thrifts and life insurance companies. It was, for the most part, a private market where available capital disappeared when interest rates rose and credit availability tightened.

HISTORICAL PERSPECTIVE

Prior to 1970, Fannie Mae provided one of the few national secondary mortgage markets through its whole-loan purchase and sale programs. Even that program was limited to government loans. The establishment of Freddie Mac in 1970 and the entrance of Fannie Mae and Freddie Mac into the conventional secondary market in 1972 began the expansion and rise in importance of secondary market activities for all mortgage lenders. This new factor manifested itself through the standardization of loan documentation and underwriting criteria and a consistent market presence that the private secondary market had never achieved.

As a result of these developments and the economic disruptions of the late 1960s, mortgage banking and the entire mortgage finance industry began to undergo fundamental changes that altered the roles of traditional participants, opened the market to new players, saw Wall Street emerge as a major supplier of mortgage capital, and radically changed the nature of the secondary mortgage market.

THE FORCES OF CHANGE

The dramatic changes in mortgage banking have been driven by a series of developments that have affected all financial services. Each development would have been significant in its own right, but in combination they have altered mortgage financing beyond recognition. The following sections discuss these forces and their impact on the business.

Mortgage Securities and Wall Street

Mortgage lenders recognized long ago that the original secondary market lacked the ability to consistently provide mortgage capital in either the amounts needed or in the geographic distribution required to adequately meet the housing needs of the nation. With no central marketplace, an awkward and illiquid investment vehicle and nonstandard documentation, mortgages could not compete in the capital markets when demands for capital exceeded the available supply from thrifts, life companies, and other portfolio lenders.

Mortgage-backed securities, which offered access to the broad investor base and capital formation abilities of Wall Street, were revived with the creation of the Government National Mortgage Association (GNMA, or Ginnie Mae) in 1968 and the issuance of the first GNMA pass-through securities in 1970. (Mortgage-backed bonds were used widely in the 1920s, but had a dismal record in the depression of the 1930s.) With government guarantees on both the underlying mortgage collateral and on the securities themselves, GNMA securities trading on Wall Street began to attract nontraditional mortgage investors. At about the same time, Freddie Mac initiated sales of pass-through securities backed by conventional residential mortgages. By the mid 1970s, residential mortgages, both government and conventional, had been accepted as viable security collateral by the investment community. The result was a rapid growth in both the volumes and types of mortgage securities in the marketplace.

In addition to reaching a huge investor base and new sources of capital, the securities markets offer a speed of execution and efficiency of pricing that the traditional secondary mortgage market cannot match. As a result, the securities markets have been the outlet for larger and larger percentages of residential mortgage production. Security markets drive mortgage pricing nationwide and heavily influence mortgage product design, as well as reducing the mortgage finance industry's reliance on mortgage portfolio lenders.

Economic Influences

During the past ten years, as mortgage securities were assuming a major role in mortgage financing, changes have occurred in the basic economics of all financial markets that have forced major alterations in the way mortgage banking operations are planned and managed. The magnitude of interest rate movements and the speed with which they occur have reached levels unknown and unanticipated prior to the 1980s. The collapse of mortgage security prices in the spring of 1987 illustrated the potential volatility of the market, which is often driven by factors totally unrelated to mortgage rates or the housing capital markets.

The effect of such volatility has been to make the mortgage banker's job of risk management much more complex and difficult. Senior management has to put into place strategies and operating plans adequate to monitor and control the risk exposure of their operations, supported by sophisticated reporting systems that provide functional managers with the information needed to carry out the plans and strategies.

Further complexities have been added to the business with the wider variety of mortgage products offered to borrowers, whose preferences shift from one loan type to another as the economic climate and expectations change. This tendency is illustrated by the changing market share of originations by fixed-rate, adjustable-rate, and balloon loans. As mortgage rates fall, fixed-rate products and balloon loans tend to dominate the market. As rates rise, lower initial rates bring adjustable products a larger share of the market. The mortgage banker's risk position changes with each shift, and swift action is required to maintain prescribed risk exposure limits.

As the economics of the marketplace have changed, so have the economics of mortgage banking. It has become a complex financial services business requiring analytical skills and financial modeling and forecasting abilities far beyond the levels necessary a few years ago.

The resources required to compete effectively have made it difficult for the small, independent firm to survive and nearly all of the medium- to large-size mortgage banking operations are now subsidiaries of larger institutions, both financial and nonfinancial.

Players in the Market

With the dominant role of mortgage securities and the impact of economic changes felt in all sectors of the mortgage finance industry, the composition of the participants in the industry has also changed. Wall Street firms, commercial banks, nonfinancial corporate giants, and traditional portfolio lenders are playing a part in mortgage banking with varying degrees of influence and success.

1. *Securities dealers* have become the primary market makers as the bulk of residential mortgage originations are used to collateralize mortgage securities, primarily through the programs of Freddie Mac, Fannie Mae, and Ginnie Mae. Many major Wall Street firms ventured into direct mortgage banking activities in the 1980s, establishing their own mortgage banking operations, buying and selling mortgages and loan servicing rights. Most of these ventures have disappeared or are serving small, specialized markets and the Street's emphasis has returned to mortgage securities and the derivative securities that have developed as the mortgage security markets matured.

2. *Thrift institutions* and the thrift industry have been decimated by the consequences of the excesses, incompetence, and fraud of the last ten years. They are no longer the major source of mortgage capital. It is estimated that some 2,000 viable institutions will remain after the cleanup is completed, but their presence in the market will be severely diminished. Most will continue to maintain a mortgage loan portfolio, but not on a scale that will make them primary sources of mortgage money as they were prior to the 1980s.

3. *Commercial banks*, particularly the large superregional banks and bank holding companies, have emerged as major players in mortgage banking. Many of the nation's largest mortgage banking operations are subsidiaries of these institutions. The banks view mortgage banking as a natural expansion of their consumer lending operations

and as a cross-selling opportunity, while the mortgage banking operation benefits from the credit facilities of the parent and the institution's financial presence in the marketplace. When the inherent conflicts between commercial banking and mortgage banking are successfully resolved by senior management, it can be a strong and effective marriage.

4. *Nonfinancial corporations and holding companies* have acquired or built some of the largest mortgage banking operations in the country with mixed results. Some operations have done very well and continue to prosper, but others have fallen victim to the goal of size for its own sake and perceived economies of scale. As in the case of commercial banks, the parent organization has to understand the business of mortgage banking and the operating disciplines that it requires if the mortgage banking operation is to succeed.

5. *Life insurance companies and pension funds* have long been viewed by mortgage bankers as prime sources of mortgage funds, but tapping the sources has not been easy. Life companies returned to residential mortgage investment in the 1980s after effectively leaving the field 20 years earlier, but most did it by setting up their own mortgage companies. Like Wall Street's venture into mortgage banking, most of these operations have been sold or shut down, although several life company mortgage banking operations continue to do well. Pension funds rarely provide mortgage bankers with direct access to funds and tend to invest in mortgages through mortgage securities.

THE IMPACT OF CHANGE

The combined effect of the forces at work in the housing finance industry has changed nearly every aspect of mortgage banking, both financially and operationally. Old axioms and rules of thumb that guided planning and strategy decisions no longer apply and new ones have short life spans. The nature of the business has become as volatile as the markets in which mortgage bankers participate.

A major new characteristic of mortgage banking today is the bewildering variety of options and alternatives available to managers in every function of the organization. Loan production, secondary marketing, loan servicing, and treasury operations must select from numerous products, market mechanisms, financing vehicles, and financial strategies that did not exist or were not open to them just a few years ago.

This array of choices is a mixed blessing. It affords the opportunity for great success but also opens the door to failure. The line is drawn between the two extremes by the ability of management to recognize and interpret the long-term implications of its choice of alternatives.

The availability of so many options has placed the burden of proper selection and implementation on the senior management of mortgage banking firms. The importance of strategic planning has never been greater, and it must be supported by careful financial analysis of the effect of strategic choices in each functional area and the combined results of the choices. Some of the primary considerations in establishing strategic approaches to mortgage banking are discussed in the next sections.

The Pursuit of Economies of Scale

One of the most striking changes in the mortgage banking industry over the past five years has been the increase in size of the major firms. Both loan production figures and the size of the servicing portfolio dwarf the figures common a short time ago. Annual loan originations of $1 billion to over $10 billion are not uncommon, nor are servicing portfolios of $10 billion and higher.

On the origination side, the influence of the securities markets has much to do with the drive for higher volumes. Formation of the collateral pools for mortgage securities is faster and more certain with high volumes, simplifying the use of Wall Street delivery mechanisms and providing more effective control over risk exposure.

Higher volumes also offer pricing advantages in the securities markets. The competition for origination market share, however, has resulted in thinner margins and less room for error on the marketing side of the operation.

Higher loan production does not appear to significantly lower the per-loan cost of origination. Loan production operates at a loss in the majority of mortgage banking firms. Data collected by the Mortgage Bankers Association of America does not indicate a correlation between greater production and lower costs.

A number of attempts have been made to reduce retail production costs through computer-based origination networks. Most of these efforts are designed to replace the loan originator and provide access to the lender through remote terminals in the offices of realtors and small mortgage originators. Some have tried to reach potential borrowers directly. Relatively few mechanized origination programs have achieved sustainable production volumes and none has succeeded on a nationwide basis.

Wholesale loan production has become a major source for mortgage bankers, fed by the increase in the number of small independent originators who do not have secondary marketing or loan servicing capability. For the wholesale mortgage banker, the lower cost of acquisition has to be weighed against the increased difficulty of quality control, but it allows access to remote markets without the overhead associated with retail production offices. Wholesalers have utilized computers to link their correspondents in networks that facilitate product pricing, loan registrations, and delivery schedules.

Loan origination losses are tolerated and justified by the industry as a cost of acquiring loan servicing rights and building the servicing portfolio. The servicing portfolio has always been viewed by mortgage bankers as their primary asset and source of steady income. The asset value has become even more important with the emergence of an active market for the purchase and sale of loan servicing rights, adding a degree of liquidity to the servicing asset that was not formerly present. For most mortgage bankers, servicing sales have become a planned source of working capital.

In contrast to loan production, loan servicing operations are subject to economies of scale, *up to a point.* There are minimum levels of fixed costs, primarily in facilities, data processing resources, and (to a much lesser degree) personnel, that are required for the varied servicing activities. These minimum resources can accommodate larger volumes without proportionate increases in the cost per loan. As a result, mortgage bankers aggressively seek to benefit from larger portfolios through expanded in-house origination programs, wholesale originations, and the purchase of servicing portfolios.

Servicing portfolio size alone, however, does not ensure lower costs or financial strength and stability. Up to $1 or $2 billion in servicing, per-loan cost declines sharply and further economies can be realized up to $4 or $5 billion. Beyond that level cost reductions come very slowly, if at all. There are indications that portfolio size may reach a point of diminishing returns, where further additions begin to increase the servicing costs. Product diversity, geographic dispersion, adequate systems support, and management control have more influence on costs than just the number of loans serviced. Loan servicing has its economies of scale, but they are not unlimited.

Large servicing portfolios are subject to financial risk as well as operational risk or rising costs. Nearly all very large servicing portfolios are built by buying servicing rights as well as through loan originations. While these purchased mortgage servicing rights (PMSR) appear on the mortgage banker's balance sheet, unanticipated periods of rapid prepayments such as occurred during the massive refinancing of loans in 1992 can cause large accounting losses. At best, these losses can be hard to explain to a board of directors and at worst, can destroy the financial base of the operation.

Can the Small, Independent Mortgage Banker Survive?

Corollary to the question of scale is the ability of the small mortgage banking firm to compete with the giants of the industry and their far greater resources. This is a question that probably has no definitive answer, but some observations and conclusions can be drawn from recent history of the industry.

Entry into the loan production side of the business is still relatively easy and can be done with minimal working capital. Numerous origination offices opened in the past few years that have successfully confined their operations to loan solicitation, selling their production to other lenders some time before closing in return for a share of the origination fees.

The next steps to putting a full-scale mortgage banking operation in place—acquiring the capability to fund loan closings through internal capital or warehouse lines of credit and establishing secondary marketing and loan servicing functions—are much more difficult.

Warehouse lines of credit can be very hard to find, even for established firms, and small mortgage bankers usually find that any lines provided will be limited and expensive. Even with premiums from servicing-released sales of loan production, most firms will find it impossible to generate the cash flows and accumulate the net worth necessary to expand and grow from within.

The economic realities of starting loan servicing operations from ground zero are even harder to overcome. Servicing requires substantial initial investment in facilities, personnel, and systems resources and the growth of the portfolio to an economic break-even size can take years. Even if the servicing is retained and subcontracted to avoid the start-up costs, the premiums from servicing-released sales must be foregone, narrowing the financial margins. Cash flow is a key factor in mortgage banking, and current conditions make it hard to generate it in sufficient volume for expansion.

The result of these factors has been a mortgage banking industry in which the vast majority of firms are subsidiaries of institutions or companies that can provide the financial support necessary to prosper and grow.

Large mortgage banking firms with strong parent organizations enjoy some critical advantages. Their financial resources give them access to cheaper sources of warehouse lines, including commercial paper markets, and an ability to buy and sell servicing. They can establish large regional or national origination networks, using both retail and wholesale programs. Larger firms can afford the financial expertise and computer support systems that have become essential to mortgage banking operations.

As has been amply demonstrated in the recent past, the level of a mortgage banking firm's competency is not a function of size. Success in the business is much more dependent on how well senior management does its strategic planning, stays focused on its primary objectives, manages its risk exposure and adapts to changing conditions. There are still well-run firms with servicing portfolios under $1 billion that have found a niche in the market and continue to prosper despite the competition from much larger and more publicized organizations.

The Problems of Risk Management

Risk has always been a basic characteristic of mortgage banking. It is what mortgage bankers get paid for. But managing the risks of the business today is tremendously more difficult and complex than it was just five years ago.

Many of the same factors that brought growth and expansion to mortgage banking have contributed to the increased risk of mortgage banking operations. Securitization and the use of Wall Street mechanisms, increased investor base, greater product variety, and geographic expansion of production sources have been accompanied by exposure to higher interest rate volatility, greater speed and magnitude of market movements, credit risk, and complexity of financial strategies and analysis. Risk management is concerned not just with minimizing losses, but with survival.

Risk arises in mortgage banking operations where it has not been evident previously. The increase in the purchase and sale of mortgage servicing is an example. Mortgage bankers have been forced to recognize that servicing rights are a financial asset as well as a business and must be managed as such. If the assumptions and forecast upon which servicing transactions are based are not carefully defined, volatile markets can create losses as great as those suffered in secondary marketing mistakes.

New opportunities are almost always accompanied by new sources of risk. Many of these are subtle and deadly, demanding skills of analysis and interpretation absent in many firms. Failure to recognize that mortgage banking is a complex financial business will ultimately end in mediocre results, if not disaster. It is not just another way to make loans. It requires an understanding of the nature of mortgage banking and adherence to the disciplines necessary to succeed.

Risk management is not a matter of hedging, of puts and calls and futures contracts. It is a matter of efficient processing, consistency of approach, effective planning, quick response to changing conditions, personnel training and expertise, capable management. Experienced mortgage bankers know this, and for many the toughest part of their job is conveying the message to parent boards and senior managers.

IMPLICATIONS FOR THE FUTURE

The past five years have demonstrated how difficult it is to project the future of the mortgage finance industry in general and the mortgage banking business in particular. Almost every aspect of mortgage lending has seen changes. Managers at all levels have been hard-pressed to assimilate and respond to new developments. Out of this period of change, however, have come certain indications of those factors that will be critical in mortgage banking operations over the next five to ten years.

1. Mortgage banking is a complex financial operation where sophisticated financial analyses and strategies drive all of the functional operating areas. The risks of the business have become so great and the margins so thin that one wrong assumption or lapse in risk management disciplines can result in financial disaster. The market exacted a heavy toll for complacency and miscalculation in 1987, when magnitudes and rapidity of movements far exceeded most mortgage bankers "worst-case" planning scenarios. There is no assurance that such volatility is an infrequent aberration and not an ever present danger with which the mortgage lender must deal on a daily basis. There have been a number of less extreme, but potentially damaging market movements since 1987. Financial expertise is a key to success in mortgage banking and its role will continue to grow. Loan production, secondary marketing, loan servicing, and risk management strategies have to be designed and imple-

mented according to comprehensive financial plans that reflect a clear understanding of the economic realities of the business.

2. The level of computer systems support for mortgage banking operations has grown faster than the ability of many organizations to respond. The pace of mortgage banking activities requires immediate access to large amounts of data and methods to manipulate the data in many ways. Even in large firms, it is not uncommon to find secondary market managers utilizing only very elementary marketing techniques (and leaving literally hundreds of thousands of dollars on the table) because of a lack of systems support. Only recently have front-end systems—including pipeline tracking, best execution models, and commitment pooling—begun to meet the needs of the business. Accurate data, instantly available, is paramount in managing the risks of mortgage banking. In many firms, the greatest source of risk may lie in the inadequacy of systems support.

3. Stand-alone mortgage banking companies continue to decline in numbers as more firms are absorbed into organizations offering a broad range of financial services. Long-standing lines of demarcation between the activities of various kinds of financial institutions have blurred with the collapse of the thrift industry and the rise in the number of troubled banks. Financial strength, not the corporate charter, determines who can do what. Many of the traditional distinctions between thrifts, commercial banks, investment bankers, and other financial services firms have been abandoned in the face of increased competition and economic necessity. Mortgage banking is a prime candidate for institutions reaching beyond their customary lines of business.

4. The chances for success by the entrepreneurial mortgage banker without enormous resources have declined to the point where such entrants into the business are confined to mortgage brokerage activities. The cost of putting in place the resources required for secondary marketing and loan servicing functions is so high and the risks so great that it is virtually impossible to expand into full-service mortgage

banking with internally generated capital. New operations require millions of dollars in capital, restricting entry into the business to well-financed companies or investor groups.

The mortgage banking business that has emerged from the last ten years is an industry whose focus has shifted from the operational side to the financial side. Loan production volumes alone are no indication of success if they do not produce a servicing asset with a value commensurate with the cost of producing it. Production, marketing, and servicing together must produce an economic gain that justifies the risk of the business. In today's environment, the real economic results, both good and bad, are often obscured in consolidated financial statements. It is easier than ever for mortgage bankers to "do a deal," but more difficult to do a good deal.

Senior management of mortgage banking organizations, along with the management of parent organizations, must have the ability to recognize the real forces that determine the long-term success of their operations, and they must base their goals, objectives, and business plans on the realities of a constantly changing environment.

Chapter 3

STRATEGIC PLANNING FOR THE 21ST CENTURY

Anthony W. Schweiger, CMB
Consultant to Mortgage Banking
Financial Services and other businesses

PLANNING PERSPECTIVE

We live in a rapidly changing world—most executives grew up with a good guy/bad guy perspective of the Soviet Union and foresaw protracted conflict with that large nation, something likely to continue for at least another 75 years. Yet unique events like the dissolution of the Soviet empire or the Perot phenomenon, along with many other industry-specific sudden and unexpected events, have clearly demonstrated that traditional planning—the kind most companies practice (i.e., planning based on probabilities)—has been rendered futile by economic, social, and political uncertainties.

Nonetheless, as Peter Drucker, the most enduring management guru of our time, recently said, "executives must commit to the future resources of time and money." The solution, he said, lies in "creating the resources of knowledge and people so that when opportunity knocks, management can turn the unexpected into advantage."

Vision and the Strategic Plan

One of a CEO's primary responsibilities is to articulate a vision for the enterprise. A vision is a statement that describes in clear-cut terms what the organization should be trying to achieve. A strategic plan used to be thought of as a road map under which the corporate vision can be achieved. However, in the 1990s, strategy is no longer an analytical exercise to determine which businesses or markets a firm should pursue. Today, it is rather a creative, holistic process that integrates decisions made at all levels, processes, resources, and organization so as to maximize the firm's ability to meet the needs of its stakeholders.

Strategy is somewhat of an overworked word in the 1990s. Businesses have strategic customers and marketing plans, and they make a variety of strategic decisions. There are ongoing efforts to develop strategies about recruiting and retaining employees, managing technology, and a host of other critical issues. Good businessmen assess the value of information and the fit between vision, the corporate culture, and strategy. In fact, there is a clear link between strategy and vision.

The terms *strategy* and *strategic planning* need a new perspective. For many managers, the strategy involved selecting the most attractive products and/or market segments and determining the appropriate investment. A number of useful tools and concepts evolved in the 1970s, providing managers with insights into the competitive attractiveness of the business and options. Most of these tools, which view business segments in terms of some variant of industry maturity and competitive position, have been valuable aids in addressing questions about expansion into new markets or businesses as well as dealing with other issues such as divestiture, restructuring, or rightsizing.

For the most part, companies are not concerned about what businesses to be in. Rather, there's a growing sense of being in a business forever. As a result, today's strategy must be more broad and dynamic than the typical market/product variety.

The critical issues for managers today are not just where to compete, in which market niche or segment, but how, with what, and with whom. Thus, strategy helps not only business portfolio managers but also the operating head, who must find ways to improve business performance.

Strategy and Stakeholders

High-performance businesses set strategies to satisfy key stakeholders by improving critical business processes and aligning resources and organization. The term *stakeholders* needs to apply to all the business's stakeholders, not just customers or shareholders, but employees and other vested interests as well. This perspective will help balance all those needs in making strategic decisions that can provide a sustainable competitive advantage.

At this macro level, the business deals not only with business lines, products, services, and markets but also whether investment is continued, increased, or retrenched. It makes decisions to enter new markets or offer new products and services. Other decisions may involve degrees of risk, raising capital, changing human resources, or managing the known resource differently. These and other similar questions are broad and strategic. They link strategy with vision.

Each business is uniquely defined by both the stakeholders it serves and the ways it goes about satisfying them. Importantly, stakeholder-based strategy versus the traditional product/market strategy involves conscious trade-offs and reinforcement of investment in the various stakeholder groups present within the business. Such groups may include, but not be necessarily limited to, the following:

Group	Strategic Issues
Employees	Compensation, benefits, training, security, as well as less tangible issues such as pride, spirit, teamwork.
Customers	New products, services, pricing methods. Less tangible issues may involve health, environment.
Owners	Dividends, earnings, stock price and P/E ratios. Less tangible issues might involve the community or social and political ones.

Operational Strategies

The second level of strategy deals with what the enterprise does and how it operates. Issues may include what operations are performed internally. Where will the particular business begin and end? What will be purchased? To what extent, if at all, will there be vertical integration? How close to the final consumer will operations reach?

Operational strategies also deal with excellence—how will the company perform each process? What advantages are gained from faster service or better products? Can quality provide a pricing or other basis for differentiation? Do we own and run the servicing system or use a service bureau?

This strategy level is similar to the traditional planning process of determining how businesses will compete, or the key success factors. However, there is one major exception. Traditional strategic processes assumed one set of factors were the basis of competition. Today, there are many patterns of operational excellence, some of which are not part of the traditional pattern of competition in the industry. Countrywide is a good example. In addition to a direct consumer origination process that eschews traditional loan officers, the company operates separate, but similar, businesses in providing services and products to the mortgage broker and correspondent sectors as well as servicing brokerages. In fact, if one closely examines the Countrywide operational strategies, they focus on operational excellence along the entire mortgage process from application, to sale of the security, to the second-tier investment bankers, and frequently the ultimate investor.

Critical Processes

For the most part, superior firms rarely have more than eight to ten broad strategic processes and rarely exceed at more than two or three. Businesses should keep planning to focus on broad, important themes.

Most importantly, top firms monitor their process strength through continuous and rigorous benchmarking techniques. Significant understanding is often obtained from comparing a specific firm's strengths and weaknesses against a competitor's.

Resources and Organization

The foundation for executing strategies is the businesses resources and organization. Resources include both capital and people. Organization defines how the resources are best leveraged or meshed to achieve the strategic objectives. Resources and organization are now seen as powerful components of strategy.

For example, will the corporate culture support or impede a specific strategy? During the 1980s we saw several businesses and even industries change process and organization in order to survive. The Chrysler Corporation story is one of the most widely known. It is unlikely the company would have survived if labor had not changed and been willing to focus on quality and make significant concessions. A number of biotechnology and software firms have had wonderful ideas, but inadequate resources and organization to bring the strategies to fruition.

Organization means the structure and policies of the corporation as well as the culture. However, the corporate culture is generally the overwhelming driver for success. Culture is shaped by policies and procedures, but also and significantly it lists the unwritten rules on how people act. A number of well-respected current management consultants and organizational specialists have concluded that people must be motivated to respond appropriately. Strategic vision and direction will be ineffective if the firm's most important resource, its people, are not focused and motivated.

Resource investments must also reinforce and further develop areas of strength, or core competencies, but only if those strengths are both strategically important and at least somewhat differentiating. In addition, resources should be flexible to respond to rapidly changing environments and remain useful over time.

Strategy formulation today, then, is the exercise of building and growing an ongoing viable business, capable of sustaining itself and living for an indefinite time period. The process begins with recognition of the limitations created by corporate history, and then defines the business in stakeholder terms. Once that focus is set, process resources and organization must be balanced skillfully to create and cultivate a high-performance business.

PLANNING TOOLS

Every mortgage business, no matter how big or small, should have a business plan. It's a wonderful management tool, as well as something bankers and others with vested interests in the firm have a need to understand.

Strategy Development

The first phase in planning is situation analysis. This typically involves:

1.   Evaluating the market and competition.

2.   Understanding industry structure and maturity.

3.   Evaluating the current business mix and performance.

4.   Defining and assessing quality.

Evaluating the Market and Competition

To create a good plan, the business should make certain it has an up-to-date understanding of the current and near-term economic and regulatory environment, the market(s) where the company operates, and the competition. During the last decade, the mortgage business has been subject to increased regulatory scrutiny. Consequently, federal and state issues, particularly new and pending ones, should be incorporated in any situation analysis.

Western businesses have not placed the same importance on business intelligence as have Eastern business cultures. Understanding what your competition does or doesn't do, how their processes and approaches create competitive advantage provides the planning enterprise with appropriate information that can drive a strategic and tactical advantage.

A large number of world-class companies have business intelligence programs that focus on key competitors and industry trends. While most mortgage lenders can't afford formal intelligence units, there are a number of readily available resources ranging from newsletters to suppliers to research groups that can be employed as needed in the planning process. Such resources include, but are certainly not limited to:

- ◆   The Mortgage Banker's Association of America

- ◆   The American Bankers Association

- ◆   The National Association of Realtors

- ◆   The National Association of Home Builders

- ◆   The Wharton Economatic Forecasting Group (WEFA)

- ◆   Private mortgage insurance companies

- ◆   Local Market Monitor

- ◆   SMR Research

- ◆   FNMA and FHLMC

With current data and intelligence, the firm can then accurately describe the current competitive economic environment and forecast the future competitive environment. Intelligence can also help challenge the underlying business plan assumptions and identify the firm's own weaknesses and vulnerabilities. Ongoing business intelligence can also help monitor competitors' reactions during implementation and assess a strategy's viability.

Understanding the Industry Structure and Maturity

A background in business life cycle and marketing dynamics may be helpful in looking at industry structure and maturity. Generally, industries are in one of four stages:

- ◆ Embryonic—introductive period—sales climb.

- ◆ Growth—lots of competitive turbulence. Contest for position and search out opportunities. Sales climb quickly.

- ◆ Mature—high level of price competition—search for efficiencies, new products or product twists. Consolidation likely.

- ◆ Aging—specialized demand or decline of sales volumes fall off unless niche approach is successful.

For the most part, mortgage banking is a mature industry with much consolidation likely to occur. However, understanding where the industry is in its life cycle can provide a framework for company planning. Managers need to recognize that their firm does not operate in a vacuum. Moreover, industry structure and maturity can and do change over time as technological and other major developments occur.

Evaluating the Current Business Mix and Performance

The next phase involves close examination of the current business mix and performance. Such an analysis typically would compare origination costs for wholesale versus retail with an appropriate implicit value for the created servicing if the product is not servicing released, as well as costs by product type and origination source. This comparative data, together with similar data on servicing and a growing available body of peer data, can help the firm make strategic decisions about products, services, and even business units. A manager may want to analyze data on one of the formats employed by the major data sources. See the Mortgage Banker's Association of America annual origination and servicing studies. Also see ICM Consultants, Valley Forge, PA, and KMPG Peat Marwick's servicing study (available only to participants).

Defining and Assessing Quality

There is a good deal of focus on quality these days, but many managers aren't really clear on the term's definition as it applies to their business. Quality must be applied to every aspect of the firm's business, from customer and employee satisfaction to minimizing rework or corrections of processing errors.

The definition of specific quality measures should be an integral part of strategy development. Each business unit needs to develop appropriate measures and then track trends to assure that quality goals are being achieved. It's important to recognize that the path to quality is a continuum—it is an ongoing process that never ends as business, customers, and the firm's objectives change over time.

The pursuit of quality is different for every company or business unit. Consistent measurement is essential to monitor defined quality. During the 1980s, the Commerce Department's Balridge Award raised the level of quality consciousness significantly in this country. Concurrently, as world trade evolved, manufacturers and suppliers were forced to meet international quality standards (ISO) if they expected to have the opportunity to compete. Many quality consultants have suggested that simply understanding the Balridge Award criteria will provide an excellent framework for assessing an individual firm's quality.

STRATEGY IMPLEMENTATION

Creating the culture for implementation is like preparing the soil for planting a tree. If you do not prepare the soil, you cannot plant the tree. Preparing the soil is tough, but once it has been prepared, planting becomes easier and the likelihood of a healthy young tree is greatly improved.

Barriers to Implementation

To assure the success of any plan, bring about change, and manage strategically, likely barriers to implementation must be understood. Perception and corporate culture are the two primary barriers that can create either success or failure. If the strategy does not seem implementable or it is not understood or acceptable to the people and teams that have implementation responsibility, then, lacking a clear go-ahead and buy-in, it will likely fail.

Reality Testing

Executive management should subject any key strategy to some reality testing. This may involve modeling or even pilot testing in controlled situations. Managers certainly need to understand the risks and rewards of a strategy before embarking on implementation. Testing can frequently provide additional information, which may modify or even eliminate a costly strategy.

Generating Shared Commitment

Belief is the strongest driver to achieve most objectives. If we believe something is possible and want to achieve it, we generally will. This perception and culture need to be well understood and managed to assure any critical strategic goal.

The best buy-in or shared commitment occurs when the strategy is well communicated and there is appropriate dialogue about implementation issues. Frequently implementation issues are perceived differently by those responsible to make them happen than they are by the strategist. Accordingly, sincere and open dialogue about such issues can effectively address concerns and fears.

Mobilizing Organizational Resources

Defining an action plan

While goals and objectives outline what will be achieved and when, action plans set forth how they will be accomplished. Plans should be appropriately detailed to make certain the key steps or tasks are outlined, allowing barriers or other implementation issues to surface early. Action plans should include:

♦ Key tasks

♦ Time frames or completion deadlines

♦ Measures to determine success (pro forma budget as well as productivity or sales goals)

♦ Where appropriate, points to decide whether to go ahead or continue

♦ Framework for periodic review and method to adjust or change

Energizing the Action Programs

Everyone in the firm shares planning implementation responsibility. Staff personnel often play roles as important as those with direct line or project responsibilities, since implementation typically requires support from many areas. Human resources, accounting, training, management information systems, facilities, legal and marketing—all may have tasks that must be accomplished in a high-quality and timely manner to achieve the strategy. Few key corporate strategies can be achieved without teamwork and a buy-in to excellence.

Executive managers should use every tool at their disposal to excite and energize the firm or business unit about the importance of their individual role in the strategy's success. Communication, feedback, and praise are key tools or techniques that cannot be overused.

Outline Guides

A guide to strategies planning and planning materials is included at the end of this chapter to assist managers in the complete planning process.

Life Cycle Planning Matrix

DESCRIPTORS/ CHARACTERISTICS	Embryonic	Growth	Mature	Aging
GENERAL THRUST	Entrepreneurship • Startup • Flexibility • Survival	Sophisticated management of markets • Growth • Develop advantageous competitive position	Critical administration • Maximize efficieny • Optimize profits	Opportunistic milking • Prolongation • Maximize profits • Survival
PLANNING SYSTEM				
• Time Frame	Long enough to encompass tentative life cycle (10 yrs.)	Long-term investment (7 yrs.)	Intermediate (3 yrs.)	Short term (1 yr.)
• Content	By service/customer	By service and program	By service/market/function	By service
• Approach	Flexible	Less flexible	Formalized	Formalized
ORGANIZATION				
• Size	Small; rapidly growing	Moderate; moderate growth	Large	Large; moderate shrinkage
• Stability	Fluctuating	Less fluctuating	Stable	Less stable
• Structure	Loose/informal; authorities/responsibilities not clearly defined, with some overlapping	Becoming more formal	Tight/formal; authorities and responsibilities clearly defined and described	Formal/pared down
• Complexity	Simple; few functions and hierarchical levels	Becoming complex; increasing number and variety of functions, divisions and hierarchical levels	Complex; multifunctional, multidivisional and multilevel	Simplified functions, divisions, levels
• Flexibility	High flexibility	Becoming more rigid	Rigid	Less rigid

DESCRIPTORS/ CHARACTERISTICS	Embryonic	Growth	Mature	Aging
MANAGERIAL MODE				
• Orientation	Task/growth/financing	Task/performance/people	People/performance	Performance/survival
• Style	Open; ad hoc; consultative	Participative; becoming more formal; delegation	Formal; leadership; delegation; control	Autocratic; tight control; expedient
• Skills	Generalist	More socialized	Specialist	More generalist
• Risk	High	Moderately high	Moderate	Low
• Time Span/Concern	Short	Long	Intermediate	Short
• Key Activity	Innovation	Planning	Systems	Control
REWARD SYSTEM				
• Main Purpose	Incentive	Incentive	Equity/incentive	Equity/incentive
• Structure of Pay Package	High variable/low fixed	Balanced variable and fixed	Low variable/high fixed	Fixed only
• Character	Loose/informal	Becoming formal	Formal/rigid	Formal/rigid
• Basis	Function worth and individual performance	Functional worth and individual and group performance	Functional worth and individual and group performance	Functional worth and individual and group performance
• Timing	Quarterly	Semi-annually—annually	Annually; some deferred for succeeding 2–3 yrs.	Annually
• Fringe Emphasis	None/insurance	None/retirement	Retirement	Retirement

Life Cycle Planning Matrix (continued)

DESCRIPTORS/ CHARACTERISTICS	Embryonic	Growth	Mature	Aging
COMMUNICATIONS & INFORMATION SYSTEM				
• Main Purpose	Rapid responsiveness	Planning	Coordination/control	Control
• Character	Informal/tailored	Formal/tailored	Formal/uniform	Little or none by direction
• Content of Reporting	Qualitative; market-oriented; unsystematic	Qualitative and quantitative; early warning system; all functions	Quantitative; work measurement systematic	Quantitative; oriented to balance sheet; systematic
• Policies	Few	More	Many	Many
• Procedures	None	Few	Many	Many
CONTROLS AND MEASURING SYSTEM				
• Main Purpose	Identify significant need for rapid response	Early warning	Improve quality of decisions	Control
• Principal Focus	Market/marketing/service development	Marketing/operations/spread	Operations/financial performance	Financial performance
• Measures Used	Few fixed	Multiple/adjustable/industry	Multiple/adjustable/industry	Few/fixed
• Frequency of Measurement	Often	Relatively often	Traditionally periodic	Less often
• Details of Measurement	Less	More who/why	Great	Less
FUNCTIONAL EMPHASIS	Market research; new service development	Marketing: organizational development	Value analysis; systems development and data processing; taxes & insurance	Operations

Life Cycle and Marketing Dynamics

Time →

	Embryonic Introductive Period	Growth Contest for Position Based on Name of the Game, Competitive Turbulence, Shakeout	Maturity and Maneuvering at a Price	Aging Specialized Demand or Decline
GENERAL CONDITIONS Business Strategies	• Initial Market development • Market penetration	• Market Penetration • Same product/new markets • New products/same markets	• Efficiencies • Consolidations • New products/same markets	• Consolidations • Little Jewel • Abandonment
Marketing Thrust	• Segment market, develop awareness of benefits • Gain trial by early adopters • Locate and remedy offering defects quickly	• Establish market dominance as quickly as possible • Strong distribution program • Staff commitment to cross-selling	• Maintain market share • Defend position against competing services through constant attention to product improvement opportunities, fresh promotional and distribution approaches	• To milk the offering dry of all possible profit • Start a new service on its life cycle
Outlook for Competition	• Few are likely to be attracted in the early, unprofitable stages, followed by the entrance of numerous aggressive emulators	• One company tends to emerge as leader • Multiple entrants occur, with duplicate products • Price and distribution squeezes impacting the weaker entrants	• Competition stabilized with few or no new entrants and market shares not subject to substantial change in absence of a substantial improvement in some offering	• Similiar competition declining and dropping out because of decrease in consumer interest
Spread Strategy	• Allocate funds against budgeted objectives	• Maximize funds commitment to cpaitalize on market dominance • Adjust pricing to meet profit and market share targets	• Parity product with investment governed by competitive rate of return • Earnings stability during interest rate cycle	• Investment aligned with yield

Life Cycle and Marketing Dynamics (continued)

	Embryonic Introductive Period	Growth Contest for Position Based on Name of the Game, Competitive Turbulence, Shakeout	Maturity and Maneuvering at a Price	Aging Specialized Demand or Decline
		← Time →		
MARKETING FUNCTIONS				
Marketing Research (Intelligence Focus)	• To identify actual developing use • To uncover any product weaknesses • Be alert for possible service failure—crash landing	• Detailed attention to product position, to gaps in model and market coverage, and to opportunities for market segmentation • Close attention to product improvement needs, to market-broadening chances, and to possible fresh promotion themes	• Intensified attention to possible product improvements • Sharp alert for potential inter-product competition and for signs of beginning product decline	• Information helping to identify the point at which the product should be phased • Watch for change in economic conditions which may prolong life
Staff Focus	• Excite and educate staff • Employee meetings and bulletins	• Promote profit contribution line areas • Frequent success bulletins	• Regular reminders to staff of profit center contribution • Employee incentive programs or sales contests	• Period staff notices on product availability
Product Design	• Limited number of models with offering designs focused on minimizing learning requirements • Descriptive material engineered to appeal to most receptive segment in design	• Modular design to facilitate flexible addition of variants to appeal to every new segment and new use-system as fast as discovered • Intensified attention to product improvement • Computerization of systems	• A constant alert for market pyramiding opportunities through either bold cost-and-price penetration of new markets or major product changes • Introduction of flanker products	• Constant pruning of line to eliminate any items not returning a direct profit

Life Cycle and Marketing Dynamics (continued)

	Embryonic Introductive Period	Growth Contest for Position Based on Name of the Game, Competitive Turbulence, Shakeout	Maturity and Maneuvering at a Price	Aging Specialized Demand or Decline
		Time ⟶		
MARKETING FUNCTIONS (continued) Product Design (continued)	• Utmost attention to quality control and quick elimination of market-revealed defects		• Constant attention to possibilities for product improvement and cost cutting • Reexamination of necessity of design compromises • Tightening up of line to eliminate unnecessary variations with little market appeal	
Pricing	• To match the value reference perception of the most receptive segments	• A price strategy for every income, from low-end to high net worth • Aggressive promotional pricing, with price cut as fast as costs decline due to accumulated experience	• Defensive pricing to preserve product category franchise • Increased attention to market-broadening and promotional pricing opportunities	• Maintenance of profit level pricing with complete disregard of any effect on market share
Advertising and Sales Promotion	• Create widespread awareness and under-standing or offering benefits • Gain trial by early adopters	• Create and strengthen brand preference with final users • Stimulate general trial • Maintain consumer franchise, strengthen institutional identification	• Blunt competition • Maintain consumer loyalty • Promotion of greater use frequency	• Phase out, keeping just enough to maintain profitable distribution

Life Cycle and Marketing Dynamics (continued)

	Embryonic	Growth	Maturity	Aging
	Introductive Period	Contest for Position Based on Name of the Game, Competitive Turbulence, Shakeout	and Maneuvering at a Price	Specialized Demand or Decline
		← Time →		
MARKETING FUNCTIONS (continued)				
Advertising and Sales Promotion (continued)	• Stress new, exclusive features			
Media Mix	• In order of value: Publicity Personal sales Mass communications	• Mass media • Personal sales • Sales promotions • Publicity • Employee sales success identification	• Mass media • Window displays	• Cut down all media to the bone—use no sales promotions of any kind
Distribution Policy	• Exclusive or selective • Market segmentation	ù Intensive and extensive • Emphasis on profit contribution to branch or profit center • Franchise correspondents or nonterritorial users	• Intensive and extensive • Employee contests or incentive programs	• Consolidate in low-overhead area

Note: This is the cycle of an industry, product, or service, and only a complex introduction may be seen to pass through all phases indicated above. The term *product life cycle* is sometimes applied indiscriminately to both brand cycles and product cycles. Most new brands are only emulative of other products already on the market, have a much shorter life cycle than the product category, and must follow a strategy similar to any single product. The graduated payment mortgage, GPM, is a good example of a complex, but single, basic product that had a relatively short life cycle.

An Outline Guide to Strategic
Plan Completion

A. SITUATION ANALYSIS

Statement of Scope

- ◆ Clearly state how much of the corporation is being profiled. For example, the XYZ division, ABC Company, etc.

- ◆ Key Statistics of Business Unit (BU)
  - – absolute sales volume, current year, and as a percent of corporate total
  - – absolute net assets, current year, and as a percent of corporate total
  - – absolute profits, current year, and as a percent of corporate total

- ◆ Market segment(s) in which the BU is currently competing, for example, the specialty X market. (Be careful to define market segment so that it properly describes the nature of the current business.) Also, state, if desired, the future market segment(s) in which the BU plans or hopes to compete.

- ◆ Products provided and end-use if needed for clarification. For example, product X for commercial use.

- ◆ If the numbers above include sale of less important products not described by the words, so state and footnote any significant skewing of the numbers. For example, the footnote may say minor products not discussed include government loans products and ARM products with no significant skewing.

Industry Description ("Industry" is defined as those firms competing directly or indirectly with the BU.)

- ◆ Dollar size of the total industry

- ◆ Growth over time (by segments, if necessary, and in relationship to GNP), both historical and future in units and dollars

- ◆ Key influences in the growth of the industry

- ◆ Cyclicality (tied to what industry indicators)

- ◆ Seasonality

- Competition
  - number of competitors—increasing or decreasing
  - names and market shares of current major competitors (quantified to extent possible)
  - how is leader's share changing—relative to BU?
  - any constraints on the leader
  - industry stability—entrants versus failure
  - foreign competitors, size and growth

- How important is this industry or industry segment to your competitors (e.g., relative profitability; emotional commitment)?

- Organizational nature of competition (freestanding company or division)

- Degree of integration, forward and backward (e.g., leaders are integrated from raw material to final product). For example, is there a CLO; how are loans originated, inhouse or outside; appraisers, document company prepares closing papers, etc.

- Competitor strengths and weaknesses

- Product-line concept and unique values offered
  - specialty

- Basis of competition (e.g., price/service/technology)
  - critical ingredients for success

- Barriers to entry

- MIS and back office
  - industry capacity situation, current year by percent utilization
  - what is optimum capacity utilization?
  - minimum economic size of incremental increase to existing plant or facilities and for entirely new plant or facilities.
  - start-up time required to build and bring on-stream incremental new plant and start up new plant
  - who is planning new capacity? when?
  - financing issues—where will funding come from?

- Existing product vulnerability
  - to new services
  - from other products

- Normal distribution channels

- Constraints (community/regulatory)
- Financial operating characteristics and trends (capacity to grow, liquidity, capital)
- Price trends (e.g., are industry prices dispersed among competitors; is there a price leader? if so, who?)
- Pricing strategy—spreads, bundling and unbundling
- Customers served
  - categories (retail, wholesale) if applicable by business unit
  - demand sensitivity for foreign (nongeographic area)
  - degree of concentration (e.g., geographic, size, other particular characteristics)

Market Description ("Market" is defined as those customers served by the industry—directly, indirectly, or both)

- Size of market segments and growth trends
- Key changes and trend in market
- Geographic distribution of market
- Customers served by market and segmented by type
- Price trends

Business Unit Description

- Share of market over time
- Share(s) of market(s) and appropriate segments
- Breadth of service line compared to competitors
- Degree of customer concentration
- Strengths and weaknesses (e.g., a particular function or process), which may or may not be competitive strengths or weaknesses
- How did the corporation enter the industry or industry segment and why?

- ♦ MIS or industry specialization strength versus competition
- ♦ Extent to which market values corporate and/or brand name
- ♦ Channels of distribution (location of branches/define other channels such as telemarketing)
- ♦ Possession of sufficient volume to justify the optimal distribution system
- ♦ MIS and facilities status
  - – capacity situation, current year by percent utilization
  - – what is optimum for you?
  - – other profitable alternative uses
- ♦ Total cost position compared with competitors
- ♦ Potential blue sky opportunities (any major opportunities not included in current plan)

Industry Maturity

- ♦ See outline for appropriate classification of the BU's industry

Competitive Position

- ♦ Try to summarize one or more real advantages over the competition—use strength and weakness analysis under "BU Description"
- ♦ Compared to competition:
  - – dominant
  - – strong
  - – favorable
  - – tenable
  - – weak
  - – nonviable

Past and Current Business Strategies

- ♦ Describe and classify by the corporate system of strategic alternatives (a BU may employ at any given time one or more strategies)

B. PLAN ANALYSIS

Key Assumptions

- ◆ Economy
  - national growth
  - regional growth
  - degree of government influence
  - degree of regulatory influence
  - competitive climate

- ◆ Industry
  - growth
  - stability
  - competitor actions
  - growth of markets from which demand is derived
  - potential threats (money center, credit union, other)

- ◆ Market
  - price trends
  - cost trends (including labor)
  - spread management (unbundling)

- ◆ Outside influences
  - corporate or group pressures (e.g., impact of previous and present corporate strategy)
  - social trends (e.g., consumerism, equal opportunity)
  - government, regulatory, antitrust

Industry Maturity

- ◆ Update the industry maturity as appropriate

Future Business Strategies

- ◆ List four to six key strategies (typically, more than four to six for each BU are not appropriate or meaningful). Strategies should be as broad and simple as possible.

Specific Programs With Key Target Dates

♦ List those major programs that are necessary to execute strategy

♦ Where possible, show cost/benefit summary

Major Issues to Be Resolved by BU and by Group Corp.

♦ Summarize critical decisions to be made so that priorities are clear

Business Functional Emphasis

♦ Rank functional emphasis needed to execute strategy
   – marketing
   – operation
   – accounting
   – human resources
   – secondary marketing
   – servicing
   – production
   – other

Interdivisional Factors Related to Plan

♦ Kind of dependency on other organizational units

♦ Degree of dependency on other organizational units

♦ Benefits provided by BU to other organizations

Acquisition Characterization

♦ Past criteria for acquisitions made

♦ Desired criteria for future acquisitions needed to implement strategy

C. PERFORMANCE

Project financial and volume performance for each BU for each year or period of the planning cycle

D. INVESTMENTS

Project required investment and expected returns for each year or period of the planning cycle

E. PERFORMANCE ANALYSIS

Past Performance Versus Past Strategy

♦ How close has the past performance followed past strategy? Describe and make judgment as to whether:
 – consistent
 – not consistent

♦ Significant changes in past performance numbers (including reasons—what went wrong)

Future Expected Performance Versus Current/Future Strategy

♦ Reasons for significant changes

Summary Characterization

♦ Capture in a summary paragraph the nature of current strategy and performance, the essence of future objectives, and the strategy (or strategies) to be employed to reach those objectives

♦ Include major reasons why

F. MANAGERIAL SYSTEM ANALYSIS

Nature of:

♦ Planning

- time frame
- format
- degree of corporate uniformity
- procedure at each level

♦ Organizing/Structure/Compensation
  - degree of choice in structure
  - degree of flexibility in compensation

♦ Communication System
  - description of method and style
  - degree of flexibility

♦ Controls and Reporting
  - system description
  - performance criteria (fixed or adjustable)
  - degree of detail

♦ Nature of Culture and Climate
  - degree of formality
  - ties with the past
  - sensitivity to changes
  - ability to respond effectively to changes

♦ Actions Required for Congruency
  - steps to be taken so that the managerial system matches strategic demands of the market

G. RISK ANALYSIS

♦ View the risk and rewards for each strategy

♦ Analyze the corporation's ability to withstand the risk assumed if the strategy fails or falls short of objectives

Chapter 4

GROWTH AND DIVERSIFICATION
Are the Benefits Always There?

Risk Analysis Group*
Coopers & Lybrand

INTRODUCTION

In August 1992 the Risk Analysis Group at Coopers & Lybrand (C&L) published an article in *Mortgage Banking* magazine dealing with two increasingly important issues to the mortgage banking industry and federal government insurance programs—growth and diversification. The trend in the mortgage banking industry towards consolidation, especially in the area of loan servicing, has resulted in fewer institutions servicing and managing loan portfolios and an increase in the average size of the portfolios serviced. The Risk Analysis Group updated the results of their earlier analysis presented in *Mortgage Banking* magazine, and their findings are presented in this chapter.

Three questions were posed for analysis. In business, is bigger really better? And what about the popular diversification advice not to

---

* The Coopers & Lybrand (C&L) Risk Analysis Group consists of 16 top management/systems analysts who work in C&L's Washington, DC, office. The Risk Analysis Group specializes in synthesizing and analyzing large data bases in order to convert raw data into management information. The members of the Group are: Director—Jim Boswell; Manager—Jean Young; Senior Associates—John Kruszewski, Xavier Gonzalez-Sanfeliu, Eunah Kim, Jim Moynihan, Teresa Luhn, and Joe Bordonaro; Associates—Anne Molitor, Derek Price, Tristan Bostone, Alex Krakovsky, Jennifer Billings, Kevin Maul, Olivier Simonis, and Michael Klein.

put all your eggs in one basket? Finally, is growth through mergers, acquisitions, and diversification everything it is proposed to be? After all, wasn't it the renowned economist Mark Twain who told us to put all our eggs in one basket, but watch them?

Even though conventional wisdom is on the side of growth through mergers and acquisitions, and diversification is a commonly sought strategic goal for many, we believe it is critical for industry professionals to question whether these strategies are everything they are cracked up to be.

On one side of the growth and diversification issue are those who argue *quantitatively* that the portfolio diversification theory, originally meant for personal portfolios only, should also be applied to business management. They insist that the soundest and least risky strategy for business management is through growth and diversification. On the other side of the same issue are the business policy analysts who argue *qualitatively* that undisciplined growth and diversification strategies may result in a reduced focus on business advantages and objectives, negating any of the presumed quantitative gains that the "number crunchers" claim result from growth and diversification.

How relevant is this issue? It is hard to think of any corporate body holding a strategic planning session that would not discuss the issue of growth and/or diversification. Much federal decision-making is molded by the policymakers' attitudes on growth and diversification, including such things as banking policy, antitrust law, and even how the savings and loan debacle is resolved.

Consolidation and geographic diversification have received increased attention from many sectors of our economy for reasons that stretch from the simple desire to improve efficiency and lower risk to the need to diversify as the only means for survival. Consider the recent spate of large bank mergers. Just within the nine-month time period between our initial analysis and our updated analysis of large servicing portfolios, the Risk Analysis Group discovered a significant drop (362 to 340) in the number of institutions managing and servicing large GNMA portfolios. Growth and consolidation is a fact of life in the competitive world. However, the question remains, is this growth and consolidation good and does it reduce the risk of the surviving industry institutions and the federal insurance programs supporting the industry? In the end, it is the American consumer who either gains or loses from the success or failure of this movement toward consolidation of federally insured portfolios and the tendency toward institutions monitoring larger and larger portfolios.

Using standardized information from 340 mortgage banking institutions that submit the status of their loan portfolios to the Government National Mortgage Association (GNMA), the Risk Analysis Group set out to evaluate the effects of growth and diversification in the mortgage banking industry. This chapter explains the results of that analysis.

PURPOSE AND FRAMEWORK OF THE ANALYSIS

Since January 1990, the C&L Risk Analysis Group has supported GNMA's efforts to monitor and actively address risk. The basis of much of the Group's risk analysis comes from the aggregation, segregation, and synthesis of more than 7.3 million home loan mortgage computer records submitted quarterly to GNMA by the institutions servicing GNMA single-family loan portfolios.

As we hinted earlier, conventional wisdom asserts that:

♦ Increased geographical diversification lowers the risk of business failure by reducing regional dependency; and

♦ Growth leads to increased efficiencies through economies of scale, which in turn improve competitive advantage.

The Risk Analysis Group decided to test this conventional wisdom by analyzing the loan portfolios of both large and small mortgage institutions with different levels of regional diversification.

For the particular analysis discussed in this chapter, the Risk Analysis Group looked at the 340 active, nondefaulted institutions, each having GNMA loan portfolios containing more than 1,000 federally insured or guaranteed home loans. The total loan sample of the analysis represents more than 7.3 million loans and $404 billion in outstanding principal. The records analyzed represented the condition of the portfolios as of September 1992.

The measurement used to evaluate *portfolio performance* was what the Risk Analysis Group calls the DQ3RATIO, the percentage of portfolio loans that are three months or more delinquent. The DQ3RATIO is central to strategic management decisions through its effect on expected future cash flows and portfolio valuation. A portfolio with a high DQ3RATIO has a high percentage of nonperforming loans and is less valuable than a portfolio with a low DQ3RATIO. The likelihood of institutional losses and a portfolio defaulting to GNMA increases as the DQ3RATIO increases.

The measurement used to evaluate GNMA's *portfolio risk* for the different size and diversification categories investigated was the standard deviation of the DQ3RATIO. A large DQ3RATIO standard deviation for a category indicates high volatility and greater risk than a category with a lower DQ3RATIO standard deviation.

The Risk Analysis Group developed its own geographical diversification index to measure the degree of diversification of a loan portfolio. The procedure for calculating the diversification index was based on the percentage of an institution's loans in each of five regions (i.e., East, Midwest, South, Southwest, and West) as defined by GNMA. Regional loan percentages of 20 percent or more were given a score of 20, while percentages under 20 percent received a score equal to the percentage itself. The minimum diversification score using this method is 20, given to those institutions that have 100 percent of their loans in one region. The theoretical optimum diversification score of 100 requires the portfolio to have exactly 20 percent of the loans in each of the five geographical regions. The following table shows how a typical diversification index was calculated.

Diversification Scoring Example

Region	Loan Percent	Diversification Score
East	43.4%	20.0
Midwest	14.3%	14.3
South	21.4%	20.0
Southwest	6.4%	6.4
West	14.6%	14.6

SIZE AND PERFORMANCE

Table 4.1 shows the results of the analysis segregated by size of institutional portfolio. As can be seen from the table, the portfolios were divided into three categories:

- ◆ portfolios with more than 10,000 loans;

- ◆ portfolios with 4,000 to 10,000 loans; and

- ◆ portfolios with 1,000 to 4,000 loans.

Note the abnormally high DQ3RATIO of the group of institutions with the largest portfolios compared to the two smaller groups. Table 4.1 shows that smaller institutions substantially outperform larger institutions in maintaining lower levels of delinquent loans.

Is it surprising that the DQ3RATIO of the largest group is significantly higher than that of the two smaller groups? Not necessarily. The economic break-even point of a loan portfolio depends upon unit processing cost factors associated with performing as well as nonperforming loans. If increased size provides economies of scale that reduce overall unit processing costs, then these economies can cover the increased costs of a higher rate of nonperforming loans. In effect, break-even analysis allows new efficiencies (reduced unit processing costs) to cover new inefficiencies (higher delinquency rates and subsequent foreclosure costs).

From an overall governmental policy viewpoint, this table may reflect a problem that is not necessarily a concern to the mortgage banking industry. The federal government covers a substantial portion of the cost of foreclosure through its FHA and VA federal home loan insurance and guarantee programs. Therefore, a business does not have to factor these losses into its break-even analysis. Much of the increased cost of reduced performance is passed to the government; thus the taxpayer eventually may cover the for increased delinquency costs.

Table 4.1   Stratification by Portfolio Size

Portfolio Size Categories (in Loans)	Number of Institutions per Size	DQ3 RATIO (Performance)	DQ3RATIO Standard Deviation (Risk Volatility)	Average Number of Loans	Average Diversity Score
≥ 10,000	145	2.43	1.013	42,442	57
4,000 to 9,900	86	2.03	1.226	6,237	37
1,000 to 3,999	109	1.93	1.322	2,230	32

Another observation about Table 4.1 is the DQ3RATIO standard deviation increases as loan size groups get smaller. This was an expected result. Due to size alone, greater volatility and risk was expected with the smaller portfolios as measured by the statistically calculated standard deviation for the DQ3RATIO. Because of this volatility, the likelihood of an institution defaulting its portfolio to GNMA is greater for the smaller portfolio groups.

In fact, historically a higher percentage of small institutional portfolios have defaulted to GNMA than large portfolios. However, the number of institutional defaults is not necessarily the best measurement for government risk. Though only 4 of the 31 previously defaulted portfolios GNMA is currently managing had more than 10,000 loans when they defaulted, these 4 portfolios represent 85 percent of the total amount of defaulted loans (approximately the same percentage that large issuers account for when looking at the entire population of 7.3 million nondefaulted loans). Large institutions might not default as often as smaller institutions, but when they do the impact is greater.

DIVERSIFICATION: A PERSPECTIVE BASED ON SIZE

Table 4.2 shows the analysis of the data when segregated into the same three size categories as Table 4.1 and further into three diversification categories:

1.   diversification scores greater than 60.

2.   diversification scores between 40 and 60.

3.   diversification scores between 20 and 40.

Remember, as defined by our diversification methodology, the higher the diversification score, the greater the portfolio's level of diversification.

An analysis of Table 4.2 argues against diversification. At first glance, diversification is not a large factor for the institutions with more than 10,000 loan portfolios. Neither the DQ3RATIO nor the DQ3RATIO standard deviations vary much between diversification categories. However, as we will examine later, DQ3RATIOs vary substantially between the five regions we analyzed. For this reason, greater volatility would be expected in the DQ3RATIO standard deviation for the less diverse portfolios. Since the volatility is not apparent in the findings, it implies some other factor must be at work. Possibly, the more targeted

Table 4.2 Diversity Score Stratification by Portfolio Size

Portfolios of 10,000 or More Loans

Diversity Score Groups	Number of Institutions per Score	DQ3 RATIO	DQ3RATIO Standard Deviation	Average Number of Loans	Average Diversity Score
≥ 60	71	2.39	1.117	60,956	75
40 to 59	41	2.47	0.859	25,873	51
20 to 39	33	2.54	.982	23,194	26
	145	2.45		42,058	57

Portfolios of 4,000 to 9,999 Loans

Diversity Score Groups	Number of Institutions per Score	DQ3 RATIO	DQ3RATIO Standard Deviation	Average Number of Loans	Average Diversity Score
≥ 60	12	2.26	0.953	6,787	75
40 to 59	21	2.46	1.449	5,982	49
20 to 39	53	1.81	1.136	6,214	24
	86	2.03		6,237	37

Portfolios of 1,000 to 3,999 Loans

Diversity Score Groups	Number of Institutions per Score	DQ3 RATIO	DQ3RATIO Standard Deviation	Average Number of Loans	Average Diversity Score
≥ 60	10	2.85	1.723	2,321	70
40 to 59	24	2.24	1.621	2,354	46
20 to 39	75	1.68	1.115	2,179	23
	109	1.91		2,231	32

*DQ3RATIO: Percentage of loans in the portfolio that are deliquent three months or more

focus of servicers of regional portfolios compared to servicers of more regionally diversified portfolios might be working to reduce the volatility in the risk.

Some facts relating to previously defaulted large portfolios are noteworthy. Of the four large institutional portfolios (loan portfolios with more than 10,000 loans) that have defaulted to GNMA, two had diversification scores above 60, one fell in the 40-59 range, and one fell in the 20-39 range. In fact, the largest of the four defaulted portfolios had a diversification index of 83.5. This leads to the conclusion that risk may be more a factor of management than of management's decisions regarding geographic diversification.

When looking at the two smaller groups of portfolios, the case against diversification seems even stronger. Table 4.2 shows the DQ3RATIOs for the 4,000 to 10,000 group and the 1,000 to 4,000 group are substantially lower for the least diversified portfolios, yet the standard deviations of the groups are not substantially different. Focus seems to be even more important for smaller entities. Note that the average number of loans in the portfolio for the two smaller groups is basically the same for each of the diversification categories.

It is probably no coincidence the largest portfolios tend to be more diversified than smaller portfolios (almost 50 percent of the large group have diversification scores greater than 60, compared to only about 10 percent for the smaller groups). To attain growth, diversification might be necessary. It is somewhat surprising the benefits of geographical diversification do not show in the analysis. At best, the analysis is neutral on the merits of geographic diversification for institutions with large portfolios. The case against diversification in smaller portfolios is more clearly apparent when the data in Table 4.2 is evaluated. These smaller institutions, on average, might lack the sophistication and resources needed to manage the potentially negative features of a diversification strategy.

DIVERSIFICATION: A PERSPECTIVE
BASED ON REGION

The Risk Analysis Group analyzed diversification from a regional perspective separately from portfolio size. Table 4.3 shows an overview perspective of the DQ3RATIO for each region, plus the DQ3RATIO for all the loans outside the particular region. For example, the DQ3RATIO for all loans in the Eastern region is 2.94 percent, while the DQ3RATIO for all loans outside the Eastern region is 2.27 percent. Worth noting, the DQ3RATIO for the entire population of loans was 2.38 percent in September 1992. Since our earlier analysis, the delinquency ratios in-

Table 4.3   Regional Performance: Home versus Away

Home Region	DQ3RATIO	Away Region	DQ3RATIO
EAST	2.94	OUTSIDE EAST (MW + S + SW + W)	2.27
MIDWEST	2.41	OUTSIDE MIDWEST (E + S + SW + W)	2.41
SOUTH	2.68	OUTSIDE SOUTH (E + MW + SW + W)	2.34
SOUTHWEST	2.01	OUTSIDE SOUTHWEST (E + MW + S + W)	2.51
WEST	1.99	OUTSIDE WEST (E + MW + S + SW)	2.51

Note: Overall DQ3RATIO = 2.38

creased in the Midwest and Western regions, though the economic problems facing the East and the South continue to show in this table.

In our analysis, we categorized each of the 340 institutional portfolios by the region where the portfolio had the highest percentage of their loans. For example, if an institution had a portfolio structured in the manner shown in our earlier example for establishing a diversification index, we would categorize the institution as an Eastern institution (the largest percentage of their loans, 43.4 percent, was found to be in the Eastern region). Table 4.4 shows a composite summary of the number of institutions, the average number of loans in the portfolio, average diversification, and the average DQ3RATIO for each regional category. Table 4.4 includes a Home versus Away matrix reflecting how each regional group performed within its own region as well as how it

Table 4.4   Institutional Performance: Home versus Away

Geographic Group	Eastern Issuers	Midwestern Issuers	Southern Issuers	Southwest Issuers	Western Issuers
Number of Institutions	44	68	66	83	79
Average Number Loans per Institution	15,389	14,162	27,285	22,508	20,562
Average Diversity Score	40	46	45	44	43
Average DQ3 RATIO	2.73	2.28	2.49	2.46	2.04

Table 4.4 (continued)

Institutional DQ3RATIOs—Home versus Away Matrix

Geographic Group	Eastern Issuers	Midwestern Issuers	Southern Issuers	Southwest Issuers	Western Issuers
EAST	**2.93**	2.81	2.69	3.41	2.96
MIDWEST	2.45	**2.14**	2.30	2.92	2.31
SOUTH	2.76	2.94	**2.55**	3.14	2.62
SOUTHWEST	1.73	1.80	2.30	**2.03**	1.78
WEST	1.89	2.53	2.34	2.28	**1.72**
DQ3RATIO OUT-SIDE HOME REGION	2.39	2.44	2.43	2.86	2.36
Regional DQ3RA-TIO (for Table 4.3)	2.94	2.41	2.68	2.01	1.99

Comparative DQ3RATIO Differences Between Regional and Institutional Performance

Geographic Group	Eastern Issuers	Midwestern Issuers	Southern Issuers	Southwest Issuers	Western Issuers
EAST	**(0.01)**	(0.13)	(0.25)	0.47	0.02
MIDWEST	0.04	**(0.27)**	(0.11)	0.51	(0.10)
SOUTH	0.08	0.26	**(0.13)**	0.46	(0.06)
SOUTHWEST	(0.28)	(0.21)	0.29	**0.02**	(0.23)
WEST	(0.10)	0.54	0.35	0.29	**(0.27)**
DQ3RATIO OUTSIDE HOME REGION	0.12	0.03	0.09	0.35	(0.15)

OVERALL DQ3RATIO AT HOME		= 2.22
OVERALL DQ3RATIO AWAY FROM HOME		= 2.51

performed in the other four regions. For example, Eastern institutions showed a DQ3RATIO of 2.93 for the East region and a DQ3RATIO of 2.76 for the Southern region. When compared against norms for the regions from Table 4.3, the Eastern group had a DQ3RATIO of 0.01 percent (2.93 - 2.94) *below* the norm for the East, and a DQ3RATIO of 0.08 percent (2.76 - 2.68) *above* that for the South. In other words, the

Eastern group performed better than the norm in their own region and worse than the norm in the Southern region.

In every region except the Southwest the regional groups performed better than the overall norm for their region. And even for the Southwest group, where performance was worse than the norms in every region, the performance was closer to the norm in its own region than in any other region. In addition, three of the home regions (i.e., the Midwest, South, and West home regions) outperformed every one of the other four comparative outside regions in their own region. Outsiders outperformed the home region institutions only in the East and the Southwest regions. Of the twenty possible locations where performance comparisons can be made between outside and home region institutions, only five show outside region institutions outperforming home institutions.

Overall, as can be seen from the bottom part of Table 4.4, when compared to population norms, every region performed better within its region than in the combined areas outside its region. This result was the same as our earlier analysis that looked at the condition of the GNMA portfolios as of December 1991. There, too, the institutions in all regions performed better within their home region than outside it. In total, the DQ3RATIO for home regions was 2.22 percent, while the DQ3RATIO for loans outside the home region was 2.51 percent. This difference between home and away delinquency rates is too statistically significant to ignore and indicates performance decrease when attention is given to areas outside an institution's core focus area.

The analysis results are worth management's attention. Though the Risk Analysis Group is unwilling to conclude that geographical diversification is a bad policy for a mortgage banking institution to pursue. They do believe the statistical analysis results show diversification policies should be well planned and cautiously considered, especially when they result in expansion into areas outside management's historically predominant focus.

CONSOLIDATION AND MEASUREMENT OF ECONOMIC AND MANAGEMENT RISK

In recent years the mortgage banking industry has experienced significant consolidation as a result of improvements in technology and an increasingly competitive environment. Table 4.5 shows how the number of institutions servicing GNMA portfolios has declined in just the last few years. Even though the overall number of loans that fall under the purview of GNMA has continued to increase, the number of institutions servicing the loan portfolios has declined by 18 percent since June 1989.

Looking at the five loan size categories of Table 4.5 shows that only the largest loan size group (portfolios with more than 10,000 loans) has increased in numbers since June 1989. As shown in the table, servicing organizations with more than 10,000 loans represent a greater share of the overall GNMA portfolio than they did only a couple of years ago. Whereas in June 1989 large institutions were responsible for servicing 82.8 percent of the GNMA portfolio, they now service approximately 88.0 percent of the GNMA portfolio. The fact that these larger portfolios tend to be more geographically diversified makes the issues addressed in this chapter even more important.

Because of the industry consolidation movement and the concern with portfolio diversification and growth and their relationship to risk, the C&L Risk Analysis Group analyzes each GNMA servicing institution's portfolio in two primary kinds of risk: (1) economic risk, and (2) management/operational risk.

Traditionally, evaluating economic risk has been the method mortgage banking regulators used to look for potential institutional problems. Determining which institutional portfolios are most affected by deteriorating regional and local economics is a necessary and valid approach to risk analysis. The C&L Risk Analysis Group is constantly evaluating regional economics to foresee problems in GNMA-serviced loan portfolios. Two of the primary economic risk factors used by the Risk Analysis Group are changes in unemployment rates and housing

Table 4.5   GNMA Issuers/Servicer Consolidation Trend

Size Group in Loans	Issuers in Group			Percent of Remaining Principal		
	JUN 1989	NOV 1991	NOV 1992	JUN 1989	NOV 1991	NOV 1992
≥ 10,000	123	149	146	82.8%	86.6%	88.0%
3,000 to 9,000	138	124	110	12.3%	9.8%	8.7%
1,000 to 2,999	121	101	83	3.3%	2.5%	2.1%
500 to 999	85	54	52	0.9%	0.5%	0.5%
≤ 500	231	211	182	0.6%	0.4%	0.4%
	698	639	573	100.0%	100.0%	100.0%

price indexes. Historically, as regional economies soured, the economic risk of an institution with loans in that region increased.

However, institutional portfolios are affected as much by management policies and operations as by regional or local economics. After analyzing previous institutional defaults, the Risk Analysis Group concluded that poor management practices account for as many of the defaults as do economic conditions. For this reason the Risk Analysis Group developed a management (or operational) risk indicator to measure how well institutions manage their portfolios. Management or operational risk, as defined by the Risk Analysis Group, takes economic factors into consideration and compensates for them. Having the universe of GNMA loans available to analyze, the Risk Analysis Group develops overall GNMA delinquency norms by year of loan origination for every 3-digit ZIP code in the country. Every GNMA-serviced portfolio is then evaluated in terms of these norms, weighted by its geographical distribution and yearly originations, to determine what the overall delinquency performance of the portfolio would be if it conformed to the universal norms for the portfolio's distribution. The actual delinquency performance of the serviced portfolio is then compared to this calculated expected norm. This measurement shows how well management is handling operations and servicing its portfolio. The management risk indicator can evaluate the effectiveness of an institution's diversification policy. Little can be done to stop institutional defaults when their portfolio lies in predominantly depressed economic areas; however, when the problems are not purely economical, but managerial, more active corrective measures can be taken.

FOOD FOR THOUGHT

A business initiating activity outside its home region, as with loan originations and purchases in the mortgage banking industry, has a hedge against economic swings at home; however, it risks sacrificing potential competitive advantages in its home market. Competitive pressures might tempt business leaders to diversify for growth without performing time-consuming, yet essential, activities, such as analyzing potential markets, investors, and competition.

Decreasing the proximity to and the familiarity with a given region or specific business makes sustaining existing competitive advantages difficult. The cost of maintaining the same level of quality control, reporting, and communication are likely to increase with diversification.

The analysis of the federally insured residential mortgage market illustrates the difficulties involved with maintaining portfolio/business performance away from a home region. Proper analysis and appraisal, essential for minimizing quality risk, become increasingly difficult outside one's home region. Comprehensive appraisals require data on local economic trends, supply-and-demand conditions, competitive dynamics, zoning laws, builders' reputations, etc. Proper field evaluations, property inspections, due diligence, and establishing strong relationships with local housing and labor authorities are difficult in unfamiliar territory.

The benefits of diversification and growth through consolidation are highly touted: lower unit costs, increased opportunities through synergistic market expansion, and a stronger competitive position in the marketplace. Nonetheless, a discussion of the benefits of growth and diversification must include related costs—all costs. For example, in the case of federally subsidized or insured business activities, insurance cost must be considered. This is a hidden cost to consolidation, as evidenced by the price of the savings and loan bailout. As legislators consider reforms to help the banking industry navigate through the current era of consolidation, they must remain mindful of the needs and objectives of the insurance programs, as well as the affected institutions.

If financial institutions with federally insured or subsidized programs are permitted to make corporate decisions without factoring in insurance costs, then seemingly reasonable business decisions can backfire onto the taxpayer. From the analysis of the mortgage banking industry discussed in this chapter, the benefits of growth and diversification are not readily apparent and are probably overstated. As commercial and mortgage banks consolidate their risk into larger and larger entities, the federal insurance and guarantee programs must find ways to improve the monitoring of their risk liability. Though the intent of consolidation might be good, the evidence presented here shows that institutions should carefully evaluate the benefits derived from such strategies.

CONCLUSION

Analyzing a large group of mortgage banking institutions shows that the gross generalization of financial theories such as "bigger is better" and "diversification lowers risk" are not sufficient, by themselves, to formulate corporate and federal policies. In fact, growth and diversification might not be as desirable as popular belief suggests. From this analysis, it appears shrewdly focusing on business strengths is more important than growth and diversification for its own sake. Finally, reiterating the most important finding of the analysis, risk might be more a factor of management than of management's decisions relating to growth and diversification.

Chapter 5

THE MANAGEMENT OF MORTGAGE BANKING COMPANIES

Jack Daly
President
Pratt • Daly Corporation

INTRODUCTION

This chapter provides an overview of those things felt to be necessary toward maximizing the success of any mortgage lending company through effective leadership and management. That is a broad-based statement and it is purposely designed as such. For the principles and fundamental strategies dealt with in this chapter apply equally well whether you are a commercial bank, savings and loan, mortgage banker, mortgage broker, mutual savings bank, credit union, or other mortgage lender. Whether your initiatives include retail, wholesale, correspondent, builder, corporate relocations, consumer direct, or another mode of origination, the principles are the same. Be you national or regional in scope, large or small, and be it A, B, or C paper that is your mainstay, the topics covered will apply. As well, the management fundamentals apply to both portfolio lenders and secondary market participants.

The game is being won by those focusing on the fundamentals—basic "blocking and tackling." The focus of this chapter will be on ten components, with a closing look at the management challenges looming ahead for mortgage lenders.

The secrets of effective mortgage lending management are not secrets at all. It involves being better, smarter, and faster than the competition. That, then, is the focus of this chapter.

FOUNDATIONS OF LEADERSHIP

Common sense tells us that managers are more common than are leaders. By understanding what is managing and what is leading, managers can grow to be leaders. Management directs and controls activities required to achieve defined purposes and goals. It involves planning, directing, organizing, budgeting, and problem-solving in order to make company systems work. But if it becomes too bureaucratic, leadership potential may be stifled.

Leadership is not in opposition to management, for it shares the aim of meeting company goals. But instead of relying on an established system, leaders get workers involved and excited. Inspired employees provide the means for a company to marshal energy, seize upon its opportunities, and cope with unexpected challenges. Leaders bring workers to their potential. They determine the urgency with which others work, and provide the focus with which management carries out its functions. Most recognize that an organization's most valuable asset is its workers—yet sometimes management forgets that assets can be managed but people must be lead.

Leadership is not management. No grief is suggested here, as both abilities are vital for success. But it is important to differentiate these disciplines. Warren Bennis, distinguished professor of business administration at the University of Southern California, states these clear distinctions between leaders and managers:

- ◆ The Manager administers; the Leader innovates.
- ◆ The Manager is a copy; the Leader is an original.
- ◆ The Manager focuses on systems and structure; the Leader focuses on people.
- ◆ The Manager relies on control; the Leader inspires trust.
- ◆ The Manager has a short-range view; the Leader has a long-range perspective.
- ◆ The Manager asks how and when; the Leader asks what and why.
- ◆ The Manager has his eye always on the bottom line; the leader has his eye on the horizon.
- ◆ The Manager imitates; the Leader originates.
- ◆ The Manager accepts the status quo; the Leader challenges it.
- ◆ The Manager is the classic good soldier; the Leader is his own person.
- ◆ The Manager does things right; the Leader does the right thing.

(Reference: Warren Bennis, *On Becoming a Leader*, 1989)

How you spend your time will define your leadership tendencies. How much of your working day is devoted to managing processes and systems and how much to helping your people grow? A manager uses power—a leader empowers through delegation and encouragement.

John Gardner said, "I like to watch great leaders in action. Unfortunately, it doesn't take much of my time." Too much time is spent managing and not enough time leading.

COMMUNICATING YOUR VISION

The challenge for the mortgage lender is an ever increasing need to manage tighter cost/expense controls, enhance revenue via increased loan production levels profitably, while maintaining or enhancing a motivated, focused work force. In order to meet such a challenge, this fourfold approach is recommended:

1. Develop and sustain a clear vision.

2. Communicate the vision.

3. Instill an action environment.

4. Create a learning environment.

Through leadership, dreams are turned into reality, with and through others. When the four factors above are put together, then such a leadership forum exists.

Vision

Max Depree, Chairman of Herman Miller Furniture, said it so well: "The first responsibility of a leader is to define a vision. The last is to say 'thank you.' In between, the leader is a servant."

The vision is the long-range goal, the result of an imaginative sense of what could be, which is both possible and credible. The vision, properly developed and communicated, is compelling—attracting and pulling people together to "make it happen." The vision, coupled with a concise, action-oriented mission statement and set of corporate beliefs (these things we believe), creates sufficient structure and guidelines to empower each of our associates to take action.

The best mission statement is the shortest. It has to be easy to memorize, and one that our associates can state verbally with pride. One mortgage lender stated their mission as:

"We create value for our customers by making home financing easy."

A few examples of corporate beliefs are:

"We believe in trust, ethics, and integrity as the cornerstones of our business partnerships" or "We believe in fostering individual growth toward personal and professional excellence."

Once the mission and beliefs are developed, the associates should be empowered to execute their functions in the fashion best suited to accomplish their mission.

Communicate

Bill Gates, the incredibly successful founder and CEO of Microsoft, described his role: "My job is to have a vision and communicate it."

Shared visions don't just happen. One way is through the concept of "cascading mission statements." Once an overall company mission is developed and communicated, each operational unit—production, operations, secondary marketing, financial, loan servicing—develops its mission statement with its associates. Then continue the process—for example, to underwriting, then to a team of underwriters, and ultimately to the level of each individual underwriter. And the same is done throughout the organization. Each associate is thereby enrolled into the mission through their participation. Each "submission" is in congruence with the overall mission. The submissions support the company mission, yet provide additional specifics, more focus, and tend to be more short-term oriented. For example, "to have our loan application approval rate exceed 95 percent in the second quarter," or "to increase our market share to____percent" or "to process an average of____loans per processor."

The Mission should excite people to action. It can be further communicated in a number of ways, such as company get togethers, newsletter, plaques, etc. The leader/manager, to be most effective, should play the very real role of "head cheerleader" with his or her associates. He or she needs to be visible with his or her associates. For those managers with team members "in the field," "out in the field" is where the leader/manager needs to be. In order to do so, the leader/manager must delegate "desk-top activities" to his or her associates. If necessary, consideration should be given to hiring an administrator to free you for your highest and best contribution.

A shared vision is a powerful tool. It doesn't just happen. It requires action.

Action Environment

Key here is alignment. An environment must be created that enables the vision to be real. Alignment develops when individuals perceive that contributing to the group is a win/win relationship contributing to their personal missions. People work for their reasons, not ours. The leader/manager must discover what those individual values are, and deliver within the overall company mission. These individual visions are then molded into a shared vision when a leader/mentor takes action and motivates others to also take action. The actions must align themselves with the vision. For example, instilling within the environment the absence of fear of being wrong or making a mistake. Or, providing access to a cross-training environment, allowing for individual personal growth.

Learning Environment

The creation of a learning environment will result in creativity and productivity. It involves delegation as opposed to a "telling" environment, encouraging associates to experiment, to take measured risks. Practice the art of asking "What is your recommendation?" People treated with respect will tend to operate in a like fashion.

Once the ingredients of the corporate success culture (vision—mission—values) have been identified along with the individual values of the associates, the company is then properly positioned to manage by objectives (MBO). This includes: goals/objectives; strategies to achieve the objectives; action plans assigning specific accountability, time lines, and measurement criteria as to performance; and company policies and procedures.

Specific objectives might include: loan production volumes (by loan product, by region, by type of origination, and at what profit/expense levels), profits, loan servicing portfolio size, sales levels, purchase levels, cost to service levels, etc.; secondary market funding capacities, portfolio capabilities, loan pricing structures, warehousing levels, etc.; automation systems, operational systems, human resource initiatives, etc.; merger and acquisition plans, and so forth.

Management cannot, however, effectively jump to the MBO activities without first creating a solid foundation for the department, region, or company by way of mission development and understanding individual values.

Picture, if you will, each department manager developing a game plan without a clear understanding of where the company is headed and what his or her associates' goals are. The underwriting department, for example, could be structured and operating on a base of priorities where turnaround time is most important, whereas loan production could be structured and operating on the basis that service to the customer in terms of working hardest to qualify the customer for the "best" loan is the highest priority. As a result, conflict ensues with each "quick no" that underwriting delivers in the interest of turnaround time, while loan production gets the rap of wanting to make any loan, regardless of its quality. This type of friction between any number of departments of a mortgage lender is not uncommon. It can be re-solved—better yet, avoided—through the up-front design and articu-lation of the company vision and beliefs.

Another demonstration of commitment to a learning environment is the Corporate University concept. More and more, larger mortgage lenders are implementing this concept, which is internally adminis-tered, while the instruction is a blend of internal outsourced modules.

The autocrat exhibits a "love of power," whereas the leader be-lieves in the "power of others." Successful leaders are recognizing this and acting as liberators with their associates in pursuing the overall mission.

ORGANIZATIONAL STRUCTURE

Company strategy and policy set directions and goals. But these broad plans must be matched by a corresponding managerial organization to carry out the strategies and action plans.

In its design the organization must be concerned with how the myriad of activities required are assigned to its people. To be effective, each person has to focus on particular segments of the total task. As well, each person's work must be coordinated with the work of others. All sorts of groupings of activities and of interconnecting links are possible, but the particular combination into subgroups and of these subgroups into larger divisions has a profound impact on the successful execution of any strategy.

For the successful mortgage lender, there is no single "right way." In fact, as a company succeeds and grows, it must change its organiza-tional structure, matching structure to strategy. Organizing calls for perception of subtle differences, imagination in designing special com-binations, judgment in balancing benefits and drawbacks, and human understanding, as those "organizational boxes" actually represent people.

When undertaking the design of the organization, be it the whole company or a part thereof, a comprehensive review of all activities and interactions is recommended. To examine only a part—say the "squeaky wheel"—is likely to lead to a remedy that creates as many new problems as it removes old ones.

Figure 5.1 depicts a traditional mortgage lending company struc-ture. Yet, two points of caution need noting. First, there exist any number of variations from this traditional structure. These variations have developed from the combination portfolio lender / secondary mar-ket operators; a number of point-of-sale initiatives; telemarketing and

Figure 5.1 Traditional Structure

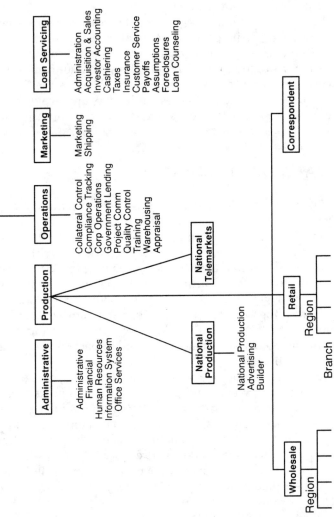

TOTAL COMPANY

Administrative	Production	Operations	Marketing	Loan Servicing
Administrative		Collateral Control	Marketing	Administration
Financial		Compliance Tracking	Shipping	Acquisition & Sales
Human Resources		Corp Operations		Investor Accounting
Information System		Government Lending		Cashiering
Office Services		Project Comm		Taxes
		Quality Control		Insurance
		Training		Customer Service
		Warehousing		Payoffs
		Appraisal		Assumptions
				Foreclosures
				Loan Counseling

National Production

National Production
Advertising
Builder

National Telemarkets

Wholesale

Region

Branch

Retail

Region

Branch

Correspondent

structures and niche revenue initiatives. Secondly, the concept of using boxes to depict organizational structure really belies the reality of the various interactions among the people who "fill the boxes." In truth, the successful mortgage lending organizational structure looks more like Figure 5.2—an ever changing atom, where individuals and departments go to the need, ignoring the "turf" suggested by the more traditional boxes. The atom organizational chart concept depicts action, fluidity, and a matching of resources to needs/opportunities. The atom organization format owns a healthy disrespect for bureaucracy in an organization. Each operational discipline has not only a right, but indeed an obligation to employ its talents to the various needs/opportunities presented to the company.

Every organization consists of more than the primary operating divisions. Questions of decentralization, the placing of staff and services, communication systems, the organization of the corporate (home) office itself, and providing the people to fill the organization, all call for attention when talking structure.

Figure 5.2   Atom Structure

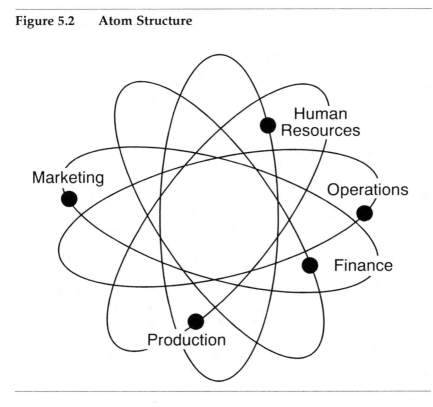

A review of each major organizational responsibility is worth noting.

Retail production is typically comprised of local branch offices manned by loan originators, loan processors, and loan closers, led by a branch manager. Residential loan underwriting is generally autonomous from the production staff, although geographically individual underwriters may reside in a retail production office. As the underwriting function is to objectively determine the creditworthiness of the borrower and collateral qualification for corporate and investor loan requirements, the separation is necessary so as to preclude conflict in the lending decision. The branch manager is responsible for originating loans through the loan originators and administrating the loan support staff. The branch manager may, or may not, be a personal producing manager, depending on the company philosophy. Regional managers are responsible for several branches and will report to the head of retail production or the senior production manager, depending on the size of the company. The production department's primary responsibility is to produce loans at a desired volume and price. In addition to retail production, several other origination avenues may exist, dependent again on the company. They include *builder business*, which can be run as a part of the retail branch or a separate focus initiative. *Wholesale/correspondent*, which involves the development of a network of company-approved mortgage brokers who perform the origination function, and the mortgage lender then offers products and pricing to the broker. Loans originated are then submitted to the lender for underwriting review. This system of origination allows the loan broker to originate without loan funding/warehouse bank lines, while allowing the lender to enhance production volumes without incurring the attendant costs of a traditional retail branch. The quality control function is generally more extensive in the *wholesale/correspondent* venue due to the third-party nature of the transactions. Because of its unique characteristics, the *wholesale/correspondent* structure typically reports direct to senior production management, and the substructure is similar to that of *retail production*. A variety of niche production initiatives exist, which may include telemarketing, consumer-direct, computerized loan originations (CLOs), etc., all of which typically report through loan production management.

The *marketing* department's primary responsibility is to ensure that all loans that are produced are either sold in the secondary market at a desired price and within a prescribed time frame or meet the desired characteristics for retention in the portfolio. The *marketing* department establishes the types of loans, interest rates, terms, and fees required by the *loan production* department. Once the loans have been originated and closed, the *marketing* department has the responsibility for shipping the loans to secondary market investors.

The *operations* department is designed to support the loan production initiatives. Functions here may include quality control, compliance, training, appraisal, warehousing, collateral control, project management, and overall lending policy and procedure. The overall scope of *operations* is to ensure compliance with internal and external lending requirements.

The *loan servicing* department is responsible for the loan once it has funded, and includes those functions incident to regular borrower interface relative to the repayment of the loan, as well as reporting and remittance of funds to the various secondary market investors. These functions may include loan setup, cashiering, investor accounting, taxes, insurance, payoffs, assumptions, foreclosures, collections, investor accounting, and acquisition/sales of loan servicing.

The balance of a typical mortgage lender organization is financial/accounting, information systems, marketing/advertising, human resources, and office services, all acting in support of the lending operation initiatives.

RELATIONSHIP SELLING

Irrespective of the type of lender, fundamental success ultimately comes down to making loans. And regardless of the fashion in which loan origination is conducted (i.e., retail, wholesale, etc.), common to all is relationships. For our purposes here we will discuss the relationship selling concept from the more traditional retail origination perspective. However, the concept is equally applicable to wholesale, builder, etc.

Mortgage lenders do not have the ability to generate substantial price or product differentials between one another. As a result, the perception of value received by the customer is critical to the success of the loan originator. Relationship selling is built on the win/win philosophy. Successful selling is the transfer of trust. Buyers want to be sure they can trust the loan originator, the company, and the product. A successful sales culture understands the value of having that culture driven by relationships developed, instead of transactions completed. To create a perceived value in the customer's eyes, the loan officer must differentiate himself or herself from all other loan officers. The loan officer must provide "value added" benefits and service by exceeding the expectations of the customer. The loan officer's goal is to know the customer and the customer's business so well that the loan officer's satisfaction of customer needs is perceived by the customer as professional counseling—*not* successful selling. Top Realtors look to the loan officer as a "financing partner," helping each to be more successful synergistically.

The Relationship Selling process is depicted in Figure 5.3. The approach is an important component to differentiation and creating positive first impressions. The purpose of the approach is to create desire for the Realtor to want to learn more about the loan officer and the loan officer's company. Next is the interview. Here the loan officer is to ask as many questions as he or she can to determine the Realtor's highest value needs. Knowing the customer means knowing what the customer really wants. Whatever solution is presented must meet the Realtor's needs, as he or she perceives them. Making a needs-fulfilling presentation is the basis for all referrals that come the originator's way. Basically, objections are needs not met. To turn objections into positive action, the loan officer must let the Realtor or borrower know that he or she shares his or her concerns, before offering additional information. Once the objections are managed and met, the loan officer has earned the right to ask for the business. As an example, "Considering what we

Figure 5.3   Relationship Selling Process

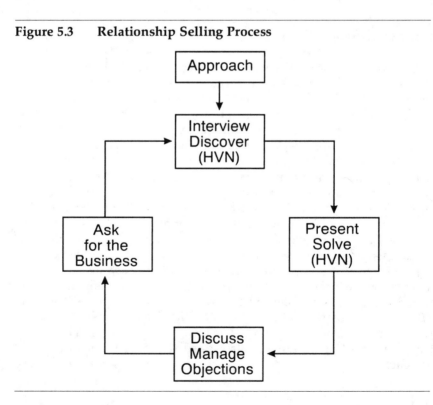

have discussed, do we have a basis for doing business together? Where do we start?"

Figure 5.4 depicts the critical path for the relationship-selling loan officer. Essentially, more work is invested in the base of the pyramid (needs analysis), thereby resulting in less time at the top of the pyramid ("selling"). Relationship selling is service oriented. The guideline for the successful loan officer is "build relationships or perish."

Figure 5.4   The Critical Path

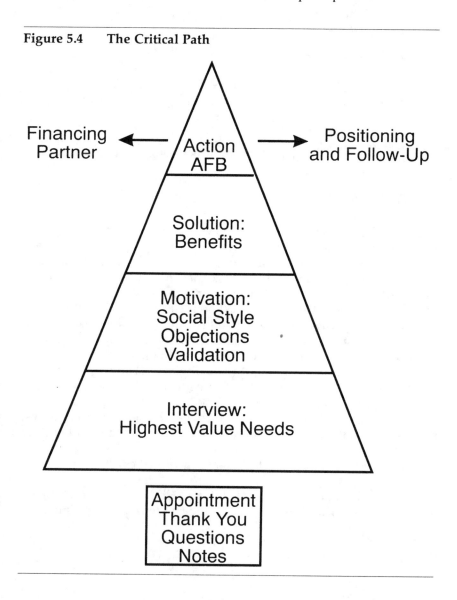

Although the loan officer is the point of sale, it is the backroom or support staff that is the moment of truth. Relationships can only be built if all parties contribute positive reinforcement to each customer contact.

The leadership/management model for the successful mortgage lender can be narrowed to five crucial areas:

♦ Recruit

♦ Select

♦ Train

♦ Motivate

♦ Coach

The balance of this chapter will focus on these key activities as they pertain to the management within mortgage lending.

BUILDING A TEAM

The mortgage lending business starts with *loan production*, for without loans the rest of the activities are unnecessary. At times this fact leads to friction within lender organizations, as loan producers adopt a prima donna persona. It's management's task, then, to temper such an attitude by conveying the reality that the loan origination staff is only as good as the people who support them. Without competitive products, competitive pricing, warehousing capability, and processing/underwriting/funding support, the loan origination efforts are for naught.

All of which points to the need for building an effective team, a team comprised of a "front room" (loan originators) and a "back room" (support groups). By "team" I'm referring to a functioning unit that is, in a word, empowered. It is whole, resourceful, decisive, dependable, and supportive. It is the role of the manager/leader to be the catalyst for ensuring that his or her associates enjoy the competitive advantage of teamwork.

Effective team-building techniques include the following:

♦ Each quarter, have loan officers "live in the shoes" of an underwriter/processor/or funder. Quid pro quo suggests that the support associates go on quarterly calls with the sales force. Mutual appreciation of one another's challenges is often the quickest route to teamwork.

♦ Conduct regularly scheduled team meetings, with agendas, while rotating the chairman.

♦ Share in unit goal- and objective setting. As well, share status and joint celebration of successes between loan officers and support groups.

♦ Encourage participation in cross-training programs.

♦ Recognition, recognition, recognition. In particular, recognition by loan officers of support staff. Too often it's the loan originators who are recognized, and not the loan support part of the team.

♦ Be an enthusiastic leader—you are the message. Watch your walk, because your associates do—and they act accordingly.

♦ Find ways for your team to win. Teams stay teams only if they continue to win.

FINDING THE RIGHT ASSOCIATES

Our future success as a company, or as an individual manager, is really dependent on the people we recruit. Nothing is more important to the manager than recruiting. Recruit good people and they will succeed despite any other company shortcomings. To accomplish this requires an investment of time—in the activity and in the candidate. Properly done, it is a active process, not a responsive solution. Consideration should be given to developing a one- to three-year plan with respect to recruiting. Too often the recruiting process begins at the time a staff vacancy arises. Yet, with our mission and objectives understood, management should regularly anticipate the staffing needs in terms of both quantity and talent.

Recruiting, like any successful relationship, must be a result of the recruiter's ability to clearly and succinctly define the profile of the position and of the highest caliber individual who will fill the position. Profiles identify the psychological, physiological, and personal attributes necessary for success in any defined position. Profiles are not the job requirement/job description. Improve recruiting performance by using the top performers in the company—loan officers, underwriters, processors, etc.—to develop models in assisting the recruiting of similar performers. Success leaves clues.

Even when fully staffed, good management calls for regular and continuous recruiting. Recruiting is the never ending process of looking for qualified candidates for employment. Keys here are ongoing communication and positioning. Similar to developing the relationship in the selling process, the recruiting activity is designed to foster and nurture a relationship with potential job candidates.

Some methods of recruiting are:

♦ Personal observation. Felt to be more effective than any other recruiting activity, personal observation requires management to be on the constant lookout for candidates.

♦ Centers of influence. People of influence within the industry know good people who would make excellent candidates. Centers of influence include mortgage insurers, title and escrow companies, and others who regularly call on Realtors and are in a position to assess potential candidates. To help them identify candidates, provide them with a position profile.

♦ Competition. Quite often the management of one lender is aware of the top performers of other lenders.

♦ Newspaper ads. Most often found to be less effective but worth considering to occasionally assess the market's talent pool.

♦ Employment agencies. While expensive, depending on the criticalness of the position, a good agency can be valuable as a solicitor/screener in the process.

♦ Keeping track of former support staff members who may have gone home to be with an infant, or gone back to school, or have taken a sabbatical and would like to work part-time.

The cost of turnover is close to the highest expense item in a company, yet this cost is seldom calculated. The benefit of ongoing recruiting is that management will never need to make a compromise choice to fill a position that was unexpectedly opened.

Once we find ourselves in need of an additional associate, through either growth or attrition, we next move to the interview.

Interviewing is an art, not a science. However, some basics have been demonstrated over time to be effective. It's these basics that will be summarily reviewed, as entire books are available on this important management responsibility of interviewing.

The first criterion for effective interviewing is to know what you are looking for, and one way of doing that is through the discipline of the previously mentioned "position profile." Additionally, this is where a job description can be of value as well.

Secondly, never hire anyone with less than three interviews. For the best results conduct three interviews, in three different locations, on three different occasions.

Third is to exercise effective interviewing skills. Too often managers hire someone because "the chemistry is right." The task is to discover the "inner person." Most people fail not because of technical knowledge but due to attitude or people-skill difficulties. Before conducting the interview, prepare a list of key questions or points to be covered. Additionally, work through the position profile, as that is the "needs list." Tips worth remembering are:

- Be aware of your personal biases and weight the interview toward being more analytic in the process.

- Don't ask yes or no questions.

- Conduct the interview outside your personal office, on neutral turf.

- Listen. The single biggest interviewing mistake is that the interviewer does too much of the talking.

- Be alert to inconsistencies.

- Watch for nonverbal clues.

- Skip around among subjects.

- Occasionally, ask the unexpected.

- Look for patterns.

- Look for changes.

- Take notes during the interview.

Biggest interviewing mistakes are:

- Too structured.

◆   You talk and don't really listen.

◆   You telegraph desired answers.

◆   You jump to conclusions.

◆   You aren't realistic.

◆   You don't project the job as it really is.

◆   You express too much power.

Selection is best accomplished when you have at least two qualified candidates. The final analysis should include:

◆   Review application.

◆   Review resume.

◆   Review interview notes.

◆   Review information gained from others.

◆   Review minimum position criteria.

◆   Compare candidate to position profile.

◆   Determine success patterns.

Lastly, if in doubt about the decision, then continue the interview
process. Too often, managers think that they can change someone after
hiring. Better to say no, and keep looking.

STARTING THEM RIGHT

First impressions are often the most lasting, and there is never a second
chance to make a positive first impression on a new employee. The
office image and work commitment created in the first month, first
week, first day, even first hour is difficult to change. Accordingly,
managers should never start someone without allocating the personal
time to commit to them, and should have a written plan to ensure the
new hire is properly welcomed and oriented.

The following is an orientation-induction checklist to be considered.

ORIENTATION-INDUCTION CHECKLIST

1.   Celebration of new hire, day one.

2. Make him or her feel welcome and secure. Tour office, introduce to all, give list of associates with nicknames. Arrange lunch.

3. Explain goals of company, office and unit, and who the key team players are.

4. Explain work ground rules.

5. Explain benefit plans.

6. Explain position mission and current objectives.

7. Define the work assignment.

8. Present education and training plans—by whom, and when. Negotiate the training contract.

9. Present work standards, responsibilities, and authorities, reporting systems, and productivity expected.

10. Make asking questions easy—where to go for help.

11. Help to be successful first day.

12. Debrief at end of first day—schedule appointment time.

13. Organize balance of week. Help to be successful; specify how.

14. Organize balance of month. Help to be successful; specify how.

15. Set quarterly objectives and quarterly progress reviews.

16. Hand-deliver calling cards.

Management's responsibility is to grow their people, therefore the training process is continuous. Training is a process, not an event. The basic goals of training are:

♦ Improve skills and productivity

♦ Reduce turnover

♦ Reduce need for supervision

♦ Improve customer service

♦ Career growth/cross-training

Managers should be personally involved in the training of their direct reports in order to set a proper example and foster the relationship.

The manager should employ a three-pronged initiative: joint calls-training calls-coaching. Take the loan production sales manager for example. The sales manager, with each of her or his loan officers, should be out in the field, making calls on Realtors. The "joint" call is where both the sales manager and loan officer participate in the discussions on the call. On the "training" call, the sales manager plays the primary role, showing the loan officer the proper steps of the call. She or he explains how and why each facet of the call is conducted. With the "coaching" call, the sales manager is silent, playing the role of an observer. Only at the end of the day, after all calls have been made, does the manager then comment on the pluses and minuses of each call, offering suggestions for improvement where needed. Each manager has "joint-training-coaching" responsibilities with her or his associates.

A number of mortgage lenders have implemented the concept of a "training contract/agreement." This agreement is between the manager and the associate, and demonstrates both the commitment and care on the part of the manager to develop his or her staff. An example of such an agreement between the loan officer and sales manager can be seen in Figure 5.5. Used regularly, such a contract will lead to an overall reduction in turnover.

As mentioned earlier, the Corporate University concept is a proven, cost-effective, technically advanced approach to human resource development.

In today's competitive environment, career growth opportunities are often more effective for recruiting new associates and for reducing turnover than the use of cash incentives. The theme of lifelong learning has moved to the forefront of successful companies in the lending industry.

GROWING YOUR ASSOCIATES

The head administrator for the New York City Health Department was asked if she believed in reincarnation. She said, "You bet I do. Every day at 5:00 p.m. I watch my employees come back from the dead to go home." Well, the lending industry might not be quite that bad, but management is forever being challenged with how to get more from their staffs while creating a positive working environment. Managers cannot motivate anyone—motivation is self-induced. Management can,

Figure 5.5   Loan Officer/Account Executive Success Agreement

This agreement between ————————————————————— and
                                              (Salesperson)

————————————————— Entered into on ————————————————
       (Sales Manager)   (Date)

is to assure as much as possible the mutual success of both parties. In consideration for professional training and management guidance,

————————————————————————————————
                      (Salesperson)

agrees to the following conditions:

1. Establish written business and personal short-term and long-term goals.

2. Establish specific marketing plans to achieve income and growth goals.

3. Complete the Initial Training Program with complete dedication and enthusiasm.

4. Set daily objectives in prospecting, selling, and other supportive

5. Provide Manager with daily feedback during initial training period, in accordance with the Initial Training Program daily guidelines.

6. Begin making quality calls within the assigned territory or marketing area during the training period.

7. Activate an on going program of attitude, skill, and knowledge development to ensure continuous personal and professional growth.

8. Cooperate with - and support - inside staff, without whom we cannot compete effectively.

————————————————   ————————————————
      Sales Professional   **Sales Manager**

however, create an environment that shows caring and in which associates will motivate themselves.

The managerial challenge for mortgage lenders is not dissimilar to that of most businesses—reduced operating budgets and increased workloads. Yet, look at the national statistics, as provided by a Public Agenda Forum Survey:

♦ Fewer than one out of every four jobholders say that they are currently working at full potential.

♦ One-half said they do not put effort into their job over and above what is required to hold on to it.

♦ The overwhelming majority, 75 percent, said that they could be significantly more effective than they presently are.

♦ Close to six out of ten Americans on the job believe that they "do not work as hard as they used to." (This may or may not be true, but it's their perception.)

In order to better tap this pent-up resource, Goethe said it well: "If you treat an individual as he is, he will stay that way. But, if you treat him as if he was what he could be, he will become what he could be." Positive reinforcement of those things people do right will do more to create a success environment than "constructive criticism."

Tactics here include:

♦ Sharing the vision, mission and goals

♦ Sharing the results and feedback

♦ Understanding individual values

♦ Effective communication as to activity in the company or department

♦ Regular performance reviews

♦ Regular recognition

♦ Appropriate rewards

Of critical importance is progress reviews. Everyone is entitled to know where he or she stands and how he or she is progressing. Progress reviews should be distinguished from compensation reviews. Compensation reviews are typically annual and deal with rewards for what's been done in the past. Progress reviews help people to look forward to what's ahead, as well as focusing on areas in which to improve. A progress review should be more focused and more frequent than the typical annual performance review. Imagine that you are a coach of a team—basketball, football, baseball, whatever. Your hopes are high for a championship season. Your team is a good one, yet competition will be tough. Now, imagine that as the coach, you decide to withhold criticisms and corrections of your players' performance until the season is over. Crazy? You bet! What team would make progress without the coach making observations on each player's performance along the way? Yet, too often as managers that is what we do—save it up for an annual performance review. The recommendation is a quarterly review, with a minimal of structure entailed. Topics covered could include objectives for the next quarter, areas for improvement, assistance needed, and summary observations.

A quick review of what a progress review is and is not follows. A Progress Review is not:

♦   A salary or compensation discussion

♦   A one-sided monologue

♦   Conducted in a superior-subordinate environment or attitude

♦   A structured interview

♦   Done in the superior's or subordinate's office or work area

♦   Done in less than an hour

♦   An intrusion into the personal life of the subordinate

♦   Threatening to either participant

♦   An employment contract for the period of the review cycle

A Progress Review is:

♦   A joint "we" communication and analysis

♦   An attempt to fully understand status

♦   A statement of expected results against which the associate will be continually reviewed

♦   Recognition of good work

♦   Suggestions for improvement—for both participants

♦   Agreement on new priorities

◆   Agreement on assistance and improvements necessary

◆   Clarification of responsibilities and authorities

◆   Verification or correction of rumors

◆   Clarification of personal and unit mission

◆   Personal and unit goal-setting

◆   Definition of self-development, education, and training needs

◆   An open-agenda—"free fire"—comfortable discussion

◆   A mutually beneficial exchange of ideas to improve personal
    and unit productivity

Figure 5.6 details the progress review procedure. Key here is adequate preparation and time investment.

Figure 5.6   Successful Results Management

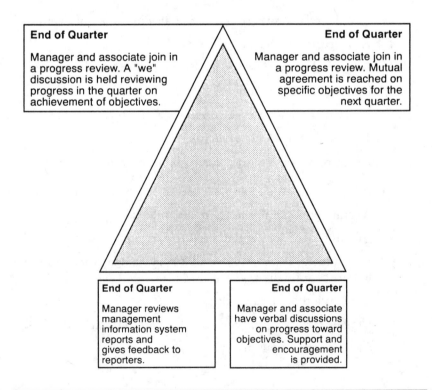

End of Quarter

Manager and associate join in a progress review. A "we" discussion is held reviewing progress in the quarter on achievement of objectives.

End of Quarter

Manager and associate join in a progress review. Mutual agreement is reached on specific objectives for the next quarter.

End of Quarter

Manager reviews management information system reports and gives feedback to reporters.

End of Quarter

Manager and associate have verbal discussions on progress toward objectives. Support and encouragement is provided.

Two closing thoughts in the area of growing your associates:

1.   People who feel good about themselves produce good results. Find people doing things right, and tell them about it.

2.   Follow the platinum rule—Do unto others the way they want to be done unto.

ACTION COMMUNICATION

Inquire from any mortgage lending individual about identifying a primary problem existing in her or his company and most frequently you'll hear "insufficient communication." Yet, it's just that communication that is the glue which bonds the successful team together. Whether it's the loan officer and processor team, or the processor and funder team, etc., the successful team is that which communicates well. For the manager, this is true for individual department areas as well as firm-wide.

The following tactics have been found to be effective when implemented within these guidelines: (1) effective communication starts with listening; and (2) follow through on what is communicated.

- Vision sharing
- Culture sharing
- Goal-setting and status
- Team meetings/staff meetings
- Progress reviews
- MBWA—Management By Walking Around
- Open-door policy
- Branch visits/department visits
- Annual meeting for associates
- Associate focus groups
- Associate surveys
- Orientation programs
- Cross-training
- Newsletters

- ◆ Audio updates

- ◆ Video updates

- ◆ Voice mail updates

- ◆ Retreats

- ◆ Intra-company competitions

- ◆ Rallies/Celebrations

- ◆ Theme days

- ◆ Casual days

- ◆ Business cards for all employees

Key for management here is to personally care. The tactics of good communication are confined only by one's imagination. And good communication will lead to the success of the team. Above all, management must remember that you communicate each and every day by serving as a role model. For you are the message!

CHALLENGES, TODAY AND TOMORROW

The challenges for mortgage lenders are significant and plentiful. The following list of ten are being faced today by managers and leaders, and they will be amplified in the future.

1. *Change*—Change in this business is a constant and with each passing day it manifests itself further.

2. *Future shock*—There are more things to do than there are doers to do them. Mortgage lending initiatives increase on all fronts, be they production, marketing, or servicing.

3. *More from less*—Expense curtailment and margin squeeze will demand further efficiencies in the deployment of both human and financial capital.

4. *Global economy*—Today, we fund our business on a global basis. How far can we be from a similar scenario in the production and servicing arenas?

5. *Time compression*—Time is our most valuable commodity. Efforts are under way in many marketplaces toward the

"One Day Loan"; current time frames from application to closing are no longer acceptable, or necessary.

6. *Government regulation*—Imagine the idyllic fantasy that this is not on the list of challenges. The safe bet is that it will continue to challenge us.

7. *Industry consolidation*—Much has occurred to date, with expectations of a continuance.

8. *New entrants*—As more mortgage lenders go public, the opportunities are highlighted for players outside the industry to enter. Coupled with the consolidation activities cited above, it provides additional inducement to enter the lending field.

9. *Work force and customer diversification*—America continues to reflect the "melting pot" culture, challenging management with additional languages, customs, etc.

10. *Automation*—With costs of technology dropping, capabilities expanding, and the compression of transaction times a given, further automation will continue.

Each of the above challenges rings a sound of opportunity. Six key thoughts aimed toward making the most of these opportunities:

1. *Focus precedes success*—Managers and leaders, first through vision and mission, must decide "where they are going."

2. *Take action*—Nike says it so well, "Just Do It."

3. *Be flexible*—Look for the better way to do it; it's out there.

4. *Risk failure*—To not risk it, ensures it.

5. *Heart*—Remember that people care more about what's in your heart than what's in your head.

6. *KAIZEN*—Get a little better every day and become the best of the best through benchmarking.

Chapter 6

LEGAL AND REGULATORY ISSUES IN MORTGAGE BANKING

Arthur B. Axelson
Partner
Pepper, Hamilton & Scheetz

Gary S. Smuckler
Partner
Pepper, Hamilton & Scheetz

INTRODUCTION

True or false? Mortgage lending and servicing can't get any more complicated. Without a doubt, false.

Two factors contribute to the increasing complexity of mortgage banking. The first of these is economics. The industry has identified and now serves the consumer's need for a wide range of mortgage products beyond the traditional long-term fixed-rate mortgage. For example, a single lender may originate and service shorter-term fixed-rate mortgages, an array of adjustable-rate products, reverse mortgages, and convertible mortgages that switch from a fixed to an adjustable rate and vice versa. In a given community, a lender may find mortgage applicants who—depending on their stage in life, economic circumstances, or career plans—demand all of these products. As financial markets and consumers become more sophisticated, this trend will continue.

The second factor is the law. The complexity of the law of mortgage banking and the risks it carries for mortgage bankers seem to be increasing geometrically. There are three reasons for this: more products and processes to regulate, more lawmakers and prosecutors getting into the act, and a better-informed and litigious population.

Volumes of law and analysis have been published in recent years on topics that were hardly known a decade ago. For example, transfers of servicing in the normal course of business were barely heard of, the process of mortgage payoff and release was a quiet backwater of the servicing department, and the topic of origination of reverse mortgages to seniors was discussed only by housing policy types.

Virtually every state has now enacted laws governing the conduct of mortgage lenders and mortgage servicers. Most states have also created regulatory bodies to oversee the industry. Now that a group of state attorneys general has made their presence felt by several major servicers on the subject of tax and insurance escrows, they and their local counterparts will almost certainly pursue other mortgage issues.

Consumers tend to stay well-informed about critical issues, as well they should. With the help of lawyers and other groups who focus these issues, many mortgage lenders and servicers find themselves defending an increasing number of claims. Many of these are unjustified, but many of them point up real weaknesses in their systems and compliance efforts. Publications and services are now available to consumers to help them identify common mistakes made by lenders and servicers. As the industry, especially servicers, concentrates into larger organizations, they become more attractive targets for class-action lawsuits.

These factors place an important responsibility on each member of a mortgage banker's staff. Although the company's sophisticated compliance efforts may have created systems designed to avoid legal trouble, those systems depend on an alert and informed individual. Getting and staying up-to-date on relevant law and regulations is an important responsibility of every member of a mortgage banker's staff.

REGULATION OF THE LENDER

Federal Housing Administration

Role in the market: The Federal Housing Administration (FHA) was established by Congress in 1934 and is part of the Department of Housing and Urban Development (HUD). The FHA was created to encourage lenders to make residential mortgage loans by providing mortgage insurance. The FHA administers several insurance programs. The basic insurance program that covers loans secured by single-family homes is known as the Section 203(b) program. A mortgage lender who wishes to originate FHA-insured loans must first become an FHA-approved lender. In addition, for a mortgage loan to qualify for FHA insurance, the loan must meet various standards established by HUD.

Lender approval process: A mortgage lender who wishes to be approved for participation in the FHA mortgage insurance program must obtain HUD approval. To obtain approval, which is commonly known as an "Eagle," the mortgage lender must meet various requirements prescribed by HUD, including having adequate staff and facilities to originate and service mortgages in accordance with FHA requirements, and meeting and maintaining net-worth requirements. Currently, a mortgage lender must maintain a net worth of not less than $100,000 to originate FHA-insured loans. In addition, the mortgage lender must maintain a reliable warehouse line of credit, which is available for use in originating FHA-insured mortgages, in an amount of not less than $250,000.

Mortgage lenders who wish to be approved for the FHA Direct Endorsement Program must meet higher standards. Under the Direct Endorsement Program, mortgage lenders are not required to submit mortgages to HUD for insurance approval prior to settlement. Instead, a Direct Endorsement lender may submit a mortgage for FHA insurance after it is closed. A Direct Endorsement lender must have five years of experience in the origination of single-family mortgages, maintain a net worth of not less than $250,000, and its underwriting and technical staff must satisfactorily complete a training program on HUD underwriting requirements. In addition, to obtain Direct Endorsement Program approval, the mortgage lender must submit 15 mortgages that have been underwritten and processed in accordance with Direct Endorsement Program requirements. If HUD determines that these initial 15 mortgages have been underwritten and processed properly, then the mortgage lender may be approved to submit subsequent mortgages for insurance after they have closed.

Mortgage requirements: To qualify for FHA insurance, a mortgage loan cannot exceed dollar limitations established by HUD. Under the 1993 HUD Appropriations Act, specific maximum dollar limitations were eliminated. Now, the maximum loan amount for FHA-insured single-family mortgages is the lesser of 95 percent of the median one-family house price in the area, as determined by HUD (with higher percentages to take into account the higher costs of two-family, three-family, and four-family residences).

HUD also sets minimum down payments for mortgages insured by FHA (generally 3 percent of the first $25,000 of appraised value plus 5 percent of any additional value), and limits the charges and fees a mortgage lender may impose upon the borrower to fees and charges for such items as credit reports, survey, title examination, appraisal and recording fees, and taxes. HUD no longer sets interest rate ceilings for

FHA-insured loans; interest rates can be negotiated by the borrower and the mortgage lender.

Obtaining mortgage insurance: A mortgage lender approved to originate FHA-insured mortgages must submit to HUD an application for insurance of the mortgage before the mortgage is executed. However, if the mortgage lender is a Direct Endorsement lender, the application is submitted *after* the mortgage is executed. If HUD approves the application, it will issue a certificate of insurance, which indicates that the mortgage is covered by FHA insurance. The borrower is required to pay a mortgage insurance premium, or MIP. For loans originated in 1991 and 1992, the annual premium is 0.5 percent of the outstanding loan balance, to be collected for five years for loans under 90 percent loan-to-value ratio and for eight years for loans of 90 to 95 percent loan-to-value ratio. Beginning in 1995, the annual premium will be 0.5 percent of the loan amount for 11 years for loans of less than 90 percent loan-to-value ratio and 30 years for loans of 90 to 95 percent loan-to-value ratio. For loans exceeding 95 percent loan-to-value ratio, the annual premium will be 0.55 percent, payable for 30 years.

Mortgagee review board: To enforce HUD requirements for the origination and servicing of FHA-insured loans, HUD created the Mortgagee Review Board. The Mortgagee Review Board has the authority to institute administrative actions against mortgage lenders. HUD has delineated various grounds for the initiation of administrative actions against mortgage lenders, including the transfer of an FHA-insured mortgage to a nonapproved lender, the use of escrow funds for any purpose other than the purpose for which the escrow funds were received, the termination of a mortgage lender's supervision by a governmental agency, failure of a mortgage lender to meet and maintain its net worth requirements, and submission of false information to HUD in connection with any FHA-insured mortgage transaction. Mortgage lenders against whom administrative action has been instituted are entitled to request a hearing before a HUD hearing officer. The Mortgagee Review Board has the authority to take remedial actions against mortgage lenders who violate HUD requirements, including issuing letters of reprimand, placing mortgage lenders on probation, suspending a mortgage lender's FHA approval temporarily, or withdrawing a mortgage lender's FHA approval for a period of time not to exceed six years, or for an indefinite period of time for egregious or willful violations by the mortgage lender.

VA-Guaranteed Loans

Role in the market: The Department of Veterans Affairs (VA) guarantees mortgage loans made to veterans who have served in the United States armed forces since 1940. Unlike the FHA, the VA does not insure mortgage loans. Instead, the VA guarantees the payment of a percentage of the mortgage loan amount in the event the borrower defaults.

Lender approval process: The VA does not have a formal approval process for lenders who submit mortgage loans to the VA for prior guarantee approval. However, a mortgage lender who wishes to originate VA-guaranteed loans under the VA's automatic guaranty program (in which prior VA approval is not required) must satisfy certain requirements. Supervised lenders (i.e., state banks, national banks, insurance companies, credit unions, and other entities that are subject to examination and supervision by an agency of the United States or of any state) may make loans that are automatically guaranteed without first obtaining VA approval.

Nonsupervised lenders (i.e., lenders that are not supervised lenders) may make loans that are eligible for automatic guaranty after first obtaining VA approval. To obtain VA approval, a nonsupervised lender must satisfy various requirements, including (1) having a minimum of $50,000 of working capital (the excess of current assets over current liabilities), and (2) having at least three years' experience in originating VA-guaranteed mortgages. The mortgage lender must also have a full-time qualified employee to personally review and make underwriting decisions on VA loans. The underwriter must have a minimum of three years' experience in reviewing credit information and making underwriting decisions and at least two years' experience in connection with loans submitted to the VA for guaranty.

VA loan requirements: Unlike borrowers with FHA-insured mortgages, borrowers are not required to pay an insurance premium for a VA guaranty. However, borrowers are required to pay an upfront guaranty fee based on the amount of the borrower's down payment. Also, unlike FHA-insured loans, interest rates on VA-guaranteed loans are set by the VA. Any discount points charged by the mortgage lender must be paid by the seller of the home being financed, and not by the borrower. The borrower can be required to pay a one-point origination fee.

The VA does not limit the dollar amount on VA-guaranteed loans. In addition, no down payment is required in connection with VA-guaranteed loans. Like FHA-insured loans, the VA limits the charges and fees a mortgage lender may impose on the borrower to charges and fees for such items as credit reports, title examination, survey, hazard insurance and recording fees, and taxes.

Federal National Mortgage Association

Role in the market: The Federal National Mortgage Association, otherwise known as Fannie Mae, was created by Congress in 1934 to provide a secondary market for FHA-insured and VA-guaranteed loans. Fannie Mae, which was originally part of the federal government, is now a privately owned corporation whose stock is traded on the New York Stock Exchange. Today, Fannie Mae purchases single-family conventional loans in addition to FHA-insured and VA-guaranteed loans. Fannie Mae also purchases multifamily loans. By purchasing loans from mortgage lenders, Fannie Mae puts money back into the mortgage markets, which in turn permits mortgage lenders to make additional mortgage loans. Fannie Mae "pools" the mortgages it purchases and sells securities backed by the mortgages in these pools.

Lender eligibility: To obtain approval to sell and service mortgage loans for Fannie Mae, a mortgage lender must meet various requirements, including demonstrating an ability to originate and service mortgage loans, being properly licensed to originate and sell mortgage loans in each jurisdiction in which it does business, and maintaining an acceptable net worth. Upon approval, a mortgage lender executes a mortgage selling and servicing contract that establishes the terms and conditions under which the mortgage lender will sell and service mortgage loans for Fannie Mae. This contract contains, among other things, representations and warranties regarding the quality of the loans sold to Fannie Mae, and the mortgage lender's agreement to originate, sell, and service mortgage loans in accordance with Fannie Mae requirements. The mortgage lender must also comply with the terms of Fannie Mae's Selling and Servicing Guides, which set forth detailed requirements regarding underwriting, mortgage delivery, and servicing. A mortgage lender's failure to comply with these terms and conditions can result in suspension from the Fannie Mae program, a demand from Fannie Mae that the mortgage lender repurchase from Fannie Mae mortgages that do not satisfy Fannie Mae requirements, and other penalties.

Underwriting requirements: Mortgage lenders who sell and service mortgage loans for Fannie Mae must be certain that the borrower and the property securing the loan meet Fannie Mae requirements. Generally, a mortgage lender may not sell a loan to Fannie Mae unless its underwriting has shown that the borrower can repay the debt, the borrower is willing to repay the debt, and the property is sufficient security for the mortgage loan. Fannie Mae's underwriting requirements include requirements that the mortgage lender obtain credit reports, bank statements, verifications of employment and deposits, verifications of income, and confirmation that borrowers have funds available for closing. Fannie Mae also requires that mortgage lenders adhere to strict appraisal requirements when evaluating properties securing loans and holds mortgage lenders responsible for the accuracy of all property appraisals obtained in connection with mortgage loans sold to Fannie Mae. Loans sold to Fannie Mae must be documented with Fannie Mae/Freddie Mac forms of promissory notes and mortgages or deeds of trust.

Federal Home Loan Mortgage Corporation

Role in the market: The Federal Home Loan Mortgage Corporation, commonly known as Freddie Mac, was created in 1970 by Congress to provide a secondary market for mortgage loans originated by federally insured thrift institutions. Freddie Mac now purchases mortgage loans from any Freddie Mac-approved lender. Although Freddie Mac by law is authorized to purchase FHA-insured and VA-guaranteed loans, it discontinued purchasing these loans in 1981 and now limits its purchases to conventional mortgages. Freddie Mac, like Fannie Mae, pools mortgage loans and sells to investors securities backed by the mortgage pools.

Lender eligibility: Like Fannie Mae, Freddie Mac purchases mortgages only from approved mortgage lenders. To be eligible, mortgage lenders must demonstrate prudent lending practices, and must maintain acceptable net worth.

Upon approval, Freddie Mac lenders enter into a mortgage purchase contract, which sets forth the terms and conditions under which the mortgage lender will sell and service mortgage loans for Freddie Mac. Freddie Mac also requires its mortgage lenders to comply with the terms and conditions of its *Sellers' & Servicers' Guide.* Like the Fannie Mae guides, Freddie Mac's *Sellers' & Servicers' Guide* sets forth detailed requirements for underwriting, delivery, and servicing of mortgages, a mortgage lender's failure to comply with the terms and conditions of the purchase contract and the *Sellers' & Servicers' Guide* may result in suspension from the Freddie Mac program, a repurchase of mortgage loans from Freddie Mac, and other penalties.

Underwriting requirements: Before selling a mortgage loan to Freddie Mac, a mortgage lender must underwrite the loan in accordance with

Freddie Mac requirements and satisfy itself that the borrower and the property securing the loan otherwise satisfy all other Freddie Mac requirements. Generally, to be eligible for purchase by Freddie Mac, a mortgage loan must be of "investment quality," which means that the loan is made to a borrower from whom timely repayment of the debt can be expected and that the loan is secured by real property providing sufficient value to recover the mortgage lender's investment if the borrower defaults. If Freddie Mac determines that a loan is not of investment quality, it may refuse to purchase the loan or, if the loan has been purchased, require the mortgage lender to repurchase the loan. Loans sold to Freddie Mac must also be documented on uniform loan instruments.

Government National Mortgage Association

Role in the market: The Government National Mortgage Association, commonly known as Ginnie Mae, was created by Congress in 1968 as a part of HUD. Ginnie Mae was created to help finance mortgages for families who could not obtain adequate housing under other mortgage programs.

Ginnie Mae's primary role is to guaranty mortgage-backed securities issued by Ginnie Mae-approved private mortgage lenders and backed principally by FHA-insured and VA-guaranteed loans. Ginnie Mae, as part of HUD, is a federal agency and its guaranty of mortgage-backed securities carries the full faith and credit of the United States.

Lender eligibility: To obtain Ginnie Mae approval, a mortgage lender must be a HUD-approved lender in good standing and must also be a Ginnie Mae- or Fannie Mae-approved mortgage servicer with experience necessary to issue and service mortgage-backed securities. The mortgage lender must also meet net-worth requirements set by Ginnie Mae.

Ginnie Mae programs: Ginnie Mae guarantees mortgage-backed securities under two programs: GNMA I and GNMA II. Under GNMA I, which is the original program, investors who purchase Ginnie Mae-guaranteed mortgage-backed securities receive payments from the individual issuers (i.e., mortgage lenders). Under GNMA II, Ginnie Mae uses a central paying agent (Chemical Bank) to issue payments on the securities so that investors receive a single monthly payment check. Securities issued under both GNMA I and GNMA II represent an undivided ownership interest in "pools" of single-family and multifamily mortgages. The purchasers of a mortgage-backed security own a pro rata share of each mortgage in the pool and receive that percentage share of all interest payments, scheduled principal payments, and principal prepayments.

Bank or BHC-Owned Companies

Role in the market: Among various possible ownership structures, a mortgage company may be directly or indirectly owned by either a national bank or a state bank, or by a bank holding company.

Prior to October 15, 1982, national banks were subject to numerous statutory restrictions on real estate loans. Today the restrictions are less burdensome and a national bank may "make, arrange, purchase or sell loans or extensions of credit secured by liens on interests in real estate," so long as the loans are made in accordance with regulations that have been issued by the Office of the Comptroller of the Currency. A mortgage company that is owned by a national bank is governed by the Federal Reserve Act and the regulations of the Comptroller of the Currency. In addition, a mortgage company that is owned by a national bank is subject to examination by the Comptroller of the Currency. All mortgage companies that are subsidiaries of a national bank are deemed HUD-approved.

State banks are subject to the laws of the state by which they are chartered and are usually regulated by a state banking commission. The requirements of a state-bank-owned mortgage company vary, depending on the individual state laws and regulations. Some states regulate and supervise state-bank-owned mortgage companies and thereby make these state banks eligible for a supervised designation for HUD purposes. However, many states do not address the issues of state banks owning mortgage companies. In many states that have no laws or regulations regarding state-bank-owned mortgage companies, they are deemed permissible since the laws and regulations contain nothing to the contrary. A few states directly prohibit a state bank from having a mortgage company subsidiary.

A bank holding company is a company that has control over either a bank or another bank holding company. Bank holding companies are regulated by the Federal Reserve Board and are restricted in the activities in which they can engage. In general, bank holding companies are prohibited from engaging in nonbank activities except for certain activities that the Board of Governors of the Federal Reserve Board has identified as being closely related to banking. One of the activities identified as being closely related to banking is the making, acquiring, or servicing of loans or other extension of credit for the account of the bank holding company or for the account of others, such as a consumer finance company, credit-card company, mortgage company, commercial finance company, or a factoring company.

Private Mortgage Conduits

Role in the market: Ginnie Mae, Fannie Mae, and Freddie Mac have been primarily responsible for the development of the secondary-mortgage and the mortgage-backed securities markets. Federal law, however, limits the size of mortgages that Fannie Mae and Freddie Mac may purchase. For loans purchased on or after January 1, 1993, the limit is $203,150 for single-family homes, with higher amounts for two- to four-family structures and homes in high-cost areas. By statute, those amounts are adjusted annually based on changes in home prices for the 12-month period ending the previous October. Mortgages that exceed these limits or that otherwise do not meet Fannie Mae's or Freddie Mac's underwriting standards are known as "nonconforming loans." Private companies, sometimes called "private conduits," have moved to fill this market, which Fannie Mae and Freddie Mac are unable to service. These companies act as "conduits" that channel funds from the capital markets to the mortgage markets by acquiring nonconforming mortgages from mortgage lenders, converting them into mortgage-backed securities, and selling them to investors.

The first private mortgage securities were issued in 1977 by the Bank of America and First Federal Savings and Loan Association of Chicago. A number of private conduits have been established since then, such as Residential Funding Corporation, Prudential Home Mortgage Company, and General Electric Mortgage Securities Corporation.

SMMEA eligibility: In addition to competing with securities issued or backed by Fannie Mae, Freddie Mae, and Ginnie Mae, companies issuing private mortgage securities have faced certain statutory and regulatory obstacles, including registration requirements of the Securities and Exchange Commission and state securities agencies. The Secondary Mortgage Market Enhancement Act of 1984 (SMMEA) helped remove some of these obstacles by exempting private mortgage securities from the registration requirements of state securities law, provided that they qualify as a "mortgage related security" under SMMEA. A mortgage related security is a security that is rated in one of the two highest rating categories by at least one nationally recognized statistical rating organization (e.g., Moody's and Standard & Poors); represents ownership of one or more promissory notes, which are directly secured by a first lien on a single parcel of real estate upon which is located a dwelling; and was originated by a savings and loan association, savings bank, commercial bank, or similar institution that is supervised and examined by a federal or state authority or by a HUD-approved lender. Because of the regulatory relief provided by SMMEA, private conduits generally purchase only mortgages that are "SMMEA-eligible."

Contractual relationship: Mortgage lenders that wish to utilize private conduits enter into purchase agreements under which the mortgage lender agrees to sell and the private conduit agrees to purchase mortgages satisfying the terms and conditions set forth in the agreement. The mortgage lender typically agrees to service the mortgages on behalf of the private conduit. The purchase agreement sets forth the underwriting and servicing standards, including loan-to-value ratios, debt-income ratios, and other standards. Often loan documentation is based on standard Fannie Mae/Freddie Mac forms. Failure by the mortgage lender to comply with the terms and conditions set forth in the purchase agreement may result in a demand that the mortgage lender repurchase mortgages that do not satisfy the private conduits requirements, termination of servicing rights, and other penalties.

Warehouse Lenders

Role in the market: Mortgage lenders require a source of funds with which to originate mortgage loans. To obtain access to loan funds, mortgage lenders establish "warehouse lines of credit" with warehouse lenders.

Warehouse lenders are institutions that make revolving credit available to mortgage lenders. The mortgage lender draws upon the warehouse line from time to time to fund mortgage loans. The extension of credit for a particular loan is paid off when the mortgage lender sells the mortgage loan to a secondary-market investor, such as Fannie Mae or Freddie Mac. Mortgage lenders who establish warehouse lines of credit typically enter into a warehouse credit agreement with the warehouse lender, under which the warehouse lender agrees to extend credit to the mortgage lender in order to originate loans, and the mortgage lender agrees to repay each extension of credit within a specified period of time, with interest.

The warehouse lender usually secures each extension of credit by placing a lien on the mortgage loan and perfects its security interest by taking possession of the original promissory note executed by the borrower, endorsed "in blank," together with an assignment of the mortgage securing the loan. To further protect its security, the warehouse lender usually takes the responsibility of delivering the loan package to the secondary-market investor for purchase. The investor, in turn, delivers the purchase price of the mortgage directly to the warehouse lender.

Mortgage Insurers

High loan-to-value ratio conventional (not FHA-insured or VA-guaranteed) mortgages of up to 95 percent of the purchase price of a home have become common. Mortgage lenders and secondary-market investors are usually unwilling to assume the higher risk of default of these loans. The private mortgage insurance industry responds to this need and provides coverage that cushions the risk of making and purchasing these higher-risk mortgage loans.

Private mortgage insurance, or PMI, generally covers the top 20 to 25 percent of a conventional loan with a loan-to-value ratio exceeding 80 percent. Mortgage lenders usually require borrowers to obtain PMI for any loan with a loan-to-value ratio above this threshold percentage. When the loan-to-value ratio drops below 80 percent, mortgage lenders and secondary-market investors may permit borrowers to discontinue PMI. Borrowers who obtain PMI are generally required to pay an up-front mortgage insurance premium at closing and one-twelfth of an annual PMI premium with each monthly installment of principal and interest under the mortgage note.

PMI should not be confused with FHA insurance. PMI is required only for *conventional loans*. Mortgage lenders do not require PMI for FHA-insured loans or VA-guaranteed loans. As discussed above, borrowers pay a mortgage insurance premium, or MIP, for FHA insurance and pay an up-front fee for a VA loan guaranty.

Private mortgage insurers also provide pool insurance for the secondary market. This insurance covers losses on mortgages in a pool backing mortgage-backed securities. This insurance will protect the purchasers of the securities backed by the mortgage pool in the event that an extraordinary number of mortgages in the pool go into default.

State Licensing

Over the past several years, licensing requirements for mortgage brokering, lending, and servicing have become the norm across the United States. In fact, approximately 85 percent of all jurisdictions now require a license for at least one of these activities.

The scope of the states' licensing requirements may vary greatly. Some states simply require that an entity register with a state before participating in a certain mortgage-related activity. Others attempt to micromanage lenders and, in addition to requiring licensing, require compliance with strict regulations concerning record keeping, office location, accounting, and origination and servicing procedures. Mortgage servicers may be required to be licensed under a variety of sections of the state code—mortgage lenders, escrow agents, and collection agents, amongst others.

Exemptions/registration: As an initial matter, lenders entering new states must determine whether an individual company needs to be licensed at all within a state, and if so, which license must be obtained. The applicability of a state's licensing statute to an individual company may depend on a great number of factors, including the type of institution, the parentage of the company, and the type of loans being made. Some state statutes specifically define which entities fall within its jurisdiction. Others set forth broad definitions, which leave much room for interpretation.

Almost universally, however, the licensing statutes set forth a list of exempt entities. These entities may be completely exempt from the licensing statutes or may merely be exempt from the licensing requirements imposed by the chapter, while still being required to comply with the regulatory requirements or to register with the state.

Often, exempt entities include those that are already regulated by another state agency—for example, banks, savings and loan associations, credit unions, and insurance companies. Others are exempt because they are mortgage lenders or servicers that are subject to licensing, supervision, or auditing by Fannie Mae, Freddie Mac, Ginnie Mae, the VA, or HUD. In addition, entities that do not maintain an office or place of business within the state are sometimes exempt.

An analysis of the applicability of a licensing statute must be performed carefully because failure to comply with a licensing statute may result in severe penalties. To assist in the interpretation of a licensing statute within a state, mortgage companies are also advised to confer with state regulators and to review any regulations that have been published by the department authorized by the state to supervise licensees. Regulations often address in much greater detail the requirements of the licensing statutes.

The license application requirements vary, however, from state to state. An application fee and the filing of a complete application form are almost always required. Some states impose a requirement that a surety bond be deposited with the state or that a specified net worth or access to a specified amount of credit be demonstrated. Some states require that an applicant maintain a physical presence in the state.

Origination and servicing: Licensing statutes often impose origination requirements on licensees. For example, many states require licensees to make certain disclosures to borrowers at the time of loan application. Lenders may also be required to disclose to borrowers a good faith estimate of all fees that must be paid as well as whether or not any fees paid by the borrower are refundable.

Other licensing statutes require that certain procedures be followed upon the acceptance of advance fees or upon the opening of an escrow account. For example, many states require that tax and insurance escrows be deposited in federally insured accounts or in accounts otherwise acceptable to institutional lenders. Some licensing statutes list fees and charges that may be imposed by the lender. Often, these charges include commitment fees, filing fees, survey fees, title insurance premiums, and attorneys' fees.

Many licensing statutes also prohibit certain actions by licensees. For example, many licensing statutes state that licensees may not knowingly advertise any false, misleading, or deceptive statement regarding the rates, terms, or conditions of a mortgage loan. Many states also require licensees to maintain samples of all advertisements for inspection by examiners.

Licensing statutes may extend their regulation into the servicing practices of licensees. For example, many states require that accountings and disclosures of escrow accounts maintained by the lender be made at prescribed times throughout the life of the loan.

Record keeping, reporting, and examination: Many states impose various record-keeping and reporting requirements on licensees within the state. In addition to requiring licensees to maintain accurate records of all loan transactions, most states set forth time periods for which all records must be maintained as well as stipulating where a licensee's records must be kept. Most often, records must be kept in the licensee's principal place of business or another place specifically authorized by the state if they can be made available within a specified time frame.

Along with record-keeping requirements, many states require licensees to make their records available to state regulators. Some states also require that a licensee pay the state an examination fee to cover the expenses of the examinations as well as any necessary travel expenses.

Situs requirements: Mortgage licensing statutes also commonly require a licensee to transact business from a principal office within the state or to designate an agent within the state for service of process. A toll-free number may also be required for out-of-state lenders or servicers. The procedure of opening a branch office in a state may also be established by statute or regulation.

Qualification to Do Business

In addition to meeting the licensing requirements imposed by a state, mortgage brokers, lenders, and servicers must consider a state's laws regarding the conduct of business by foreign corporations. Every state, as well as the District of Columbia, has a statute that requires corporations that are incorporated in a foreign state to obtain a certificate of authority before transacting business in the state.

While foreign corporation statutes are quite similar from state to state, the slight differences that exist in definitions and terminology may make the difference in determining whether a company needs to obtain a certificate of authority to conduct its proposed activities within the state. Unfortunately, the state attorney general offices and the secretary of state offices in each state are unlikely to provide much insight into the interpretation of these statutes. Additionally, there has been very little case law on these statutes that would aid in interpretation.

Most states do not set forth a definition for "transacting business" or "doing business." Rather, states list a number of activities that are deemed not to be "transacting business" or "doing business." These exempted activities are usually only applicable to companies that do not maintain an office within the state in question. Once an office is maintained within a state, a company is almost certain to be deemed to be "transacting business" or "doing business" and, therefore, must obtain a certificate of authority.

In most states, two exempted activities apply to mortgage lenders and servicers and may, depending upon the scope of their activities, serve to exempt them. These activities are "making or acquiring evidences of debt, mortgages or liens on real or personal property" and "securing or collecting debts or enforcing any rights in property securing the debts."

The process of qualifying to do business within a state is usually simply a matter of paying an annual fee, completing an application, and appointing a resident agent. The consequences for failure to obtain a certificate of authority most often are the inability to bring a lawsuit within the state, the payment of any back fees and taxes, along with the payment of a monetary penalty. The monetary penalty may range from $500 a year to $5,000 a month. Corporate acts performed and contracts entered into while a foreign corporation is not qualified are usually not invalidated.

REGULATION OF THE LOAN—STATE AND FEDERAL

Overview of the Federal Statutes and Regulations

Every stage of a mortgage loan from advertising and application through loan processing, closing, and servicing is regulated by either federal or state law, or both. The statutes and regulations impose both substantive and disclosure requirements and are generally intended to protect borrowers from abusive lender practices. The panoply of statutes and regulations address issues as diverse as the permissibility and disclosure of settlement costs to equal credit and fair housing concerns. Addressed below are the principal statutes and regulations affecting mortgage lenders. These laws are addressed in the order of the various stages of a mortgage loan: application, processing and approval, settlements, and servicing.

Application, Processing, and Approval

The enactment of the Home Mortgage Disclosure Act (HMDA) in 1975 stemmed from a rising public concern about credit shortages in urban neighborhoods. Congress had determined that the failure of financial institutions to provide reasonable home financing to qualified applicants in certain areas had been a contributing factor in the decline of some urban areas.

The goals of HMDA are to (1) provide information to the public indicating whether financial institutions are serving the credit needs of the neighborhoods they serve, and (2) to assist public officials in targeting private-sector investments to the areas where they are most needed.

Applicability of HMDA: HMDA applies to mortgage lenders generally, even if a lender is not a depository institution such as a bank, savings association, or credit union. Exempt institutions include for-profit mortgage lending institutions (other than banks, savings associations, and credit unions) holding assets which, combined with those of any parent corporation, did not exceed $10 million on the preceding December 31. An exempt for-profit mortgage company must also have originated fewer than 100 home-purchase loans in the preceding calendar year.

The data compilation and reporting requirements are applicable to home-purchase and home-improvement loans (including refinancings of both) as well as to applications for home-purchase and home-improvement that did not result in loan originations. Data is also required for purchase of these types of loans.

Data compilation requirements: HMDA requires covered entities to compile information on loan type (such as conventional, FHA-insured, or VA-guaranteed), the purpose and amount of the loan, the type of action taken on the loan, the date on which any action was taken, and whether the property relating to the loan is to be owner-occupied.

Information must also be compiled regarding properties in any geographic area in which the entity has a home or branch office. This information includes the metropolitan statistical area number, as defined by the U.S. Office of Management and Budget, state and county codes, and census tract numbers.

Finally, covered entities must compile data regarding the race, national origin, sex, and annual income of the applicant.

Reporting requirements: The above information must be recorded on a Loan/Application Register (HMDA-LAR), and transactions must be reported for the year in which a final action was taken. The HMDA-LAR must be submitted to the financial institution's regulatory agency by March 1 for the previous calendar year. The Federal Financial Institutions Examinations Council then produces a disclosure statement for each financial institution. Within 30 days of the receipt of this disclosure statement, the lender must make the statement available to the public.

Fair Lending

There are several federal fair lending statutes that impact upon every stage of the lending process—from the advertising of services to the taking of an application, the determination of creditworthiness, and the origination, servicing, and collection of a loan.

Three federal laws that provide protection to consumers are briefly outlined below. Lenders should be aware that the requirements of these laws may in some ways overlap and that certain actions may trigger the requirements of more than one federal "fair lending" statute.

Equal Credit Opportunity Act: The Equal Credit Opportunity Act (ECOA) and its implementing regulation, Regulation B, are applicable to all persons who, in the ordinary course of business, regularly participate in deciding whether or not to extend credit.

The purpose of ECOA is to promote the availability of credit to all creditworthy applicants. It prohibits discrimination on the basis of race, color, religion, national origin, sex, marital status, or age. ECOA also prohibits creditors from discriminating against applicants whose income in whole or in part derives from public assistance or applicants who have in good faith exercised any right under the Consumer Credit Protection Act.

ECOA and Regulation B address the taking and evaluating of applications, as well as the actual extension of credit. As an initial matter, ECOA prohibits creditors from in any way discouraging applicants or prospective applicants from applying for a loan. ECOA also limits the type of information that may be requested of a credit applicant. Creditors may not request any information about an applicant's spouse or former spouse unless the spouse will be permitted to use the account, will be contractually liable on the account, the applicant is relying on the spouse's income as a basis of repayment, the applicant resides in a community property state or property on which the applicant is relying as a basis for repayment is located in a community property state, or the applicant is relying on alimony or other maintenance payments for repayment. Creditors may not inquire about marital status of an applicant or the sex of an applicant except under very limited circumstances. Creditors also may not inquire as to an applicant's birth control practices, intentions concerning childbearing, or capability to bear children. Creditors also may not inquire as to an applicant's race, color, or national origin.

The above bases for discrimination are also applicable to the evaluation of applications and the extension of credit. Generally speaking, in evaluating applications and handling loans once they have been originated, creditors may consider any information that they have obtained about an applicant or borrower, so long as this information is not used in a manner that discriminates against the applicant or borrower on a prohibited basis.

Creditors are further prohibited from requiring the signature of an applicant's spouse or other person, except a joint applicant, on any document if the applicant qualifies for the loan on his or her own. If an applicant requests unsecured credit, relying in part on property the applicant owns jointly with another person to establish creditworthiness, the signature of this other person may be required only on necessary instruments.

Creditors must notify applicants within 30 days after receiving a completed application whether the creditor has approved the requested credit, is making a counteroffer, or is taking adverse action (e.g., refusing to grant credit) on the application. Notification of an adverse action must be in writing and contain a statement of the action taken, the name and address of the creditor, a prescribed ECOA notice (which is set forth in the Act), the name and address of the federal agency that administers compliance with respect to the creditor, and either the principal reasons for the action taken or a disclosure of the applicant's right to obtain such a statement, and from whom it can be obtained.

Creditors failing to comply with ECOA's requirements are subject to civil liability for actual and punitive damages. Liability for punitive damages is restricted to nongovernmental entities and is limited to $10,000 in individual actions and, in class actions, $500,000 or 1 percent of the creditor's worth, whichever is less.

Various federal agencies enforce ECOA, depending upon the type of creditor. The Federal Trade Commission enforces ECOA for mortgage bankers. Companies affiliated with financial institutions are regulated by the agency regulating that financial institution.

Fair Housing Act: Smilar to ECOA in purpose, the Fair Housing Act prohibits lenders from discriminating in housing-related activities such as the sale or rental of housing as well as in lending activities. The prohibited bases for discrimination under the Fair Housing Act are broader than those under ECOA. Under the Fair Housing Act, lenders may not discriminate against any person because of race, color, religion, national origin, sex, handicap, or familial status. It should be noted that neither ECOA nor the Fair Housing Act is intended to coerce lenders into extending credit when it is not, in their good business judgment, prudent to do so. Rather, these acts are intended to prohibit discrimination based upon specified bases. Lenders that provide loans for the purchase, repair, or improvement of housing must comply with both ECOA and the Fair Housing Act.

The Fair Housing Act is wider in its scope than ECOA, in that it regulates "any person or other entity whose business includes engaging in residential real estate-related transactions," which includes lenders, real estate brokers, rental agents, sellers of real estate, and appraisers.

The Fair Housing Act makes it unlawful for lenders to deny a loan or any other financial assistance for a real estate-related transaction on the basis of the race, color, religion, familial status, national origin, handicap, or sex of the loan applicant, a person associated with the loan applicant, an owner or prospective owner of the property, any lessees, or any tenants. Lenders are also prohibited from discriminating in determining the amount of credit that will be extended, the interest rate, the duration of a loan, or any other loan terms.

Certain acts have been determined by courts to be discriminatory under the Fair Housing Act. These acts include "redlining" (denying loans in certain neighborhoods even though applicants may be eligible for credit), making excessively low appraisals of property, creating a racially exclusive image (portraying applicants in advertisements as being of a certain race), and the establishment of excessively burdensome loan application standards.

HUD has established certain actions that have been deemed to be indicative of compliance with the Fair Housing Act. These actions include the required displaying of an equal housing opportunity logotype, statement, or slogan as well as the use of models of different races in advertisements. Lenders should provide a printed copy of the non-discrimination policy to employees and clients.

The Department of Housing and Urban Development has been charged with the enforcement of the Fair Housing Act. Aggrieved persons may file a discrimination complaint with HUD and HUD will investigate the complaint and attempt to resolve the grievance. Aggrieved persons may also sue anyone who they feel has unlawfully discriminated against them. In addition, the Attorney General of the United States may sue for an injunction against anyone that displays a pattern of noncompliance with the Fair Housing Act.

Fair Credit Reporting Act: The Fair Credit Reporting Act (FCRA) regulates the consumer reporting industry as well as users of consumer credit reports by placing disclosure obligations on the users of consumer reports and ensuring fair, timely, and accurate reporting of credit information. FCRA also restricts the use of reports and requires the deletion of out-of-date and inaccurate information contained in consumer reports. Lenders are most likely to be affected by the requirements of FCRA as "users" of consumer reports.

FCRA defines a "consumer reporting agency" as any person or entity that, for a fee, for dues, or on a cooperative nonprofit basis, regularly engages in whole or in part in the practice of assembling or evaluating consumer credit information or other information on consumers for the purpose of furnishing consumer reports to third parties, and that uses any means of interstate commerce to prepare or furnish consumer reports. Lenders providing consumer credit information other than their own experience with the consumer to other lenders will fall within this definition and, therefore, must comply with the requirements set forth in FCRA for consumer reporting agencies.

Consumer reporting agencies may issue consumer reports only in certain circumstances. A report may be furnished in response to the order of a court having jurisdiction to issue such an order or a subpoena issued in connection with proceedings before a federal grand jury or in accordance with the written instructions of the consumer to whom it relates.

Consumer reporting agencies may also issue consumer reports to persons who it believes intend to use the information (1) in connection with a credit transaction involving the consumer on whom information is being furnished, (2) for employment purposes, (3) in connection with the underwriting of insurance involving the consumer, (4) in connection with the determination of the consumer's eligibility for a license or other benefit granted by a governmental instrumentality required by law to consider an applicant's financial responsibility or status, or (5) in connection with an otherwise legitimate business need for the information involving a business transaction with the consumer.

FCRA requires users of consumer reports who make a credit decision based on a credit report to disclose this fact to the consumer. The consumer must then be provided with the name of the consumer reporting agency that provided the credit report. (Note that the denial of credit based upon a credit report is an example of a situation that triggers the requirements of two acts—ECOA and FCRA.) This disclosure is usually included in the lender's adverse action notice.

When credit for personal, family, or household purposes is denied, or the charge for such credit is increased because of information obtained from a person other than a consumer reporting agency, the user of the information must, within a reasonable period of time, and upon the consumer's written request received 60 days after learning of the adverse action, disclose the nature of the information to the consumer. The user of the information must disclose to the consumer his or her right to make such a written request at the time the adverse action is communicated to the consumer.

Other disclosure requirements are imposed on credit reporting agencies. These disclosure requirements are required in order to provide consumers with an opportunity to correct any inaccuracies in their consumer reports. Lenders that also act as consumer reporting agencies must comply with these provisions.

Liability may be imposed on lenders acting as either users of credit reports or as consumer reporting agencies. Civil liability under FCRA can include actual damages and punitive damages, as well as court costs and attorneys' fees. FCRA also authorizes civil liability for negligent as well as willful noncompliance. FCRA is enforced by the Federal Trade Commission.

Real Estate Settlement Procedures Act

Scope: The Real Estate Settlement Procedures Act (RESPA), which is administered by HUD, was enacted by Congress in 1974 to provide mortgage loan applicants with the disclosure of information about the costs and procedures involved in loan settlement. The timing and content of the various disclosures and who has the obligation of providing them depends on the stage of the loan application process. RESPA was also enacted to prohibit kickbacks and other undisclosed or unearned fees from being unknowingly or improperly passed on to borrowers. Revisions to RESPA were enacted by the Cranston-Gonzales National Affordable Housing Act of 1990 to require disclosures relating to escrow accounts and the transfer of mortgage servicing.

RESPA applies to "federally-related mortgage loans" which, as originally enacted, were defined as loans secured by a first lien on one-to four-family residential real property if the loan proceeds were used in whole or in part to finance the purchase of the property. There were exemptions from this definition, including, for example, property that contained 25 or more acres and property that was purchased for resale or investment. The definition of a federally related mortgage loan, and thereby the coverage of RESPA, was dramatically revised with the enactment of the Housing and Community Development Act of 1992. In addition to first lien purchase money mortgage loans, federally related mortgage loans now include subordinate mortgage loans and refinancings of existing mortgage loans, whether or not a transfer of title is involved. Additionally, the exceptions were deleted.

In connection with the expansion of RESPA's coverage in October, 1992, Regulation X, which implements RESPA, also underwent extensive change as of December 2, 1992. Unlike RESPA, which had undergone numerous revisions since its passage in 1974, Regulation X had been revised only once since its enactment in 1976. Although RESPA's coverage was expanded to include subordinate mortgage loans, Regulation X states that RESPA does not apply to mortgage loans that are not secured by a first lien. Regulation X is expected to be amended to apply to second mortgage loans by the Spring of 1993.

To aid lenders in complying with RESPA and Regulation X, lenders had previously relied on informal HUD counsel's opinions and HUD staff interpretations to determine their conduct. However, those interpretations were withdrawn as of December 2, 1992, but may continue to be used to determine the validity of conduct under Regulation X as it existed prior to December 2, 1992. Future interpretations will be published in the *Federal Register* as interpretations, interpretive rules, or commentary.

Good faith estimate: RESPA requires that a good faith estimate of settlement costs (GFE) be delivered to or placed in the mail to a loan applicant no later than three business days after the application is received. Both the mortgage lender and the mortgage broker, if any, must provide the GFE, unless the mortgage broker has an exclusive relationship with the lender. In that case, only the lender need provide the GFE. The GFE consists of an estimate, expressed as either a dollar amount or a range, of the charges the borrower will be likely to incur at or before settlement, based on common practice in the locality. HUD has created a model form for the GFE disclosure that lenders may, but need not, use.

In addition to an estimate of expected settlement costs, if the lender requires the borrower to use a particular provider of settlement services, such as an appraiser, credit bureau, or title insurance agent, and the borrower will be paying for any part of such service, the GFE must also clearly state that the use of a particular service provider is required and that the estimate is based on the charges of that provider. The name, address, and phone number of the provider, as well as the nature of any relationship between the lender and the required provider, must also be disclosed.

Disclosure of broker fees: When RESPA was enacted in 1974, the use of mortgage brokers was uncommon. Lenders originated mortgage loans primarily through walk-in business at their retail offices. During the 1980s, lenders began originating an increasing number of loans through mortgage brokers. By using mortgage brokers, lenders were able to expand their markets by originating loans in areas where they did not maintain retail offices. Many lenders and mortgage brokers took the position that the fees charged by mortgage brokers for their services were not required to be disclosed under RESPA, especially broker fees that were not paid directly by the borrower, such as yield spread premiums. However, HUD has recently made its position clear that RESPA requires the disclosure of mortgage broker fees, however denominated, whether paid directly or indirectly by the borrower or the lender (including servicing release fees, yield spread premiums, and discount points remitted by the lender to the mortgage broker) on both the GFE and HUD-1 Settlement Statement.

Controlled business arrangements: A controlled business arrangement is an arrangement by which a person in a position to refer business incident to a settlement service refers business to a provider of settlement services, and the person referring business has either an affiliate relationship with or a direct or beneficial ownership interest of more than 1 percent in the settlement service provider. Controlled business arrangements do not violate Section 8, the anti-kickback provision of RESPA, if certain conditions are met. First, the borrower must be provided with a controlled business arrangement disclosure statement at the time of the referral, setting forth the nature of the relationship, including the ownership and financial interest, between the provider of settlement services and the referring party, and an estimated charge or range of charges generally imposed by the provider. The disclosure must be provided on a separate piece of paper no later than the time of the referral or, if the lender requires the use of a particular provider, at the time of loan application, in which case the controlled business arrangement disclosure may be a part of the GFE. Second, the person referring may not *require* the use of a particular provider. Third, the only thing of value, i.e., compensation, that is permitted to be given to the person referring the business is a return on ownership or franchise interest.

Computerized loan origination: Computer loan origination services (CLOs) are a relatively new practice in the mortgage lending industry. CLOs are computer programs that allow borrowers, for a fee, to access loan information from various potential service providers. They necessarily require a computer service for borrowers to see different financing options and are usually offered by mortgage brokers. In order to promote increased consumer information and awareness, HUD has taken the position that payments by a borrower for a CLO are not a kickback if the borrower is provided with a disclosure that includes an itemization of the services provided and the fees to be charged on a form prescribed by HUD. The disclosure must be provided by the CLO provider whenever it is anticipated that the borrower will pay for the CLO service.

Civil liability and enforcement: HUD has enforcement powers over violations of the anti-kickback provisions of RESPA, which include the disclosure provisions that relate to broker fees, controlled business arrangements, and CLOs. Whoever violates these provisions will be fined no more than $10,000 and/or imprisoned not more than one year *per* violation. Whoever violates the provisions will also be liable for up to three times the amount of the settlement service charge involved in the violation. Injunctive relief by HUD, state attorneys general, or state insurance commissioners may also be obtained. Successful parties may also be awarded court costs and attorney fees.

Notice of transfer of servicing: RESPA was revised in 1990 to require disclosures relating to the transfer of mortgage loan servicing. In addition to requiring, at the time mortgage loan servicing is actually transferred, notices by the transferor and the transferee of mortgage servicing, which are discussed later in this chapter, lenders must also provide an initial mortgage servicing transfer disclosure at the time of loan application.

The provisions of Regulation X that implement this section of RESPA have not been finalized, but are contained in an interim rule. In the interim rule HUD has provided a model for the initial mortgage servicing transfer notice; however, the language contained therein is not mandatory except for the applicant's acknowledgment.

This initial mortgage servicing transfer disclosure must be provided to each applicant for a federally related mortgage loan, by each person who receives such an application (either a mortgage lender or a mortgage broker). This disclosure must be provided at the time of application. If a face-to-face interview occurs at application, the disclosure must be provided at that time. Otherwise, the disclosure must be placed in the mail, first-class, within three business days after receipt of the application. The disclosure must state (1) whether the servicing of the loan may be transferred while the loan is outstanding, (2) the percentage of loans made by the lender for which servicing has been sold, assigned, or transferred during the most recently completed three calendar years, (3) the best available estimate of the percentage of loans originated by the lender for which servicing may be transferred during the 12-month period beginning on the date of origination, (4) a summary of the information required to be disclosed upon the actual transfer of servicing, and (5) a summary of the procedures applicable when a borrower has an inquiry for the loan servicer.

Truth in Lending

Scope: The Truth-in-Lending Act (TiLA) was enacted in 1968, and was simplified and revised in 1979. It was enacted to provide consumers with information about the cost of credit to enable them to compare different credit programs. TiLA is administered by the Federal Reserve Board (FRB). Like RESPA, TiLA is a disclosure statute. TiLA and its implementing regulation, Regulation Z, apply to entities that regularly extend credit to consumers, if the credit is primarily for personal, family, or household purposes and is subject to a finance charge or is payable in more than four installments according to a written agreement. Exempt from TiLA is consumer credit that is not secured by real property and is for an amount in excess of $25,000. In addition to setting out rules for the disclosure of the terms of consumer credit before the consumer enters the transaction, TiLA also requires disclosure on a periodic basis, provides for billing error resolution, and regulates how a lender advertises loan programs. TiLA also requires that the note for a loan secured by a residential one- to four-family property contain a maximum interest rate if the note allows for an increase in the annual percentage rate.

TiLA contains different disclosure rules, depending on whether the credit is open-ended or closed-ended. Open-ended credit, which includes home equity lines of credit, is defined as consumer credit offered under a plan in which (1) the creditor reasonably contemplates repeated transactions, (2) the creditor may impose a finance charge from time to time on an outstanding unpaid balance, and (3) the amount of credit extended is generally made available to the extent any outstanding balance is repaid. Closed-ended credit is defined as everything other than open-ended credit. Traditional first-lien mortgage loans are made on a closed-ended, or nonrevolving basis, and so we have discussed the closed-ended credit requirements below.

The terms "finance charge" and "annual percentage rate" are terms of art whose comprehension is critical to any lender's compliance efforts. There are special disclosure rules applicable to these terms, and they alone are responsible for several pages of official staff commentary published by the FRB. The finance charge is the cost of consumer credit expressed as a dollar amount. The annual percentage rate is the cost of credit as a yearly rate. Regulation Z provides detailed rules for calculating the finance charge and the annual percentage rate.

Timing and format requirements: TiLA has strict requirements for its disclosures. These requirements relate to the actual content of the disclosures as well as the order, spacing, segregation, and relative prominence of the various disclosures.

In closed-ended credit transactions, creditors must provide disclosures before consummation of the transaction, which is the time that a consumer becomes contractually obligated. These disclosures are discussed below under "Settlements." The closed-ended credit disclosures must be provided in a form the consumer may keep, must be grouped together and segregated from any other information, and must not contain any extraneous information. The finance charge and annual percentage rate, when required to be expressed with a corresponding amount or percentage rate, must be more conspicuous than anything except the lender's name. Further, the itemization of the amount financed must be separate from other required disclosures. The RESPA GFE may be substituted for the itemization of the amount financed.

If the information necessary for an accurate disclosure is not known to the lender, the lender is permitted to make the disclosure based on the best information reasonably available, if the lender states that the disclosure is an estimate.

For residential mortgage transactions (purchase money or initial construction loans secured by the borrower's principal dwelling) that are subject to RESPA, good faith estimates of the disclosures required before consummation (discussed below under "Settlements") must also be delivered or placed in the mail no later than three business days after the lender receives the borrower's written application. This timing requirement coincides with the time period within which the RESPA GFE is required to be provided.

Additionally, if the transaction is secured by the consumer's principal dwelling and the annual percentage rate may increase after consummation, then additional disclosures must be provided at the time an application form is provided to the consumer, or before the consumer pays a nonrefundable fee, whichever occurs earlier. If the application is taken over the telephone or reaches the lender through an intermediary, agent, or broker, these additional disclosures must be delivered or placed in the mail no later than three business days after receipt of the application. These additional disclosures are (1) the booklet entitled *Consumer Handbook on Adjustable Rate Mortgages* and (2) a loan program disclosure for each variable-rate program in which the consumer expresses an interest.

The variable-rate disclosure for each loan program must contain certain disclosures, including the index or formula used in making adjustments and a source of information about the index or formula; an explanation of how the interest rate and payment will be determined, including an explanation of how the index is adjusted, such as by the addition of a margin; the frequency of rate and payment changes; and a historical example, based on a $10,000 loan amount, illustrating how payments and the loan balance would have been affected by interest rate changes implemented according to the terms of the loan program.

Civil liability and administrative enforcement: Lenders that violate the TiLA provisions, including both open- and closed-ended disclosure requirements and rescission requirements, will be subject to civil liability. The civil liability provisions are set out in the TiLA statute and include amounts that may be recovered and the permissibility of class-action lawsuits. Because lenders most often use preprinted forms and standard procedures, mistakes can be quite costly. In an individual action, lenders may be liable for actual damages, an automatic statutory penalty equal to twice the amount of the finance charge (with $100 and $1,000 minimum and maximum caps), plus court costs and reasonable attorney fees. In a class-action lawsuit, lenders may be liable for actual damages, an amount equal to the lesser of $500,000 or 1 percent of the lender's net worth, plus court costs and reasonable attorney fees.

Although TiLA and Regulation Z are interpreted and administered by the FRB, enforcement for TiLA is divided up among various federal regulators, depending upon the type of institution. For example, compliance with TiLA is enforced by the OCC for national banks, the OTS for savings and loan associations, and the FTC for mortgage lenders and anyone else for whom regulation is not specifically administered by another agency. When the finance charge or annual percentage rate is inaccurately disclosed, the regulators may require restitution, that is, adjustments to the affected accounts to ensure that borrowers are not required to pay a finance charge in excess of the finance charge actually disclosed or the dollar equivalent of the annual percentage rate actually disclosed, whichever is lower. TiLA sets guidelines under which agencies are not mandated to require adjustments.

Lenders can protect themselves from civil liability and administrative enforcement by curing any violation within 60 days of discovering an error, provided no proceeding has yet been brought. The lender must notify the person concerned of the error and make whatever adjustments in the appropriate account are necessary to ensure that the person will not be required to pay an amount in excess of the finance charge actually disclosed or the dollar equivalent of the annual percentage rate actually disclosed, whichever is lower. Additionally, civil liability may be avoided if the lender shows by a preponderance of the evidence that the violation was not intentional and resulted from a bona fide error notwithstanding the maintenance of procedures reasonably adapted to avoid such errors. Finally, acts or omissions that result from good faith compliance with any rule, regulation, or interpretation by the FRB are not subject to civil liability and administrative enforcement.

Adjustable-Rate Mortgages

Coverage: The adjustable-rate mortgage (ARM) is a financial product that has grown from a rarely used innovation of the early 1980s into one of the most common types of residential mortgage financing. Rather than a fixed rate for 30 years, which does not permit lenders to keep pace with inflation, ARM loans offer shorter periods of rate inflexibility, and are, to some extent, a gamble for both lender and borrower. The interest rate of an ARM loan is tied to an index that floats up and down with the money market. As ARM loans have proliferated and are now purchased without hesitation by the major secondary-market players, the options being offered have similarly multiplied. There are ARM loan products on the market that adjust anywhere from six months to one, five, or seven years. In addition to the variety in the length of time between interest rate adjustments, ARM loan programs offer different margins, rate caps, and indices on which the interest rate is based. This hodgepodge of loan programs presents a daunting challenge to any servicer, particularly one that services pools of loans originated under various ARM programs by different lenders.

State law: ARM loans were originally suspect, and, although the various federal agencies authorized federally chartered lenders to originate them, state statutes and regulations often precluded state-chartered lenders from offering ARMs. The Alternative Mortgage Transaction Parity Act, which was part of the Garn-St Germain Depository Institutions Act (Garn-St Germain) of 1982, was enacted to grant non-federally-chartered institutions the authority to make, purchase, and enforce "alternative mortgage transactions" (which includes ARMs), despite contrary state law, as long as they follow regulations issued by the appropriate federal agency. In those states that prohibit or restrict the making of alternative mortgage loans, mortgage bankers and state-chartered savings and loan associations can take advantage of this federal preemption under Garn-St Germain by following the guidelines of the OTS, while state-chartered banks must follow OCC requirements for ARM loans. States were given a three-year window period in which they could act to override this federal preemption, and only Arizona, Maine, Massachusetts, New York, South Carolina, and Wisconsin chose to do so. Each of these states' laws must be researched to see what, if any, restrictions the state has placed on alternative mortgage instruments. The law of the states that have not overridden Garn-St Germain must be researched because if the state law does not contain any restrictions on ARMs, the state-chartered lender need not follow the federal regulations in order to take advantage of the federal preemption. However, if the state does have restrictions on ARMs, the lender, in order to take advantage of the Garn-St Germain preemption, must ensure that any requirements imposed by the relevant federal agency are followed.

In order to take advantage of the Garn-St Germain federal ARM preemption, housing creditors that fall under the jurisdiction of the OTS (e.g., mortgage bankers) must follow the OTS requirements for adjustable-rate mortgages. These requirements permit lenders to adjust the interest rate, payment, balance, or term to maturity on a loan as specified in the loan contract and also permit loans to be non-, partially, or fully amortizing. OTS requires that adjustments correspond directly to the movement of an index that measures the rate of inflation if the index is readily available to and verifiable by the borrower and is beyond the lender's control.

Disclosure requirements: In addition to substantive requirements, the OTS imposes disclosure requirements on ARMs. First, for closed-ended loans with a term of more than one year, the TiLA early ARM disclosures discussed above must be provided at the earlier of providing an application form to a borrower or the payment by the borrower of a nonrefundable fee. Within three business days after receipt of a written application for an ARM loan, the lender must also disclose in writing, in plain language, in one or more documents separate from the loan documents (1) the rights of the lender under a due-on-sale clause if there is one in the loan contract, (2) required information relating to any late charge or prepayment penalty, (3) required information relating to escrow payments, and (4), if the loan is non- or partially amortized, a statement of information that will be contained in the notice of maturity and how far in advance the notice will be given, whether the lender has unconditionally obligated to refinance the loan, and whether there will be a large payment due at maturity.

Additionally, the OTS requires adjustment notices (1) at least once a year if there is an interest rate adjustment without a corresponding payment change, and (2) between 25 and 120 calendar days before payment at a new level is due. Adjustment notices must disclose the current and prior interest rates; the index values upon which those rates were based; the extent to which the lender has foregone any increase in the interest rate; the contractual effects of the adjustment, including the payment due after the adjustment is made; a statement of the loan balance; and the payment that would be required to fully amortize the loan at the new interest rate over the remaining term, if this payment amount is different than the payment actually due.

ARM errors: Since 1989, ARMs have been the subject of much media attention because of the discovery of a fair amount of ARM loan adjustment errors. These errors resulted from the confluence of the many features of various ARM programs discussed above in addition to human error, such as entering the incorrect interest rate into servicing software. Following the initial discovery of errors, subsequent audits conducted by regulators revealed an inconsistent pattern of errors, resulting in both the under- and over-charging of interest in amounts ranging from a few dollars to several times the amount of interest that would have been due had the loan been adjusted correctly. The Task Force on Consumer Compliance of the Federal Financial Institutions Examination Council, which is composed of members of the FRB, OCC, OTS, FDIC, and National Credit Union Administration, issued interagency examination procedures and is working on correction procedures. Fannie Mae has also been developing procedures for its servicers to follow upon discovery of ARM errors in a Fannie Mae portfolio.

Appraisals and Appraisers

Federal action: With the enactment of the Financial Institutions Reform, Recovery and Enforcement Act of 1989 (FIRREA), much attention and regulation has been focused on appraisals and appraisers. FIRREA established requirements for appraisals on federally related real estate transactions and requires that appraisals be performed "in accordance with uniform standards, by individuals whose competency has been demonstrated and whose professional conduct will be subject to effective supervision." All states were mandated to establish appraiser licensing and certification requirements by December 31, 1992. Therefore, lenders must ensure that the appraisers that they select are operating in compliance with state laws.

An appraisal of the property to be mortgaged is necessary in order to verify that the value of the property will support the loan amount anticipated. As a general rule, a property must be appraised within the 12 months preceding the date of the mortgage and the note. If the appraisal report is more than four months old, the appraiser will be required to reinspect the exterior of the property and to review current market data to determine if the value of the property has declined. If it is determined that the value of the property has declined, a new appraisal must be obtained.

Selecting an appraiser: Federally related real estate transactions having a transaction value of more than $100,000 must be appraised by at least a state-licensed appraiser, if not a state-certified appraiser. (For loans or other extensions of credit, the amount of the loan or extension of credit is the "transaction value.") Appraisals obtained in connection with all federally related transactions that have a transaction value of $1 million or more must be conducted by certified appraisers. Nonresidential federally related real estate transactions having a transaction value of $250,000 or more, other than those involving appraisals of one- to four-family residential properties, also require a state-certified appraiser.

An appraiser will be deemed to be "certified" if he or she has satisfied the criteria for certification issued by the Appraisal Qualifications Board or the Appraisal Foundation, and passed a state-administered examination that is consistent with the Uniform State Certification Examination issued or endorsed by the Appraisal Qualifications Board or the Appraisal Foundation. In order to be a "licensed" appraiser, an appraiser must pass state examinations and meet state experience and educational requirements.

Appraisal requirements: For all federally related transactions, appraisals must conform to the Uniform Standards of Professional Appraisal Practice (USPAP) adopted by the Appraisal Standards Board of the Appraisal Foundation. Appraisals must:

♦ Be based on the market value of the property

♦ Be written and presented in a narrative format or on forms satisfying these requirements

♦ Enable the reader to ascertain the estimated market value of the property and the rationale for this estimate

♦ Report and analyze prior sales of the property

♦ Report appropriate deductions and discounts for any proposed construction, or any completed properties that are partially leased or leased at other than market rents as of the date of the appraisal

♦ Include a statement that the appraisal assignment was not based on a requested minimum valuation, a specific valuation, or approval of a loan

♦ Contain sufficient supporting documentation

♦ Include a legal description of the property

♦ Identify and separately value any personal property, fixtures or intangible items,

♦ Follow a reasonable valuation method that addresses the direct sales comparison, income, and cost approaches to market values

♦ Disclose whether information deemed pertinent to the completion to the appraisal is unavailable.

Furthermore, if the property is and will continue to be income-producing, the appraisal must report current revenues, expenses, and vacancies. The appraisal should analyze and report a reasonable marketing period for the subject property and report on current market conditions and trends that will affect projected income.

Depending upon the institutional lender to which a mortgage will be sold, certain exhibits must be attached to appraisals. These exhibits may include a street map showing the location of the property, photographs of the subject property, and a sketch of all improvements on the property, indicating building dimensions.

In order to ensure that an appraisal is accurate, the mortgage lender must provide the appraiser with accurate data. A copy of the complete sales contract for the property will provide the appraiser with most of the information needed. The mortgage lender must make the appraiser aware of all closing costs, loan fees, and interest rate buy-downs, amongst other financial information. Mortgage lenders should also inform appraisers of any environmental hazards located on the property or nearby.

State Application, Disclosure, Lock-In, Commitment, Processing Requirements

Just as licensing requirements for mortgage brokers, lenders, and servicers have been increasing in recent years, the regulation of the activities and practices of these entities has increased as well. These regulations are intended to provide safeguards for borrowers and potential borrowers and, to a certain extent, ensure uniformity in mortgage lending practices within each state. Of course, procedures and forms will differ from lender to lender within each state. However, states are showing an increased concern that the processing of applications by mortgage companies is fair and timely.

Typical disclosure and commitment requirements: At the time of a loan application or upon loan commitment, many states require that disclosures be made regarding terms and conditions of the proposed mortgage loan, as well as the terms and conditions of the commitment itself.

Usually, loan originators are required to disclose the principal amount of the loan, the term of the loan, the initial interest rate and, for an adjustable-rate loan, how the rate will be determined and any limitations on rate changes. Other required disclosures include the monthly payment of principal and interest, a statement as to whether a balloon payment will be required, the conditions under which the mortgage loan may be assumable, and a statement as to whether any funds will be escrowed.

Loan originators must also usually disclose the time during which the commitment is irrevocable, the amount of fees and charges payable at the time of commitment, and the expiration date of the commitment. Most states also require a disclosure stating that a borrower who signs a commitment and then fails to close the loan at the scheduled time may lose certain commitment fees and charges.

Typical lock-in requirements: Before the acceptance of any points or a lock-in fee, mortgage lenders are usually required to provide an applicant with a lock-in agreement, which is signed by the mortgage lender and the applicant. The lock-in agreement must identify the property to be mortgaged, and it must set forth the principal amount and term of the loan, initial interest rate and points, commitment fees, and lock-in fees. It must also disclose the length of the lock-in period.

Most states require that the length of the lock-in period be a time period during which the lender can reasonably expect to close the loan. The consequence of failing to close the loan within the lock-in period must also be set forth. Most states require lenders to honor the locked-in rate and points of the loan if the loan does not close within the lock-in period through no fault of the applicant.

States also usually set forth circumstances under which a lock-in fee must be refunded to the borrower. A lock-in fee usually must be refunded if the property appraisal is less than the anticipated loan on the property or if an applicant who has provided complete credit information is determined not to be creditworthy.

Diligent and timely processing: States are now commonly requiring mortgage companies to process loan applications in a timely manner and to act diligently in the mortgage loan process so as not to cause delays in loan closings. There has been case law in at least one state holding a mortgage lender liable for the negligent processing of a mortgage loan.

Settlements

Mortgage loans sold to investors are usually required to be documented on standard forms. Investors also usually require standard forms or standard covenants for the credit documentation supporting the mortgage loan and for the documents pertaining the sale of the loan to them. Fannie Mae and Freddie Mac have jointly published a uniform set of loan documents for conventional loans for each state, or, in some cases, for multistate purposes. These uniform single-family first-lien mortgage loan documents include security instruments for all 50 states, the District of Columbia, Puerto Rico, and the Virgin Islands; notes for ten jurisdictions and multistate notes, riders, and various addenda for special fact situations. Riders may be required for a planned unit development or condominium regime, for a two- to four-family home, or for an adjustable rate. Fannie Mae and Freddie Mac have published numerous riders and notes for the various ARM programs that they purchase. Fannie Mae and Freddie Mac also publish mortgage documents for single-family second mortgages and multifamily loans.

Lenders selling to Fannie Mae or Freddie Mac must use the Fannie Mae/Freddie Mac mortgage documents that are current for the jurisdiction in which the property is located. The Fannie Mae/Freddie Mac form of security instrument for each state contains uniform covenants covering the majority of the borrower's representations, warranties, and obligations. The instruments also contain additional nonuniform covenants that set out specific requirements, procedures, or protections permitted or required under that state's law. The model forms may require specific modifications for a particular state, and in that case, the investor has either provided for certain permitted changes or must approve the proposed changes, which must comply with applicable law. Investor requirements for the endorsement of the note and the assignment of the security instrument are also critical. They must comply with applicable state law requirements as well as satisfying investor guidelines. For loans that are FHA-insured or VA-guaranteed, lenders are required to use appropriate FHA and VA language and forms. Private investors require Fannie Mae/Freddie Mac uniform instruments or their own specialized covenants.

RESPA Requirements

Uniform settlement statement (HUD-1): HUD requires settlement agents to provide a disclosure of settlement costs on the HUD-1 Settlement Statement (HUD-1) at closing. The settlement agent must permit the borrower to inspect the HUD-1 during the business day immediately preceding settlement. Copies must be provided to the borrower, the seller, the lender, and/or their agents.

Only one HUD-1 need be prepared and provided in any transaction, even if there are multiple borrowers. Instructions on the proper completion of the HUD-1 are set out in Appendix A to Regulation X. All charges imposed in the transaction, including mortgage broker fees, must be separately disclosed.

Escrow disclosure: RESPA was revised in 1990 to require disclosure of escrow account requirements in connection with escrow accounts maintained for the purpose of paying taxes, insurance premiums, and other charges with respect to federally related mortgage loans. HUD has issued a proposed rule setting forth the escrow account disclosure requirements; no final rule has yet been promulgated. HUD has stated that it will not seek penalties for actions taken by a lender or servicer prior to the effective date of the final rule. Although the proposed rule was issued prior to the expansion of RESPA's coverage, the proposed rule states that it applies to *any* first-lien mortgage loan (i.e., including refinancings), if an escrow account is established.

If the lender requires the establishment of an escrow account at closing, makes an escrow account a condition for making the loan, or agrees to establish an escrow account voluntarily before closing, then the required initial escrow account disclosure must be provided at closing, either as a separate disclosure or as an addendum to the HUD-1. If an escrow account is established subsequent to closing, the initial disclosure statement must be provided within 45 calendar days of the establishment of the escrow account. Annual escrow account statements must also be provided within 30 calendar days after the end of the escrow account computation year.

The initial escrow account disclosure required at closing must itemize the estimated taxes, insurance premiums, and other charges reasonably anticipated to be paid from the escrow account during the first 12 months after the account is established and must disclose the anticipated due dates of the charges. In the proposed rule, HUD has set out a required format for the initial escrow account disclosure statement.

Regulation X also contains limits on the amount the lender is permitted to require the borrower to maintain in the escrow account. At settlement, the lender cannot collect more than an aggregate sum greater than the amount necessary to pay the taxes and insurance premiums for the time period between the last date on which the charges would have been paid and the first installment payment due under the mortgage, plus one-sixth of the estimated total of taxes and premiums to be paid during the following 12-month period. In any given month, the borrower's escrow payment may not exceed one-twelfth of the amount of estimated taxes and insurance premiums reasonably expected to be paid for the following 12 months, plus one-sixth of the estimated total of the amount of taxes and insurance premiums to be paid during the following 12-month period.

Failure to provide the required escrow account disclosures is a violation of RESPA, and the lender (or servicer with respect to annual escrow account statements) will be assessed a civil penalty of $50 per violation, up to a $100,000 cap per lender per 12-month period.

Notice of transfer of servicing: As discussed in the section "Transfer of Servicing" below, RESPA was revised in 1990 to require a notice by the transferor and transferee of mortgage servicing within 15 days of the effective date of transfer. At settlement, the lender and the servicer accepting the transfer of servicing may each provide a notice (or they may combine their respective notices into one notice) containing the information required to be provided at the time servicing is actually transferred. If the lender and the transferee servicer provide these disclosures at settlement, the notices need not be provided within 15 days of the transfer as would otherwise be required.

The disclosure must contain (1) the effective date of the transfer; (2) the name, address, and toll-free or collect-call telephone number of the new servicer; (3) the toll-free or collect-call telephone number of an individual employed by both the new and the old servicer or the department of each servicer that can be contacted by the borrower to answer servicing transfer inquiries; (4) the date on which the present servicer will cease to accept payments and the date on which the new servicer will begin to accept payments, which dates must be identical or consecutive; (5) any information concerning the effect of the transfer, if any, on the terms or continued availability of optional insurance; and (6) a statement that the transfer does not affect the term of conditions of the security instruments other than terms directly related to servicing.

TiLA

As discussed above, certain TiLA disclosures must be provided for closed-ended credit before consummation. These disclosures are subject to the segregation and other format requirements discussed above with respect to the early disclosures for closed-ended credit. The required disclosures include items such as the finance charge; the annual percentage rate; the number, amounts, and timing of the payments; and an identification of the security interest taken by the lender. If the annual percentage rate may increase after closing, certain variable-rate disclosures are also required.

Rescission requirements: Under TiLA consumers have a right to rescind a transaction in which a security interest is taken in the consumer's principal dwelling. The right of rescission is granted under TiLA to anyone whose ownership interest is or will be subject to the security interest, even if that person is not obligated on the debt. This right does not apply to certain transactions such as a purchase-money mortgage or a refinancing by the same lender of existing debt already secured by an interest in the consumer's principal dwelling.

The lender must provide each consumer who has a right to rescind two copies of the notice of the right to rescind. The notice must be on a separate document and must clearly and conspicuously disclose the taking of a security interest in the consumer's principal dwelling, the consumer's right to rescind the transaction, how the consumer may exercise the right to rescind, with a form for that purpose designating the address of the lender's place of business, the effects of rescission, and the date the rescission period ends. The rescission period lasts until midnight of the third business day following consummation, delivery of the notice of the right to rescind, or delivery of all material disclosures, i.e., the annual percentage rate, the amount financed, the finance charge, and the total of payments, whichever occurs last. Typically, all three triggering events occur simultaneously at closing.

In order to exercise the right of rescission, consumers must notify the lender of their rescission by mail, telegram, or other written communication. The notice is considered given when mailed or sent. If the consumer exercises the right of rescission then the security interest created by the transaction is void and the consumer is not liable for any amount paid, including any finance charges. During the rescission period, money may not be disbursed except in escrow.

Consumers may waive or modify their right to rescind if the lender determines that the credit is needed to meet a bona fide personal financial emergency. In order to waive rescission, the consumer must provide the lender with a written and dated statement describing the emergency, specifically waiving or modifying the rescission period. The statement must be signed by all consumers that have the right to rescind and may not be on a preprinted form. Lenders should not encourage consumers to waive the rescission period.

Title Insurance

Lenders and secondary-market investors require mortgagee's title insurance policies, naming the lender as the insured, to protect the lender from such risks as a hostile claim of ownership against the borrower. An owner's policy, naming the borrower as the insured, is usually issued in connection with the mortgagee's policy. Investor requirements must be taken into consideration when originating the loan. These requirements cover such matters as the nature and scope of the coverage, required endorsements, and permitted exceptions from coverage. Properties that are condominiums or in a PUD may be subject to additional investor-imposed title requirements. The investor may require the title policy to be on a certain form, usually the American Land Title Association standard policy form, and may further restrict which insurers it will accept.

Hazard Insurance

In order to protect the property on which it has taken a lien and in order to sell a mortgage to an institutional lender, a lender requires hazard insurance. A hazard insurance policy must usually protect at least against fire and other usual perils and should cover 100 percent of the present replacement cost of the property.

The insurance carrier must be licensed and authorized to do business in the state in which the mortgaged property is located and must have a prescribed insurance rating. Additional hazard insurance requirements must be met if the secured property is a condominium or planned unit development.

Flood Insurance

If improved property has been identified by the Secretary of Housing and Urban Development or the Director of the Federal Emergency Management Agency as being in a Special Flood Hazard Area, flood insurance must be maintained by the borrower in an amount at least equal to the lesser of 100 percent of the insurable value of the facilities or the maximum coverage available under the National Flood Insurance Administration program applicable to the property. Lenders are responsible for determining whether the property is located in a special flood hazard area by checking a flood insurance rate map or a flood hazard boundary map.

No federal officer or agency (such as FHA, VA, or SBA) can approve a loan for acquisition or construction purposes in any area identified as having special flood hazards unless the community in which the area is situated is participating in the national flood insurance program. Flood insurance is available only to communities participating the national flood insurance program.

Under the National Flood Insurance Act, federal entities responsible for the supervision of various lenders are required to ensure that lenders notify purchasers (or obtain adequate notification that the seller has notified the purchaser), in writing, that the property they intend to purchase is in a flood hazard area and whether or not flood insurance is available. This notice must be provided in a reasonable amount of time before the purchaser signs any documents related to the proposed transaction. Additionally, lenders must notify purchasers that in the event of a flood disaster damaging their property, federal assistance will be available.

State Laws

States have imposed restrictions on the settlement process separate from the requirements discussed above that are imposed by federal law, any federal agency insuring the loan, or the ultimate investor. These requirements relate to, among other things, who may conduct loan closings and the permissible form of funds brought to settlement.

Wet settlement acts: Many states have "wet" settlement, or good funds, laws regulating a variety of procedures in connection with loan settlement. A "wet" settlement implies that funds are available for disbursement to the borrower by the time of settlement, as opposed to a "dry" settlement, which is a loan that closes and goes on record prior to funding. These statutes may state what form the funds being provided by the lender to the settlement agent must take, may impose disclosure requirements on the settlement agent, or may set out required time frames between the receipt of loan proceeds from the lender and disbursal to the borrower. When examining a particular state's wet settlement law, it is important to note what types of loan transactions the law applies to. For example, the statute may place restrictions on the settlement agent or on loan proceeds only in connection with purchase money mortgage loans.

When a state law requires that funds provided by the lender to the settlement agent take a particular form, cash, wired funds, certified checks, or cashier's checks are usually permitted, as are checks drawn on a financial institution within a particular geographic or regulatory area, such as a Federal Reserve District. The statute may also dictate the timing of events, such as prohibiting a settlement agent from disbursing loan proceeds until after recordation of the security instrument and may also prohibit collecting interest until funds have been disbursed, in which case the settlement agent may have to advance funds for recording costs.

Miscellaneous disclosures: State law may require disclosures at closing in addition to any disclosures required at the time of application for a loan. These disclosures may be part of a consumer protection statute, a real estate statute, a licensing statute, or a wet settlement statute. Frequently, disclosures are required to be placed on loan documents themselves, such as a statement that the borrower should not sign a document—such as the note, security instrument, or loan agreement—if it contains any blank spaces or a certification or affidavit stating that funds were disbursed at the time of execution of the mortgage. When the disclosures take the form of a certification or affidavit, it may be the lender or settlement agent who is required to sign instead of the borrower. Disclosures and/or certifications may also relate to the preparation of the loan documents, such as a statement of who prepared the documents.

Delivery, Custodian, and Assignment Requirements

Lenders selling mortgage loans to institutional lenders must be aware of and be in compliance with requirements for delivery of mortgage loans, custodian requirements for mortgage documents, and assignment requirements.

Delivery packages delivered to institutional lenders are received by the institutional lender's document custodian for review. The delivery package must contain the original note, other legal documentation of the mortgage loan, copies of recording receipts, documents that summarize general characteristics of the mortgage loan, and an assignment of the mortgage to the institutional lender.

The assignment of the mortgage to the institutional lender may not contain a recitation that the assignment is "without recourse." The assignment must be in recordable form. Therefore, lenders must be aware of specific state requirements regarding the recording of mortgages or deeds of trust. The assignment, should not, however, be recorded. On the assignment, the lender should include the date of execution, the lender's name, the borrower's name, a legal description of the property, recording information related to the mortgage, the date of the mortgage, an authorized signature, and an appropriate notarization if this is required by state law.

Servicing

Escrow administration: Mortgage lenders typically require the establishment of escrow accounts in connection with mortgage loans in which the borrower deposits funds to pay taxes, insurance premiums, and other charges with respect to the property securing the loan. The escrow account enables the mortgage lender to pay these amounts when they come due, thus avoiding any tax delinquencies or lapses of hazard insurance coverage on the property. RESPA sets standards for the calculation of the amount that the mortgage lender can require the borrower to deposit into the escrow account. RESPA limits the initial deposit into an escrow account to an amount equal to the sum sufficient to pay the taxes, insurance premiums, and other charges with respect to the property for the first payment period (usually one month) plus a cushion equal to two months' escrow deposit. The mortgage lender may not require the borrower to pay on a monthly basis more than one-twelfth of the total amount of the total estimated annual taxes, insurance premiums, and other charges, plus an amount necessary to maintain the two-month cushion. If the mortgage lender determines that there will be a deficiency in the escrow account, the mortgage lender may require the borrower to make additional deposits into the escrow account to eliminate the deficiency.

Escrow analysis: RESPA requires the mortgage lender to notify the borrower not less than annually of any shortage of funds in the escrow account. Under 1990 amendments to RESPA, RESPA requires the servicer of the loan to provide the borrower annually a statement disclosing the amount of the borrower's current monthly payment, the portion of the monthly payment being placed in the escrow account, the total amount paid out of the escrow account during the period, and the balance of the escrow account at the conclusion of the period. HUD issued proposed rules implementing this RESPA requirement in December of 1991. No final rule has yet been issued.

Interest on escrow accounts: Most mortgage lenders, as a rule, do not pay interest on escrow accounts, unless required to do so by state law. Approximately 15 states have enacted laws requiring mortgage lenders to pay interest on escrow accounts. The required interest rates generally range from 2 percent to 5 percent per annum, or are based on the institution's passbook savings account interest rate. Generally, interest earned on the account must be deposited into the escrow account and used to pay taxes, insurance premiums, and other charges related to the property as they become due. Some of these states otherwise requiring interest on escrow accounts do not require mortgage lenders to pay interest on escrow accounts under certain circumstances, such as escrow accounts established in connection with loans having loan-to-value ratios of less than 80 percent, or loans over a certain amount, such as $100,000. Federal legislation requiring the payment of interest on escrow account balances has been proposed in Congress. It is not clear whether this federal legislation, if enacted, will preempt state law requirements regarding the payment of interest on escrow accounts.

Transfers of Servicing

RESPA also requires mortgage lenders to disclose to borrowers certain information regarding the transfer of mortgage servicing. RESPA requires the seller of servicing to notify the borrower not less than 15 days before the date of the transfer of servicing and requires the purchaser of the servicing to notify the borrower of the transfer of servicing not more than 15 days after the date of the transfer. In these notices, the seller and purchaser of servicing are required to provide information regarding the effective date of the transfer, the name and telephone number of the seller and purchaser of the servicing, the date on which the seller of the servicing will stop accepting payments and the date on which the purchaser will begin accepting payments, and whether the terms of the mortgage will be affected by the transfer.

Payoff and Release

Many states have enacted laws that impose requirements on the payoff and release of a mortgage. Some states require the mortgagee to provide a payoff statement in writing upon the written request of the mortgagor within a specific time period. Furthermore, some states impose requirements as to the contents of the payoff statement. Depending on the state, many have imposed specific restrictions as to time period in which the mortgagee must deliver an executed, recordable release of the mortgage. The mortgagee often has an obligation to execute and deliver a release within 10 to 60 days after receipt of payment of the mortgage in full. Depending on the state, various penalties are imposed on the mortgagee upon the failure to discharge a mortgage or to execute and acknowledge a deed of release after full payment and performance of the terms of the mortgage. The penalties can include damages resulting from its failure to discharge the mortgage, attorneys' fees, and additional penalties. Some states provide for certain exceptions to the specified time period for delivering an executed release.

Some states permit a mortgage to be released by indicating the release in the margin or face of the recorded mortgage record, while others require a separate recordable deed of release. The statutes of each state should be reviewed to determine if the state has adopted a specific form for discharging a mortgage.

Foreclosure

The foreclosure method used to obtain title to property varies depending on the law of the state where the property is located.

In some states foreclosure is a judicial process that requires that an action be brought in a state court. The attorney files a complaint with the court, personally serves the mortgagor with notice of the action, advertises the foreclosure over a required period of time in a local publication, obtains a judgment from the court, and then obtains a court order to sell the property to satisfy the court judgment. Notice must normally also be given to all junior lienholders. Under a judicial foreclosure, some states provide for a statutory right to reinstate the mortgage at any time until a final judgment of foreclosure is entered or the foreclosure sale is held. Furthermore, some states provide for a redemption period, which allows the mortgagor to pay off the debt during a specified period after the foreclosure sale and regain title to the property.

In states having nonjudicial foreclosure laws, a public sale is conducted pursuant to a power of sale, which is specifically set forth in a nonuniform covenant of the mortgage. Depending on state law, various types of notice may need to be provided prior to the nonjudicial sale of the property. The notice of sale must usually contain the description of the property being sold, the date and time of the sale, the terms of the sale, and the date and place of recording of the mortgage. Notice must generally be given to all junior lienholders.

Under either type of foreclosure, the sale is conducted by a designated public agent or official and in a place accessible to the public. Good foreclosure practice generally obligates the lender to conduct and advertise its sale in a manner likely to get the highest bid at the auction-style foreclosure sale. Ideally, if the property value is substantial, the successful bidder will be a third party who will bid more than the secured indebtedness, so that the mortgage lender will be made whole and any excess can be paid to the defaulting former homeowner. Generally, however, the property is worth no more than the indebtedness plus the costs of the sale, so the defaulting former home owner gets nothing and the mortgage company is forced to buy the property in exchange for its debt. To avoid the expense and to preserve their credit rating, some borrowers elect, with the mortgage lender's approval, to grant a deed in lieu of foreclosure.

FHA/VA and Private Mortgage Insurance Claims

In general, when an FHA-insured loan goes into default, there are three options that are available to HUD and the lender. First, HUD can make temporary mortgage assistance payments on behalf of the borrower. Second, HUD can accept an assignment of the mortgage from the mortgagor. Third, the lender can foreclose on the mortgage and sell the property. In general, no action can be taken by a lender unless at least three full monthly mortgage payments are due and unpaid, and a notice of intent has been mailed to the mortgagor.

If HUD provides temporary mortgage assistance payments, the amount of the HUD assistance payment will be based on the mortgagor's financial circumstances. Assistance can continue for as long as 36 months under the temporary mortgage assistance program, at which time the mortgagor must resume full mortgage payments. In addition, any payments that are made by HUD under the temporary mortgage assistance program must be repaid with interest, according to a schedule prepared by the mortgagor and HUD. HUD may place an additional lien on the property to ensure repayment of the loan.

When a loan is assigned to HUD, HUD pays off the mortgage insurance and then becomes the owner of the mortgage. The mortgagor continues to make the payments to HUD and the loan servicing becomes the responsibility of the local HUD office. In addition, in connection with the assignment of the mortgage, HUD may provide the mortgagor with forbearance assistance. Forbearance assistance may allow all or a portion of the payments due under the mortgage to be postponed for a specified period of time; however, the payments must eventually be repaid. If the mortgagee forecloses on the property and takes title under the state law, it may then convey title to HUD.

If a VA-guaranteed loan goes into default, the VA may require the holder, upon penalty or otherwise losing the guaranty or insurance, to transfer and assign the loan to VA upon receipt of payment in full of the balance of the indebtedness remaining unpaid as of the date of the assignment. The VA then handles the disposition of the property and uses the proceeds from such sale to cover the cost of the acquisition of the loan. In the alternative, the VA may pay off the guaranty, leaving the responsibility for the disposition of the property with the lender. When the VA chooses this alternative, the payment by the VA becomes a debt owed by the borrower to the U.S. government. However, the VA can, in certain instances, waive the debt obligation if the default was caused by circumstances beyond the borrower's control.

If a lender forecloses on a loan insured by private mortgage insurance, a claim can be made against the lender's master policy. It is important to note that there have been cases that have held that insurance may be rescinded if the mortgage was part of a fraudulent financing scheme or a lender's material misrepresentation of loan terms.

Fair Debt Collection Practices Act

Purpose: The Fair Debt Collection Practices Act (FDCPA) became effective March 20, 1978, and was enacted to prevent the use of abusive, deceptive, and unfair debt collection practices by debt collectors. The FDCPA specifically states that the purpose is to "eliminate abusive debt collection practices by debt collectors, to insure that those debt collectors who refrain from using abusive debt collection practices are not competitively disadvantaged and to promote consistent state action to protect consumers against debt collection abuses."

Scope: The FDCPA is applicable only to consumer debts (i.e., debts incurred for personal, family, or household purposes) and not to debts incurred from business transactions. In addition, the FDCPA defines a debt collector as any person who uses any instrumentality of interstate commerce or the mails in any business the principal purpose of which is the collection of any debts, or who regularly collects or attempts to collect, directly or indirectly, debts owed or due or asserted to be owed or due another. Recently, the scope of the FDCPA has been expanded to include an attorney that falls within its definition of a debt collector.

Communication with the consumer or a third party: In   general, the FDCPA provides that without the debt collector receiving the prior consent of the consumer directly, or the express permission of a court, a debt collector may not communicate with a consumer at any unusual time or place that should be known to be inconvenient to the consumer. A debt collector shall assume that the convenient time for communicating with a consumer is after 8:00 a.m. and before 9:00 p.m., local time at the consumer's location. Furthermore, if the consumer is known to have retained an attorney, the debt collector may not contact the consumer directly, unless the attorney fails to respond within a reasonable period of time or unless the attorney consents to the direct communication with the consumer. A debt collector also may not contact the consumer at his or her place of business if the debt collector knows or has reason to know that the consumer's employer prohibits the consumer from receiving such communications.

Under the FDCPA, if a consumer notifies a debt collector in writing that the consumer refuses to pay a debt or that the consumer wishes the debt collector to cease communication with the consumer, in general, the debt collector may not communicate with the consumer with respect to the debt. Generally, a debt collector may not convey any kind of information about the debt to anyone other than the consumer or his attorney, unless it has received prior written consent by the consumer or express permission of a court of competent jurisdiction.

Prohibition against harassment: The main purpose of the FDCPA lies in the three sections that deal with harassment or abuse, false, or misleading representations, and unfair or unconscionable practices. Under the FDCPA, a debt collector may not use or threaten to use violence or any other criminal means to harm a physical person, property, or the reputation of any person; use obscene or profane language; publish a list of consumers who allegedly refuse to pay debts, except to a consumer reporting agency; advertise for the sale of any debt to coerce payment of debt; and cause the continuous ringing of a telephone.

Examples of false or misleading representations that are prohibited by the FDCPA include the use of any false representation or implication that the debt collector is affiliated with the United States or any state; the false representation of the character, amount, or legal status of any debt; or the threat to take any legal action that cannot legally be taken or that is not intended to be taken. In addition, a debt collector may not engage in any unfair or unconscionable practices, including the collection of any amount, including interest, fees, or charges incidental to the principal obligation, unless the amount is expressly authorized by the agreement that gave rise to the order. A debt collector also cannot take or threaten to take any nonjudicial action to dispossess or seize the property if there is no present right to possession of the property claimed as collateral through an enforceable security instrument.

Under the FDCPA, a debt collector must provide the consumer with written validation information of the amount of the debt being collected within five calendar days of the initial communication with the consumer unless the required information is included in the initial communication, or unless the consumer has paid the debt. The written notice is required to contain certain disclosure information. If the consumer notifies the debt collector in writing, within 30 days of receiving the notice, that the debt is disputed or that the consumer requests the name and address of the original creditor, the debt collector must cease all collection action until the debt collector obtains and mails to the consumer verification of the debt or the name and address of the original creditor.

Civil liability: A private civil action may be brought under the FDCPA within one year from the date of the debt collector's violation, in any appropriate United States District Court. In an individual action, liability is limited for actual damages plus punitive damages for up to $1,000. The court in determining the amount of liability will consider the frequency and persistence of noncompliance, and the general culpability of the defendant's conduct. In addition, if a suit is brought in bad faith and for the purpose of harassment, the court may award attorneys' fees and costs to the defendant.

Right to Financial Privacy

Scope: The Right to Financial Privacy Act of 1978 (RFPA) became effective on March 10, 1979, and provides customers of financial institutions with a certain amount of privacy as to their financial records. Prior to the enactment of the RFPA, customers of financial institutions had no way of knowing that their personal records were being turned over to a government authority. In addition, customers had no available means of challenging the government's access to their personal financial records. The RFPA establishes specific procedures that the government must follow in order to obtain financial information about a customer from a financial institution. Specifically, a financial institution shall not release the financial records of a customer until the government authority seeking the records certifies in writing to the financial institution that it has complied with the terms of the RFPA.

The RFPA applies to customers of a financial institution and defines a customer as any person or authorized representative of a person who utilized or is utilizing any service of a financial institution, or for whom a financial institution is acting or has acted as a fiduciary in relation to an account maintained in that person's name. In general, for a governmental agency to obtain information from a financial institution about a customer, one of the following conditions must be satisfied: (1) the customer has authorized disclosure of the records that are being sought, (2) the records are disclosed in response to an administrative summons or subpoena, (3) the records are disclosed in response to a search warrant, (4) the records are disclosed in response to a judicial subpoena, or (5) the records are disclosed in response to a formal written request by a government agency that follows the procedures set forth in the RFPA.

Notice and record-keeping requirements: The RFPA requires that notice be given to a customer prior to the financial institution releasing any customer financial records. In addition, the notice shall provide the customer with an explanation of the purpose for which the records are being sought. However, there is an exception to the customer notice provision if the government obtains a delay of notice order from the appropriate court. The RFPA provides specific circumstances in which the courts will grant an order of delay. Once the proper notice is given to the customer, the customer is provided a period for challenging the request for the customer's financial information.

The RFPA requires the financial institution to keep a record of each time a customer's financial records are disclosed to a government authority pursuant to a customer authorization. In addition, the customer has the right, unless the government authority obtains a court order, to obtain a copy of the record that the financial institution maintains regarding such disclosure. Any financial information that is obtained under the Act is not permitted to be transferred to another governmental agency or department unless the transferring agency or department certifies in writing that there is reason to believe that the records are relevant to a legitimate law enforcement inquiry within the jurisdiction of the receiving agency or department.

Civil liability: Any agency or department of the United States, or financial institution that discloses financial records or information contained therein in violation of the Act is liable to the customer to whom the records relate for (1) $100, without regard to the volume of the records involved; (2) any actual damages sustained by the customer; (3) punitive damages as the court may allow, where the violation is found to have been willful or intentional; and (4) in the case of any successful action to enforce liability under the Act, the costs of the action together with reasonable attorney fees as determined by the court.

II

Programs for Mortgage Origination:

Meeting the Need for
Mortgage Finance

Chapter 7

METHODS OF MORTGAGE LOAN ORIGINATION

John F. Macke
VP Financial Planning & Analysis
Inland Mortgage Corporation

Rick L. McGuire
Senior VP and Chief Production Officer
Inland Mortgage Corporation

INTRODUCTION

Most mortgage bankers would agree that new loan production is the lifeline of all mortgage banking. This theory is based on the fact that without the continuous infusion of new mortgage production, servicing portfolios would eventually perish. Not coincidental to this thinking is the fact that loan production has been the cornerstone on which most successful mortgage banking operations have been built. Whether a mortgage banker chooses to hold new production in a servicing portfolio or sell the servicing rights for cash, the *most basic value-creating function in mortgage banking is the ability to produce new mortgage loans.*

Mortgage origination systems take various forms. The most popular methods being used today would fall into the categories of Retail, Correspondent, Wholesale, and Consumer Direct. These forms of production will be discussed later in this chapter. Historically, the main goal of any loan origination system was to minimize the cost of servicing acquisition. It was a conceded fact that you could not originate mortgages at a profit, and thus mortgage bankers talked in terms of "cost of origination." However, recently, with the advent of affordable technology, mortgage bankers are demanding more from their production systems. Now the search is on for ways not only to make the origination process more efficient, but also to make loan production a reliable profit center, instead of simply a process that creates servicing value. This trend toward profitable loan production systems will likely continue into the next century.

A cursory examination of the basic revenues and costs of a typical retail production system highlights the problems of trying to become profitable in loan production. Assume a lender collects from a borrower an origination fee of 1 percent of the principal balance of the loan and an additional 0.25 percent in miscellaneous fees. Directly deducted from these revenues is the loan officer's commission, which typically ranges from 0.50 percent to 0.60 percent, leaving the mortgage banker 0.65 percent to 0.75 percent to cover the costs of processing, underwriting, closing, and shipping the loan. Cost containment is crucial in trying to squeeze any profit out of such a scenario. Interest margins and secondary marketing gains are two potential sources of profits for the originator, albeit unreliable and potentially risky ones. Another problem for the retail originator is the relatively high amount of fixed costs that are necessary to maintain a retail operation. As in any business, fixed costs are great in high volume periods, but can be lethal when volume declines.

Factor into this equation intense competition and an uncertain regulatory environment and the true nature of the mortgage origination industry can begin to be seen. Due to the real and perceived homogeneity of mortgage products, competition is direct and intense. Traditionally, price has been the battlefield, but as originators try to differentiate themselves with niche strategies, other factors are becoming important. Examples of such factors are service quality, location, availability, and product line. Regulatory uncertainty is a way of life for mortgage originators. Due to the political appeal of widespread home ownership, the government has never let a free market exist in the housing market. Oftentimes regulation is based more on politics than on prudent market management, which can have enormous negative ramifications for mortgage lenders. Lenders, however, have to live with poor regulations until a reversal can be obtained, and they often suffer throughout the life of an ill-fated regulation.

These challenges facing the retail originator have caused some mortgage bankers to abandon this form of loan production altogether. Some companies see Correspondent and Wholesale production as the principal means of eliminating the need for retail production. These production systems basically buy production from retail lenders and pay a service release premium, thus avoiding most of the headaches retail origination causes. However, cost containment, competition, and regulation are as much a part of wholesale and correspondent lending as they are of retail.

This chapter is designed to expand on the topics discussed here and give the reader a flavor of the mortgage production industry from the perspective of a participant in the industry.

METHODS OF PRODUCTION

Traditional Retail

The traditional retail production system consists of a branch system staffed by a sales force of loan officers (also known as originators, loan representatives, account executives, etc.). Loan officers make sales calls on people in a position to refer borrowers. The most obvious mortgage referral sources are realtors and homebuilders. Realtors and builders need home buyers to attain financing approval quickly and smoothly in order to transact their business more effectively. Other sources of referrals are financial planners, attorneys, insurance agents, and leasing agents.

Retail loan officers strive to convince these referral sources to use their services instead of their competitors.' To do this, they must give these people what they want, which is a successfully closed loan. To achieve this goal, a retail production system must have four important features:

1.   A highly trained professional staff

2.   Competitive mortgage products

3.   Reasonable rates

4.   Quality service

Ironically enough, realtors and builders do not automatically refer their customers to the mortgage company with the lowest price in town. Anyone who has been in the mortgage industry for any length of time knows that the price of mortgages is set by the laws of supply and demand, which are greatly influenced by economic and political factors well beyond a mortgage company's control. To try to consistently be the "lowest price in town" is not only unwise, it can be suicidal for the company. Therefore, realtors and builders who understand the mortgage business rely not solely on price, but on the quality of service a mortgage company can give their customer. After all, the "lowest price in town" does not mean anything if the loan does not close.

To achieve this high level of service, it is imperative to have a highly trained, professional staff. In the early 1980s it was not uncommon for the loan approval process to take 45 to 50 days. With the new technology available today, this processing time has been reduced by at least 50 percent and is continuously decreasing. It is conceivable that in the next few years the time from loan application to loan approval will take only a few hours. With this in mind, mortgage companies are putting a much greater emphasis on training loan processors, closers, and loan officers. Although product knowledge and knowledge of agency requirements will always be a critical element of top-quality employees, their responsiveness to customer needs is becoming more important to the ultimate success of the organization.

Training retail production employees involves making them aware of the many different mortgage products available today. It was not so long ago that there were only one or two options available to a borrower. With the advent of such products as ARMs, buydowns, balloons, two-steps, reverse mortgages, housing programs, etc., it is now possible to qualify a multitude of borrowers in a multitude of ways. The right program for one borrower may not be as suitable to another in the same financial position because of extraneous factors such as relocation potential, upward mobility, family plans, etc. A good loan officer will be able to listen to his or her customers' future plans and needs and put them into a mortgage program that best fits their particular situation.

Retail Branch Structure

Individual retail branches consist of a branch manager who oversees a staff of loan officers, processors, closers, and any other support staff necessary to run a smooth operation. As discussed earlier, loan officers

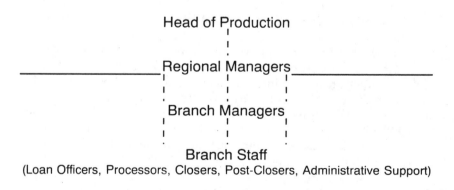

Head of Production

Regional Managers

Branch Managers

Branch Staff
(Loan Officers, Processors, Closers, Post-Closers, Administrative Support)

obtain loan applications from people referred by realtors, builders, and others. In the traditional retail system, these loan officers are paid a commission of anywhere from 50 to 60 basis points on all loan applications that close. Obviously, it is in their best interest to have a competitive price, good products, and a high-quality support staff to make this happen. Loan officers, therefore, rely on their branch manager for support in obtaining these things. These needs filter up from the branch manager to a regional manager (who oversees several branch managers) to the Head of Production.

It is the Head of Production's responsibility to juggle the needs of the branches with other corporate goals. For example, a company will not be profitable if their price is too aggressive, nor will they be profitable if their price is not aggressive enough, since the only way to be profitable is to create production. Therefore, the Head of Production normally oversees pricing and product line development. He or she monitors the needs of the entire company and tries to formulate a plan that successfully integrates them.

The regional manager is responsible for relaying the needs of the branches to upper management. Conversely, he or she must relay corporate goals to the managers and loan officers in a way that they will accept and strive to achieve. Regional managers are critical constituents in a successful retail company, as they must often act as the intermediary between the goals of the sales force and the overall goals of the corporation.

A branch manager can be much more focused. His or her primary responsibility is to increase market share by having quality loan officers, marketing products aggressively, and running a smooth back-office operation. A branch is only as strong as its people, and it is the manager's responsibility to recruit and retain quality employees. The branch manager is another critical link in the retail production chain because he or she can motivate the staff to buy into corporate goals. The majority of branch personnel do not deal with the Home Office or upper management, and their leader is their manager. How their leader reacts to corporate decisions will determine how the support staff reacts to them.

A loan officer in a retail branch drives the entire loan origination process. Realtors and builders send their business to a retail branch based on a relationship a loan officer has developed with them. A loan officer has a high-profile, hands-on approach that cannot be duplicated. They may not send their business to "ABC Mortgage Company," but rather to "John Smith" because of the relationship that has developed between John Smith and the realtor. One of the branch manager's most important tasks is to keep loan officers motivated and satisfied, since the loan officer is building a clientele that is likely to follow should he or she move to another mortgage company.

Some companies have been moving away from the traditional retail approach and going toward either Correspondent or Wholesale lending. (These methods will be discussed in detail later in this chapter.) A retail production branch, with its many fixed costs, is most cost-efficient in a market with large production volume. A wholesale/correspondent system can be more cost-effective in low and intermediate volume markets because it has relatively few fixed costs.

Why, then, would not all companies move in the direction of creating a Wholesale or Correspondent production system? One reason is the fact that a well-run retail system can be the most cost-effective method of acquiring servicing rights. A retail branch of a strong retail production company with a top-notch branch manager and excellent loan officers can produce loans cost-efficiently in almost any market environment, because this branch will produce the volume necessary to cover their fixed costs. An experienced retail production manager knows these kinds of branches are possible. Another favorable aspect of retail production is quality control. It is much easier to control the quality of retail originations simply because one's own employees are doing the originating, processing, and closing. Therefore, the production company controls the loan from point of sale to closing.

Even with these positives, the mortgage industry as a whole has been moving more and more toward the wholesale method of mortgage banking. According to one survey (an ICM Consultants survey reported in *The ICM Journal*, October 1991), in 1986 more than 80 percent of all mortgage banker volume was retail originations; by 1990 this percentage had fallen below 50 percent.

Correspondent Lending

Correspondent lending is best viewed as being one step removed from the point of sale in retail lending. Basically, correspondent lenders purchase completed application packages from smaller retail originators referred to as "mortgage brokers," or simply "correspondents." Mortgage brokers compete in the retail market and sell their production, generating profits by collecting service release premiums from the correspondent lender. This system allows correspondent lenders to produce a large volume of business without incurring large fixed costs. The correspondent lender's greatest expense is the service release premium paid to the broker, and thus the cost burden is shifted from fixed cost to variable cost. Therefore, only minimal cost is incurred on loans that do not close. The brokers maintain the "bricks and mortar" of the business and lose money on loans that fall out.

A typical correspondent lending structure would be as follows. The correspondent lender, or "investor," registers brokers that meet his financial and business requirements. The investor faxes prices to all registered brokers daily. Some lenders show the price of the mortgage separate from the service release premium; others add them and show only a single "net" price. In either case, since brokers are free to price as they choose, they generally add the two components together and may subsidize mortgage prices with service release premiums to be more competitive on the street. The broker then originates and processes applications and delivers the completed application packages to the investor to be underwritten, closed, and funded. Since correspondent lenders are performing value-added services (e.g., underwriting, closing, funding) and providing brokers with a ready market for their completed applications, the service release premium paid is usually less than the full value of the servicing rights acquired. Generally speaking, the more value-added services the investor provides, the less the service release premium will be.

A key aspect of this structure is that it provides a place in the production market for brokers. Brokers are typically experienced lenders who have left larger financial institutions to venture out on their own to originate mortgages. Correspondent lending allows these people to continue in the mortgage-lending field, which benefits consumers by increasing competition and thereby keeping prices lower.

Some brokers simply originate mortgages, collect their fees and service release premiums, and achieve their desired income by adjusting their production volume. However, sometimes as brokers gain experience, they become more aggressive in marketing their production by locking their loans with investors at the point they feel will maximize their profit. An example can better illustrate this point. Assume a broker takes an application and locks a borrower in at the current market price of 99 percent (1 percent discount), but the broker believes interest rates will fall. So, he does not lock the loan with an investor. If, as the loan is processed, rates fall as the broker expected, he may be able to lock the loan with an investor at 100 percent and thus make an additional 1 percent on the loan. However, if interest rates rise and the loan is ready to close, the broker may have to lock the loan with an investor at 97 percent and thus lose 2 percent on the loan. Prudent brokers will take limited marketing risks only on a portion of their production, if they take marketing risks at all, and thus limit their potential losses.

One of the most important benefits correspondent lenders provide for their brokers is funding. Since most brokers run smaller operations and maintain minimum net worth on their balance sheets, banks are hesitant to extend warehouse lines of credit to them. By using the correspondent lender's financial strength to obtain funds to close their loans, brokers are able to originate large volumes of mortgages. Recently, changes in the Real Estate Settlement Procedures Act (RESPA) have made using third-party funding a distinguishing feature of brokers. RESPA requires a broker to completely disclose all fees earned, including pricing gains and service release premiums, on loans funded by an outside source (i.e., a correspondent lender). For loans closed using internal funds, less disclosure is required.

Wholesale Lending

Wholesale lending is similar to correspondent lending in that the wholesale lender (or "wholesaler") is purchasing production from other lenders. In the case of wholesale, however, the mortgages have already closed and are being held in warehouse by the originating lender. The selling lender in a wholesale relationship is not necessarily a mortgage broker selling all production service released. In fact, a correspondent lender may sell some of its production to a wholesaler, if that wholesaler accepts third-party originations. Other mortgage lenders may sell their nonconforming jumbo mortgages to a wholesaler specializing in that type of product.

Wholesalers are further removed from the retail point of sale than correspondent lenders. Wholesale production appeals to servicers interested in acquiring new product in a continuous stream as opposed to buying bulk servicing at a lump sum. The service release premium paid by wholesalers is typically a little greater than that paid by correspondent lenders and, in some cases, can be nearly as much as prices paid for bulk servicing packages. Generally, wholesalers require their sellers to make representations and warranties regarding the quality of the product being sold. Since the sellers have the financial strength to make meaningful reps and warranties, wholesalers feel more insulated from the possibility of fraud and other origination problems and thus are comfortable paying a higher price for the servicing. Wholesalers will base pricing for each selling originator partly on the amount of risk they perceive is related to buying that lender's production. Thus, wholesalers buying third-party product from a correspondent lender may pay a lesser service release premium than they would for product purchased from a large retail originator, because the wholesaler is further removed from the point of sale when buying third-party product.

Retail originators selling to wholesalers can assume marketing risks similar to those described above in the Correspondent Lending section. However, these lenders are able to close loans with their own funds and are not relying on an outside funding source to close loans. Therefore, there is less potential for borrowers to be hurt by a lender that reneges on a lock-in commitment. Again, since these originators are generally larger and more financially fit than brokers, they are less likely to risk damaging their reputations by reneging on lock-in commitments.

By examining the marketing opportunities of the mortgage sellers in correspondent and wholesale relationships, one can begin to understand the risks to which the investor/wholesaler is being exposed. On the buy side, prudent pipeline management would dictate that the mortgage pipeline be well hedged against interest rate risk. However, in a retail environment, where each loan is represented by an individual borrower, fallout patterns are less volatile than in the wholesale arena. In wholesale, groups of loans are being represented by a rational, profit-seeking individual. If market movements create the opportunity for large gains, originators have the incentive to cancel their lock-ins and re-lock with another wholesaler. Some wholesalers recognize this fact and allow lock-in flexibility for their customers. Other wholesalers monitor fallout very closely and will terminate relationships with lenders they suspect are abusing their lock-in privileges in this manner. These latter lenders believe that strong relationships built on mutual trust and respect are better for both entities in the long run than are short-term marketing gains.

Relationships are the foundation of correspondent and wholesale lending. Investors want servicing value and are willing to be partners with originators and pay for servicing value. Correspondent and wholesale lenders are well aware of the intense competition for mortgage loans. Indeed, many wholesalers also operate, or have operated, retail production systems. The underlying philosophy is to allow the originator to battle for production and collect his rewards as he produces loans, while the wholesalers and correspondent lenders collect their rewards over time through servicing. These production methods have literally exploded in popularity over the last few years, and many hail them as the wave of the future as they cause the demise of the traditional retail originator/servicer. Others agree wholesale and correspondent lending are indeed attractive, but believe nothing can beat a well-run retail system in regard to overall cost, control, and quality of production.

Consumer Retail

The most recent innovation in mortgage production has been the advent of direct to the consumer marketing strategies. Lenders have attempted to access borrowers through advertising, telemarketing, direct mail, and computerization. Affordable technology is a driving force behind this trend. The key to these strategies is to eliminate the steps typically performed by a loan officer and move a loan directly into processing. This is usually best accomplished through technology. As was seen earlier, a great deal of expense can be eliminated if a company can negate, or at least lessen, the need for production personnel.

Although telemarketing and direct mail strategies have been around for a while, faster, less expensive computers have enabled companies to more efficiently pinpoint their marketing efforts, and some firms are beginning to operate profitable production systems using these techniques.

Another form of the direct marketing concept is the Computerized Loan Origination systems (CLOs) that are beginning to operate in some parts of the country. Larger national lenders are even aligning themselves with large realtor multiple-listing software companies to create a tight link with the home buyer from the first realtor contact. It takes little foresight to see the power of having mortgage payments calculated under varying scenarios printed on every realtor's listing sheet, with a mortgage company's name and phone number emblazoned across the bottom of the printout. A wholesaler could operate a CLO clearinghouse system for his top five correspondents by listing five prices daily either on listing sheets or on a computer terminal in a realtor's office, and thus show competitive rates and secure the acquisition of all servicing rights on loans originated through the clearinghouse. Also, with personal computers entering households faster than either VCRs or microwave ovens did, self-service mortgage application systems may appear in the not too distant future. Since CLO systems are such a new concept, no one can be sure of exactly how many different ways lenders will use them.

Marketing directly to consumers, with or without the involvement of realtors, is a trend that appears to be here to stay. A few companies are making large investments in technology in hopes of capturing a large share of this emerging market. Increasing computer literacy rates among both mortgage bankers and consumers will aid the establishment of this market segment, and over time, may ensure that it becomes the preferred mode of mortgage production.

PROFITABILITY OF LOAN PRODUCTION

Mortgage bankers constantly face two primary questions regarding operational strategy. The first is, "If the net present value of our servicing operation is less than the price we could receive for selling our portfolio, should we not sell our portfolio and abandon mortgage servicing?" The second question would be, "If the 'all-in' net cost of origination in our production system is greater than the price being paid for bulk servicing packages, should we not abandon loan production?" The latter of these two questions is the basis for assessing the profitability of loan production. There are many factors that impact this decision besides simple economic considerations.

Most originators probably answer the second question above by saying that their net cost of origination is far less than prices being paid for bulk servicing. Depending on how the net cost is calculated, some originators may be incorrect in this assumption. The basis of this assumption is the belief that mortgage originators are *adding value* to the mortgage product by producing servicing rights. Producers are not only originating mortgage loans, but they also are creating servicing rights, and by performing this service they naturally create a profit margin over a company that simply comes in after the fact and buys servicing rights. Again, whether or not this is always true is the topic of much debate.

One of the prime considerations to which both originators and servicers pay attention is *GAAP reported earnings*. Retail originators argue that GAAP earnings only tell half the story, since GAAP accounting requires retail originators to expense the entire cost of production in the year of origination (FAS 91 notwithstanding). Wholesalers, correspondent lenders, and bulk purchasers are allowed to capitalize and amortize their cost of purchased servicing, and are thus able to report greater book earnings in the year of acquisition. Retailers would argue that you must level the playing field before you make economic decisions. Some securities analysts argue that the securities markets are more concerned with GAAP earnings than they are with true economic value being created. Other industry analysts insist that ignoring economic reality is misleading when evaluating the mortgage industry.

Another of the considerations to which mortgage originators pay close attention is *control*. To many, purchasing bulk servicing equates to losing control of what goes into a servicing portfolio. These originators believe a well-trained, professional staff of mortgage producers can deliver higher value servicing than can be obtained through bulk purchases. Being able to track a loan's performance in a servicing portfolio and provide feedback to the loan's producer has great value that cannot be equaled with the reps and warranties provided by a bulk servicing seller.

Another attraction of operating a loan production system in conjunction with a servicing operation is the *"self-hedging"* nature of this relationship. When interest rates are falling, servicing portfolios experience greater runoff that must be recaptured. Mortgage originators, however, thrive in times of falling interest rates and, in most cases, can easily more than replenish runoff. Without a production system, a servicer would be required to increase bulk acquisitions and, although prices for existing servicing would be discounted due to higher prepayment assumptions, prices for new lower-rate product would likely be increasing due to the fact no one would know if interest rates had bottomed out or not. Secondary marketing gains are also easier to obtain while rates are falling. These gains lower the cost of origination, and make loan production even more profitable. Conversely, in periods of rising interest rates, servicing portfolio runoff slows but it does not stop. Mortgage origination also slows, and secondary marketing gains can turn into losses. Hopefully, a production system can, at a minimum, replenish portfolio runoff. Some servicing rights may have to be sold to pay for the losses of the production system, however, servicing prices would be greater due to slower prepayment expectations. The servicer without a production system would also be experiencing slower prepayment but would have to enter the bulk servicing market and pay the higher prices to maintain the status quo. Basically, mortgage originator/servicers are less impacted by interest rate swings than strict originators or servicing-only companies. This lessened interest rate sensitivity creates a more stable earnings pattern over time, which is very attractive to mortgage bankers and the investment community as well.

THE MORTGAGE ORIGINATION INDUSTRY

It would be an understatement to describe the mortgage origination industry as simply "dynamic." From the early 1980s, when savings and loans were powerful residential lenders and adjustable-rate mortgages were brand new, until the early 1990s, when wholesale and correspondent lending were experiencing annual growth rates of 50+ percent and S&L market share had dropped dramatically, the mortgage industry has not been the same two years in a row. Considering all the forces that can impact mortgage lending, it is little wonder the industry is so volatile. Besides natural economic cycles, many other factors can create dilemmas for lenders. Mortgage originators must contend with political policy, fiscal policy, and monetary policy in the government sector. As mentioned previously, misguided and unexpected regulation creates extremely difficult situations for the industry. Natural disasters, such as earthquakes and hurricanes, place a tremendous strain on the insurance and housing industries, both of which directly impact mortgage originators. Environmental concerns regarding the timber industry inflate lumber prices, which depresses home building, and again mortgage producers are affected. In addition to these considerations, originators must deal with the ever increasing demands of the consumer.

In spite of the seemingly endless list of reasons not to participate in the mortgage origination market, competition in the industry is very intense. Bank deregulation and its impact on overcapacity in the industry and the S&L crisis contributed greatly to the large number of mortgage originators now in business. Years ago, mortgage lending was dominated by depository portfolio lenders (e.g., S&Ls) who were supported by government mandated interest rates on deposits. Since a nice interest rate margin was easily maintained, these lenders had an easy time making profitable mortgage loans. This situation bred overcapacity in the industry. When banking was deregulated, and interest rates were allowed to float with supply and demand, not only were more firms (e.g., commercial banks) interested in entering the industry, but the potential for lower profit margins had developed. As has been well-chronicled, many S&Ls reacted horribly to deregulation, creating the S&L crisis and leaving many experienced mortgage loan officers out of work. Many of these loan officers started their own mortgage brokerage offices, and some combined to form mortgage banking operations. Commercial banks also increased mortgage banking activities in hopes of increasing market share and expanding cross-selling opportunities.

The role of mortgage bankers in the industry underwent an interesting evolution during this period. Prior to banking deregulation, when portfolio lenders dominated mortgage lending, mortgage bankers were viewed mainly as government loan originators. Government loans were harder to originate, process, and underwrite, since the government borrower was typically a more marginal credit risk. The federal government had created FHA insurance and the Government National Mortgage Association (GNMA) to provide mortgage insurance and a secondary market for these mortgages to encourage their origination. However, portfolio lending was much less onerous and with a protected interest rate margin, portfolio lenders saw little need for secondary markets for their mortgage production. Therefore, mortgage bankers who took the time and trouble to learn how to participate in the government lending programs accepted this role because the amount of competition was limited (due to the perceived rigors of the programs). Mortgage bankers also had secondary markets for conventional product through FNMA and FHLMC, however, portfolio lenders were typically more aggressive in pursuing this market segment, which put mortgage bankers at a disadvantage. With deregulation, the S&L crisis, and ensuing regulation, mortgage bankers found themselves in a much more attractive market position. As S&Ls failed, borrowers turned to mortgage bankers to fill the void. Banking regulators required financial institutions to clean up their balance sheets and specifically looked hard at real estate loans. The ability to turn mortgage originations into mortgage-backed securities (MBSs) smoothly and efficiently became a virtual necessity in the new environment. MBSs could be sold into the secondary market and quickly removed from the originator's balance sheet. Mortgage bankers, not having the luxury of a depositor base, had already developed these skills and were able to continue to operate as efficiently as ever, while other financial institutions struggled to master these new abilities. The result has been a large and rapid increase in market share for mortgage bankers over the last few years.

Competitive Factors

Because borrowers perceive little difference in the mortgage they receive from different mortgage lenders, price is a major determinant in their selection process. However, many borrowers accept advice from a third party when making their selection. Typically, these third parties, such as realtors and home builders, have experience with the mortgage process and have a vested interest in seeing the mortgage approved, if at all possible. These referrers realize lowest price does not necessarily mean best price. Therefore, price, although very important, is not the only competitive factor in the mortgage industry. Originators also compete on the basis of service quality and product line width.

Since price is such an important criterion in a borrower's selection process, mortgage bankers work very hard to reduce costs to enable them to offer a lower price. Efficient secondary marketing execution and warehouse funding programs can also enhance a lender's pricing latitude. Some lenders subsidize prices by factoring in servicing value created by obtaining the mortgage. The price issue is more occluded in wholesale and correspondent lending when there is only one net price given to brokers, which includes an amount for a service release premium. However, the wholesale market is just as price conscious as is the retail market, basically because in the end it is the borrower borrowing from a retail lender that is driving the market.

Service quality is another area in which mortgage bankers are aggressively competing today. As mentioned previously, realtors, builders, and other referral sources will rely on and be loyal to a mortgage lender from whom they receive excellent service. In mortgage lending, service quality embodies product knowledge, courtesy, speed, accessibility, and responsiveness. Service quality often separates lenders with competitive prices from the pack and is a cornerstone of competitive strategy. On the wholesale/correspondent side, a recent survey (Mortgage Guaranty Insurance Corporation, 1991) indicated that brokers value service quality slightly higher than price when asked about the most important qualities in a wholesaler.

Originators producing agency (GNMA, FNMA, and FHLMC) product also need to satisfy the agencies' quality requirements to maintain their ability to participate in the agency programs. Due to the agencies' obligation to MBS investors to consistently produce quality collateral for their securities, all three major agencies have increased their quality control efforts in recent years. By continuously improving the quality of agency mortgage originations, agency backed MBSs are able to attract capital at consistently narrow spreads over Treasury securities and thus lower the cost to the consumer. Any deterioration in this quality level could cause investors to require higher yields, which would raise the cost of mortgages and slow demand.

Another strategy mortgage originators are beginning to utilize is a product line strategy. Some lenders believe offering the widest possible product line gives them a competitive advantage, and others believe a very narrow product line is best. Yet others believe that the optimal product line is somewhere in the middle. The narrowly focused product line strategy is based on the belief that focusing all organizational energy on learning and originating one product type will make the organization most proficient in the market for that product. Some lenders have gone 100 percent government, others have focused solely on conventional product. The proponents of a wide product line believe that mortgage lending is already a narrow focus, and that in itself gives them an advantage over banks and other financial institutions. They believe a lender should be known as *the one source for mortgages*, not simply as a lender for only a certain market segment. And, of course, there are people taking an intermediate approach who think offering products originated in extremely small volumes is a waste of company resources. These originators offer popular products and products they believe may become popular as market conditions change.

CONCLUSION

The following points should be considered key in this chapter:

1. Loan origination is the lifeline of all mortgage banking.

2. There are various methods of loan production, all of which are viable and constantly changing.

3. Gauging the profitability of loan production often involves examining the entire organization's profitability over time.

4. The mortgage industry is a dynamic, competitive, volatile industry which reacts to a variety of forces.

5. The only constant in mortgage origination is change.

Although the last point was not explicitly explained, it is as important as the other four. As one begins to understand the loan production business, it becomes apparent that there is no certainty. That fact could be no truer than it is today. Methods of production are changing. Products are changing. Demographics are changing and will continue to change in ways that will dramatically affect mortgage lending. The economy and the overall economic environment are changing. Technology is advancing at unprecedented rates. Securities markets are becoming more sophisticated and yield driven. The political climate is changing, which causes uncertainty in the regulatory environment. Basically, nothing is certain except the belief that service quality, cost efficiency, and hard work will be the admission tickets to the loan production industry. And the standards for these three items are continuously being raised due to this constant change.

An important feature of this environment is that it is exciting. And this excitement attracts a wide range of personalities to the business, which makes for a very interesting work environment. The loan production industry constantly tests its participants' abilities to react to change and stand up to challenges. This testing environment builds strong teams and quickly highlights employees who cannot handle pressure.

A final comment must be made on the need for strong leadership in a loan production company. The dynamics outlined above should highlight this need clearly. The importance of loan production, the debate over the "best" method, the volatile environment, and the difficulty in accurately assessing profitability combine to necessitate leadership that is both strong and flexible. Leaders must have the ability to stay the course through temporary changes in the environment, and the vision to recognize permanent changes. The rest of the organization at times will be ready to change course, and at other times will cling to the status quo. They will continually look to their leaders for guidance and empowerment. These leadership challenges will continue and increase as the industry evolves.

Chapter 8

LOAN PRODUCTION MANAGEMENT

John J. Jacobs IV, CMB
Executive VP Production and
Secondary Marketing
BancPlus Mortgage Corporation

INTRODUCTION: THE FUNCTION AND PURPOSE OF LOAN PRODUCTION

The making of loans has existed since it became necessary for people to finance their purchase of real estate. This chapter will examine the function and purpose of loan production, and the management techniques that have evolved into the modern loan production philosophies of today. Making real estate loans has become one of the largest industries in the United States. A home purchase is still the single largest transaction most families ever make.

Real estate loans were investment vehicles for institutions that took in deposits and paid interest on them. Loans were a method by which an institution could take in funds from depositors at one rate of interest and lend money to borrowers at a higher rate. This practice was the basis for the savings and loan industry. They were very successful and profitable at this activity until the mid-to-late 1970s, when interest rates began to rise sharply. Savings and loan institutions had always borrowed from the public in the form of savings deposits. They borrowed short-term and lent their funds long-term. This was a good strategy, given that interest rates on deposits were capped by law, and there was a positively sloping yield curve. Then interest on deposits were allowed to float and become a competitive process with the enactment of Regulation Q. This historically profitable positive spread between short-term interest paid to depositors and long-term interest received on real estate loans began to disappear. Interest paid on deposits began to approach the interest rates received from real estate borrowers. Eventually, short-term rates were higher than the long-term interest rates on the loans in their portfolio, which caused an obvious financial dilemma.

To remain a profitable activity, the savings and loan industry had to develop mortgage instruments that would allow them to adjust the interest rates on the mortgages they made whenever the interest on their deposits changed. These new instruments were called Adjustable Rate Mortgages or ARMs. The next development was the maturing of the secondary market for mortgage-backed instruments. With a mortgage instrument and a market for the mortgages, the modern mortgage banking era was born. So too was the need for a mechanism for originating mortgages, and servicing the mortgages that were sold into the secondary market, given that investors neither were experienced at servicing mortgages nor wanted to service them. The thrifts had always serviced the loans they made in the past, but now they wanted to diversify their loan portfolios with loans from other parts of the country or with products they were unwilling to make themselves. The new liquidity provided by the secondary market created a place to sell loans and a place to acquire loans.

Mortgage bankers were a minor part of the overall real estate lending equation at this point. They acted as agents or brokers to primary lenders that did not wish to hire, train, and pay for mortgage origination capacity. Mortgage bankers sold all their loans into the secondary market, either to individual lenders through whole loan transactions, or to institutional investors for pooling into mortgage-backed securities enhanced with government guarantees. Mortgage bankers knew that there were profits in servicing the loans that were being sold to investors. This business of mortgage servicing was the driving force in creating mortgage banking firms.

Loan Production

What is the purpose of a mortgage production operation? The modern mortgage banker is in business to create mortgage servicing of its own or to sell the rights to service the loans it makes to others.

Mortgage servicing rights are separate from the loan itself. Mortgage bankers do not wish to own the loans they make. They simply want to have the right to service those loans. The rights associated with servicing have monetary value. Their value depends on whether the rights are retained or sold to another. If retained, the value is realized over the life of the loan. A fractional portion of every mortgage payment made by the mortgagor is retained by the servicer as payment for collecting the payment and remitting the investor's portion. Additionally, the servicer is responsible for seeing that the real estate taxes and the hazard insurance policy on the real estate are paid and in full force. This *servicing fee* is predetermined and fixed.

If the mortgage originator does not service loans or does not wish to service certain loans, the servicing rights can be sold to a firm that wants to service them. The value of the servicing rights are then realized upon sale rather than over the life of the loan. The value of the servicing rights is the present value of the expected cash flows generated primarily from the servicing fee income. The servicer makes certain assumptions about the loans' cash flows and their duration. This calculation determines the amount that a servicer is willing to pay to acquire the servicing rights. (See Figure 8.1.)

If mortgage servicing is valued as the present value of the servicing fee cash flows over its expected life, then any purchase price that is less than that amount will make the loan more profitable. If a firm services loans but does not produce them, it is then subject to the market price for the mortgage servicing it wishes to acquire. To reduce the volatility of this pricing, many firms have decided to produce the loans

Figure 8.1   Servicing Value

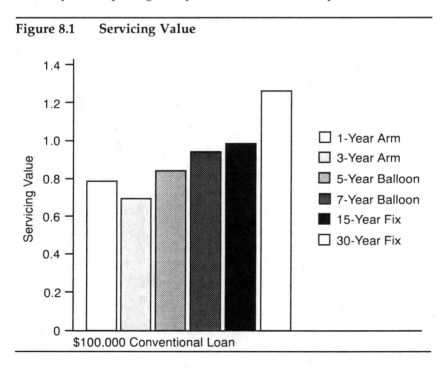

they service. This integration of mortgage production and mortgage servicing has many positive benefits.

It would be an inefficient loan producer that could not produce a mortgage at a cost less than the price needed to purchase the same servicing rights from another company. Thus, **cost of acquiring servicing rights is the primary reason for producing mortgage servicing rather than buying it.**

Servicing rights may not be available or affordable when a firm wishes to acquire them. If they produce their own, the flow and availability is much more predictable. The resources of the firm can then be more efficiently utilized.

The quality of the mortgages underlying the servicing rights is always a concern. If the mortgage quality is high (that is, the loans are made to borrowers that make their payments on time), then the profitability of the servicing will be much higher (remembering that the fee income from servicing rights is fixed). Profitability is enhanced by having loans that have lower costs associated with their servicing. A delinquent loan is much more expensive to service, and thus the margin of profit on that loan will be lower than on a nondelinquent loan (see Figure 8.2). The quality of the loan underlying the servicing rights can be controlled if your own employees are producing the loan.

Figure 8.2   Deliquent versus Nondeliquent Loan

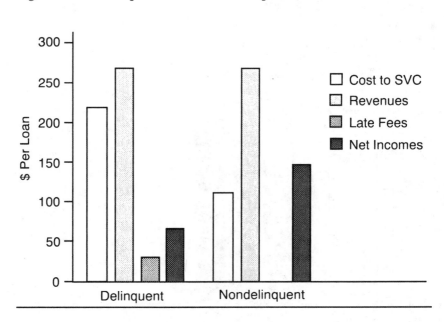

Loan Production as a Servicing Hedge

Firms that service loans make several assumptions about the loans they service and value them accordingly. The primary determinants of mortgage servicing value are loan life and delinquency. At times of low interest rates, mortgages pay off at higher than normal speeds due to refinancings and mortgagors moving up in housing size. Both of these events cause the value of the portfolio of servicing rights to plunge. A natural hedge against this "runoff" is loan production to replace the loans that are paying off. If the loans in your servicing portfolio are paying off at a high rate, it is likely that the loans of other servicers are also paying off. This will mean that there are many more loans available to be made. Thus, this higher production at times of high runoff will partially or completely offset the loss of loans out of your company's portfolio, creating a natural hedge (see Figure 8.3).

TYPES OF LOAN PRODUCTION

Mortgage banking firms tend to count all the loans they acquire during the year as *loan production*. Loan production, however, takes several distinct forms. It is appropriate that each category be identified. There are three categories of loan production:

Figure 8.3   Production as a Servicing Hedge

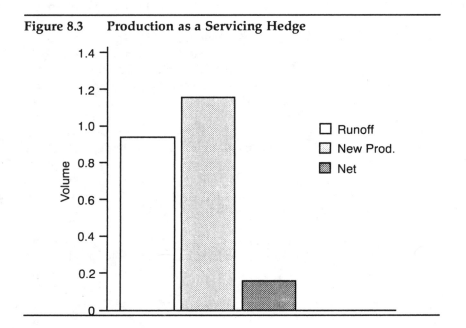

1. Retail
   Production

A retail loan is one that is originated, processed, underwritten, and funded by a company's own employees. A company loan
officer typically solicits a loan application
from a real estate agent or a home builder.
These are the two primary sources of loan
production. Other possible sources are customers of the firm, such as bank depositors;
relocating employees of a company; or call-in
business. These loan applications are then
documented, underwritten, closed, and sold
to a mortgage servicer or some other secondary market participant.

2. Wholesale
   Production

A wholesale loan is one that comes to the
firm fully processed. All that is necessary to
complete the loan is to underwrite and fund
it. There are many firms, called *loan brokers*,
that solicit the loan application and process
the loan, but must seek out a larger firm to
take on the credit risk and marketing risk.
These larger firms are called *wholesalers*.
Their function is to provide underwriting expertise, fund the loan, and deliver it to an investor. The wholesaler provides the broker a
guaranteed yield at application at which it
will close the loan. The relationship is such
that the loan broker keeps the origination fee
paid by the buyer and the wholesaler gets
the loan for its servicing portfolio. In this arrangement both parties, the loan broker and
the wholesaler, work in a symbiotic way. The
broker provides the loan application, and the
wholesaler provides the loan investor. This is
an efficient and mutually rewarding relationship. Each party considers the loan as their
loan production.

3. Correspondent
   Production

This channel of loan production is a combination of retail and wholesale production.
The originating company completes the lending process through the loan funding phase,
and then sells the loan to a mortgage banker

who wants to service loans. The sale of the loan is generally at a predetermined yield. The correspondent is usually a mortgage banker that has no servicing capacity or one that does not wish to service loans. It wants to realize the value of the mortgage servicing soon after the loan closes, not over the life of the loan like the servicer. This value received for selling a correspondent loan is called a *servicing release premium*. This premium represents the net present value of the loan's cash flows over its expected life.

It is hard to determine the market share of the loan broker and the originating mortgage banker, since most firms count all loan production as though it were *their* loan originations. This means there is a double counting. The wholesaler calls his loan fundings *loan production*, as does the loan broker. Often correspondent lenders count their annual funded volume as loan production too. *Every loan is a retail loan for someone*. This is the only true loan production, all other loan production is really loan acquisition.

WHY ENGAGE IN RETAIL LOAN PRODUCTION?

Many companies have examined this very question in recent years. With the proliferation of loan brokers and mortgage bankers willing to sell their loans on a servicing released basis, mortgage servicing can be acquired without incurring the cost and headaches of establishing retail loan production capability. The reasons for being in loan production are as varied and as persuasive as the reasons for not being in the business. The common reasons for being in loan origination are:

- ♦ The cost of acquiring mortgage servicing can be controlled, since the entire lending process is conducted by company employees.

- ♦ The quantity and geographic location of the loans produced can be managed, given that the firm determines where branches are located and how they are scaled.

- ♦ The quality of the loans can be controlled, given that company employees originate, process, and underwrite each loan before it is funded.

♦ It is a natural hedge against servicing portfolio runoff.

♦ Mortgage loan production produces a financial loss that helps offset servicing profits, thus reducing taxable income.

♦ The value of the servicing rights created are off of the balance sheet and thus are not taxable until earned or sold.

Many firms have exited the loan production arena. Their inability to manage the process has soured them on the enterprise and has turned them to the loan acquisition channel instead. The common reasons for their abandonment of this activity are:

♦ The fixed costs associated with operating branch locations are high.

♦ Slow method to build capacity into high volume, because it takes time to hire staff, lease space, acquire office equipment, and build a pipeline.

♦ It is expensive to exit the business.

♦ The firm must hire personnel to originate, process, underwrite, and fund the loans produced, making it a people-intensive business.

♦ A large investment is required in capital, time, and people.

♦ Regulatory complications and complexities are many, as states continue to enact licensing legislation.

♦ The "mind-set" differences between servicing and production personalities makes the management of these two businesses incompatible.

Because of these real and perceived issues many mortgage banking firms have elected to enter either the wholesale or correspondent business. Accounting rules have played a major role in creating the viability of these two forms of loan production.

Accounting practices dictate that the costs associated with the production of retail loans must be expensed in the month in which the loans were produced. If the same loan servicing is purchased rather than produced by company employees, the cost of acquiring the servicing rights can be capitalized and placed on the balance sheet to be amortized as the income from the servicing rights is earned monthly. This accounting difference has created a strategy for servicing rather than producing it simply to gain the more lenient accounting treatment. The economics of the business take a backseat to the accounting. In the vast majority of cases, mortgage servicing can be produced internally at a cash-flow cost far below that of purchased servicing (see Figures 8.4 and 8.5).

BRANCH OFFICE STRATEGIES

There are many options to consider when opening a loan production office: Where will it be located? Will it be a large or a small branch? Will it be part of a regional cluster of branches or entirely remote? Will the processing and closing be centralized or within the branch? These are just a few of the decisions that must be made when opening a branch and developing a network strategy.

Before any of these specific questions can be answered, the firm must look at its macro plan for being in the business of loan production. It must look at its strengths and weaknesses, and its overall corporate mission statement. The loan production effort should draw on the firm's strengths and help in fulfilling the corporate goals.

"Good, Fast, or Cheap"

In performing any service-related business, such as mortgage loan production, the firm should decide how it is going to play the game. What niche will it occupy? There are three possible levels of service. A service

Figure 8.4   Retail Origination Break-Even

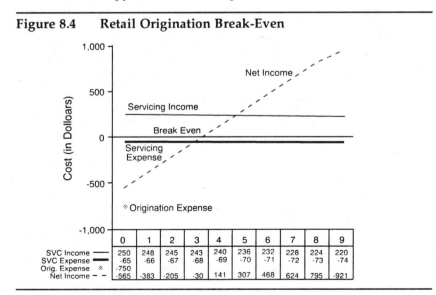

	0	1	2	3	4	5	6	7	8	9
SVC Income	250	248	245	243	240	236	232	228	224	220
SVC Expense	-65	-66	-67	-68	-69	-70	-71	-72	-73	-74
Orig. Expense	-750									
Net Income	-565	-383	-205	-30	141	307	468	624	795	-921

Figure 8.5   Correspondent Origination Break-Even

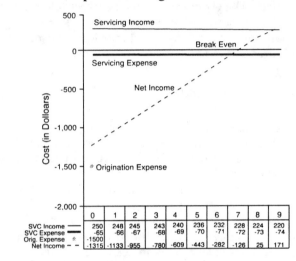

	0	1	2	3	4	5	6	7	8	9
SVC Income ——	250	248	245	243	240	236	232	228	224	220
SVC Expense ▬	-65	-66	-67	-68	-69	-70	-71	-72	-73	-74
Orig. Expense ✳	-1500									
Net Income – –	-1315	-1133	-955	-780	-609	-443	-282	-126	25	171

provider can only provide two of them. They cannot provide all three, because one of the possible outcomes precludes another. The three outcomes are: (1) the firm can provide excellent service *(GOOD)*, (2) it can provide it quickly *(FAST)*, or (3) it can perform with a low cost to the customer *(CHEAP)*. An example of this trade-off is the "One-Hour Film Processing Center." They provide one-hour, quality film processing. The cost of this service is **high,** however. Providing the first two characteristics of service, GOOD and FAST have precluded it from being CHEAP. To continue the analogy of film processing, one could choose to send the film away to be processed via a mailer. This will allow for a GOOD and CHEAP outcome but not a FAST one.

So, too, in loan production one must decide the level of service that is going to be provided and what is going to be traded away. Hopefully, the analysis of the firm's strengths and weaknesses will allow this trade-off to be at a minimum. The firm with excellent automation may already have sunk the costs for its computer system, and thereby can provide good and fast service. The branch network should be established to capitalize on this company attribute.

Branching Philosophy

Mortgage origination companies have one of three perspectives: it can be a local company serving only one or two markets, a regional company serving a distinct region of the country, or a national lender serving multiple regions of the country. Many companies have started out as a local or regional lender and have grown to a national one. The decision about what markets to serve is not always a cognitive one, company ownership or lack of capital for expansion may "make" the decision for management.

Branch Scale

Should the branches be large ones or small ones? There is a common belief that large anything is always better because of the theory of "economies of scale." This is an overrated concept. Several mortgage loan production cost studies have shown that there are little or no economies of scale in loan production. Small branches can perform at a cost of production equal to or better than large branches. The small branches tend to do better year in and year out. Mortgage loan origination is a cyclical business. This cyclical production curve is the primary reason that economies of scale cannot be achieved in loan production. In any five-year period there is usually one very good year, one very poor year, and three mediocre years. The small branches, because of the lower fixed costs of operation, tend to provide lower costs of production in four of the five years. Only in the very good year do large branches provide lower costs.

When setting up a loan production branch, one should have a scale of operation in mind. A range of loan production is to be expected from a given branch size and personnel configuration. This scale should be supported by the study that has been done of the market in which the branch is to be opened, both historically and in the future. (Scaling a branch and measuring performance will be discussed in a later part of this chapter.)

Centralized versus Decentralized versus Semi-Decentralized

With the increasing use of computer power and other technologies in loan production, many firms have utilized these technologies so that the processing of the loan files and the closing and funding of the loans can be done from a centralized location. These centralized facilities do provide a certain economy of scale. It is much harder to have excess capacity in a centralized center than in a remote branch. A center can accommodate specialists, such as government loan processors and conventional loan processors, loan closers, loan funders, and loan shippers. Many times these functions must be performed by the same personnel in a branch.

The concept of GOOD, FAST, or CHEAP also comes into play when deciding whether you should have centralized or decentralized processing and/or closing. Some firms have fully centralized these two functions, others have centralized just one, i.e., closing. The strengths of the firm can help with this decision, but ultimately it comes down to GOOD, FAST, or CHEAP. It has been shown that centralized processing and/or closing is the cheapest method of conducting these activities, but the trade-off every time is the FAST or the GOOD element. These trade-offs may only be perceived, but if the customer thinks that the service and speed are not as good from a centralized center, they will have a reason not to use your company. If the cost to the customer is low enough, that is, CHEAP enough, that may overcome this objection. The decision will differ from firm to firm. GOOD service may be worth a higher cost to some customers, but not to others.

A decentralized system utilizes branch personnel to perform all functions within the branch location. Service is usually GOOD and FAST, but not CHEAP. There is a high probability of excess capacity in one of the functional areas.

A middle-of-the-road strategy might be the semi-decentralized concept. This is a strategy where processing and/or closing centers are in regional areas rather than fully centralized or in the branch (decentralized). These regional centers are located where there are clusters of branches. The remoteness of the processing or closing is perceived to be minimal, such as 50 miles away. Invariably the costs of this operation are somewhere between those of the centralized centers, which are the least expensive, and the decentralized branch operations, which are the most expensive. The trade-offs between cost and service to the customer are possibly more acceptable.

This strategy is most effective when there is a branching structure, with a main branch office and smaller origination branches in the same geographic area. Many times this is called the "Hub and Spoke" method of origination. This method lends itself well to a semi-decentralized structure and allows for reduced cost of branch management. Typically, the manager of the "hub" branch is also responsible for the "spoke" branches.

The correct branching strategy depends on what is appropriate for each individual firm. There is no **correct** strategy for all firms to follow. The strengths and weaknesses, as well as the overall objectives of the firm, will help guide management in selecting the right strategy.

SALES FORCE CONCEPTS

Every production operation must have a method of selling its product. In mortgage banking there are several different sales force concepts that have been proven effective. Usually, the most effective concept will depend on the loan products to be offered, and the source of the customers. If a lender has an attractive loan product that is in high demand, and not easily provided by others, it will not have to hire the same kind of sales force as a company with more-generic products.

Commissioned Loan Officers

The loan products of today are predominantly determined by the availability of secondary market investors. This heavy reliance on the secondary market by nearly all mortgage originators has created a product line offering that looks strikingly similar from company to company. With these commodity-like product lines, companies must rely on strong sales forces for their sales. The normal compensation for these salespersons is commission income. The commission is based on the size of the loan being made. The primary reason for this form of compensation is to create a variable cost of sale rather than fixed costs. In times of high volume, the costs of sale are high, but so are revenues. In low-volume periods, when revenues are low, so are the costs of sale. This form of compensation is the most prevalent in the mortgage banking industry.

Salaried Loan Officers

Salaried loan officers are usually associated with companies that have either a unique loan product or access to a customer base that is not easily accessed by others. As an example, a savings and loan association making loans for its own portfolio, not the secondary market, will typically hire salaried loan officers. This is a less expensive form of sales force, since salaried loan officers' costs are fixed and not variable. When the company's own loan product is creating the loan demand, and not the salesperson, the compensation does not have to be as high as when the salesperson is solely responsible for the sale. While a variable cost structure is generally preferrable to a fixed one, the overall compensation paid to a salaried loan officer is generally much less than that of a commissioned loan officer over the same range of sales volumes.

An example of a captive customer might be the home-building company. It is relatively common for high-volume home builders to have a mortgage lending capability. The loan officers they employ are usually on salary since the builder provides the customer.

Combination Loan Officers—Salary and Commission

Another sales force strategy is to use a combination of salary and commission to compensate the salesperson. This is a compensation method that tends to attract a more risk-averse loan officer, one that would trade the upside potential of a commissioned existence for the more predictable income stream of a salary. The total compensation paid by the firm will be less for this combination arrangement than for a commissioned loan officer over the same range of production volume. The negative for the firm is that the least productive loan officers tend to like this form of compensation. Several national companies have opted for this form of compensation for their sales force. The salary usually covers a certain fixed dollar amount of loan production, and the commission is paid on production above that threshold. The incentive for the loan officer is to exceed the threshold as early in the month as possible. (See Figure 8 6.)

Recruitment, Training, and Retention

The single hardest aspect about sales force management is the recruitment and retention of top-notch loan officers. There is a strategy to be

Figure 8.6   Loan Officer Compensation

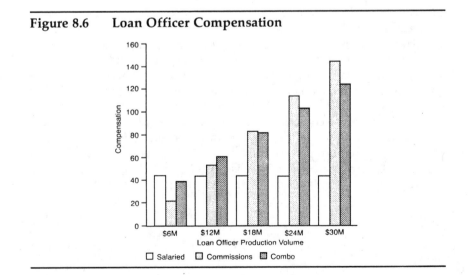

considered in recruiting high-quality, as well as high-quantity, loan officers. The question is, do you hire experienced loan officers or do you grow your own? The obvious advantage when hiring experienced salespeople is their record of success at loan originations in the past. They come to you with preconceived notions about how the business should be conducted, and are at times hard to manage. The overiding benefit is obvious. They are immediately productive. Retention is always a question mark, since they left the last company to come with you. A loan officer's customer base is portable. The customers, realtors, and builders, do business with individual loan officers, not with mortgage companies. The customers belong to the loan officer, much like a stockbroker's. If the stockbroker changes firms, clients tend to change with him or her. When loan officers change companies, their customers change with them.

The hiring and training of salespeople with no prior experience has several advantages over hiring the experienced: (1) you can train them to understand the business your way, (2) they are more loyal because they know no other company, and (3) their expectations about what the company can do for them are not as high.

The biggest negative to hiring and training inexperienced loan officers is the big investment in time it takes to make them productive. Unlike engineering or architecture, the business of mortgage banking cannot be prepared for academically. A business and sales background are a great help, but virtually everything a mortgage originator needs to know must be learned on the job. Only the largest of the mortgage bankers have the financial strength and corporate patience to hire and train loan officers with no previous experience. The loan producer is the life's blood of most mortgage companies. Their recruitment, training, and retention should be one of the highest priorities.

BRANCH MANAGEMENT

The role of the branch manager is a very interesting and multifaceted one. The branch manager must be a combination sales manager and plant manager. A typical mortgage origination branch office is a small mortgage factory. It has some of the same dynamics and characteristics. It is rare that a good salesperson is also a good manager of minute details. A mortgage origination branch is responsible for the handling of a loan from application through to its closing. Learning the intricate details of investor guidelines and legal requirements has many pitfalls. A branch manager needs to know them and avoid them. This attribute differentiates a good branch manager from a poor one.

Sales Manager or Plant Manager?

With the need for a manager to be both sales manager and plant manager, and the mind-set differences this requires, many mortgage companies have struggled for years wondering whether the manager should be primarily a salesperson or a plant manager. Some companies have structured the branch manager's position such that he or she must produce loans like loan officers, deriving the majority of their income that way, while others compensate their managers to manage the processing, closing, and funding functions within the branch. There does not seem to be a clearly best approach. It is more costly to have branch managers managing only, without loan production to help offset their salary and other expenses. The main determinant seems to turn on branch size. Large branches require more managing and can bear the expense of a nonproducing branch manager, while most small branches do not need full-time management and can ill afford the associated costs. It is still a matter of corporate strategy and preference. As long as the trade-offs are understood, one is as defensible as the other.

Duties and Responsibilities

The structure the firm has chosen as its production strategy will dictate the duties and responsibilities of the branch. If processing and closing have been centralized, then the branch will be responsibile for taking the loan application and communicating the status of the processing to the customer. The branch acts more as a coordinator in the home lending process. Some would say that this frees the sales personnel to do what they do best, **sell**; and removes them from that which they do less well, **process paper**.

If the lending process is decentralized, then the duties of the branch are many. It is responsible for processing the loan application, issuing the closing documentation, and funding the loan. There are several post-closing functions that also must be performed, such as securing the follow-up documents, the title policy, and the recorded legal instruments. If the loan was a government loan, in addition to those documents mentioned, the branch must also order the loan guaranty from either HUD or VA. The strengths and management skills of the branch manager can vary greatly depending on the responsibilities that the branch must carry out. The more functions that the manager is required to manage, the more management skills are needed.

The Branch Manager as Plant Manager

One of the most difficult tasks that a branch manager has is managing the clerical staff—hiring personnel that are competent in performing the processing and closing of the loan files, but also hiring those individuals that are sensitive to the sales effort. A good processing and closing team can supplement the efforts of the sales force. A great sales force will be ineffective if the loans they originate do not get processed and closed in a timely way.

It has been mentioned that a loan production branch is similar to a loan factory. Many of the principles that apply to running a manufacturing facility apply to running a successful branch office. The most important decision that must be made is selecting the *scale of operation*. How big should the branch be? The most appropriate size is that which is compatible with the marketplace. A very large branch in a small market is doomed to fail. The costs of operation will preclude it from ever achieving an acceptable cost of production. A branch that is too small has less risk, but may never realize the potential that it could if properly scaled.

Branch Capacity

Assuming that this concept of "scale of operation" is understood, the second most important principle is that of *branch capacity*. Few managers really understand this principle. Only at capacity will the lowest costs of production be realized. Any level of production below capacity will not allow costs to be minimized.

How do we measure capacity? This is quantified by establishing standards of performance for every clerical staff person, i.e., files processed per month, closings per month, etc. The standard will probably differ from person to person based on their individual skill level. An inexperienced processor would not be expected to process as many units per month as an experienced one. Once these standards have been established, a branch potential or capacity can then be quantified based on the number of processors and closers. **Capacity is completely determined by the number of processors and closers, not the number of loan officers.** The clerical staff should know the standard of performance that is expected of them. Staffing considerations are then relatively easy to make once these standards have been established and the branch's capacity determined. If the branch consistently performs at 75 percent of capacity, it might be time to reduce the clerical staff. Conversely, if capacity is consistently being exceeded, it might be time to add a clerical worker rather than pay the overtime (see Figure 8.7).

Branch Manager Compensation

Compensation specialists will tell you that establishing a compensat ا plan is simple—you **compensate for the activities you wish to promote.**

Many compensation plans have created activities that were not in the best interest of the firm. Compensating a branch manager should be consistent with this principle. If compensation is too heavily weighted toward a certain activity at the exclusion of another, you can rest assured that the activity that has the highest compensation potential will receive the most emphasis. If you pay a branch manager for producing loans and do not pay him or her for controlling costs, loans will get produced and costs will be ignored. Remember, compensate for the activities you wish to promote.

Developing the ideal compensation plan is much like searching for the Holy Grail. We know it is out there but no one has found it yet. Most modern mortgage banking firms have developed compensation plans centered on a producing branch manager. We have found that the most cost-effective branches tend to be those where the branch manager has some production responsibility. They are usually compensated on their own production much like a loan officer, through a commission. The other components of their compensation package will vary greatly from firm to firm. Possible compensation would be an override on the monthly production of the loan officers that work for the manager. This would be an incentive for the manager to hire productive loan officers.

Figure 8.7   Capacity Analysis

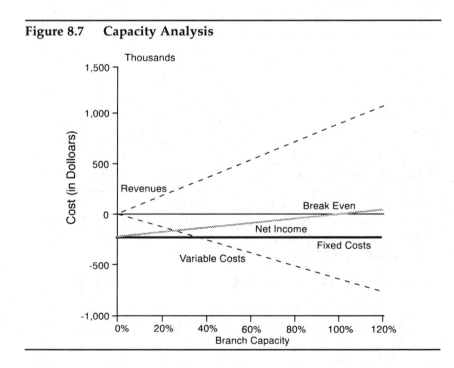

Compensation for some measure of branch profitability is also fairly customary. Profitability is a misnomer in the loan origination business. Loan production does not produce a profit. Within the industry it is common for a company to produce loans at a net cost of breakeven to over 100 basis points of loss. Mortgage bankers are willing to produce loans at a loss on the front-end to realize the long-term profitability of the servicing. Most firms budget a loss in production. Profitability would then be considered any improvement on the budgeted loss. Some firms actually create the illusion of branch profitability by giving the branch a credit for producing mortgage servicing. This credit is usually calculated on the value of the servicing created. This method is less preferred because it allows for a great deal of subjectivity in the calculation. A loan produced in one part of the country may be worth more than a loan produced in another part of the country. Giving equal credit for that loan is going to be a windfall for one of the branches. If branch manager compensation is then dependent on this value-added calculation, one of the managers will be slighted. Typically, there is some compensation for improving on the profitability of the branch, regardless of how it is calculated.

Some compensation plans look at the performance of the loans produced from the branch and either credit the branch for good loan performance or "ding" the branch for poor performance. This performance criteria could be for delinquency or default characteristics. Poor loan performance would mean that the manager's compensation would be negatively impacted in some way. He or she would be financially tied to the quality of the loans produced. This is a less common component of a branch manager's compensation package.

Other possible components of manager compensation might be: underwriting performance, quality control criteria, internal audit results, fallout ratios, or the mix profile of the branch's loans. The determinants of manager compensation grow each year as the industry evolves and experiences areas of concern. Compensation considerations help involve the branch manager in the management of these areas of concern. The branch manager is the first line of defense and involving him or her is an appropriate management tool.

BRANCH PRODUCTION SUPERVISION

As mortgage banking has matured, the management level under most scrutiny has been the *branch production supervisor*. This position carries several possible titles: Area Manager, District Manager, or Regional Manager. The one sure fact is that there are fewer production supervisors per production employee today than there were even five years ago. The primary cause for this reduction is cost. The position is nearly always on the officer level, either vice president or senior vice president, with compensation to match.

To understand why this position has been reduced over the last few years, one must examine the branch production supervisor's role. They have historically been responsible for the hiring of the branch managers, and in many instances, the sales force. They helped report the pipeline numbers and direct the clerical activities of processing and closing.

With the widespread and virtually universal use of computers to manage the inventory of loans in the branch pipeline, the need for this liaison and information link between the branch and home office has been much reduced. Front-end processing systems can report new loan registrations to the Marketing Department for pipeline management as well as communicate application processing activities, forms generation, document preparation, and loan funding. Many companies have gone to a form of centralized processing and/or closing of the loan files, which has reduced the need for the number of branch supervisors that were once needed before the use of computers and centralized services.

The modern mortgage origination company has increased the number of branches that a branch supervisor can manage, thus reducing the overall number of supervisors. This has been accomplished by structuring branch networks in creative ways. For instance, using "Hub and Spoke" type branches reduces the need for several well-trained branch managers by asking one well-trained manager to assume the responsibility for several smaller, less-full-service branches as well as their primary branch (see Figure 8.8). The use of geographically oriented branching clusters positions the supervision closer to the action and increases responsiveness.

To whom loan production reports in the organization has long been debated. Typically it reports to the president or chief operating officer. Occasionally, it might report to a level below the president having responsibility for the Marketing Department activities as well as Production Department. This might be a preferred arrangement since Production is so dependent on products and pricing. If the same person is responsible for Marketing and Production, a natural balance between the two areas is achieved. If one activity is emphasized at the expense of the other, one person can be held accountable. When Production and Marketing report separately to the president, one division's poor performance might be blamed on the other. Substandard Production performance can be blamed on poor product offerings or pricing, while Marketing losses can be blamed on the need for pricing below costs. (See Figures 8.9 and 8.10.)

Figure 8.8   Hub and Spoke Organization Chart

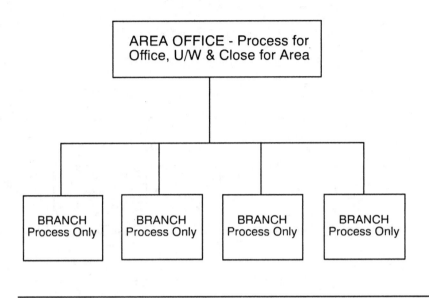

Compensation

Branch supervisors are typically compensated by a salary, a monthly production override calculated in basis points, and a year-end performance bonus. The philosophy of the compensation is to create a variable component to this level of management's pay structure, both monthly and yearly. If the production activities are successful, compensation will typically be high, but if activity is poor, compensation will be low. The override component is encouraged so that the intra-year cyclical production curve is as constant as possible. The manager will be compensated higher for greater monthly loan-closing volume. (See Figure 8.11.)

SUMMARY

Several different schemes have been tried in an attempt to produce loans without branches and loan officers. To date all have failed. Consumers seem to want personalized service when buying a home. Much like going to the doctor, the process of buying and financing a home is a traumatic one, even for the experienced buyer. They want to have a person to call and consult with as well as someone to reassure them throughout the transaction. Computerized services and other forms of

Figure 8.9   Origination and Servicing Firm

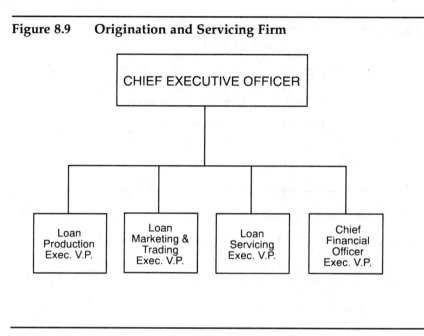

Figure 8.10   Origination and Servicing Firm

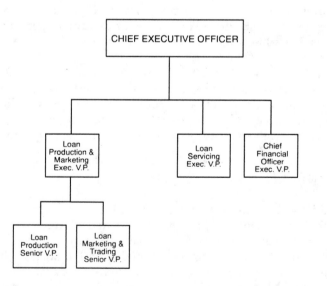

Figure 8.11   Production Curve

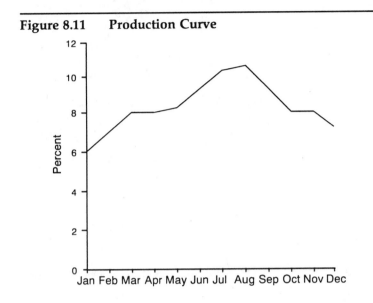

impersonal contact cannot provide this aspect for the borrower. Mortgage loan production will continue to be best provided by individuals and companies with high levels of commitment to customer service and automation enhancements. Loan providers are realizing that they must improve their service and exploit the use of automation. Very soon all loan officers will be able to take a loan application from a borrower with the aid of a computer that will electronically compile income, credit, and appraisal information almost instantaneously. The information will then be underwritten using artificial intelligence. Loan decisions that take two to four weeks today will take hours or minutes in the years ahead. It will be neccessary for the loan production manager of the future to be saleperson, plant manager, and also computer literate. The ability to adapt to a changing landscape is what *management* is all about.

Chapter 9

MORTGAGE BROKERS: A SPARTAN EXISTENCE

Howard Schneider
Freelance Writer

INTRODUCTION

Mortgage brokering sounds straightforward: loan officers can work out of small shops, keeping their overhead low and being able to react quickly to local market changes. By avoiding the costs of buildings, secondary marketing staff, and corporate managers, they'll be able to make a living just from origination fees.

But a mortgage broker is also a business owner—not a field rep. Management and regulatory considerations thus add to the challenge of originating loans in a stiffly competitive marketplace.

As financial institutions and mortgage bankers have closed retail offices during the past few years, mortgage brokers have grown to dominate the market in some parts of the country. In 1984, "there were not five mortgage brokers in the state of New York," says Ralph LoVuolo, Sr., president of Deer Park, New York's LoVuolo & Company, Inc. By 1991 there were almost 2,000.

H.A. "Tony" Davis, past president of the Illinois Association of Mortgage Brokers and head of his own firm, Preferred Mortgage As-

Reprinted by permission of *Mortgage Banking*, a Publication of the Mortgage Bankers Association of America.

sociates, Ltd., in Lombard, says Chicago-area title companies claim brokers account for 55 percent of all Illinois loans. One reason for the trend is that realtors have become more receptive to working with brokers, Davis adds. "The change in the real estate community over the last three to four years is like night and day."

Due to this emergence of mortgage brokers in residential lending, it's not surprising that "states are looking pretty hard at them," says Andrea Lee Negroni, an attorney in the nation's capital and author of *Residential Mortgage Lending: State Regulation Manual* (published by Clark Boardman Callaghan). Brokers, she adds, "have been regulated with laxity for the last five to ten years."

National Association of Mortgage Brokers (NAMB) Executive director Michael Hoogendyk notes that most states currently have loans concerning mortgage brokers, and new legislation is being considered in numerous states. Regulations vary widely, although uniformity among state laws is one goal of the three-year-old American Association of Residential Mortgage Regulators (AARMR). In addition, AARMR serves as a clearinghouse for reports of fraud, making it tougher for a bogus originator to transfer his operation to another state.

GREATER MARKET SHARE

Wholesale lending also is booming. Countrywide Funding Corporation started its wholesale division in 1987. In fiscal year 1991 the wholesale division brought in $1.4 billion, or 31 percent of the Pasadena-based firm's total volume, according to Standard & Poor's.

By the summer of 1991, Countrywide was buying from $250 to $300 million each month in mortgage broker originations, says Jerry Baker, managing director of production and support divisions. According to Standard & Poor's, wholesale loans were making up 39 percent of Countrywide's business by September of 1991.

As a result of such increases in purchased originations, particularly from mortgage brokers, Freddie Mac and Fannie Mae have begun asking if there is more risk from loans originated by a third party. Freddie Mac now buys such loans only on a negotiated basis.

Fannie Mae is asking seller/servicers to track delinquencies on brokered loans separately from retail originations, says director of loan acquisition Roy Downey. But he adds that "the majority [of brokers] are doing a very good job."

Mortgage bankers aren't the only firms making use of mortgage brokers. For instance, people who walk into branch offices of California's Western Federal Savings, based in Marina del Rey, won't find anyone who will take a home loan application. Instead, they are given a toll-free number to call and are referred to one of the thrift's approved mortgage brokers. Vice President Pat Briggs explains that "we don't want to compete with our brokers in any way."

Western Federal started relying on mortgage brokers in 1983, after attempting to work with home builders and also trying retail originations. Officials say buying loans from brokers gives Western Federal cost savings and makes competition with larger thrifts easier.

WHO ARE BROKERS?

The growth of mortgage brokering is reflected in NAMB's membership. In March 1988, the Phoenix-based group had 440 members. But just three years later that number had risen to 1,200. Besides lobbying governmental and regulatory bodies, the association is seeking to increase public awareness of mortgage brokers. NAMB members are also eligible to earn the professional designation of Certified Mortgage Consultant (CMC).

Despite the numbers of competing mortgage brokers, they seem to have no difficulty discovering funding sources. "Wholesalers seek us out," LoVuolo reports. "Our fax machine goes most of the day. We look at them all." With one person working as both processor and underwriter, plus six producers, LoVuolo expects $40 million in annual fundings. He sells primarily to four wholesalers, but the firm is approved by at least four times as many.

Brokers don't fit into molds any more than Western Federal acts like a traditional thrift. Some mortgage brokers have staff underwriters, in-house training, and marketing programs that include conducting phone surveys of clients and referrals sources after every deal.

D. L. Herndon III, owner of Westlake Village, California's The Herndon Company, ran several mortgage firms and also had experience in public accounting before opening his brokerage business. Now he works mainly with self-employed borrowers. Herndon's loan packages thus often contain both personal tax returns and business cashflow statements.

In order to get a loan approved, Herndon finds that changes might be needed in a borrower's business finances. For instance, when an entrepreneur has substantial personal funds invested in his firm's inventory, Herndon might suggest the person get a business line of credit to pay for the inventory and then transfer some cash into a personal savings account.

Because many entrepreneurs must personally guarantee their corporate debts, at first glance their credit reports might cause lenders some concern. Herndon says he "knows how to position" the borrower's financial statements to give lenders a clear picture of how much cash is available to make home payments.

In addition to working with realtors, Herndon gets referrals by keeping in touch with past clients. Community bankers also refer customers to him when they don't have a mortgage that suits one of their clients.

BIG LENDER STRATEGIES

Some large-volume lenders—such as Bank of America and Norwest Mortgage Corporation—combine retail and wholesale production strategies, notes Stuart Feldstein, president of SMR Research Corporation in Budd Lake, New Jersey.

Yet other big lenders avoid certain aspects of the wholesale business, or stick with in-house originations altogether. In February, 1991, Columbia, South Carolina's Fleet Mortgage Group "ended relationships with brokers," says Executive Vice President Richard Duncan. Although the firm is a major player in wholesale production, retail originations, adds Duncan, allow a lender to have "better control over employees."

One factor that influenced Fleet's decision to stop using mortgage brokers was the administrative needs for processing loan packages from many different brokers. Even receiving packages in which documents are in a different order makes the task harder, Duncan notes. "To be effective, you have to have some flexibility" when dealing with brokers, he adds.

Ann Tierney, a vice president at GE Capital Mortgage Services in Cherry Hill, New Jersey, says the firm works with 270 correspondents. But because of its volume appetite, GE works with mortgage banking companies, not brokers.

"Stronger financial standing" is required of correspondents, Tierney says, because of increased risks in home lending. At the end of 1990, GE required correspondents, Tierney says, because of increased risks in home lending. At the end of 1990, GE required correspondents to have net worths of at least $500,000. By the end of 1992, they were required to have $1 million in net worth and other requirements to do business with GE, according to Tierney.

FINDING FUNDS

Despite their small size and lack of sizeable net worth, mortgage brokers can have surprisingly sophisticated operations. Mark Ross, CMC, president of Tucson's Prime Capital, Inc., works with two dozen wholesalers as well as "200 private investors" he has found over the years. With these sources Prime Capital originates "'A' to 'D' paper," Ross says. Lower-rated loans are "very well-secured" by collateral, and loan-to-value ratios are a maximum of 70 percent; most are at 50 to 60 percent, he adds.

Customers are found by referrals from traditional sources, as well as from recreational vehicle dealers and home improvement-related firms, such as pool and fence companies. In addition to originating residential paper, Prime Capital also does commercial property loans and second mortgages.

Ross presents private investors—such as doctors or pension funds—with the borrower's credit report and a property appraisal in order to help them decide whether or not to fund the loan. Prime Capital succeeds in a medium-sized city, although most mortgage brokers are found in urban areas that have "a lot of real estate transactions," says Hoogendyk.

HOW BROKERS WORK

Some brokers rely on advertising, mailings, or telemarketing for business prospects. However, most find that referrals from realtors, financial institutions, and past clients are the best ways to get business, says former NAMB president C. Kent Miller, CMC, president of Gilroy, California's Monterey Mortgage.

Brokerages are managed to fit individual philosophies. For instance, Donald Henig, president of Island Mortgage Network in Islandia, New York, says purchase loans made up 85 percent of his business in late 1991, because he didn't want to hire staff for refinancings that would go away when rates rise.

On the other hand, at the same time, current NAMB president Diane Kelly, president of Virginia Mortgage Exchange, Inc., in Annandale, Virginia, was soliciting previous clients for refinancings. It was "a marvelous time" to turn a second mortgage into a new first, she explained.

Brokers originate loans for less than do many traditional lenders by avoiding both nonproducing managers and excess capacity. "All of us have a tendency to be understaffed," says Kelly. "You work until the job's done." Kelly has six employees in her 40-year-old firm. But she adds that often, mortgage brokers are in "a mom-and-pop shop," consisting simply of an originator and a processor.

Balancing staffing to meet the volume of loans is "a very, very difficult problem," adds Henig. "It's something you have to keep your eye on every day. You want to give the best service, but you don't want overhead."

Tying compensation to results also makes brokers efficient. For instance, D.L. Herndon pays his staff on a per-deal basis. "I want everyone to care about the business as much as I do," he says, "and have the same vested interest as I do."

Some brokers pay wholesalers to process their loans, while others try sharing an office or franchising to save on overhead. Franchising is seen as a way to save on marketing costs by combining the resources of numerous offices. One mortgage brokering franchise, Amerimac Equifirst Mortgage, in San Jose, even uses "Wheel of Fortune" hostess Vanna White as its spokesperson, according to Hoogendyk. But observers note that some franchises provide limited training, which "can give neophyte [loan officers] a false sense of security."

REGULATORY BLUES

Because brokers work with consumers, their activities are coming under greater scrutiny—particularly at the state level. Regulatory practices range in severity from no oversight in Mississippi to requirements of a $25,000 net worth and annual fees costing thousands more in Illinois.

Having minimal capital requirements to enter the business or to participate in table funding programs are points of contention for mortgage brokers, who often are thinly capitalized. Attorney Negroni notes that "you can't always tell who the good guys are based on how much capital they have."

Florida brokers take 24 hours of classes on mortgage finance before being licensed and must disclose the fees they receive. Only New Jersey and Arizona also require mortgage brokers to pass a test, says Negroni. But she advocates that feature, which "regulates competency, not solvency."

LICENSING REQUIREMENTS

Different states use various regulatory bodies to watch over mortgage brokers. For instance, the state banking commission regulates brokers in Florida, while the department of real estate does so in California, which requires just a real estate brokerage license to get into the business.

In Illinois, brokers are licensed annually and examined every other year, says Commissioner of Savings and Residential Finance Jack Seymour. Loans also are spot-checked, bonding is required to establish a third-party review of brokers, and a $25,000 minimum net worth is necessary. Seymour says this reserve isn't meant to provide funds for buying back bad loans, but instead is an indicator of overall economic health. "People do desperate things when they run out of money," he explains.

It's not uncommon for mortgage brokers to see most regulatory action as threatening. "Regulations from the state level are running rampant," contends Henig. "More regulations are coming every week," adds the former NAMB president. "Every one of them is scary." Yet despite increasing governmental oversight, mortgage brokers will not be regulated out of business, Negroni says.

Because the mortgage brokerage industry is fairly new, some observers claim that regulators aren't always familiar enough with mortgage brokering to adequately oversee it. Negroni charges that regulators in certain areas "are not well-versed in mortgage banking."

James Brodsky, an attorney with the Washington, D.C., law firm Weiner, McCaffrey, Brodsky, Kaplan & Levin, notes that varying state regulations will make it more difficult for a national lender to manage a large retail network. Wholesaling thus should increase, he adds, but brokers will start being held increasingly accountable for the quality of loans they originate.

To give an overview of how legislators are thinking, Brodsky cites the following trends in state law requirements covering mortgage brokers:

- net worth and broker bonding requirements;
- fee limits;
- written agreements with customers;
- increased disclosure to borrowers and investors;
- identification of lenders used;
- licensing as a lender before table funding is allowed.

Although similarities are apparent, Brodsky says, "states move in non-uniform ways. They deal with abuses or problems they see." Randall Holland notes that as director of the Florida banking department's finance division, he is working for a political appointee. When constituents make complaints about originators, both his field examiners and the state's legislators tend to act.

Other states see similar patterns. For instance, calls for protection both from wholesalers and consumers helped usher in Illinois' stringent mortgage broker licensing requirements. Seymour estimates that brokers spend $4,000 to $6,000 annually to pay for license fees, annual audit fees, examinations, and state spot-checking of loans. Broker Davis says the figure is actually as high as $8,000.

When the law passed in 1987, mortgage brokers and out-of-state servicers who were affected by the Illinois Mortgage Banking Act were outraged. Seymour notes that the industry had not been regulated before then in the state. So it was a shock when licensing fees jumped overnight from $500 a year to around 10 times that amount.

Yet, Illinois is home to just 300 mortgage brokers, says Davis, while LoVuolo says the situation is different in New York where "there are just too many people in the business." He notes that New York requires only a $500 fee and does no testing of mortgage brokers. Thus, competition increases with easier entry into brokering.

But while Illinois has no education or experience requirements for mortgage brokers, Arizona licensees must have three years of real estate lending background, take a required course, pass two exams and post a $10,000 bond.

Yet that doesn't bother Tucson broker Mark Ross. "Cosmetologists go to school," he notes. And because "instances of fraud get big press," Ross would like to find ways of discouraging these practices.

At the federal level, Brodsky explains that officials at HUD, Freddie Mac, and Fannie Mae are stressing net worth, quality control, and internal audit of mortgage brokers.

BAD APPLES

The incidence of mortgage origination fraud in Illinois is "very small," says Commissioner Seymour. But since such activity puts a firm at risk, "you don't engage in mortgage fraud on a one- or two-case basis." He recalls one Chicago mortgage firm "which had been around for years" that had double-sold hundreds of loans.

"We want the crooks out of here just as bad as anybody else," says the NAMB's Hoogendyk. But he contends that when lenders don't underwrite all the loans they buy, they leave the window open for certain unsavory characters who will become brokers and sell fraudulent loans.

Most fraud occurs with a new mortgage broker or in a geographic area that is new to San Jose's First Franklin Financial Corporation, says CEO Bill Dallas. By not spending enough time researching brokers' backgrounds, Dallas notes that fraud "is almost always our fault." In addition, First Franklin tries to "make brokers responsible" for their loans by letting them know what percentage become delinquent, Dallas says.

But at GN Mortgage in Canoga Park, California, president William Jacobs began filing criminal reports and prosecuting mortgage brokers who practice fraud in an effort to get them out of the business.

Negroni says that "distressed borrowers" facing foreclosure or falling property values are the most likely victims of fraud. She suggests mandating a "'change-your-mind' period of 48 to 72 hours" after an application is taken, and also letting mortgage brokers collect fees only if an application is approved.

WHOLESALER PERSPECTIVE

To guard against fraud and related problems, Countrywide looks at the experience of each mortgage broker and his or her employees, says Executive Vice President Rick Cossano. References are checked and physical inspections of the broker's offices are done before approval, he adds. Although Countrywide doesn't keep a list of brokers to avoid, the firm does "share informally with other wholesalers" the names of brokers that aren't approved to do business with them, Cossano notes.

Working out of 17 regional offices, Countrywide's wholesale underwriters were rejecting about one third of all broker applications as of September 1991, according to Standard & Poor's. Countrywide has approved 3,000 mortgage brokers nationally, says Cossano, who adds that three quarters of the firm's wholesale business comes from one fourth of those brokers.

Most wholesalers work only regionally, although at times these smaller lenders then sell broker-originated mortgages to national wholesalers. Using mortgage brokers allows a smaller firm to quickly access a large sales force. As borrowers began showing a preference for fixed-rate loans, Western Federal decided to offer mortgage brokers its first-ever fixed-rate mortgage product. Six weeks after being unveiled, it accounted for about one third of Western Fed's home loan volume.

LENDER-BROKER RELATIONSHIPS

"The longer you work with someone, the more you know how they work," says Preferred Mortgage's Davis. "Trust develops." Attempting to "make my client a real person" in the eyes of the wholesaler "helps make a deal go," adds LoVuolo. To do so, he often will visit wholesalers to discuss a loan even before sending in the application.

Brokers claim there's no conflict in being paid by a borrower, while following a wholesaler's guidelines. "We work for the customer," explains Davis, "and represent the wholesaler." He adds that 40 percent of all loans need additional "explanations to substantiate why they should qualify."

Many mortgage brokers expect to see closer business ties with wholesalers emerging in the future. Even small favors can help, they note. One broker says that often wholesalers will fax rate sheets first to their top producers. When rates are falling, getting new prices 15 minutes before the competition can help a broker get a loan he's been working for.

Brokers and wholesalers agree rates are important in determining where the business goes. If a wholesaler is off the market by more than 25 basis points, he won't get many loans. But even great rates can't guarantee a wholesaler return business. For instance, Ross describes his relationship with wholesalers as "love-hate." Although he needs the funds, inconsistent requirements and underwriting standards are "frustrating."

Most mortgage brokers today complain that wholesalers are asking for more documents than in the past, taking more time reviewing them—and then asking for some more documents. One broker complains of loans that "are processed to death."

Repeated requests for more information can irk a mortgage broker, who often has an anxious real estate agent or home buyer on the other line. It's not surprising that each side of the business doesn't always understand the other. But generally, mortgage brokers and wholesalers think well of each other and describe their relationship in positive terms.

But that doesn't stop mortgage brokers from wanting to see more perks from wholesalers. In addition to marketing and training support, more financial incentives are expected to be offered by wholesalers in the future.

Miller adds that co-op advertising is an anticipated benefit. A wholesaler would pay part of the cost of advertisements that a mortgage broker uses to promote the wholesaler's product.

Today, some wholesalers provide incentives, such as better rates, in return for reaching certain volume levels. In addition, faster underwriting, documents and funding, as well as daily pipeline reports, are benefits some wholesalers give preferred customers.

One mortgage broker sees the practice of offering rebates giving way in the future to providing mortgage brokers with a share of servicing value and income. Doing so would provide an incentive to the broker to originate quality loans and guarantee him or her some cash flow to cover overhead during lean times. Although wholesalers generally don't talk about such matters, the mortgage broker says "some wholesale lenders are making those kinds of things available for a select few, based on volume."

Consumers benefit from a healthy partnership between wholesale lenders and mortgage brokers. Wholesalers bring operations efficiency to home lending, while brokers are the human side of the business. "We go to our closings," says Davis. "It's nice to see people move into homes."

Chapter 10

AUTOMATED MORTGAGE ORIGINATION SYSTEMS

D. William Mulcahy
Director of Consulting
Mortgage Flex Systems, Inc.

INTRODUCTION

Mortgage originators, compared to other participants in financial services, have been slow to adopt automation and to exploit and effectively utilize its capabilities. Although virtually every mortgage lender has at least some origination automation, not many lenders have fully integrated automation into the origination process to obtain significant operating advantages. In an increasingly competitive and consolidating market, where most mortgage lenders offer the same products at more or less the same price, industry leaders recognize that quality service is what, in the long run, offers the best opportunity to obtain a competitive edge. Integrating automation, and redesigning origination processes to take advantage of automation tools, is critical to obtaining that service advantage. Although many major originators have reached this conclusion, there are still ample opportunities for the effective user of technology to differentiate service and obtain significant market advantage through exploiting the features of the more advanced automated system capabilities available today.

This chapter will briefly review how we got to where we are today, analyze features available in the best currently available automated systems, and look at where the best future opportunities for improved performance through automation will come from.

ORIGINATION AUTOMATION OVER THE LAST DECADE

The recognition of economies of scale has long driven development, implementation, and integration of automation in the mortgage servicing sector. Although origination automation has become common during the last ten years, several factors weighed against the high level of integration and benefit obtained by mortgage servicing and by other financial industries:

♦ Originations have typically relied on production from small branch offices. While most financial services have attempted to centralize operations, mortgage operations (i.e., processing and closing) have remained distributed, with a limited number of operations people at each branch site. Many lenders are now moving to centralizing operations, in a single market, regionally, or nationally.

♦ Market fragmentation. Until recently, the biggest originators with the largest number of small branch offices commanded only a small portion of all mortgages originated. Only in the last five years have the top-producing lenders commanded more than a negligible share of total originations.

♦ Limits to available technology. The mainframe-based origination systems that were initially available were ill-suited to the small distributed operations dominating the industry. Early personal computer systems were not capable of integrating the full range of automation activities. In addition, the paper-intensive nature of origination operations was not significantly helped by impact printer technology. Feeding preprinted forms into a printer is barely an improvement over typewriters. Laser printing has probably led more originators to accept technology than any other development.

♦ Difficulty of use. Related to the previously mentioned factor, early origination systems were difficult to use and, given the dispersed location of system users, it was difficult to train people to use and support it.

♦ Mortgage originators have historically emphasized marketing. Branch managers typically have been drawn from among the top salespeople in an organization, and they continue to focus on their sales strengths while failing to develop the operational skills that they previously did not need. This has led to a lower perceived need for automation and less comfort in implementing and using automation in a branch environment.

♦ Lack of competitive pressure to automate.

Technological developments, notably the dramatically increasing power and lowering prices of personal computers and laser printers, have done much in the last few years to spur software development and implementation. Most lenders actively producing loans today have automated many elements of the origination process. The ability of automated lenders to survive the extreme production spikes experienced in 1986, 1991, and 1992 made clear to those who had not yet automated the need to do so. It also indicated for many other originators the need to upgrade their current systems to take advantage of new market and technological developments. Following is a review of some of the key system capabilities that any mortgage lender should expect their automated origination system to have. Given the diverse functions encompassed by the origination process, it would not be practical to attempt to define all aspects of origination automation in this forum. The focus will be on significant features most commonly encountered in automated systems.

COMMON FEATURES OF CURRENT AUTOMATED SYSTEMS

Whether an originator has automated via vendor products, internally developed applications, or a combination of the two, a number of key features are regularly encountered. Systems will vary primarily in the sophistication of the functions they offer and the level of management control that they ultimately afford. The following is a by no means complete list of capabilities that are common (or should be common) to all systems. Some features are only present in the more sophisticated systems. Current origination systems should be able to:

♦ Quickly and accurately prequalify potential loan applicants based on their personal financial data and detailed loan program criteria. The emphasis should be on providing clear and useful information to consumers, either directly from the originator or via an intermediary such as a realtor, builder, or broker. An example of what this analysis could include is contained in Figure 10.1.

Given the ready availability and low price of prequalification systems, either as a stand-alone system or as part of an overall automation strategy, it is surprising that automated prequalifying is not more prevalent.

♦ Produce all required origination, processing, underwriting, closing, and other required documents. Automated mortgage systems have sometimes been criticized for concentrating on producing paper instead of streamlining the process itself. As long as processing is driven by investor or third-party requirements for paper, however, this must continue to be a necessary element of automated systems.

♦ Integrate data throughout the system. Data entered when registering a loan should carry through to processing, underwriting, closing, secondary marketing, and any other function without further data entry. It seems ludicrous to mention this at this point in time, but many of the early systems (including some still in use) required separate data input for each module. The better systems will offer full integration, or integration capabilities with subsystems (i.e., appraisal, credit, spreadsheets, and judgment systems) and systems not strictly related to originations (secondary marketing, servicing, and accounting systems).

♦ Laser printing of documents. This again seems obvious, but some lenders, particularly if they are using systems developed prior to the late 1980s, may be continuing to use impact documents. Laser printing eliminates the need to keep inventories of preprinted forms, allows a significant number of documents to be printed without human intervention, and reduces errors. Batch printing of documents is standard, with most systems offering the capability of predefining a group of required documents. More-sophisticated systems will have the capability of defining processing and closing requirements to allow the system to identify needed forms instead of forcing intervention by a human expert.

Figure 10.1 Buying Estimate

Assumptions —	Monthly Income:	$ 5,000
	Monthly Debt Payments:	$ 340
	Cash Available:	$ 35,000

	15-YR FIXED	30-YR FIXED	7-YR BALLOON	1-YR TR ARM
Int.\Qual. Rate:	8.000	8.250	7.750	6.250
Sales Price:	$138,485	$168,372	$174,565	$181,539
Loan Amount:	124,637	151,535	157,108	163,385
Down Payment:	13,848	16,837	17,457	18,154
Closing Costs:	4,067	5,216	4,853	5,203
Cash Required:	17,915	22,053	22,310	23,357
Qualify Rate:	8.0000	8.2500	7.7500	7.2500
P&I:	$1,190	$1,140	$1,130	$1,110
Taxes:	144	175	182	189
Insurance:	35	42	44	45
PMI:	29	44	48	50
Total Payment:	1,399	1,402	1,404	1,395
LTV:	90%	90%	90%	90%

Last Rate Update: 02/01/93

♦ Allow flexible loan program design. The system should be able to define the loan programs offered by a lender, with the capability of defining the types of programs that may be offered in the future. Many specialized loan products devised in the 1980s were undermined by the inability of systems to quickly respond to market opportunities.

♦ Automate loan program pricing. An automated system should provide all system users with the ability to access current system prices as soon as they go into effect. The better systems will automate this or allow input from a pricing subsystem (i.e., a spreadsheet tied to an on-line pricing service) to eliminate or minimize the need for data entry.

♦ Control pricing. Advanced systems will automatically adjust pricing to account for different factors specific to a loan, rather than depending on the product knowledge of the originator or loan input staff. Some of the factors that should be weighed in such adjustments are:

♦ Occupancy (Owner-Occ., Investor)

♦ Minimum Loan Amount

♦ Loan Use (Purchase, Refinance)

♦ Maximum Loan Amount

♦ Property Type (1 Family, 2-4 Family)

♦ Branch

♦ Temporary or Permanent Buydowns

♦ State and County

♦ Origination Type (Retail, Wholesale)

♦ Affinity Groups

♦ Documentation Type

♦ Loan Program
♦ Combination of any or all of the above features

This feature, if utilized at the point of origination, will eliminate or greatly reduce misquoted or mispriced loans.

♦ Define investor and underwriting guidelines on the system. This capability of advanced systems will restrict registration of loans that cannot be approved, funded, or sold. Using factors such as those defined above, the result will be more valid and usable pipeline reports.

♦ Manage the mortgage pipeline. Any automated system should be capable of tracking and reporting on all loans by status level. The best systems will be those offering the greatest flexibility in reporting. Report sort capabilities should tie to Loan Program, Loan Originator, Branch, Processor, and Status Code, with an ad hoc reporting capability tied to user-defined variables preferred.

♦ Item tracking. Historically, knowledge of what is going on with a loan application has required possession of the physical loan file. This factor has undermined the economies of scale possible from centralizing processing. Origination systems should be able to track all of the items required to process, underwrite, approve, and close a loan, thus allowing anyone with system access to know what is happening with that loan. Tracked items may comprise documents printed by the system, inadequacies in the loan application, additional data required, alternative documents, or underwriting conditions. The most sophisticated systems will allow expert definition of items needed for a loan and automatically generate entries to drive reports, loan approvals, closings, and fundings. On-line reporting capabilities should enable a manager to sort and display items for a loan based on the following criteria:

Item Type	Item Status	Secondary Sorts
♦ Processing	♦ All items	♦ Item priority
♦ Underwriting	♦ Received items	♦ Item ordered date
♦ Closing	♦ Unreceived items	♦ Subtype (i.e., all verifications)

♦ Item tracking offers the best way to manage the origination work flow and eliminate the tedious manual status reports that require significant processing time. Everyone with system access will have loan information immediately, and can thus control the flow of information to interested parties, such as loan officers, realtors, and brokers. This capability will be present whether the loan file is 20 or 2,000 miles away.

♦ On-line underwriting. With all data for a loan entered in a system and all additional information required for the loan defined via a tracking mechanism, underwriters will be able to evaluate and underwrite loans on the system. This will again allow everyone with system access to have loan information immediately.

♦ Automate all required reporting to investors and regulatory agencies. Data entered in the system for processing and closing the loan should feed any required reports without further data input. Where possible, data should be formatted for electronic data transmission.

♦ Enable full compliance with industry standards and requirements. Although this would seem to be another restatement of the obvious, it is important to look at the technology used in developing an automated system to determine how quickly the system can be updated to stay current with a constantly evolving external industry. This is particularly relevant in an industry where many practices are dictated by governmental and quasigovernmental agencies seemingly immune from marketplace realities and pressures.

♦ Provide utilities for originators with a minimal level of technical proficiency. These utility functions should allow originators to create their own custom documents and reports, and define and store data not otherwise tracked within the system. Products that emphasize these capabilities have gained some market presence by promoting the ability of lenders to have significant input into the design of their own system. Such systems typically sacrifice some level of performance and management control, while requiring significant effort prior to implementation to design and set up the system.

While there are many other capabilities common to most origination systems, these elements are inherent in and critical to the success of the more effective systems. Mortgage lenders wishing to automate or to upgrade their current automation should consider a systems solution that meets these capabilities in a way consistent with their business objectives. In defining a systems solution, factors beyond system capabilities should be weighed, including (but not limited to) whether to develop a system internally or purchase an existing vendor product, and what type of system operating environment (distributed or centralized) is desired.

Internal Development or Purchase

There are a variety of effective mortgage origination software products available on the market today. However, some lenders will determine that no existing product meets their perceived unique operating needs. Before making the decision to develop, the mortgage originator should be sure to weigh some of the hidden costs associated with software development. Among them:

♦ Significant time involvement is required by end-users (i.e., processors, closers, loan officers, management) to define the system. If not, it will be unlikely to meet their needs.

♦ Unless the originator already has an internal development staff, they will have to hire and manage programmers.

♦ Software development has a steep learning curve, in this case exacerbated by multiple governmental and quasigovernmental regulatory bodies.

♦ The aforementioned regulatory agencies ensure that development efforts are being directed at a moving target.

♦ Programming resources will have to remain on staff to keep the program current with industry changes and to stay abreast of technological developments.

♦ Compliance personnel will need to be continually involved to verify that the system remains consistent with ongoing legal and regulatory requirements.

♦ Training, documentation, and support are the elements most often overlooked in analyzing development costs. All will require dedicated resources on an ongoing basis. In the long run, support may require more of a time and money investment than the actual development.

♦ Internal developers are not subject to the market pressures that vendors are—branches generally cannot go elsewhere when an internally developed system does not meet their needs. If a vendor does not keep its system current with changing market requirements and technological developments, mortgage originators are quite capable of picking a product that does.

Internal development of an origination system can be accomplished successfully. Given all of the costs involved, however, it would seem to make sense only for the largest mortgage lenders. A number of lenders have made significant development investments with little or nothing to show for it. Those originators who have successfully developed their own in-house systems have generally found the costs significantly higher and the benefits considerably lower than they anticipated.

Distributed or Central Systems

With early origination systems, the type of operating environment was more or less dictated by the state of the technology. Up through the mid-1980s, lenders wanting to automate originations had little choice but to utilize a centralized mainframe system or branch-based minicomputers. Early microprocessor-based networks were fairly limited in the number of users that could be supported and the number of transactions that could be processed effectively. Hardware distinctions are less critical today than is the issue of whether the originator wishes to create, own, and maintain data in a distributed mode (i.e., at the branch level), centrally at a home office location, or some combination of the two. The critical issue is to determine who needs access to which information, and how often they need to have that information. Table 10.1 suggests possible solutions for different business situations.

Table 10.1

Function	Takes Place At	System Approach
Processing	Branch	Distributed or central
Processing	Centralized	Central
Underwriting	Branch	Distributed or central
Underwriting	Home Office/Regional	Central, or data transfer needed
Closing	Branch	Distributed or central
Closing	Home Office	Central, or data transfer needed
Secondary Marketing	Home Office with batch reporting	Distributed
Secondary Marketing	Home Office with "real-time" pipeline	Central

FUTURE TRENDS IN ORIGINATION AUTOMATION

Origination systems have reached a certain maturity level with a number of common features and characteristics. Following are some of the best future opportunities for increased efficiency through effective use of automation.

♦ Mortgage originators have made a significant effort over the last few years to introduce automation. Having for the most part won that battle, originators can now focus on actually using their automation tools to run their business more effectively.

♦ Mortgage systems have successfully automated traditionally manual and tedious tasks. The more sophisticated systems already have some expert capabilities of analyzing data entered. An increasing emphasis will be placed on evaluating data entered to identify, for example, an acceptable loan application and to reject applications that do not meet lender-defined standards for completeness.

♦ Automated loan officers. This has been a hot topic for years, yet few lenders have accomplished this to any significant extent. Technological developments (i.e., portable laser emulation printers) have now made this feasible. Taking the loan application is the most significant element of the mortgage origination process yet to be automated, and offers the best opportunity to identify needed information at the beginning of the process.

♦ Automated underwriting via an Artificial Intelligence (AI) system. Many lenders are currently evaluating or beginning to implement links with AI systems. AI potentially offers the benefits of more consistent underwriting and greatly reduced costs. The intention of an AI system is not to eliminate human underwriters but to limit their involvement to the more difficult judgment situations. Industry estimates for the percentage of loans that could be automatically underwritten range between 50 and 80 percent. Assuming two hours per loan underwriting time, the typical underwriter can review 1,000 loans a year. Lenders will get maximum use of underwriting resources if those 1,000 loans represent difficult decisions while the automated system is making calls on an equal number of obvious approvals, and rejecting loans with inadequate information to make a decision.

♦ Better flow of information between different systems and subsystems. In the absence of a standard industry format for data transmission, developers have had to develop their own formats for exchanging data with other systems. At the time of writing, an MBA data exchange standard appears likely in the near future. This should do much to facilitate the flow of information between different systems. Given the increased emphasis on wholesale business, the flow of information between brokers and correspondents is an area where an increasing automation focus will be placed.

♦ The time is right for automated mortgage counseling in real estate offices. Computerized Loan Origination (CLO) networks have been tried before with minimal success. Technical limitations and regulatory restrictions were among the factors limiting the success of such ventures. Recent RESPA changes ease some of the restrictions on CLOs and make it more attractive to set up such a venture. Advances in point of sale technology provide realtors with the sophisticated screening mechanisms to provide expert knowledge and provide a comfort level to lenders receiving loans from this delivery channel.

CONCLUSION

Automation offers the best opportunity for mortgage originators to offer consistent, high-quality, cost-efficient, customer-oriented service. Powerful technology is easily available now to any originator wishing to automate, while continuing technological developments will expand the scope and power of origination automation in the near future.

To some extent, introducing automation to mortgage originations has been the easy part. Attaining immediate and ongoing operational efficiencies by using automation is the challenge that originators will need to focus on now and into the foreseeable future.

Chapter 11

PIPELINE FALLOUT: DEFINITIONS, QUANTIFICATION, ANALYSIS, AND APPLICATION

Don M. "Dusty" Lashbrook
Senior VP Marketing
Maryland National Mortgage Corporation

INTRODUCTION

In most areas of the country, competitive pressures require mortgage lenders to guarantee the rate and points to the mortgage applicant from the time of application until closing for a specified period of time—from 45 to 90 days, based on processing and closing times for the local area. This practice introduces a new risk to the lender—fallout and the uncertainty in predicting it on the basis of market conditions.

When analyzing your options in regard to hedging a pipeline of mortgages, it becomes apparent that the most cost-effective and risk-adverse program consists of selling the mortgages that will close for delivery in a time frame that coincides with your ability to physically make delivery after the closing occurs. Given the fact that the rate and point guarantee must be made available at or near the time of application, one can see that it is impossible to predict with 100 percent accuracy the loans that will actually close based only on credit approval. Add to this the effect that interest rate movement during the lock period has on the applicant's desire to close and one can see how complex and important the task of fallout projection can be to the profitability of the operation.

Fallout can be defined in a number of different ways, and different organizations may choose to define it in a way that fits their particular needs. For most organizations, fallout should be viewed from a risk management perspective and from the viewpoint of processing efficiency. First, let's define "fallout" as it relates to interest rate risk management.

From the perspective of interest rate risk management, an application should be considered fallout only if the rate and point structure is guaranteed for a specific period of time and the loan does not close for any reason during the lock period, as locked. In its purest sense, "fallout" is defined as the amount of locked loans that do not close, expressed as a percent of all locked loans during a specific period of time.

When looking at fallout from the perspective of application and processing efficiency, only those applications that do not close, regardless of the terms and the actual time frame in which they close, must be considered as fallout. This measure of fallout has little or no relevance to the interest rate risk management function, but it is an extremely important tool when measuring the efficiency of a production unit and in particular the originator/processor team. This chapter will look at the fallout analysis process in depth, discussing the causes and effects and relating the results to the day-to-day operations within a mortgage lending operation. When reading this chapter, bear in mind that the preciseness of the fallout analysis may be done to the degree that is necessary for each mortgage operation's needs. Fallout may be computed on as broad a scale as the corporate level or as precise as by loan officer, by product, or for each loan purpose. The level to which a company takes the analysis may be dependent upon systems, staffing, and the accuracy required within the operation's risk management function.

PULL-THROUGH/FALLOUT RANGES

When analyzing fallout, the analysis is being performed to determine the percentage of loans that will close; either from the locked-in pipeline for hedging purposes or from the overall pipeline for the purpose of processing efficiency analysis. "Pull-Through" and "fallout" are commonly used terms within mortgage banking. Either term can be used and tracked, provided the reader realizes that they are direct opposites.

The initial analysis that needs to be performed has to do with the establishment of the *range* of pull-through or fallout to the preciseness established by the individual company. The levels to be determined and their definitions are as follows:

Minimum pull-through percentage: The lowest historical percentage of closures regardless of market movement, production source, or quality of applications (by definition, cannot be less than zero percent).

Maximum pull-through percentage: The highest historical percentage of closures regardless of market movement, production source, or quality of applications (by definition, cannot be less than 100 percent).

An example of a Pull-Through Range Chart is shown in Figure 11.1. The area between the minimum pull-through percentage and the maximum pull-through percentage can be identified as the *variable pull-through percentage*. This percentage, defined as the difference between the maximum and minimum pull-through percentages, is the percentage of applications/locks whose closure is influenced by market movement, production source, and application quality, all of which will vary from time to time.

The variable pull-through percentage is the percentage of applications or locks that present an ongoing challenge in regard to its prediction, its control, and the management of its effects on the opera-

Figure 11.1   Pull-Through Range Chart

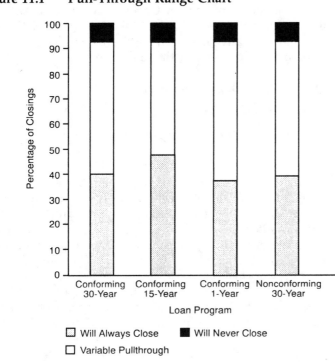

tion. From the perspective of interest rate risk management, the minimum pull-through percentage allows for hedging with no-basis risk/no-cost vehicles, such as mandatory forward sales while the percentage of locks above the maximum pull-through percentage requires no hedging. The variable pull-through percentage will require different hedging techniques. From the perspective of processing efficiency, staffing and financial projections require at a minimum the percentage of applications included in the *minimum pull-through percentage* and should *never* include a percentage in excess of the *maximum pull-through percentage*.

The focus of this chapter will be on the quantification and control of the variable pull-through percentage and an in-depth analysis of the factors that influence this percentage.

FALLOUT ANALYSIS

Fallout analysis must be based on historical data along with a current analysis of trends regarding the sources of fallout. As with any statistical analysis, the more quality data available from the past, the more accurate the analysis. One should remember that current applications/locks and their ultimate disposition will influence the future calculations of this percentage. It is imperative that each application or lock be tracked throughout the mortgage process for the following:

1.   Ultimate disposition of the application

2.   Reason for cancellation

3.   Stage of application when cancellation occurred

The pipeline system in use must have codes established that allow for the proper recording of the above. In regard to disposition, loan applications either close or they are canceled. If they cancel, it is for a reason. The reason is key to your determination of fallout, its causes, and how these causes may change over time with market movement, market conditions, and the sources of production. The more detailed the coding, the more information can be obtained from the analysis. An example of a cancellation code table can be found in Figure 11.2, along with the definition of each. The reason for cancellation must be viewed in conjunction with the stage at which the cancellation occurs in light of the loan purpose.

Two other factors need to be recorded in order to later utilize the data collected.

1. Daily pricing of individual loan programs

2. Revisions to the lock that affect program, rate, discount points, or final lock expiration date

SYSTEM CRITERIA

The pipeline management system should have the capabilities to allow for quantification of all lock-ins during a specific period of time. This period should be able to be altered if the analysis period changes (monthly locks, quarterly locks, annual locks, or locks from a longer or shorter period of time). The system should be able to calculate the following:

1. The total population of lock-ins for the analysis period

2. The total dollar amount of loans locked during the analysis period that close during their lock term with no changes to program, lock term, interest rate, or discount charged

3. The price movement for each individual locked loan from the time of lock until closing or cancellation

For maximum analysis of the above information, the system should be able to sort based on the following criteria:

Figure 11.2 Cancellation Code Table

Code	Reason for Cancellation
C1	Program noncompliance
C2	Incomplete application
C3	Withdrawn by applicant
C4	Credit denial prior to underwriting
C5	Credit denial—underwriting
C6	Recision by applicant

1.   Loan product

2.   Loan purpose

3.   Stage of application

4.   Production source

When reviewing historical data from the perspective of processing efficiency, the total population changes to include *all* applications taken regardless of lock-in. The total closings include all loans closed regardless of changes to critical terms or the time frame in which they close.

Loan purpose can be as simple as "purchase" or "refinance," but improved forecasting can be seen if the purpose portion is further narrowed into the following categories:

P   — Purchase

PF   — Purchase by first-time home buyer

NC   — Refinance with no cash-out

CO   — Refinance with cash-out

AC   — ARM conversion

The tracking of multiple processing stages is dependent on the procedural discipline that the company has for detailed tracking of the loan as it moves through the processing and closing function. The accuracy of the fallout projections will increase proportionally with further stage definition. Recommended stages to use would be:

1.   Pre-application/phone application

2.   Application

3.   Submitted for underwriting

4.   Suspended for conditions

5.   Loan approved

6.   Papers drawn/closing set

7.   Loan closed/in recision (refinance only)

8.   Loan closed

9.   Canceled

SOURCES OF FALLOUT

The sources of fallout, as evidenced by the cancellation codes, not only give the makeup of the fallout but provide insight into the production and processing team.

A high percentage of *incomplete applications* should be investigated as to the sources of production. This source of fallout can be easily controlled with policy changes regarding pre-application and phone lock-ins and with originator education/training and correspondent lock-in requirements. If pre-application locks are required due to competitive pressures, the risks associated with them can be managed if these types of locks can be quantified and the expected lower pull-through factored into the overall pull-through expectations. When these types of locks are given, emphasis must be placed on making sure that pre-apps that don't become full applications within a specified period automatically cancel from the pipeline system. Once a loan is in process, applicants are frequently asked to provide additional information. It's important that time constraints be placed on the applicant as well as regular follow-up until the item is actually received or it is determined that the loan should be canceled.

Fallout due to *program noncompliance* is one source that can be almost totally controlled through system edits, production education, information flow, or a combination of all three. This source is the most frustrating to secondary marketing executives, as the fault lies completely with production. The occurrence of this source is being lessened by the fact that many front-end and pipeline systems edit for the majority of program parameters prior to the acceptance of a lock-in. Most mortgage bankers assume that fallout due to *credit denial* is a relatively static percentage with little or no value gained from ongoing analysis. On the contrary, much can be gained from analyzing these numbers on a regular and ongoing basis. The information that may be derived from credit denial analysis is:

1. Identification of loan officers/correspondents with an unusually high percentage of denials

2. Identification of approval/rejection percentages for underwriters

3. Makeup of credit denials (credit, appraisal, cash shortage, etc.)

The above information allows for training programs to be set up to improve the approval percentages of loan officers. It also allows training to be done with correspondents with poor percentages or in extreme cases, suspension of the correspondent's ability to register new loans. Analysis of the reason for credit denial may provide insight into market area trends that may be useful in establishing policies in cases where a market is exhibiting declining values (i.e., restriction of cash-out refinances, high LTVs, or certain product types).

Processing delays normally occur during seasonal peaks and also during volume surges due to dramatic interest rate drops, but they may be a sign of procedural breakdowns within the production entity. This fallout source is discovered when analyzing the volume of extensions or the average time from application to closing. A note of caution needs to be relayed in regard to fallout due to processing delays. In some areas of the country the rate and point guarantee *must* be extended if the delay in processing is due to no fault on the part of the applicant. Though lock-in policies (extension at the worse of the original price or the price at the time of relock) may appear to provide protection to the secondary marketing area for this type of risk, state requirements may dictate that extensions be treated otherwise. During periods of high volume with processing delays, it may prove beneficial to lengthen lock terms and price for later delivery.

The most volatile source of fallout is, without doubt, the fallout exhibited due to *applicant withdrawal* or their "threat" to withdraw. While not the only reason for withdrawal, *interest rate volatility* and, in particular, the ability of the applicant to obtain lower rates and points from another lender at any time during the application and closing process is the primary reason.

Interest rate volatility is also the major contributing factor in the applicant's decision not to follow through with a pre-application or to provide follow-up information after the application is in process. Though important to understand the other influences on pull-through, it is absolutely imperative that the mortgage banking operation understand how interest rate volatility affects its pipeline and that models are developed that accurately reflect the correlation.

EFFECTS OF INTEREST RATE VOLATILITY

Applicants today are much more aware of the current rates and points that are available than in the past. The media keeps mortgage interest rates on the "front page" and aggressive loan officers follow up on applications they "lost" due to pricing. If the market improves after the application has been made, they may attempt to persuade the applicant to "walk" for better rates and points. This practice becomes even more prevalent when rates have moved dramatically or when application levels are low. The use of alternative documentation has allowed for quicker processing of mortgage loans. The ability to process loans faster allows the applicant to withdraw at a later point in the application process and still obtain loan approval and close prior to contract expiration (in the case of purchases). These factors have increased the effects of interest rate volatility by influencing applicants to withdraw and reapply with only minimal movement in rates and/or points. In the case of refinances, the problem is even more pronounced, since the applicant is not under the constraints of a contract deadline in regard to closing. Differences exist among product types also. Applicants seeking loans with nonconforming loan amounts usually exhibit the most reaction to interest rate volatility as they tend to be better informed of current rates, and a small difference in rate or price on a nonconforming loan equates to a larger dollar savings than it does on a loan with a conforming balance. Nongeneric products will exhibit less change in fallout based on interest rate volatility, since the applicant may have chosen the loan program due to certain features such as documentation, maximum loan amount, or LTV, which may not be readily available with another lender. Given these influences, one can see that the correlation between interest rate volatility and the change in fallout must be calculated based upon purpose on a product-by-product basis.

CALCULATIONS

As stated previously, the reason for keeping historical records of fallout is to develop the ability to forecast the percentage of loans (both locked and unlocked) that will close for management purposes. The historical records must include the change in interest rates during the time frame sampled, since the largest contributor to the variation in fallout is withdrawal due to interest rate volatility. When quantifying fallout, each loan must be tracked from application to closing or cancellation. The following should be calculated for each product by purpose for loans registered during the period of time examined:

1. *Dollar* amount locked during period examined (for interest rate risk management) or dollar amount of applications during period examined (for efficiency and staffing management)

2. *Dollar* amount closed from the above population with no changes to critical terms (i.e., rate, points, product, lock expiration date) or in the case of efficiency analysis, dollar

amount of all loan applications from the period examined that eventually closed

3.   Percentages closed on each of the items above

4.   Average discount change (+ or -) from the date of lock until date of cancellation or closing

Once computed, the above information may be used to construct pull-through/fallout charts. The initial task is to determine the pull-through when no pricing movement exists. The period of time examined may have to be chosen *based* upon your knowledge that no market movement occurred during the period. The same procedure can be used to complete the graph including the establishment of the minimum and maximum pull-through percentages (a sample pull-through graph can be seen in Figure 11.3). When computing the pull-through percentages for processing efficiency analysis, be sure that the period of time examined is broad enough to ensure that all applications are either closed or canceled.

USE OF INFORMATION—RISK MANAGEMENT

All mortgage banking operations where locks prior to closing are offered must utilize some form of fallout analysis, even if it is only an educated guess.

To a large extent, the success of the hedging program will be dependent upon the ability to project pull-through. The procedures described in this chapter provide the basics required to compute pull-through based on historical data. The pull-through percentages can be utilized in many ways. The majority of firms multiply the percentage by the population to determine the expected pull-through, with the resulting number hedged with the appropriate financial instrument or instruments in some combination. The hedging program should be set up with the idea that the credit markets are dynamic, changing each minute of the market day. The changing pricing scenario continually changes the expected pull-through of each individual loan since the applicant's tendency to withdraw will change as the market moves. Since the true pull-through can be a moving target, volatility assumptions must be established. The conservative operation will always sell forward the amount equal to the minimum pull-through percentage but layer optional coverage up to the amount equal to the maximum pull-through percentage. A more cost-efficient approach may be to

Figure 11.3   Pull-Through Graph

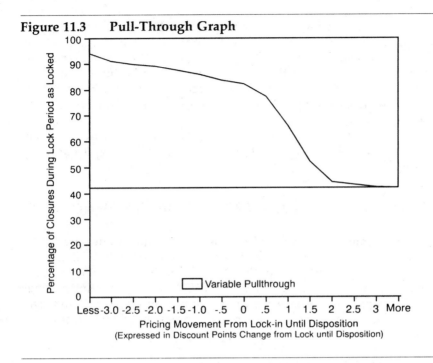

project the potential volatility based on a market analysis and extend the mandatory forward sales to the expected pull-through, less the change that would be expected due to potential volatility, with optional coverage up to the expected pull-through, plus the change that would be expected due to potential volatility. Below is an example of this approach:

Product Type:	30-year conforming fixed-rate loans
Total Locked Pipeline:	$10,000,000
Average Price versus Current Market:	–1.0%
Expected Pull-Through:	74.5% (calculated based on purpose, stage, and price)
Volatility Assumption:	± 1.5%
Projected Pull-Through Within Volatility Range:	67% - 86%
Recommended Coverage:	$6.7 million of FNMA MBSs sold for future settlement. $2.0 million of OTC put options purchased for the future delivery of FNMA MBSs.

An alternative approach may be to analyze the pricing of each individual loan in relation to the current market and the potential change in pricing due to volatility. Those loans that would constitute no market risk even at the extremes would be excluded from any hedging program until they close. Expected pull-through would be applied to the remaining loans on an individual basis, with the collective risk hedged.

Any combination of hedging programs may be used. Each company must select a program that manages the risk in line with corporate policies.

USE OF INFORMATION—PROCESSING EFFICIENCY

The establishment of projected closings by product allows marketing to inform various areas of the company of the volume that will need to be handled well in advance of the closed loans. The normal time frame from application to closing is from 45 to 60 days. By projecting closings based on applications each month, personnel and cash-flow management can be improved. The functions or areas that benefit from such an analysis are:

1. Origination income projection

2. Warehouse management

3. Post-closing review

4. Securitization/loan delivery

5. Loan funding/cash management

6. Projection of gain/loss on sale of mortgages

7. Servicing volume projections

8. Final documentation management

9. Quality-control review

A loan not only moves through the pipeline in a predictable, orderly fashion but it also moves through the back office in the same predictable manner. Creation and distribution of volume projections based on historical pull-through to each affected area will provide each area with the opportunity to manage the personnel aspects associated with fluctuating volume. Figure 11.4 shows an example of a management report that provides volume projections to each area.

Figure 11.4   Closing Volume Projections/Time Table

Volume ($1000)	Closing Month		Volume ($1000)	% of Pull-Through	Post Closing/ Delivery Month	Whole Loans	Securities	Total	Funding Month	Q.C. Month	Total (10%)	120-Day Final Documen-tation Delivery
375,000	March	A	300,000	0.80	April	60,000	240,000	300,000	May	June	30,000	August
365,500	April	A	292,400	0.80	May	45,000	247,400	292,400	June	July	29,240	September
325,000	May	P	273,000	0.84	June	55,000	218,000	273,000	July	August	27,300	October
345,000	June	P	286,350	0.83	July	57,000	229,350	286,350	August	September	28,635	December

P = Projected
A = Actual

CONCLUSION

The percentage of applications that close affects almost every area of a mortgage banking operation. The ability to accurately predict not only the expected percentage but the expected change in the percentage is crucial to the success of the operation. The analysis can be taken to whatever level of precision required, based on the particular operation. The level of sophistication will be dependant upon systems, staffing, and the company's needs. The value added will be directly proportionate to its accuracy. The process of fallout analysis is dynamic, with certain fallout sources subject to reduction through management controls once the sources are identified and quantified.

III

Opportunities in the Secondary Market

Chapter 12

PIPELINE MANAGEMENT SYSTEMS AND STRATEGIES

Will Technology Used by Mortgage Lenders Ever Catch Up With the Rest of the Secondary Mortgage Market?

John P. McMurray
Senior VP of Secondary Marketing
BancPlus Mortgage Corporation

INTRODUCTION

With the advent of increasingly sophisticated mortgage securities tailored specifically to investor needs, an increasing share of residential mortgage loans are originated for sale into the secondary market rather than for bank, thrift, or insurance portfolios. Mortgages represent a large and growing part of the U.S. credit market. Figure 12.1 shows the magnitude of the primary mortgage market. All of the mortgage bankers' loan origination volume and now much, perhaps even most, of the volume originated by other types of financial institutions are sold directly into the secondary market instead of going directly into a mortgage portfolio.

All mortgage loans start as applications, which must be processed, underwritten, closed, and packaged before they can be sold into the secondary market. The application becomes a loan after the lender funds the mortgage transaction. However, a closed loan is not saleable in the secondary market until it is packaged as a "whole loan" or mortgage-backed security. Industry tradition dictates that the prospective borrower be offered a rate lock at the time of application. Pipeline hedging refers to the process of hedging the "pipeline" of rate-locked

Figure 12.1   Residential 1–4 Mortgage Originations

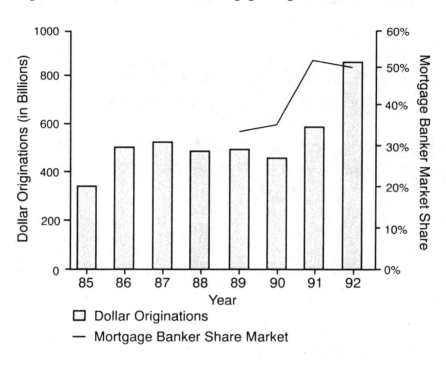

mortgage applications/loans until the packaged loans are sold into the secondary market.

Two types of pipeline risk must be hedged: interest rate risk and fallout risk. Interest rate risk occurs because mortgage prices decrease and increase as interest rates rise or decline. If interest rates rise, the locked mortgage applications and unsold loans lose value, exposing the mortgage lender to losses. Fallout risk results from some locked applications not becoming loans. A lender does not know with certainty which loans are available for sale until after each application either falls out or closes into a loan. Given the size of the primary mortgage market and the risks involved with transforming mortgage loans into a saleable secondary market product, the reader might expect mortgage lenders to employ sophisticated pipeline management systems and techniques.

The pipeline management systems and strategies employed by most mortgage lenders have not kept pace with other developments in portfolio management and the valuation of fixed-income securities.

This chapter's intent is to describe some of the more significant short-comings in the systems and approaches currently employed by many lenders and to suggest alternatives.

HEDGING VERSUS SPECULATION

Like portfolio management, the first step in pipeline management is to set objectives. Hedging the pipeline against interest rate and fallout risk is an appropriate objective for mortgage lenders, since their business is making mortgage loans. In the mortgage industry, however, the term "hedging" is often used to describe activities that are not hedging. Before delving into the specifics of pipeline hedging, some general comments regarding hedging are in order. A simple graph illustrates the difference between speculation and hedging. Figure 12.2 shows three lines. The first line, which slopes up and to the right, represents a long asset position with an initial purchase price of 100. If the market price increases above 100, the long position is profitable. And, at market

Figure 12.2   Long and Short Asset Positions

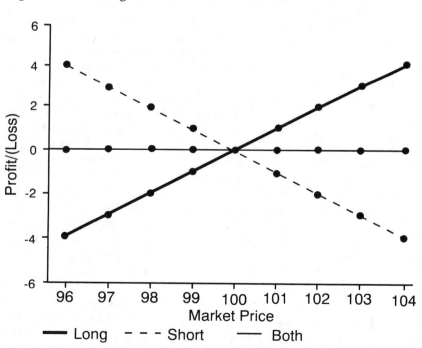

prices below 100, the position is unprofitable. The second line, which slopes downward to the right, represents a short-sale position with an initial sales price of 100. A short position is the exact opposite of a long position. If the market price increases above 100, the position is unprofitable. At market prices below 100, the short position is profitable. The third, horizonal, line is a combination of the long and short positions. For any market price, gains in the long position offset losses in the short position and vice versa. It would be speculative to hold either a naked long or naked short position by itself. A long position could be fully hedged by simultaneously entering into a short position. A fully hedged position entails no market risk.

As Figure 12.2 illustrates, speculative and fully hedged positions differ in their risk and reward profiles. A speculative position can be profitable or unprofitable, depending upon post-transaction market price movements. A fully hedged position is protected from adverse price changes, but it also gives up the benefit from positive market price movements. Pipeline hedging strategy choices are similar to those in Figure 12.2—one can be long, short, or fully hedged. Being fully hedged protects one from adverse market moves but also precludes one from benefiting from positive market movements.

An ideal pipeline hedge preserves asset value over a wide range of market fluctuations. Yet, many mortgage lenders use the term "hedging" to describe speculative or semispeculative activities. One of the more popular sessions at the MBA's (Mortgage Bankers Association) National Secondary Conference is titled "Here's the Market—What Would You Do?" The MBA is merely accommodating the approach used by many lenders. Instead of carefully evaluating their pipelines and constructing an appropriate hedge, these lenders try to predict the future market conditions. If rates are expected to decline, sales are postponed to create a long pipeline position. For those lenders that lack the ability to foresee future interest rates, a better approach is to construct a hedge that protects the pipeline over a range of rate movements. In other words, "Here's your pipeline—what would you do?"

While a few mortgage lenders practice overt pipeline speculation, others claim to pursue fully hedged pipeline strategies when they actually engage in disguised speculation. The disguise can be intentional or inadvertent. Intentionally disguised speculation usually results from a lender's desire to follow a speculative strategy while placating bank or investor requirements to be fully hedged. Inadequate pipeline systems create much of the inadvertently disguised speculation. Lenders that believe they are fully hedged end up long or short as a consequence of their systems' shortcomings. Inconsistent objectives also cause disguised speculation. For example, competitive factors often force lenders to price lock-ins below the secondary market price. Nevertheless, these same lenders wish to be fully hedged *and* overcome the shortfall priced into the initial lock. Pursuing a fully hedged strategy precludes the lender from recovering any of the initial pricing loss. Although the loss might be reclaimed through speculation, a speculative strategy risks making the loss even larger.

Pipeline management strategies span a wide spectrum of risk: from outright speculation to fully hedged. Lenders should understand the risks associated with a speculative strategy and the opportunity costs associated with a fully hedged strategy. Though each lender decides at which point on the risk spectrum it intends to operate, all lenders require a pipeline system capable of accurately assessing interest rate and fallout risk. In short, successful pipeline hedging requires knowledge of pipeline behavior and a reasonable hedging objective.

MORTGAGES

Mortgages and mortgage securities rank among the more complex fixed-income instruments. While mortgages are callable by a prepaying borrower, the exercise of this embedded option is often based on unpredictable and seemingly irrational factors. Figure 12.3 compares the price changes for a 10-year Treasury note with an FNMA 30-year, fixed-rate pass-through security. The comparison covers upward and downward interest rate moves of three hundred basis points. Like the Treasury note, the 30-year, fixed-rate mortgage possesses a significant amount of interest rate risk. The mortgage's call feature makes its price-rate relationship less attractive than the Treasury note's.

Different mortgage instruments respond differently to the same rate movements. Figure 12.4 compares the price changes that occur for an FNMA 30-year, fixed-rate pass-through and an FHLMC 5-year balloon pass-through. Notice that the 5-year balloon has less price sensitivity than the 30-year, fixed-rate. The 5-year is particularly less vulnerable to upward rate movements because of its balloon feature. One of the nation's largest mortgage origination companies incurred pipeline hedging losses when it hedged its balloon pipeline with short forward sales of 30-year, fixed-rate mortgage securities during a period of falling rates. Duration and convexity measurements are one of the easiest and most convenient, though not the best available, methods to evaluate an instrument's price-rate relationship.

A significant amount of interest rate risk accompanies most mortgage instruments. As a result, mortgage pipelines contain a correspondingly significant interest rate exposure. Despite the complexity of mortgages, successful pipeline interest rate risk management requires a familiarity with how each mortgage instrument responds to changes

Figure 12.3   Price-Rate Relationshop

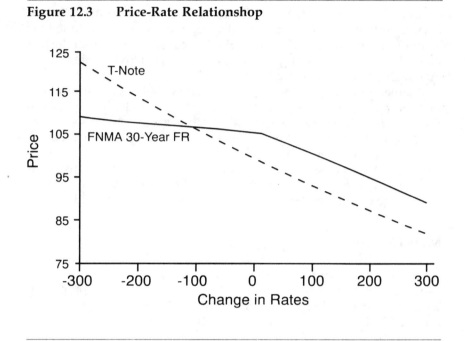

in the interest rate environment. The interest rate environment encompasses not only the absolute level and direction of interest rates but the slope of the yield curve and volatility of rates. Mortgage lenders should integrate existing fixed-income valuation technology for modeling mortgage price behavior into their pipeline systems and hedge construction.

FALLOUT

Not all mortgage applications become loans. Some applications are declined in the underwriting process. Other applications abort for reasons unrelated to the mortgage transaction. Even once an application is approved, the applicant can choose to close or not to close. Moreover, besides the embedded call option inherent in almost all mortgages, pipelines involve a second applicant/borrower owned option. Locked applications represent put options exercised at the applicant/borrower's discretion. Applications which do not close, for whatever reason, are referred to as fallout.

   Fallout complicates pipeline management considerably. The lender does not know with certainty how many or which loans a locked

Figure 12.4   Price-Rate Relationship

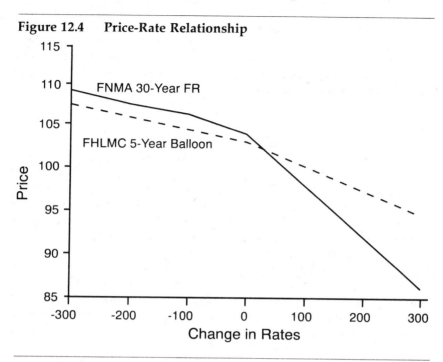

pipeline will yield until after each application closes or falls out. If the fallout projection is too low, the lender will end up with more loans than anticipated and an underhedged position. Fallout projections that are too low frequently take place in a rising-rate environment. Rising rates combined with an underhedged position will generate losses. On the other hand, if the fallout is higher than expected, an overhedged position will result from too few loans. An overhedged position in a period of declining rates will create losses.

In spite of the enormous hedging consequences of fallout, many lenders take a careless approach to projecting and managing fallout. At the end of a conference cocktail party, the author overheard the director of the capital markets area for one of the nation's largest mortgage lenders comment to one of his traders: "Let's reduce our fallout projection from 40 to 30 percent; these applications are going to close." There are more sober and sophisticated approaches to managing fallout.

Measuring Fallout

Those mortgage lenders that bother to measure fallout at all typically do so by dividing loans that ultimately fund by the loans that were originally put into process as applications. Applications may relock, change rates, switch programs, or cancel and reactivate before they eventually close. Most lenders erroneously use this "eventual closing" rate for hedging purposes. Once a fallout rate is assigned, net lock-ins (total lock-ins less projected fallout) are managed as closed loans. While some lenders vary fallout rates according to market conditions, they still base fallout projections on eventual close rates:

Eventual Closing Rate = Closings ÷ Applications
Eventual Fallout Rate = 100% – Eventual Close Rate

Enhanced accuracy results from measuring closing percentages on lock-ins rather than applications. When a lock-in does not close, it counts as fallout. Consider an example. A loan locks at 9.00 percent. It then relocks at 8.50 percent and closes. Under the traditional eventual closing approach, the closing rate would be 100 percent and the fallout zero percent. One application yields one closed loan. Measuring the example using the lock-in method, the close rate would be 50 percent and the fallout rate 50 percent. Two lock-ins were necessary to close a single loan. The author refers to this approach as "lock-in termination." All lock-ins terminate in one of several ways:

CLOSING—the loan can close and fund. A closing percentage should be calculated by dividing closings by lock-ins.

CANCELLATION—the borrower or seller can cancel the application. Sometimes cancellations reactivate and then relock.

REJECTION—underwriting may reject the borrower's credit or the property (appraisal).

EXPIRATION—the lock-in may expire.

RELOCK—the loan may relock. A relock can mean a change in rate, price, program, or expiration date (an "extension").

In the remainder of this chapter, the closing rate using the lock-in termination method will be referred to as "LIT" closing rate. Likewise, fallout based on lock-in terminations will appear as "LIT" fallout rate:

LIT Closing Rate = Closings ÷ Lock-ins
LIT Fallout Rate = 100% – LIT Closing Rate

The eventual closing measurement does not account for relocks and reactivations. However, these practices have tremendous cost—

particularly on hedging activities. Applications may close, but at different terms from the original lock. For example, at one company, eventual closing rates on applications run near 75 percent. LIT closing rates though, are closer to 55 percent and go below 20 percent for some branches. If the 75 percent ratio was used for hedging, an overhedged position would often result. Further, because program and rate switches are not properly anticipated, the eventual close approach can leave some product lines overhedged while others are underhedged. This hedge imbalance can occur even in a flat market.

Attempts to accurately measure fallout without considering each loan will fail. Further, individual lock-in transactions must be accounted for within loan level. Meaningful summaries can be generated only after the results from each lock-in are evaluated.

Pricing Fallout

Most mortgage lenders refuse to recognize the importance of lock-in exercise efficiency and fallout pricing despite the consequences they have on hedging success or failure. An example demonstrates the standard mortgage industry technique:

In this example, the loans that close and become inventory are assumed to have the same price (98) as the beginning pipeline. Stated differently, the example assumes inefficient lock-in exercise and price random fallout. Except for underwriting rejections, the exercise of the lock-in option is seldom totally inefficient. Whenever possible, applicants will decide to close when their lock is better than the market and decide not to close if their lock is worse than the market. Because the price of fallout applications almost always differs from the price of applications that close, the final inventory price will seldom match the

Pipeline	Fallout/Close Ratios	Inventory Price
$1,000,000 @ 98	25%/75%	$750,000 @ 98

pipeline. Table 12.1 shows the unlikely pipeline that experiences price random fallout. Table 12.2, a pipeline identical to the one in Table 12.1, shows an example of how efficient exercise of the lock option degrades final inventory price. Perfect exercise efficiency means that only those lock-ins with prices equal to or better than the current market close. Lock-ins priced worse than the market do not close. Tables 12.1 and 12.2 show the extremes of exercise efficiency. Most real-world pipelines are somewhere between perfect efficiency and inefficiency (price random fallout). An efficient pipeline is much more difficult to manage

Table 12.1   Price Random Fallout

Beginning Pipeline	Locked Price	Closed Loans	Closed Price
$90,000	99.00	fallout	99.00
90,000	98.00	$90,000	98.00
110,000	97.00	110,000	97.00
90,000	96.00	90,000	96.00
90,000	95.00	fallout	95.00
$470,000	97.00	$290,000	97.00

Table 12.2   Perfectly Efficient Exercise

Beginning Pipeline	Locked Price	Closed Loans	Closed Price
$90,000	99.00	$90,000	99.00
90,000	98.00	90,000	98.00
110,000	97.00	110,000	97.00
90,000	96.00	fallout	96.00
90,000	95.00	fallout	95.00
$470,000	97.00	$290,000	97.93

than an inefficient pipeline. A very high degree of exercise efficiency almost guarantees disappointing hedging results.

In addition to considering lock-in exercise efficiency, one should calculate pipeline price dispersions. Dispersion measures the price spread or variance of a specific segment of the pipeline. Price dispersion affects LIT closing ratios and the final weighted average price of the closed loan inventory. Tables 12.3 and 12.4 are similar to Tables 12.1 and 12.2. Although the weighted average prices of the beginning pipelines are all identical, the price variance or dispersion of the pipelines in Tables 12.3 and 12.4 is lower. In the unlikely event that all fallout is price random (as in Tables 12.1 and 12.3), dispersion has no impact on

Table 12.3   Price Random Fallout (low dispersion)

Beginning Pipeline	Locked Price	Closed Loans	Closed Price
$90,000	98.00	fallout	98.00
90,000	97.50	$90,000	97.50
110,000	97.00	110,000	97.00
90,000	96.50	90,000	96.50
90,000	96.00	fallout	96.00
$470,000	97.00	$290,000	97.00

Table 12.4   Perfectly Efficient Exercise (low dispersion)

Beginning Pipeline	Locked Price	Closed Loans	Closed Price
$90,000	98.00	$90,000	98.00
90,000	97.50	90,000	97.50
110,000	97.00	110,000	97.00
90,000	96.50	fallout	96.50
90,000	96.00	fallout	96.00
$470,000	97.00	$290,000	97.47

the final price of the closed loans. Low dispersion mitigates some of the harmful effects of high efficiency. Note the price difference in the closed loan totals between Table 12.2 and Table 12.4; the pipeline in Table 12.4 benefits from lower dispersion. Like high lock-in exercise efficiency, high dispersion makes pipeline hedging more difficult.

Dollar-weighted standard deviation is one method of measuring pipeline price dispersion. Each dollar in the pipeline represents one observation. The standard deviation of price is calculated for all of the observations related to a single rate/product type. Do not combine rates or products; this calculation must be performed for each unique rate/product type in the pipeline. While calculating dispersions is a useful exercise, the best approach is to measure and project closing/fallout probabilities at the loan level. Loan level probabilities handles the issue of exercise efficiency as well as dispersion. See Table 12.5 (inefficient exercise) and Table 12.6 (efficient exercise).

Projecting Fallout

A lock-in represents a put option the lender has granted to the borrower, usually at no cost. Several factors affect whether a lock-in terminates as a closing or a fallout. The following variables appear to have significant relationships to LIT closing/fallout probabilities:

Table 12.5   Price Random Fallout

Beginning Pipeline	Locked Price	Closing Probabilities	Expected Loans	Expected Price
$90,000	99.00	61.7%	$ 55,532	99.00
90,000	98.00	61.7%	55,532	98.00
110,000	97.00	61.7%	67,872	97.00
90,000	96.00	61.7%	55,532	96.00
90,000	95.00	61.7%	55,532	95.00
$470,000	97.00		$290,000	97.00

Table 12.6   Efficient Exercise

Beginning Pipeline	Locked Price	Closing Probabilities	Expected Loans	Expected Price
$90,000	99.00	92.6%	$ 83,298	99.00
90,000	98.00	74.0%	66,638	98.00
110,000	97.00	61.7%	67,872	97.00
90,000	96.00	50.8%	45,748	96.00
90,000	95.00	29.4%	26,444	95.00
$470,000	97.00		$290,000	97.46

CURRENT MARKET versus LOCK-IN PRICE—Lenders that vary fallout rates normally use overall market condition or direction. How a loan's locked price compares to the market price is much more important. If a loan is locked at a price better than the market, it has a higher probability of closing no matter what has happened to rates. Like an option, a lock-in can be in-, at-, or out-of-the-money. An in-the-money lock has a price better than the current market and a higher probability of closing. An out-of-the-money lock has a worse price and a lower closing probability.

VOLATILITY—Increased volatility depresses closing ratios for in- and at-the-money lock-ins and increases closing ratios for out-of-the-money locks.

TIME to EXPIRE—Unless the lock-in is out-of-the-money, longer expiration dates have lower closing probabilities. With more time, an in-the-money lock-in has more opportunity to become out-of-the-money. In other words, the market can improve past the locked price.

PURPOSE/PRODUCT—Refinance lock-ins exhibit higher exercise efficiency than purchase transactions. Unlike the refinance applicant who has an existing loan, the purchase applicant must close the loan to purchase the house that he or she has selected. Conventional applicant/borrowers typically exercise their lock-ins more efficiently than government (FHA/VA) borrowers. Government applicant/borrowers tend to be less sophisticated and their discount points are often paid by the seller.

SOURCE—Correspondent and wholesale customers generally have the highest and lowest fallout rates. Their in-the-money lock-ins usually close and their out-of-the-money lock-ins normally fall out. Ergo, wholesale lock-ins exhibit higher lock-in exercise efficiency. The industry trend toward wholesale notwithstanding, retail loan production is generally easier and cheaper to hedge.

Some of the more sophisticated mortgage lenders compare the weighted average price on a particular product line and coupon to the market price to assign a fallout rate. For example, at-the-money pipelines may have a 60 percent expected close rate and one point out-of-the-money pipelines may have a 45 percent expected close rate. Although this method is better than the usual "guess," it is far from ideal. A market versus pipeline price comparison does not incorporate the other nonprice factors that influence fallout, such as source, time to expiration, and volatility. One measurement, delta, encompasses most of the factors.

Delta measures an instrument's sensitivity to a directional price change. Closed loans, for instance, have deltas of 1. The value of the closed loan increases or decreases 1 percent for each 1 percent increase or decrease in market prices. Lock-ins, which are short put options, have deltas that can range from 0 to -1. Deltas for at-the-money short puts approach -0.5 as expiration nears. Lock-in deltas can be correlated to LIT closing rates. Higher delta (absolute value) lock-ins will have higher LIT closing probabilities. The delta-LIT closing rate relationship will vary from company to company. Lenders with efficient pipelines tend to have steep and concave delta-LIT closing functions. In contrast, the delta-LIT closing rate functions for less efficient pipelines tend to be flatter and less concave. Source and pricing policies, especially for relocks and transfers, influence this relationship. Figure 12.5 depicts two pipelines: X and Y. Pipeline X's closing function is steeper than pipeline Y's. Delta can be calculated using the Black's commodity model or a binomial option pricing model. Even though these models are widely used, care should be exercised in implementation. Both models assume a log-normal price distribution and should be modified for mortgage applications.

The stage of application processing influences fallout. Before a loan is underwritten, lock-in exercise is less efficient. Underwriting

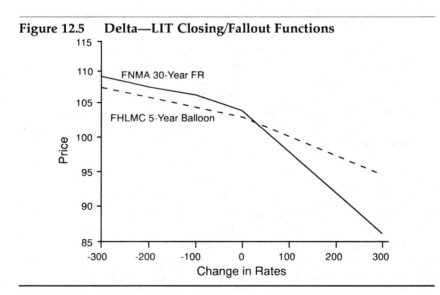

Figure 12.5   Delta—LIT Closing/Fallout Functions

decisions are price random and some locked applications with better than current market prices get rejected. Once approved, fallout tends to decline and exercise efficiency increases. Whenever possible, delta-closing correlations should be evaluated at each processing stage.

Fallout behavior varies considerably from lender to lender because their sources, product lines, policies, and policy enforcement differ. Each lender should be intimately familiar with its fallout behavior. A decent pipeline system incorporates all of the nuances associated with fallout at loan level.

DELIVERY

All investors have specific delivery requirements, whether they purchase whole loans or securities. These requirements affect potential gain or loss and should be included in any pipeline management system. In its simplest form, a pipeline mark-to-market consists of marking commitments to sell, loans in the warehouse, and expected closings from the pipeline. Combining the gain or loss for each component produces an overall projected gain or loss.

While easy to calculate, this approach has several major deficiencies. One is that the timing of the gains and losses is not apparent. A pipeline typically spans three or more delivery months. If the mark-to-market on the pipeline, for instance, shows a gain of $26,250, it is helpful to know if the projected gain is $8,750 for the next three months or losses of $50,000 for the next two months and a gain of $126,750 in month three. The traditional approach uses one month's settlement price to mark all loans to market. However, the loans will be delivered in several different settlement months. Using a "close in" or near-month settlement price inflates projected gains and understates projected losses. Conversely, using an "out" settlement month understates gains and overstates losses.

Consider the example in Table 12.7, where $5 million in FHA/VA applications are locked in with an 8.00 percent note rate at an average cost (the price the application was locked in at) of 98. Aggregate fallout is projected to be 40 percent. These applications will close and be available for delivery to the investor over the next three months. The "drop" between settlement months is 12/32, and the current market prices for the next three forward settlement months are 99.5, 99.125, and 98.75. Under the traditional approach, the cost is subtracted from the market price (99.5 − 98 = 1.5) and multiplied by the loans expected to close ($5 million less 40 percent fallout = $3 million). Depending on which settlement month is used, the projected *pipeline* gain is either $45,000, $33,750, or $22,500.

Table 12.7   Traditional Mark-to-Market

Pipeline (loans)	Forward Sales
market price = 99.125	market price = 99.125
$5,000,000 @ 98.000 less 40% fallout	$3,000,000 @ 98.875
$3,000,000	$3,000,000
× 1.125% [99.125 −98.000]	× (0.25) [98.875 −99.125]
$33,750	($7,500)

Mark-to-Market = $33,750 + (7,500) = $26,250

A delivery-based pipeline system spreads the position over the three settlement months. The lock-in expiration date along with the timing requirements for investor packaging is used to slot each locked application into the appropriate settlement month, as in Table 12.8. Although the average fallout is 40 percent, it varies significantly from month to month:

In month one, the applications are locked at a price worse than the current market and have low (absolute value) deltas. These loans

---

Table 12.8   Delivery-Based Mark-to-Market

	Month 1	Month 2	Month 3	All months
Market price	99.500	99.125	98.750	
Pipeline	1,500,000	2,000,000	1,500,000	5,000,000
Cost	97.000	98.000	99.000	98.000
Fallout	70%	40%	10%	40%
Net pipeline	450,000	1,200,000	1,350,000	3,000,000
Expected cost	98.125	98.625	99.063	98.747
PL mark-to-market	6,188	6,000	(4,219)	7,969
Forward sales mark-to-market				(7,500)
Total mark-to-market				469

are "out-of-the-money." Consequently, fallout is much higher, since most applicants will not close.

The fallout in month two is the same as the overall 40 percent average.

Month three consists largely of high delta applications, which are locked at a price better than the current market. These locks are "in-the-money." Because applicants in month three have a better price than the market, the fallout is much less.

In the fallout section of this chapter, the reader learned how fallout degrades the pricing or cost of the loans that close. Notice that "expected cost" has been worsened by fallout pricing dynamics. The $469 gain calculated using the delivery approach in Table 12.8 is less than the $26,250 calculated using the traditional mark-to-market approach.

Up to this point, the delivery discussion has focused on the loan side of the mark-to-market. A mark-to-market includes forward sales and possibly other hedge vehicles. The forward sales are normally marked to market as a short position in the traditional approach shown in Table 12.7. The delivery-based approach acknowledges that loans, packaged as GNMA mortgage-backed securities in the example developed here, will be delivered into the forward sales. Therefore, loans are allocated to forward sales currently in place. The allocated gain or loss is then calculated by subtracting the cost of the loans (long position) from the price of the forward sales (short position) and multiplying the result by the amount of the forward sales, as in Table 12.9. Rather than selling a GNMA II to cover the $450,000 position in month one, these loans are carried over and combined with month two.

A delivery-based pipeline system offers substantial advantages over the traditional approach. Overall accuracy as well as the timing of gains and losses in the mark-to-market is far superior to traditional techniques. Further, the delivery approach allows for more-precise forward selling. Imprecise forward selling hurts hedging performance due to the cost of pairoffs and rolls.

SCENARIO ANALYSIS AND SIMULATION

Most pipeline systems calculate a static net position and mark-to-market using daily mortgage pricing. In order to properly construct a hedge, the pipeline system should incorporate a scenario analysis or range of market conditions. The pipeline system inputs a range of upward and downward interest rate changes (parallel yield curve shifts) to stress test the pipeline and hedge position. A thorough pipeline system also accommodates nonparallel yield curve shift scenarios. Earlier, modeling mortgage prices was stressed. Upward and down-

Table 12.9   Calculating Allocated Gain/(Loss)

	Month 1	Month 2	Month 3	All months
Market price	99.500	99.125	98.750	
Pipeline	1,500,000	2,000,000	1,500,000	5,000,000
Cost	97.000	98.000	99.000	98.000
Fallout	70%	40%	10%	40%
Net pipeline	450,000	1,200,000	1,350,000	3,000,000
Expected cost	98.125	98.625	99.063	98.747
Net pipeline		1,650,000	1,350,000	3,000,000
Expected cost		98.489	99.063	98.747
Forward sales		1,500,000	1,500,000	3,000,000
Forward sales price		99.000	98.750	98.875
Net position		150,000	(150,000)	0
Allocated gain/(loss)	0	7,670	(4,688)	2,983
Net position gain/(loss)	0	955	0	955
Mark-to-market	$0	$8,625	($4,688)	$3,938

ward *price* changes cannot be substituted for interest rates changes because different mortgage instruments, and even different coupons for identical mortgage instruments, respond differently to the same move in rates. Loan level fallout probabilities are recalculated in each scenario to simulate fallout behavior as the market improves and deteriorates.

Besides stress testing the existing hedge, one can simulate contemplated hedging strategies using the pipeline system's scenario analysis feature. Trades that comprise each hedging strategy under consideration can be input into the pipeline system. The scenario analysis is then run with the trades under consideration. Multiple strategies can be considered over a range of market conditions before actually implementing a specific hedging strategy. Scenario analysis and simulation helps alert a lender to hedge shortcomings and ineffective hedging strategies while there is still time to take corrective action.

SUMMARY

In the hierarchy of practices in the fixed-income markets, mortgage pipeline hedging occupies one of the more primitive branches. Existing techniques and technology are now available to remedy mortgage lenders' minimal methods. Lenders can realize an appreciable improvement in their pipeline hedging performance by concentrating their efforts in a handful of critical areas.

Hedging versus Speculation. Lenders should understand the difference between hedging and speculation. Realistic hedging objectives should be set. Given that pipelines consist of short puts, which were given away for free, and that mortgages are negatively convex, it is certainly not reasonable to expect consistent pipeline trading profits if loans are priced at or better than the secondary market price. Consistent losses are likely from a probabilistic standpoint—especially if hedging costs are considered.

Mortgages. Lenders should understand mortgage pricing dynamics and incorporate these into their pipeline systems. Understanding mortgage pricing dynamics can benefit the lender in nonpipeline areas like the purchase and sale of servicing rights.

Fallout. Although it may appear simple on the surface, complex factors determine fallout behavior. Lenders must understand their fallout functions and incorporate these functions into their pipeline systems at loan level. A pipeline with high exercise efficiency is more difficult and expensive to hedge than a pipeline with lower exercise efficiency. Lenders should be aware that pricing policies and enforcement affect exercise efficiency. Lenient policies and/or lax enforcement are expensive.

Delivery. Investors and security dealers have very specific delivery time frames. Lenders should understand these time frames and the potential impact on hedging performance. Delivery requirements should be programmed into all pipeline systems.

Scenario Analysis and Simulation. Pipeline systems should include a scenario analysis feature to assess the impact of changing market conditions and different hedging strategies.

Chapter 13

FANNIE MAE: PROGRAMS FOR MORTGAGE BANKERS

Frank Demarais
VP Product Development/Marketing
Fannie Mae

INTRODUCTION

The Federal National Mortgage Association, more commonly known as Fannie Mae, is the largest provider of funds for home mortgages in the United States and the most active participant in the secondary mortgage market. This chapter introduces you to Fannie Mae and its secondary market operations and surveys the range of products and services that Fannie Mae offers to primary market lenders that wish to sell or swap their mortgages in the secondary market.

FANNIE MAE—THE USA'S HOUSING PARTNER

Fannie Mae is a federally chartered, shareholder-owned, and privately managed corporation. Historically a leader in the mortgage finance industry, Fannie Mae is the fifth-largest corporation in the United States, based on assets, and the nation's largest investor in American home mortgages.

Fannie Mae's mission is to provide financial products and services that increase the availability and affordability of housing for low-, moderate-, and middle-income Americans. Fannie Mae fulfills its mission by creating an efficient and reliable secondary market for residential mortgage loans. Fannie Mae has provided over $1 trillion to finance homes for more than 18 million families over the past 55 years.

What Is Fannie Mae?

The federal government established the Federal National Mortgage Association in 1938 to help solve the housing finance problems of the Great Depression by providing an outlet for FHA loans and later for VA loans. In 1968, Congress split the corporation into two separate organizations: the current Fannie Mae and the Government National Mortgage Association, or Ginnie Mae. Ginnie Mae continues to be owned and managed by the federal government within the Department of Housing and Urban Development and purchases exclusively government-insured and government-guaranteed loans. In contrast, Fannie Mae became entirely shareholder-owned and expanded the scope of its business to include a wide variety of conventional mortgages. Fannie Mae now operates under a unique federal charter and is subject to oversight by both the Secretary of the Treasury and the Secretary of Housing and Urban Development.

Fannie Mae's Role in the Secondary Market

Fannie Mae channels funds between primary market lenders that originate mortgages and capital market investors that purchase securities backed by those mortgages. Fannie Mae purchases residential mortgages from approximately 2,800 mortgage banking companies, savings and loans, commercial banks, and other primary market lenders across the nation, and thus replenishes their funds for additional lending.

Fannie Mae also expands the availability of funds for home mortgages by issuing Mortgage-Backed Securities (MBS) in exchange for pools of mortgage loans from lenders. Fannie Mae guarantees the timely payment of principal and interest on its MBS to security holders, attracting capital market investors who might not ordinarily invest in mortgages, and provides a link between the residential and capital markets.

FANNIE MAE'S PRODUCTS

Fannie Mae offers a wide variety of products to help lenders achieve their business objectives—whether these involve obtaining a source of funds for new loan originations, accommodating the changing needs of the marketplace, restructuring a loan portfolio, or obtaining a source of fee-based income.

Whatever a lender's financial goal, Fannie Mae will purchase for cash or swap for MBS a broad assortment of current production or seasoned loans. Depending on the type of loan, lenders can sell or swap their mortgages using Fannie Mae's standard terms or they can negotiate a transaction to meet their particular needs.

Fannie Mae currently purchases and swaps more than 50 mortgage products through the Standard Commitment Window, such as

♦ 10-, 15-, 20-, and 30-year, fixed-rate mortgages

♦ 1- and 3-year adjustable-rate mortgages (ARMs) indexed to Treasury securities or to 11th District Cost of Funds

♦ FHA/VA fixed-rate and graduated-payment mortgages

♦ 15- and 30-year biweekly mortgages

♦ 5- and 7-year two-step ARMs

♦ 7-year balloon mortgages with refinance option

The mortgages that Fannie Mae will purchase or swap must meet eligibility requirements for maximum original loan balances, property types, occupancy status, and loan-to-value ratios.

Congress limits the maximum (conforming) loan amounts that Fannie Mae may purchase or insure. These limits are set annually based on a survey of changes in home sales prices. In 1993, Fannie Mae can purchase or swap single-family first-mortgage loans with maximum original balances of $203,150 (except for loans secured by properties in Alaska, Hawaii, or the U.S. Virgin Islands, where the limit is 50 percent higher). Higher limits apply to loans secured by two- to four-family dwellings.

Eligible property types include first mortgages secured by one- to four-family residences, including units in approved condominiums, cooperatives, and planned-unit developments. Through its multifamily program, Fannie Mae also purchases conventional multifamily loans secured by income-producing residential properties of five or more units. Occupancy eligibility includes loans secured by properties that are owner-occupied principal residences, second homes, or investment properties.

Maximum allowable loan-to-value ratios depend on several factors, but generally range from 70 percent to 95 percent. Mortgages with loan-to-values greater than 80 percent require mortgage insurance to reduce Fannie Mae's exposure to 75 percent of the property's value.

Flexibility in negotiating sales or swap transactions is a key feature of Fannie Mae's product offerings. The marketing staff at Fannie Mae's regional offices works with lenders to design transactions that meet lenders' specific needs, and Fannie Mae makes every effort to price any segment of a current production or seasoned portfolio that a lender wishes to sell for cash or swap for MBS.

Affordable Housing Initiatives

Fannie Mae has developed a number of special mortgage products to meet the needs of specific borrower categories. Many of these products are designed to help lenders meet their community lending objectives.

Households of modest means face significant barriers to home ownership, including accumulating the down payment and closing costs, establishing a credit history, and managing housing expenses that often exceed standards permitted in traditional mortgage lending. To expand home ownership opportunities for these households, in 1987 Fannie Mae created the Office of Low- and Moderate-Income Housing to emphasize its commitment to providing products and services that would assist lower-income borrowers. Fannie Mae currently offers six community lending products that have been developed in partnership with lenders, mortgage insurers, public agencies, and not-for-profit organizations:

The Community Home Buyer's Program has built key flexibilities into the standard underwriting requirements, allowing borrowers in this program to qualify for 30-year, fixed-rate mortgages with loan-to-value ratios of up to 95 percent and allowing greater flexibility in debt-to-income ratios. A significant feature of the program is the 3/2 Option, which allows home buyers to meet the minimum 5 percent down payment with 3 percent from personal resources and 2 percent from a gift from a family member, a grant, or an unsecured loan from a not-for-profit organization.

Fannie Neighbors helps lenders target traditionally underserved neighborhoods—home buyers in low- and moderate-income or minority census tracts with incomes up to 140 percent of the area median income (150 to 165 percent in some high-cost areas).

The Community Seconds Mortgage consists of three components: a 5 percent down payment, a fixed-rate first mortgage, and a subsidized second mortgage of at least 20 percent of the property value. The keystone of this product is the subsidized second mortgage, normally issued by a state or local housing agency or a not-for-profit corporation, to help close the affordability gap for lower-income borrowers.

The Lease-Purchase Mortgage enables not-for-profit organizations to purchase (and often rehabilitate) homes that they then lease to lower-income families with an option to buy. Fannie Mae will purchase 30-year, fixed-rate first mortgages issued by lenders to qualifying not-for-profits and will permit a one-time assumption by the renters when they are ready to buy the home.

The Community Home Improvement Mortgage Loan is designed to help lenders revitalize older housing stock in neighborhoods they serve. Home buyers who are purchasing houses that need modest repairs can obtain a loan to finance the purchase of the home plus repair work of up to 30 percent of the property's value, based on an appraisal that includes the value of the repairs.

The Community Land Trust Mortgage Loan enables not-for-profit corporations, known as community land trusts, to own and lease land at affordable prices. A community land trust sells homes and leases the land to low- and moderate-income households. Fannie Mae will purchase mortgages on property situated on land held by a community land trust if the lease contains provisions for continued use of the land to assist low- and moderate-income persons.

Fannie Mae helps lenders offer reasonably priced mortgage credit to other groups that have traditionally been underserved. These initiatives include **Magnet**, an employer-assisted housing product, in which Fannie Mae will purchase the first mortgage, while the employer provides assistance with the down payment, closing costs, and/or ongoing monthly payments.

Fannie Mae also works with government and social agencies to provide a way for cash-strapped older homeowners to convert their home equity into cash and yet remain in their homes for life. Fannie Mae purchases the **Home Equity Conversion Mortgage** (HECM), which is an FHA-insured reverse annuity mortgage designed by HUD.

In addition to these products, Fannie Mae continues to work to expand the market for mortgage products and securities that address the needs of rural Americans, and that provide more flexible forms of renovation financing.

CASH PROGRAM

Fannie Mae's cash program enables lenders to sell their newly originated or seasoned loans to Fannie Mae for cash quickly and profitably.

Lenders may sell single loans, or groups of loans, against flexible commitments that match the demands of origination processes (or pipeline), selecting from a range of delivery dates and pricing options that match pipeline needs. There is no minimum submission amount for a cash commitment. Lenders may commit to 10-, 30-, 60-, or 90-day deliveries, with prices dependent on the short-term carrying costs. Products and prices are posted on wire services, such as Telerate and Knight Ridder, and are distributed over Fannie Mae's PC-based MORNET electronic communications system.

A key feature of the cash program is its flexibility to meet lenders' needs for nonstandard delivery or negotiated pricing. Fannie Mae works with lenders through account management teams assigned to each regional area. These account teams will work with lenders to negotiate individual pricing, underwriting, or delivery characteristics.

Pricing Options

Lenders who wish to sell fixed-rate loans to Fannie Mae for cash may choose the standard (par), premium, or discount pricing option. Standard pricing calculates all purchases at par (100 percent) for delivery of a net note rate equal to or greater than the posted required net note rate. The premium and discount pricing options allow delivery of net note rates above or below the posted rate in exchange for prices that reflect a premium above or discount below par. Lenders submitting loans eligible for premium or discount pricing may also elect a Cash Flex commitment, which allows delivery of a range of five consecutive net note rates at predetermined prices. The Cash Flex option is a hedging mechanism that accommodates management of a pipeline that has various note rates, which are subject to fluctuations in market rates and the timing of borrower closings. Adjustable-rate mortgage commitments offer options for various combinations of net note rates, net margins, and lifetime rate caps for standard ARM products.

Remittance Options

Many of Fannie Mae's cash products are offered with a choice of remittance options for the monthly principal and interest cash flow. The most commonly used option, the Actual/Actual (A/A) remittance, requires next-day remittance of any receipt of principal and interest, but only the amounts actually received. The Scheduled/Actual (S/A) remittance option, which is mandatory for biweeklies, requires a monthly remittance of scheduled interest, whether received or not, and actual principal.

Delivery Requirements and Options

Delivery of the closed loans can be made at any time during the commitment term, but must be completed before the commitment expires. Funding of the sale usually occurs within two to three business days after delivery.

To meet the terms of a standard (mandatory) delivery commitment, a lender must deliver eligible mortgages that meet all of Fannie Mae's underwriting and legal criteria and that, in aggregate, meet at least 95 percent of the commitment amount. If a lender is unable to deliver the required amount, it may substitute other loans that meet the terms of the commitment, or it may repurchase (pair off) a portion of the commitment. Fannie Mae charges a fee representing market price movement for the amount paired off.

Fannie Mae also issues optional (standby) commitments that commit Fannie Mae to purchase a designated dollar amount of mortgage loans from a lender but do not obligate the lender to sell the loans to Fannie Mae. The yield is established if and when the lender converts the standby commitment to a mandatory delivery commitment. The combined term of the standby and mandatory commitments can be up to 14 months.

To reduce errors in delivery and to speed funding, Fannie Mae offers several methods of delivery. Fannie Mae's MORNET system incorporates a software package—the Cash Delivery System—that enables lenders to prepare and transmit loan and commitment data electronically: lenders may either key in the data by hand using a personal computer or import it directly from an origination system. The software then edits and formats the data for electronic transmission to Fannie Mae. Lenders may also submit data via magnetic tape or hard copy.

MBS PROGRAM

Fannie Mae's MBS program enables lenders to pool their loans and exchange them for one or more Fannie Mae Mortgage-Backed Securities. The MBS is an investment instrument that represents an interest in a pool of mortgages. Each month the principal and interest payments from borrowers (as well as any unscheduled payments) are passed through to the MBS investor at a specific interest, or coupon, rate. Fannie Mae MBS are popular with investors because Fannie Mae guarantees the timely payment of principal and interest to holders of its MBS. MBS swap transactions can involve as little as one loan of the same mortgage product, thus providing lenders with access to the trading and pipeline management flexibilities of a market that is second only to U.S. Treasuries in liquidity.

Lenders who swap for MBS can retain the security as part of their own investment portfolio (swap and hold), sell to another investor (swap and sell), or use it as collateral to increase their borrowing capability. Fannie Mae's Customer Service Trading Desk acts as a broker for lenders who wish to swap and sell, obtaining the best price available from capital market dealers and handling all of the details of the sale.

MBS Pooling Requirements

Fannie Mae's MBS pooling requirements offer lenders flexibilities that match the requirements of their loan origination process. Each group of mortgages pooled for an MBS swap must contain a single mortgage product (for example, all 30-year, fixed-rate mortgages). The mortgage note rate in each pool must support the coupon (pass-through) rate, plus minimum servicing, plus a guaranty fee required by Fannie Mae. Lenders negotiate the guaranty fee, generally 25 to 35 basis points (bp) (0.25 to 0.35 percent), based on the product. MBS coupons generally trade best at one-half percent increments (7.50 percent, 8.00 percent, 8.50 percent, etc.), and lenders should pool their loans to take advantage of these coupons. For example, 8.00 percent, 30-year, fixed-rate loans with a 25bp guaranty fee and a 25bp minimum servicing fee could be pooled in a 7.50 percent MBS coupon.

In determining what loans to include in a specific coupon, lenders can use Fannie Mae's guaranty fee "buydown" and "buyup" features to reduce the spread required for the guaranty fee or to sell excess servicing to Fannie Mae. For example, if a lender wants to include a 7.875 percent mortgage in an MBS with a coupon rate of 7.50 percent, it can buy down the guaranty fee from 25bp to 12.5bp for a fee, and maintain the 25bp minimum servicing. Similarly, if a lender wants to include an 8.125 percent mortgage in the same 7.50 percent MBS, instead of keeping 37.5bp servicing on top of the 25bp guaranty fee, it can sell the excess 12.5bp servicing to Fannie Mae in return for a buyup fee. The buyup/buydown feature allows lenders to sell loans without taking excess servicing, thus maximizing current income.

The MBS program allows pooling of just one loan at a time in current production mortgages in a multilender pool, known as a Fannie Major. Each month, Fannie Mae establishes Majors pools for specific MBS coupons, and lenders can deliver multiple individual submissions against these pool numbers throughout the month. Lenders service these separate submissions as a single pool. All lenders receive MBS equal to their submission amount, but the pool backing the loans represents all the loans submitted by all the lenders. Investors value pool size, and therefore lenders that have small pool submissions can benefit from the price and trading advantages of a large pool. Single-lender pools require a minimum submission of $1 million.

Fannie Mae MBS can generally be traded for settlement as much as 120 days in the future with a wide range of securities dealers and investors. Fannie Mae offers the services of its Customer Service Trading Desk (CSTD) to approved lenders to facilitate these favored trades. The CSTD offers services in trading the MBS and in financing the MBS prior to sale through repurchase agreements (repos), which enable the lender to borrow funds at short-term rates to carry the MBS until future settlement. For MBS traded through the CSTD, a transaction known as As Soon As Pooled can be employed to fund a pool of loans 2 days after delivery—and as many as 5 to 30 days before the MBS is issued.

MBS Deliveries

The MBS delivery process is efficient and fast. Lenders deliver their notes and assignments to a document custodian of their choice, whose purpose is to ensure the accuracy and safety of the documents. A MORNET software application, PoolSub, can be used to edit and transmit the loan schedule data, and the lender must submit the pool documentation package to Fannie Mae within 24 hours of transmission. Fannie Mae issues the MBS in an electronic form to the lender's account or the designated investor's account within six business days if the MORNET transmission is error free.

For a current production pipeline, Fannie Mae's MBS process allows loans closed near the end of a given month to be processed into MBS for settlement in the middle of the next month. If loans cannot meet the conventional monthly settlement date established by the Public Securities Association (PSA), Fannie Mae's As Soon As Pooled option allows those loans to be funded and removed from more expensive warehousing.

Remittance Options

Fannie Mae's MBS program offers remittance options that help lenders better manage their monthly principal and interest (P&I) cash flow. The MBS program uses a Scheduled/Scheduled (S/S) remittance, requiring scheduled principal and interest, whether or not received. Standard remittance requires all scheduled monthly payments for the current month and any unscheduled, or prepaid, principal for the prior month to be paid on the 18th day of the month.

Fannie Mae will allow reductions in the negotiated guaranty fee when lenders agree to remit cash flows earlier than the standard monthly remittance date. One option, known as MBS Express, reduces the guaranty fee by 1.5bp (0.015 percent) if the unscheduled P&I from the prior month is remitted on the 4th business day of the month rather than the 18th calendar day. Another option, the Rapid Payment Method, reduces the guaranty fee by 3bp (0.03 percent) if the full monthly payment—scheduled and unscheduled P&I—is remitted on the 10th rather than the 18th of the month following collection and reporting. These reductions in guaranty fee can be translated into higher upfront proceeds when used with the buyup/buydown feature.

Derivative MBS Structures

One reason why the MBS market offers such efficient and consistent pricing for a wide array of products and coupons is the development of derivative MBS structures that match mortgage characteristics to investors' needs. Fannie Mae has pioneered and developed markets in REMICs (Real Estate Mortgage Investment Conduits) and in Stripped MBS (or "strips"). Each of these structures involves putting MBS securities into a new trust, which then separates the cash flow into different combinations of principal and interest, and in the case of the REMIC, into different maturity dates. Most new production MBS become collateral for a REMIC or a strip after the primary lender sells it to a dealer or to Fannie Mae's Customer Service Trading Desk. The flexibilities of these structures have ensured an uninterrupted flow of investment dollars into the mortgage market despite the large swings in demand triggered by recent refinancing opportunities.

DOING BUSINESS WITH FANNIE MAE

Fannie Mae requires its approved lenders to meet certain minimum net worth, operational, and staffing criteria. Once approved by Fannie Mae to sell loans, lenders seeking to conduct business with the Customer Service Trading Desk must also apply for and receive CSTD approval. Fannie Mae coordinates all of its lender relationships out of five regional offices: Atlanta, Chicago, Dallas, Pasadena, and Philadelphia. Each regional office has a team of marketing, lender administration, underwriting, and quality control staff assigned to that region. Fannie Mae is dedicated to meeting housing needs in all markets and constantly seeks opportunities to apply its programs to specific needs—expanding its program features and flexibilities and providing cost reductions, broader availability, and speedier executions.

Fannie Mae publishes an extensive series of customer education materials (in addition to the information formalized in its *Selling* and *Servicing Guides*) and regularly conducts local customer training seminars. The information in this chapter represents a synopsis of the information included in a publication titled *Welcome to Fannie Mae*. Lenders interested in learning more about Fannie Mae may call the Fannie Mae Home Office at (202) 752-2837 for a free catalog of all Fannie Mae seminars and educational publications.

Chapter 14

FREDDIE MAC: PROGRAMS FOR MORTGAGE BANKERS

Warren A. Raybould
Senior VP Marketing and Sales
Freddie Mac

INTRODUCTION

The secondary mortgage market has become an essential business tool for mortgage originators, and a vital part of the U.S. economy. The secondary market ensures a steady and plentiful supply of capital to lenders so they can originate mortgages in virtually any interest rate environment. The secondary market engineers this capital flow by purchasing mortgages originated in the primary market, repackaging them into securities, selling those securities to investors around the globe, and then using the capital earned from these sales to purchase more mortgages from lenders.

Freddie Mac pioneered this process, known as securitization, for conventional mortgages, as well as many of the investment tools needed to attract large amounts of capital from global financial markets. By tapping global markets, securitization has helped to eliminate capital shortages in lending, bring efficiencies and innovation to the housing finance industry, and reduce the cost of mortgages to American consumers.

This process has worked so well that today two of every three mortgages originated in the United States are sold to the secondary market. Indeed, between Freddie Mac and Fannie Mae, the secondary market has financed mortgages that represent fully half of the nation's corporate debt, a level exceeded only by the U.S. Treasury, and one that is expected to continue to grow.

Nowhere is this growth more evident than at Freddie Mac. The company was created in 1970 primarily to serve portfolio lenders. But the restructuring of the primary market, which began in the 1970s and continued through the early 1990s, resulted in other kinds of lenders relying more on the secondary market to keep mortgage capital flowing even as interest rates took a roller-coaster ride. Lenders of all kinds soon embraced the practice of selling their mortgages to the secondary market, to reduce the risk that changing interest rates could pose to their holdings.

As a result, Freddie Mac's annual purchase volume skyrocketed from a few billion dollars in the 1970s to more than $190 billion in 1992. Further, Freddie Mac's customer base experienced a massive transformation. As recently as a decade ago, fewer than one in ten Freddie Mac customers were mortgage bankers. In 1992, however, mortgage bankers comprised a majority of the company's customer base, a figure that continues to increase in 1993.

Because of all these changes, Freddie Mac has structured its programs to make it easier and more profitable for mortgage bankers to conduct secondary market transactions with the company. This chapter summarizes the types of single-family mortgage products Freddie Mac purchases, and the programs that faciltate there product sales. It will describe the major features and benefits of each program, and the key elements of transactions, and is based on Freddie Mac's programs as of June 1993. More-detailed information can be obtained through Freddie Mac account representatives, the *Sellers' and Servicers' Guide* and other Freddie Mac publications.

ELIGIBLE MORTGAGES

Leaners can sell their mortgages for cash, or swap them in exchange for Participation Certificates (PCs), Freddie Mac's brand of mortgage-backed securities. The following types of mortgages are eligible for sale to Freddic Mac:

♦ **15-, 20- and 30-year Fixed-Rate Mortgages.** Since most borrowers prefer the stable payments of the traditional 30-year loan, this type of loan has been a popular mortgage product Those who can afford higher payments can obtain lower interest rates by borrowing at shorter terms (15 or 20 years). This way, borrowers can reduce long-term interest expenses and build up equity faster. For lenders, the fixed-rate mortgage is easy to service, features low and predictable costs, and generally yields lower default rates.

◆ **5- and 7-year Balloon/Reset Mortgages.** Freddie Mac buys fixed-rate mortgages with 5- or 7-year maturities and a 30-year amortization. These balloon/reset loans offer borrowers low, fixed start rates in the initial 5- or 7-year period, and, if the borrower meets certain conditions, the ability to reset the remaining 23- or 25-year loan balance. Lenders can use this mortgage type to attract borrowers who plan to remain in their homes for a short period of time, but want the security of being able to extend their mortgage after the initial period if their plans change.

◆ **30-year Adjustable Rate Mortgages.** Freddie Mac buys rate-capped, adjustable rate mortgages (ARMs). These mortgages offer borrowers even lower start rates than balloon/resets, but, usually, earlier adjustments. Freddie Mac buys ARMs that adjust after one, three, or five years. Annual rate adjustments on these mortgages are generally capped at 1 or 2 percent, and are tied to the indices for U.S. Treasury notes or the 11th District cost of funds. These mortgages also feature life-of-loan rate caps, and some ARMs include an option to convert to a fixed rate. Low start rates and the security of rate-change limits are the main attractions to borrowers seeking ARMs. For lenders, rate-capped ARMs minimize default risks and offer more flexibility in pipeline management through Freddie Mac's extended commitment and delivery schedules.

CASH PROGRAMS

Cash Programs offer lenders ease of convenience, speed, and competitive prices. Lenders can sell Freddie Mac single loans, or groups of loans and, under certain conditions, loans originated by third parties.

Freddie Mac offers three Cash Programs: Gold Cash; Required Net Yield (RNY) Cash; and ARM Cash. Gold Cash and RNY Cash are outlets for 15-, 20- and 30-year fixed-rate and 5- and 7-year balloon/reset mortgages, while ARM Cash is, as its name implies, the sole outlet for adjustable rate mortgages.

Lenders can locate prices for all three Cash Programs through the major information networks such as telerate, or by calling Freddie Mac's mortgage rate line. Prices and required net yields may change at any time during the business day, depending on market conditions. Under Cash Programs, lenders can take out commitments to sell with a single phone call or computer link and receive funding within a few days.

Gold Cash

When selling fixed-rate and balloon/reset mortgages, Gold Cash is used if the mortgage coupon is at or below Freddie Mac's posted maximum eligible coupon. The price Freddie Mac quotes to lenders is tied to the mortgage securities market.

RNY Cash

RNY Cash is a vehicle for two types of mortgages sales: (1) participation interests (less than 100 percent of the mortgage balance being sold) of fully amortizing, fixed-rate mortgages; and (2) 15- and 30-year fixed-rate and balloon/ reset loans, with coupons above the maximum eligible note rate. The RNY, posted for each eligible product, is the amount of interest that Freddie Mac must receive for each mortgage it purchases. Because lenders can choose from two remittance cycles, they can either hold the payment and earn interest on the funds, or choose Accelerated Remittance Cycle (ARC) for fixed-rate mortgages and trade in float for a higher cash price upfront.

ARM Cash

Lenders sell 30-year, 1- and 2- percent annual rate-capped ARMs through ARM Cash. The interest rate is tied to the one-year Treasury index, is constrained by life-of-loan caps, and can be converted to the fixed rate, subject to certain conditions. ARM Cash works well for new production ARMs that are originated to match Freddie Mac's program parameters. Freddie Mac usually posts 24 ARM cash plans, giving lenders a wide range of start rates to offer borrowers.

CONSIDERATIONS IN CASH SALES

There are several seller considerations in cash sales including contract commitment requirements, delivery periods, remittance cycles, and pricing.

Contract Requirements

Through the Cash programs, lenders can sell whole loans with mortgage balances between $1,000 and $10 million. Lenders must use separate contracts for each mortgage type; keep servicing spreads of at least 25 basis points for Gold Cash and RNY Cash, and at least 37.5 basis points for ARM Cash; and deliver the full contract commitment amount within certain tolerance levels and agreed time periods.

Purchase Contracts and Commitments

Lenders sell their loans to Freddie Mac using either one-time purchase contracts or master commitments.

Lenders that sell regularly to Freddie Mac, or sell more than one type of mortgage product, often prefer master commitments. Master commitments give lenders flexibility in the dollar amount of each type of product they sell within a total contract commitment amount established over a fixed period of time, usually between six months and one year.

Master commitments help lenders to manage efficiently their loan sales in a changing marketplace. For instance, lenders can use the same master commitment to sell various types of mortgages through either the Cash or Swap program, apply certain negotiated underwriting waivers automatically to loans, and lock in other vital contract features such as the buyup ratio.

One-time contracts, as the name implies, cover one loan commitment and one mortgage product. Once lenders deliver mortgages sold under that commitment, the contract is fulfilled. The next time lenders want to sell mortgages to Freddie Mac, they must execute another contract.

Freddie Mac allows a certain leeway, know as a purchase tolerance, between the aggregate dollar amount of mortgages a lender commits to sell and the aggregate dollar value of the loans actually sold. In both master commitments and one-time purchase contracts, lenders have a 2.5 percent purchase tolerance level above or below the commitment/contract amount, or $10,000, whichever is greater. Lenders who deliver mortgages that fall below this level must "pair off" the amount of the shortfall. If the contract price is no higher than the current price, Freddie Mac will pay lenders at the contract price; otherwise, Freddie Mad will reprice the excess amount

Lenders selling through the Gold Cash Program have a choice of two commitments, summary and detail. In summary commitments, lenders lock in prices for a specific 51-basis-point range within the eligible posted range for any given day, and then receive prices for each one-eighth percent coupon. In detail commitments, however, lenders select a specific note rate within the eligible range posted for the day, and they receive a price quote based on a single note rate. Lenders receive the same prices no matter which commitment path they choose. Summary commitments are best for covering a range of coupons in the pipeline, while detail commitments are designed for specific note-rate pricing on loans with note rates that are not set on an exact eighth percent.

Delivery Periods

The delivery period represents the number of days between the date of a purchase contract acceptance and the date when Freddie Mac must receive all required mortgage documentation. Freddie Mac's delivery periods are based on calendar, not business, days.

Both the Gold Cash and RNY Cash programs offer a choice of delivery periods of 10, 30, 60, and 90 days. Gold Cash includes additional options of 15 and 45 days. Different prices and RNYs are posted for different delivery periods. The shorter the delivery period, the higher the price and the lower the RNY. Also, the lower the RNY relative to a note rate, the greater the amount of servicing lenders receive.

The ARM Cash Program has no such range of delivery periods with different prices. Instead, Freddie Mac posts a last delivery date under each ARM plan. There are about 90 days between the first possible commitment date and the last delivery date.

Remittance Cycles

Once lenders sell mortgages to Freddie Mac, they generally remain the servicer for those mortgages. They will continue to receive monthly principal and interest (P&I) payments from borrowers, and forward them, less a servicing spread (the amount lenders keep to service mortgages), to Freddie Mac each month. The remittance cycle sets forth the timing of that monthly payment to Freddie Mac. A faster remittance cycle brings lenders a higher price for their mortgages.

Under Gold Cash, lenders have the option of two different cycles: Gold and First Tuesday. Under Gold remittance, which is Freddie Mac's standard remittance cycle, lenders forward P&I to Freddie Mac on the third business day after the 15th of the month. First Tuesday remittance is self-explanatory: lenders forward P&I on the first Tuesday of the month after they are due from the borrower. RNY Cash gives lenders the choice of First Tuesday or Accelerated Remittance Cycle (ARC), which works similiarly as Gold remittance. ARM Cash sales requires First Tuesday remittance.

Pricing

Under Gold Cash, Freddie Mac gives lenders competitive prices for premium (high-coupon), current rate (Par) and discount mortgages. Freddie Mac posts a 100- to 150-basis-point range of mortgage coupons and the indication prices for each one-eighth coupon within that range. The company posts the coupon that is priced closest to par, and the coupons that are 50- to 75-basis points above and below the par. Base prices are quoted using the Gold remittance cycle and a servicing spread of 25 basis points.

Under RNY Cash, Freddie Mac pays lenders at par if their mortgage coupons are at least equal to the minimum gross yield (which is the RNY plus servicing spread). While lenders will not receive premium prices for their premium mortgages, they will receive more servicing income in addition to the par price.

Under ARM Cash, Freddie Mac posts prices for both convertible and nonconvertible ARMs under each plan. Prices are quoted as a percent of par. Freddie Mac pays premium, discount, and par prices for ARMs. The price that lenders receive depends on the market conditions at the time they take out a commitment. Unlike Gold Cash prices, ARM Cash prices do not assume any specific servicing spread.

Cash indication prices and RNYs—based, where applicable, on mortgage product, note rate, and delivery period—are posted between 10 a.m. and 4 p.m. EST daily on the major market information vendors, including Freddie Mac's MIDANET for the PC, Telerate, Knight-Ridder, and Bloomberg. Lenders also may call Freddie Mac's mortgage rate line at 703/438-8800. For a firm price commitment, however, lenders must call Freddie Mac's commitment line or for Gold Cash sales, they can access firm prices through their personal computer using Freddie Mac's Gold Connection software.

Sales Transaction

Lenders can make commitments to sell their loans by calling Freddie Mac's commitment line, or if selling through the Gold Cash program they can input data into a personal computer using the Gold Connection software. Whether lenders use the commitment line or Gold Connection, they provide the same information to Freddie Mac. Once a lender agrees to the firm price quoted to them, their next step is to complete the necessary documentation and submit it to Freddie Mac before the delivery date. Lenders will be funded within a few days.

SWAP PROGRAMS

Lenders may swap mortgages for a Participation Certificate, Freddie Mac 's brand of a mortgage-backed security. Once a PC is obtained, some lenders immediately sell the security through a dealer for cash. This is known as swapping and selling, or forward selling. Other lenders will swap and hold the Freddie Mac PCs in their portfolio. PCs are often used as collateral to obtain a variety of low-rate financing. Further, risk-based capital regulations encourage lenders to hold mortgage-backed securities, since they require less capital to be held against them than a portfolio lender holding mortgages.

PCs represent undivided interests in a group, or pool, of mortgages. The financial community regards these securities as sound investments. Using Freddie Mac's Swap Programs, lenders can enhance their liquidity and increase the flexibility of their pipeline management.

A PC generates an income stream that is used to pay investors. In a cash or a swap transaction, the P&I on each loan in a pool is "passed through" to the investor. The borrower pays P&I to the lender which, as the servicer, takes out a servicing spread and passes through the principal and the remainder of the interest to Freddie Mac. Then, Freddie Mac takes out its guarantee fee (the company's compensation for guaranteeing payments to the investor) and passes through the principal and remaining interest to the PC holder.

Freddie Mac offers Gold PCs and WAC ARM PCs. Lenders receive Gold PCs by swapping their eligible fixed-rate and balloon/reset mortgages, and WAC ARM PCs by swapping eligible adjustable rate mortgages.

Gold PCs are Freddie Mac's premiere security and the fastest-paying conventional mortgage pass-through security in the market. Indeed, investors receive funds from Freddie Mac just 15 days after borrowers' P&I payments are due to lenders. This quick pass-through feature makes Gold PCs a mortgage-backed security that is attractive to investors and typically commands a higher price than other mortgage-backed securities. Another reason for their popularity is that investors can use Gold PCs as collateral. And finally, because Freddie Mac guarantees the timely payment of monthly P&I—regardless of whether borrowers actually make their payments or not—investors believe these securities to be a sound investment.

WAC ARM PCs are also considered to be a sound investment. They differ in that the company guarantees the ultimate payment of principal and the timely payment of interest. When securitizing their ARMs, lenders have complete flexibility in selecting mortgage coupons, margins, life-of-loan caps, and adjustment dates. This flexibility allows lenders to easily form large pools, which may bring higher PC prices. When WAC ARM PCs are used as collateral for borrowing, they may bring lower financing rates than unsecuritized ARMs.

Guarantor and MultiLender

Freddie Mac features two Swap Programs: Guarantor and MultiLender. The major difference between the two relates to securities ownership. A Guarantor Swap gives lenders PCs that are backed exclusively by their own mortgages. A MultiLender Swap, on the other hand, offers lenders a prorated share of a Gold PC that is backed by mortgages Freddie Mac purchases from several lenders. Further, the Guarantor Program requires lendrs to swap at least $1 million worth of mortgages at a time, while they use the MultiLender Program to swap as little as $1,000 worth.

Balloon/reset mortgages, as well as both conventional and FHA-VA fixed-rate mortgages can be swapped through the Fixed-Rate Guarantor Program. Lenders can swap only conventional fixed-rate and baloon/rest mortgages through the MultiLender Program.

Eligible ARMs can be swapped through the WAC ARM Guarantor Program. This Program makes it easy for lenders to form large pools. PCs backed by larger pools particularly trade well because there are no specified ranges for mortgage coupons, margins, life caps, and adjustment rates. The PCs that lenders receive from ARM swaps have coupons based on the calculated weighted average of the underlying mortgage coupons. The PC coupon is recalculated each month to reflect adjustments in the mortgage coupons as well as in the total unpaid principal balances (UPB) of the underlying loans.

CONSIDERATIONS IN SWAPS

Many of the same considerations affecting cash sales also play a role in swaps, such as determining which mortgages are eligible for a particular Program, and choosing commitment types and remittance cycles. But swaps involve other considerations as well, including forming mortgage pools.

Whole Loan versus Participation Interests

Lenders may swap both whole loans and participation interests in the Fixed-Rate Guarantor and MultiLender Programs. But only whole loans may be swapped through the WAC ARM Guarantor Program. For whole-loan deliveries, the swap amount is the UPB of the mortgages.

For participation interests, the swap amount is the total UPB of the mortgages multiplied by Freddie Mac's participation percentage, which is generally 50 to 95 percent of the mortgage amount.

Minimum Swap Amounts and Servicing Spreads

For the Fixed-Rate Guarantor Program, lenders must swap at least $250,000 for 15-, 20-, and 30-year fixed rate loans, and $1 million for balloon/reset mortgages. The minimum swap amount in the WAC ARM Guarantor Program is $500,000, while lenders may swap as little as $1,000 worth through the MultiLender Program. The servicing spread for eligible fixed-rate mortgage swaps, including balloon/resets, is normally 25 basis points, but ARMs can be swapped with spreads that range from 37.5 to 200 basis points.

Purchase Contracts and Master Commitments

Loan commitments work almost the same way in Cash and Swap programs. For instance, lenders can choose between one-time purchase contracts and master commitments. But, unlike the Cash Programs, lenders swapping with Freddie Mac have an additional choice between mandatory master commitments and optional master commitments. Lenders utilizing optional master commitments can choose to deliver a partial amount of a loan commitment, although they must "purchase" the option with an up-front fee.

As with Cash programs, Freddie Mac allows a certain purchase tolerance for mortgages or lenders' deliveries against a commitment. In mandatory master commitments, lenders have a 10 percent tolerance level above or below the promised amount. Lenders using optional master commitments can err only over the stated amount, and only up to 10 percent. Lenders who deliver mortgages that fall outside these tolerance ranges must pay a pairoff fee of 12.5 basis points.

Lenders using one-time contracts may use optional or mandatory delivery. The purchase tolerance for each one-time contract under mandatory delivery is plus or minus 5 percent of the contract amount, or $100,000, whichever is greater. Optional deliveries are available only on a negotiated basis and are subject to the same purchase tolerances exceeding a loan delivery. Both deliveries are subject to the same pairoff fee as master commitments.

Pooling Mortgages

Under Freddie Mac's Swap Programs, lenders need to form a pool of mortgages before they swap. Because PC investors take a close look at the mortgages underlying the securities, the value of lender PCs is greatly influenced by how lenders pool, or stratify, their mortgages.To obtain optional securities pricing, lenders should keep the range of mortgage coupons and maturities within the mortgage pools they form as narrow as possible. The more lenders learn about the indicators investors use to predict cash flows and prepayment rates of PCs—the primary considerations in influencing an investor's rate of return—the easier it is to create more-valuable securities.

One quick way investors gather basic PC information is through the use of Freddie Mac pool prefixes that identify specific mortgage and pool characteristics. The first two characters of the pool prefix provide traders and investors with an indication of what type of mortgages are in the pool. Separating loans by mortgage type according to pool prefixes is the first step in forming successful pools. Through Freddie Mac's software system called MIDANET for the Personal Computer, lenders can sort, analyze, and organize their loans to create the pool that brings the best possible price or value for their PC.

In the Fixed-Rate and MultiLender Programs, lenders may pool eligible 20-year mortgages separately or with 30-year loans. Pooling 20-year mortgages separately, however, brings a higher PC value for lenders. In the WAC ARM Program, lenders must pool their eligible ARMs by the same index, adjustment period, convertibility option, and rate cap.

Guarantee Fee Adjustments

Lenders can adjust their guarantee fee through buyups and buydowns, and by swapping with recourse. These options allow lenders to better manage their servicing income and receive the best possible PC coupon.

In the Fixed-Rate Guarantor and MultiLender Programs, mortgages in a pool with note rates above the minimum mortgage note rate bring lenders additional servicing income each month unless they use buyups to sell Freddie Mac the additional yield. Servicing income above a 25-basis point servicing spread for fixed-rate mortgages may be regarded as excess servicing by the IRS. If lenders retain excess servicing, the IRS may require them to allocate some portion of their mortgage investments to the retained servicing, which in turn may influence lender tax gains or losses when they sell PCs.

With Freddie Mac's note-level buyups and buydowns, which are offered through both the Fixed-Rate Guarantor and MultiLender Swap Programs lenders can mix note rates within one pool and still minimize their retained excess servicing. Lenders can buy down their guarantee fees to zero (in exchange for cash to Freddie Mac), or buy up to as much as 12.5 basis points (and receive cash from Freddie Mac).

But lenders do not need to buy up or buy down by the same amount for all the note rates in the pool. Instead, lenders need only adjust their guarantee fee on each note rate to the extent necessary for it to support the PC coupon they request, and to leave them with the servicing spread they desire. The range of adjustment possibilities provides lenders with the utmost pooling flexibility.

Lenders in each the Swap Program also can reduce their guarantee fee by negotiating swaps with recourse. That is, they agree to buy back loans that go into foreclosure, and to pay foreclosure costs. Lenders that swap without recourse transfer the risk of loan default to Freddie Mac, but cannot adjust their guarantee fee downward.

Remittance Cycle

Under the Fixed-Rate Guarantor and MultiLender programs, lenders have three remittance options: Gold, First Tuesday, and Super ARC. Gold and First Tuesday work the same as they do in the Cash Programs. Super ARC is similar to the ARC option used in Cash Programs, but also allows lenders to convert much of their float income into a lower guarantee fee. Under Super ARC, lenders remit to Freddie Mac on any set date before the 16th of the month in which P&I is due them. Under Gold and First Tuesday, lenders do not have to advance scheduled principal payments they have not yet received from borrowers. However, under Super ARC, they do.

Lenders swapping through the WAC ARM Program may choose from the original remittance cycle (which is operationally the same as First Tuesday) and ARC. Lenders using ARC, which operates similar to ARC under Cash Programs, can reduce their guarantee fee by four to six basis points.

Swap Transaction

Lenders conduct swaps with Freddie Mac by working through their Freddie Mac representative. Through MIDANET, lenders can provide essential information, including, where applicable, mortgage product, requested servicing spread, commitment amount, swap options, weighted average remaining maturity, remittance cycle, and requested settlement date. Freddie Mac and lenders then electronically exchange contracts and forms. Lenders are wired PCs in an amount equivalent to the mortgage pools they swap.

For lenders who previously arranged for forward sales through Freddie Mac's Securities Sales and Trading Group (SS&TG) or another dealer group, Freddie Mac sends PCs to the buyers, who then wire lenders cash.

After Issuance of a PC

Once lenders have swapped for either a Gold PC or an ARM PC, they may choose to hold it to use as collateral.

But lenders also may choose to sell their PCs. With more than $3 trillion in outstanding securities, the mortgage-backed securities market is a very liquid and dynamic market. PCs are typically sold into the "forward market"—a trade agreed to on one day with settlement (delivery of the PCs in exchange for payment) occurring at a later date. Despite the large size of the mortgage securities market, forward selling into the marketplace is relatively easy.

Freddie Mac's SS&TG and other dealers price mortgage-backed securities in 32nds—1/32 of 1 percent above or below par (the original principal balance of a loan pool). At par, investors pay $1 for every $1 they will receive in the future. At a discount, or below par, investors will pay less than $1 for every $1 of principal, which is generally the case for PCs backed by mortgages at below-market coupons. At a premium, or above par, investors will pay more than $1 for every $1 in principal, which generally occurs when PCs are backed by pools of mortgages with above-market coupons.

SS&TG creates markets in Freddie Mac securities, and provides financing for Gold and WAC ARM PCs. With no obligation, SS&TG will provide lenders with up-to-the-minute market pricing on all PCs, and also assist lenders with pooling strategies for loans they plan to sell into the capital markets. Since SS&TG is part of Freddie Mac, lenders are assured of a reputable and financially strong trading partner that can handle all lender trading and hedging activities with ease.

Generally, lenders forward sell their mortgages for one reason: as interest rates rise, fixed-rate mortgages decline in value. To reduce interest-rate risk, many lenders forward sell their PCs to hedge their mortgage pipeline and protect the value of their assets. To sell PCs, lenders perform many of the same activities they do to acquire the PCs. For instance, lenders must inform the dealer of the trading characteristics of a PC pool. This includes the pool amount, mortgage type, PC coupon and requested settlement date. Dealers provide the lenders with bids once the dealers have the critical information.

One alternative funding mechanism is the Early Funding Program, offered exclusively by SS&TG. It allows lenders to forward sell PCs through Freddie Mac and receive payment before the issue date.

Lenders receive 100 percent of the proceeds from the forward sales as early as five days before Freddie Mac forms the pool.

By taking advantage of Early Funding, lenders can use their proceeds to pay down lines of credit and to originate more loans. The program is especially beneficial when borrowers rush to refinance mortgages in a falling interest-rate environment. Because of Early Funding, lenders can continue to serve their borrowers without overextending their credit lines. Further, since an early-funding trade is generally considered a sale of assets, it results in a smaller, cleaner balance sheet.

Whether lenders choose to hold or sell their PCs, they will find that the financial community is eager to invest in transactions supported by these mortgage securities. Freddie Mac, a key player in the conventional, mortgage, pass-through securities market since 1970, has issued more than $293 billion in Gold PCs and more than $71 billion in WAC ARM PCs. A 19-member dealer group of securities dealers, including SS&TG and a variety of major national and regional firms, maintains an active market in Freddie Mac securities.

CONCLUSION: MEETING LENDER NEEDS

Freddie Mac ensures that mortgage originators have the right mix of programs, and flexible program features, to meet consumer demands regardless of the interest rate environment. Securitization, market liquidity, and loan standardization have been the company's hallmarks. Freddie Mac remains responsive to lender needs by purchasing a wider variety of loans, and by continually refining programs to meet the changing nature of the lender business.

For example, one such need lies in affordable housing. Making housing more accessible to borrowers and tenants of low and moderate means, without increasing credit risk and decreasing profitability, is a challenge that the primary and secondary markets jointly face. Indeed, redefining the term "investment-quality loans" may well be to the 1990s what establishing the secondary market for conventional loans was to the 1970s.

That is why Freddie Mac is developing a comprehensive national delivery system that relies on the company's strengths—securitization and standardization—to provide lenders with the capital they need to make loans in areas serving borrowers and renters of low and moderate means. In this manner, Freddie Mac and mortgage originators can expand the umbrella of traditional housing finance system to serve more people.

It is this pursuit of effective, long-term solutions within proven business systems that has allowed Freddie Mac to provide lenders with the Cash and Swap programs necessary to become more profitable and competitive, to create the investment tools necessary to meet originator demands for ever increasing amounts of mortgage capital, and to keep mortgages relatively inexpensive for home buyers. As the primary and secondary markets move ahead together, they can ensure that this system works to their mutual satisfaction, and works for more Americans with each passing year.

Chapter 15

SECONDARY MARKETING AUTOMATION

Douglas D. Foster
VP Secondary Marketing
Alliance Mortgage Company

INTRODUCTION

The value of an automated work system is the sum of the benefits it provides to the user. The statement is simplistic and self-evident; yet nowhere is it more applicable than with automated secondary marketing systems. This chapter explores the most common features available in secondary marketing systems today, never losing sight of the initial premise.

A STARTING POINT FOR SECONDARY MARKETING SYSTEMS EVALUATION

Although they share many of the same challenges, no two mortgage banking firms are alike. Their objectives, policies, and marketing philosophies are developed over time based on their own experiences. Therefore a realistic systems evaluation begins internally with an examination of the basic functions that the system is to support. What are the marketing objectives and how are they currently being achieved? All internal secondary marketing functions should be reviewed, analyzed, prioritized, and (if it has not already been done) documented in detail. Next, consideration should be given to how each of these functions can be improved or made more efficient through automation. Perceptive visualization should result in a valuable "wish list" of expected improvements resulting from automation.

The initial process helps to form a set of expectations concerning the ideal automated secondary marketing system, which in turn establishes a foundation for subsequent systems evaluation. It is important because a systems evaluation should be user-based, not systems-based. The user should be looking for features that directly benefit his or her operation, with a goal of clearly understanding why specific system features will or will not provide the desired benefit (see Table 15.1). Without the internal examination, the systems evaluation can too easily become a score-keeping exercise, with the winner being the system with the most "bells and whistles." Unfortunately, the loser is the user.

COMMON SECONDARY MARKETING SYSTEM FEATURES

This section analyzes four general categories of features common to many automated secondary marketing systems: These are (1) position

Table 15.1   Preliminary Systems Evaluation Procedures

Action	Benefit
List current marketing objectives and the basic methods by which they are being achieved.	Identification of areas where automation may be evaluated.
Analyze, prioritize, and document each function.	Lays the foundation for a greater understanding of howautomation can improve operations.
Consider and document possible ways automation can improve each function.	Identification of key features to look for in an automated system.

measurement, (2) evaluation, (3) profitability measurement, and (4) commitment tracking.

POSITION MEASUREMENT

The position report is the primary vehicle used by most mortgage bankers in assessing and managing the net position. An automated secondary marketing system should produce a position report that assists the hedger in the following activities:

♦ Co-tracking inventory (long position) and coverage (short position)

♦ Assessing pipeline risk and incorporating it into the hedging strategy

♦ Adjusting short positions for implied values

♦ Mark-to-market

CO-TRACKING THE LONG AND SHORT POSITIONS

The probability of success for any hedge (whether a whole loan or MBS forward sale, an OTC option, or a substitute sale) is increased when its progress can be tracked against the progress of the hedged asset. Changes in value on both the long and short positions are specific to product type, interest rate ranges, and delivery periods. Without the ability to compare long and short positions with this degree of specificity it becomes difficult, if not impossible, to ascertain the overall net position.

An effective position report can show a net position (i.e., long position less short position) by user-defined interest rate ranges and delivery periods for each mortgage product type. To accomplish this, the system should provide tables in which ranges of dates or interest rates can be established by the user and linked directly to mortgage product types. This is illustrated in Table 15.2.

The number of interest rate and date ranges allowed should not be too limited.

The position report groups locked loans using their product type designation, interest rates, and lock-expiration dates or closing dates. Unallocated closed loans should be similarly grouped and reported. These two categories (locked and closed) plus any purchase commitments, constitute the long position. For trades (short position), the user

Table 15.2   Position Reporting Parameters for Product Type X

Delivery Periods (By # of days or by dates)	Interest Rate Range
_____ to _____	_____% to _____%
_____ to _____	_____% to _____%
_____ to _____	_____% to _____%
_____ to _____	_____% to _____%
_____ to _____	_____% to _____%

should be able to specify via data input the exact mortgage product being hedged, the range of interest rates to which this hedge applies, and the ending date for interest rate risk protection. The system uses this information to "match" the hedge to the hedged mortgages. Optional and mandatory commitments should be separately reported. The result is a net position reported for each grouping. The report should also show the percentage of the locked pipeline covered, both by mandatory and total coverage. (Closed loans should be deducted out of both the long and short positions before percentages are calculated.) Table 15.3 illustrates the basic format.

PIPELINE RISK AND THE NET POSITION

Traditionally, many mortgage bankers have preferred that the rate locked pipeline be reported in the long position at the amount expected to close, not at the amount locked. There exists another school of thought concerned with the amount expected to close "under water" (market value less than cost). Each takes a different approach in determining the optimum amount of pipeline coverage. However, in either approach an outcome is predicted depending upon specific variables. A system that is flexible in allowing the user to establish assumptions regarding the likelihood of a particular outcome can function effectively under either of the two methodologies. Variables most commonly associated with influencing the likelihood of closing or of closing at less than market value are:

♦ The direction and magnitude of changes in market rates since the original rate lock

♦ Time until closing

♦ Refinance versus purchase money mortgage

Table 15.3   Position Report for Product Type X

Rate Range
8.0%–8.5%

	Period 1	Period 2	Period 3	Totals
Long Position				
In-Process	566,000	1,270,000	940,000	2,776,000
Closed	780,850	0	0	780,850
Commit. to Buy	0	500,000	1,000,000	1,500,000
Total Long	1,346,850	1,770,000	1,940,000	5,056,850
Short Position				
Mandatory Sales	866,000	1,000,000	400,000	2,266,000
Optional Sales	200,000	500,000	1,000,000	1,700,000
Subst. Sales (M/O)	0	600,000	200,000	800,000
Total Short	1,066,000	2,100,000	1,600,000	4,066,000
Net Position	280,850	(330,000)	340,000	290,850
% Mand. Cov.				53%

- ♦ The term of the original rate lock
- ♦ The source of business (wholesale versus retail)
- ♦ The type of loan (fixed versus ARM, 30 year versus 15-year, etc.)
- ♦ Recent market volatility

Sophisticated matrices have been developed that allow the user to establish outcome probabilities based on some or all of the above variables in combination. For example, in the more traditional hedging approach, a 30 percent fallout probability might be assigned to a 15-year, fixed-rate wholesale loan with an original rate lock of 60 days and with 10 days remaining until expiration that is valued at 1 percent above the current market (in-the-money for the lender). The position report program identifies the variables in the loan selection process and assigns the correct fallout percentage. In the alternative hedging approach the program would assign an optimum coverage percentage based on a different set of variables (such as recent market volatility).

Obviously the ability to establish outcome probabilities and incorporate them into positioning is a major benefit of an automated secondary marketing system. However, without empirical data, the assumptions behind them amount to no more than speculation. The system must be able to produce meaningful historical statistics linking outcomes with independent variables. The user should have control over the time period to be reported, and should be able to manipulate the variables in any combination for historical reporting purposes. With the greater levels of historical reporting sophistication in recent years, many mortgage bankers have found that some of the traditional fallout assumptions have simply not held true. A good secondary marketing system should make these determinations possible.

ADJUSTING SHORT POSITIONS FOR IMPLIED VALUES

Associated with a short transaction, an implied value may be defined as the equivalent dollar value of the long position hedged by the short. The need to consider implied values arises in substitute sales (the sale of an alternative asset as a temporary substitute for the sale of the hedged asset) and options transactions, either MBS OTC or exchange traded. For substitute sales transactions, the implied value is the product of the dollar amount of the substitute asset sold multiplied by the hedge ratio. (The hedge ratio is the dollar amount of the substitute asset that must be sold for every dollar of the hedged asset.) For options transactions, the implied value is the product of the dollar amount of the underlying asset multiplied by the hedge ratio and by the delta. (The delta is the ratio of the movement in the price of the option to the movement in the price of the underlying asset.)

As an example, consider a put option on an 8 percent MBS (MBS OTC option) purchased to hedge 8.5 percent fixed-rate conforming mortgages. Currently the option is 1 percent out-of-the-money. Because the option is out-of-the-money, any increase in the value of the underlying security will not be equally matched with an increase in the value of the option (i.e., the delta is less than 1.00). Therefore the contract amount included in the short position must be adjusted for this disparity in price movements by multiplying it by the delta. This example assumes that the asset being hedged can be delivered into the short sale if the option is exercised; therefore, the hedge ratio is not applicable.

For options transactions, both the purchase of calls and the sale of puts create negative implied values, thus increasing the net long position.

Transaction	Implied Value Equals. . .
Sale of Substitute Asset	$ of asset sold × Hedge Ratio
Any option transaction	$ of underlying asset × Hedge Ratio × Delta

A system that calculates or accommodates user input of hedge and delta ratios and then automatically employs them in reporting hedging transactions at their implied value within the net position provides a significant benefit in accurate position reporting.

POSITION MARK-TO-MARKET

One of the areas best served by secondary marketing automation is in the mark-to-market of the position. Most mortgage products and most hedging transactions can be valued with prices quoted from a computerized financial information service.

An efficient mark-to-market begins with the automatic transfer of information from the financial information service to the automated secondary marketing system. Normally the transfer is accomplished through an intermediary, i.e., a Lotus 1-2-3 or Excel spreadsheet. Some mortgage bankers, however, use what is known as a digital data feed. The information is passed via phone line to a "gateway" box and then directly to the users data base.

The advantage of using a spreadsheet as an intermediary over a direct feed is that the user is able to manipulate the data using common spreadsheet formulas. For example, most financial information services report forward MBS prices only on the current coupon. For other coupons, only the spot price is reported. The spreadsheet can be used to calculate the expected "drop" on noncurrent coupon MBS. Another advantage of using the spreadsheet as an intermediary is that the same market information used in the mark-to-market can be used to calculate retail origination pricing or wholesale buy pricing, often on the same spreadsheet. The information can then be printed to rate sheets for distribution, or can be exported directly into the origination system.

Knight-Ridder Systems has recently introduced an automated spreadsheet interface called MoneyCenter for Windows. The advantage this has over traditional spreadsheet interfaces is that the spreadsheet can be updated continuously with live market prices. This is made possible through the multi-processing capability of Microsoft Windows, and eliminates the need for periodic user intervention in order to bring the most recent market prices to the spreadsheet.

Whichever interface method is used, the spreadsheet information is put into a specific columnar format required for import into the secondary marketing system and is then sent to a print file. An import program residing within the secondary marketing system captures the information in the print file as instructed by the user.

The secondary marketing system must be capable of matching the correct market price to the correct piece of inventory or coverage. This means the mark-to-market utility must be sensitive to interest rates, delivery periods, and product types. This is easily accomplished by relating it to the position reporting parameters described earlier in this chapter. Table 15.2 may be extended to include another column called "mark-to-market instruments," each tied to a specific product type and interest rate range, with multiple prices corresponding to the different delivery periods. (See Co-tracking The Long and Short Positions.)

There are two principal methods for calculating a mark-to-market on the position, either of which should yield the same result. The first matches loan inventory (long position) to compatible trades (short position) and calculates a gain or loss based on the difference between the buy price on the loan inventory and the sell price on the trades, plus the value of any rate differential. Whatever is left over after the matches are made is then marked-to-market. If the net position is long, the remaining loans are marked-to-market. If the net position is short, the remaining trades are marked-to-market.

The alternative mark-to-market methodology first performs a mark-to-market on the long position then separately marks-to-market the short position without first netting the two out against each other. The two results are added together to arrive at the total mark-to-market.

It bears repeating that the results of the two mark-to-market methodologies should be identical. In practice, the first method is most often performed directly on the position report due to its long and short matching format. The second method may be performed on separate mark-to-market reports.

A mark-to-market should allow user flexibility in the treatment of rate differentials, i.e., the difference between the interest rate on the asset and that of the mark-to-market instrument. Most mortgage bankers prefer to mark their conforming pipeline to market using MBS. Because MBS prices are usually quoted in $\frac{1}{2}$ percent increments, there is a range of loan interest rates that may be linked to one mark-to-market instrument. Changes in accounting and tax rules regarding the treatment of excess servicing has led many mortgage bankers to look to eliminate excess servicing through guarantor fee buyups and buydowns, while others prefer to weigh buyups and buydowns against the present value of the excess servicing before making a decision.

The system should permit the user to treat rate differentials in the mark-to-market in a way that is consistent with how they are being treated in the ultimate loan disposition. If the user always uses guarantor fee buyups and buydowns, the mark-to-market should be able to employ the current buyup/buydown ratios in valuing rate differentials. On the other hand, if the user customarily retains and capitalizes excess servicing, rate differentials should be valued using sophisticated prepayment models with user prepay assumptions and discount rates. These same prepayment models may also be used within the system in gain-on-sale reporting and best execution.

EVALUATION

The secondary marketing manager is frequently faced with decisions involving a selection among complex alternatives. These decisions almost always involve large and uncertain cash flows. Many mortgage bankers do not have the tools to adequately evaluate these alternatives.

A good secondary marketing system allows the user to harness the power of the computer to perform complicated and exhaustive analysis virtually instantaneously, making it possible to identify market opportunities. Two areas where this is most beneficial are best execution and optimum pooling.

BEST EXECUTION

In recent years both FNMA and FHLMC have greatly expanded the number of options sellers have in doing business with them. Different methods of pricing for loans and securities as well as multiple ways of remitting collections have created new challenges for mortgage bankers. These options can be evaluated through the use of a best execution model.

A best execution model should have the ability to isolate and value various cash flows. For example, for each of the remittance options offered by FNMA and FHLMC (i.e., ARC, RPM, First Tuesday, etc.) there are three separate cash flows, as follows:

1. Principal and interest collections and remittances

2. Prepayment collections and remittances

3.   The difference between the number of days' interest collected on a payoff and that which is required to be remitted to the investor.

For each remittance option, the requirements differ for all three variables. Therefore, each variable has a different float value depending on the remittance option. A best execution model should be able to assign a float value to each component using a realistic cash flow model (PSA, CPR, or some variance thereof) with user-defined prepayment assumptions, discount rates and short-term reinvestment rates for the float. The system will assign the number of days funds are held based on the remittance option, but should be flexible in allowing the user to change these assumptions. Table 15.4 displays the relevant inputs and outputs for a current best execution model.

The model shown in Table 15.4 also allows the user to evaluate buying the guarantor fee up or down, to value excess servicing, and to compare cash versus MBS execution.

OPTIMUM POOLING

Optimum pooling involves grouping loans for sale or securitization in such a way as to maximize their overall value. Often this must be balanced against specific investor requirements regarding the characteristics of the loans eligible to be pooled.

A secondary marketing system should automate this process. An example best illustrates: Assume that a secondary marketing manager has determined that the maximum price for a pool of ARMs can be obtained if the current rates, months to roll, life caps, and maturities all fall within specific ranges. At the same time, the investor has placed restrictions on the amount or percentage of loans matching certain criteria. For example, no more than 10 percent of the pool may be cash-out refinances with LTVs over 60 percent, no more than 5 percent of the loans can be in second-home condominiums, and no investor loans are permitted. Without an automated system, the process of finding and allocating loans to the pool that meet the pooling parameters without violating the investor restrictions is time-consuming. With an automated system, the process will take little longer than the time it takes to enter the pooling criteria and restriction parameters into the system.

Some systems will automatically find the best allocation combination based on tolerances and whether the user would like to overfill

Table 15.4

MORTGAGEFLEX SYSTEMS					**ASRPICBP**
BEST EXECUTION MODEL					REPORT DATE 04/24/92
INVESTOR COMMITMENT - POOL 1					
PRODUCT TYPE - CONF CONVENTIONAL FIXED			FIXED POOL (30 YR)		
TOTAL AMOUNT	163,250		WAC 8.2182	WAD −0.036753	

Revelant Information

	Scene 1 2 FNMA Case S/A	Scene 2 4 FNMA MBS-Std	Scene 3 8 FHLMC 1st Tues	Scene 4 9 FHMLC-Gold/ARC
Remit Option				
Description				
New Rate	7.97000	7.50000	7.50000	7.94000
Price	100.000000	98.7500000	98.625000	100.00000
Guarantor Fee	0.0000	0.2500	0.2200	0.0000
Gr. Buyup Fee%	0.00000	0.00000	0.00000	0.00000
Gr. Buydn Fee%	0.00000	0.00000	0.00000	0.00000
Service Fee	0.2500	0.2500	0.2500	0.2500
P&I Float Days	13	11	27	12
P/O Float Days	28	26	7	7
P/O Int. Diff	7	−8	0	0
FL. Reinv. Rate	6.15000	6.15000	6.15000	6.15000
Pooling Fees $	0	0	0	0
Delivery Fees %	0.00000	0.00000	0.00000	0.00000

Best Execution

	Scene 1 FNMA Case S/A	Scene 2 FNMA MBS-Std	Scene 3 FHLMC 1st Tues	Scene 4 FHMLC-Gold/ARC
Description				
Price Difference	−59.99	−2100.62	−2304.68	−59.99
Total Fees	0.00	0.00	0.00	0.00
Present Value-Ex Service (discount)	−14.50	1896.32	2157.02	245.16
Book Gain/(Loss)	−74.49	−204.30	−147.66	185.17
Present Value-Total Float	648.35	347.57	475.95	259.50
Total Present Value of Income Stream	573.86	143.27	328.29	444.67

or underfill a commitment to maximize value. Without automation, this can also be a long process.

PROFITABILITY MEASUREMENT

In the secondary mortgage market today there are a multitude of methods for disposing of mortgage loan assets. This, along with unprecedented changes in tax and financial reporting rulings, has created new challenges in recording the profitability from secondary marketing transactions.

A good system should be able to report the gain or loss resulting from any of the myriad of available methods of disposition. For whole loan sales the system should be able to store and utilize multiple prices under flex/summary pricing options, or be able to calculate discounts and excess servicing values under more traditional required net yield pricing. Servicing released premiums received as well as commitment or delivery fees paid should also be accounted for.

For MBS transactions, the amount of buydown/buyup fees paid or received at either the commitment level or note level should be reported. The system should link pools with multiple trades and vice versa, reporting the results in one total.

Many of the major private conduits as well as FNMA/FHLMC are now pricing loans based on perceived credit risk. A system should allow the user at the commitment level to specify how pricing may be affected by certain credit risk attributes such as LTV, and then automatically make the pricing adjustments in the P&L report for loans that match the established criteria.

The ability to account for deferred loan fees under FASB 91 and include them in the P&L report is also important to some lenders.

COMMITMENT TRACKING

If one had to choose one word to describe what is most important in a secondary marketing commitment tracking system, that word would undoubtedly be "flexibility." The tracking system must be versatile in supporting the needs of various personnel performing different functions. To meet these needs, the system must allow the user to control (1) how commitments are selected, grouped, and sorted; and (2) the level of detail in which they are to be reported.

For example, senior management or the marketing committee desires to see a report summarizing the settlements during the month by investor or by transaction type, including P&L results. The secondary marketing manager requires a report on master commitments, showing how much is available and how much has been delivered under specifically restricted categories. Accounting personnel need detailed warehouse bank reports showing the loans currently warehoused, the amount of the line used, and the average turnaround time. Finally, shipping personnel require reports showing which commitments have yet to be filled as well as detail reports providing information on individual loans that have been allocated to commitments. A few examples of these reports are included in the appendix to this chapter.

REQUIREMENTS FOR SUCCESS IN SECONDARY MARKETING AUTOMATION

This chapter has taken a user's perspective in evaluating secondary marketing systems, i.e., from the point of view of the secondary marketing department. In reality, a successful secondary marketing system must be compatible with the operations of the mortgage banking firm as a whole, and must be supported by a knowledgeable technical staff, both internally and with the vendor.

Issues that must be thoroughly evaluated are hardware requirements (mainframe versus PC-based), operating system compatibility, interface with existing front-end or servicing systems, licensing agreements, continued vendor business viability, user friendliness at all levels, and available levels of support.

This requires the involvement of all levels of management as well as various functional areas such as the Information Systems department and the Internal Audit department. A discussion of their specific involvement and of the issues each must consider is beyond the scope of this chapter. That is not to deny their importance in the overall success of secondary marketing automation.

Appendix

REPORT DATE 12/24/91
PAGE NUMBER 1

POOL #	MASTER COMM #	POOL TYPE	POOL AMOUNT	AMOUNT ALLOCATED	SECURITY PRICE	SECURITY RATE	ISSUE DATE	SETTLE DATE	PURCHASED DATE	CURRENT P&L
91OCTPC01	91080983	OCT 30YR GOLD 9.0%	1,000,000	977,750	99.5937	9.0050	10/01/91	10/15/91		4,551
91OCTPC02	91080983	OCT 30YR GOLD 9.0%	1,000,000	976,250	99.4843	9.0050	10/01/91	10/15/91		2,947
91OCTPC03	91080983	OCT GOLD 30YR 9.0%	1,000,000	1,954,700	101.0937	9.5050	10/01/91	10/15/91		-1,743
91OCTPC04	91080983	OCT 30YR GOLD 9.0%	1,000,000	1,002,750	100.9375	9.5050	10/01/91	10/15/91		-2,059
91OCTPC09	91080983	OCT 30YR 9.5% GOLD	1,000,000	1,008,200	104.5937	10.0050	10/01/91	10/15/91		43,695
91OCTPC11	91080983	OCT 30YR GOLD 8.5%	1,000,000	1,003,500	100.0000	9.0050	10/01/91	10/15/91		2,468
91OCTPC12	91080983	OCT 30YR GOLD 9.0%	1,000,000	980,350	101.5000	9.5050	10/01/91	10/15/91		2,773
91OCTPC13	91080983	OCT 30YR GOLD 9.0%	1,000,000	1,001,400	101.7500	9.5050	10/01/91	10/15/91		1,092
91OCTPC14	91080983	OCT GOLD 30YR 9.0%	1,000,000	1,010,700	101.2187	9.5050	10/01/91	10/15/91		11,468
91OCTPC15	91080983	OCT 30YR GOLD 8.5%	1,000,000	978,250	100.2343	9.0050	10/01/91	10/15/91		7,374
91OCTPC05	91080983	OCT 30/5 GOLD 8.0%	1,000,000	976,500	100.9375	8.5500	10/01/91	10/21/91		-1,009
91OCTPC06	91080983	OCT 30/5 GOLD 8.0%	1,000,000	985,450	101.0468	8.5500	10/01/91	10/21/91		1,212
91OCTPC07	91080983	OCT 30/5 GOLD 8.0%	1,000,000	976,550	101.0000	8.5500	10/01/91	10/21/91		2,454
91OCTPC08	91080983	OCT 15YR GOLD 8.5%	1,000,000	1,003,650	100.5312	8.9900	10/01/91	10/21/91		5,570
91OCTPC10	91080983	OCT GOLD 30/5 7.5%	1,000,000	977,100	99.7812	8.0500	10/01/91	10/21/91		4,248
91OCTMBS01	L01602	OCT 30/7 MBS 8.0%	1,000,000	991,650	99.8906	8.5000	10/01/91	10/21/91		4,058
91OCTMBS02	L01602	OCT 30/7 MBS 8.5%	1,000,000	984,600	101.6250	9.0000	10/01/91	10/21/91		18,059
** REPORT TOTALS	17 RECORDS PRINTED		17,000,000	17,789,350						107,158

POOL DETAIL INFORMATION REPORT

POOL NUMBER 91OCTPC01   OCT 30YR GOLD 9.0%

SETTLEMENT DATE: 10/15/91   DELIVERY DATE:

REPORT DATE 12/24/91
PAGE NUMBER 1

STATUS CODE	LOAN PROGRAM	APP #	BORROWER	INTENT	PROPERTY TYPE	PURPOSE	CASH OUT	LOAN AMOUNT	ORIGINAL LOAN AMOUNT	CURRENT INTEREST RATE	POINTS	DISCOUNT POINTS	NET MARKET POINTS	MATURITY	MARGIN	LIFE CAP	FIRST CHANGE DATE	LOAN TO VALUE	FIRST PAYMENT DATE	DOC TYPE
60	CF300	25003171	DENSMORE	2ND	CONDO 1	REFI	NO	75,000	75,000	9.1250	2.1250		0.6250	361				50.37%	11/01/91	1
60	CF300	25003171	RANDLE	00	CONDO	PURCHASE	NO	118,750	118,750	9.1250	2.0000		0.6250	362				90.00%	10/01/91	1
60	CF300	40003900	PETERSON	00	CONDO	REFI	YES	168,000	168,000	9.1250				366				80.00%	06/01/91	1
60	CF300	60011192	MORGAN	00	SFR	REFI	NO	136,500	136,500	9.1250	-0.1250		-0.1250	362				39.00%	10/01/91	1
60	CF300	72027782	CLARDS	00	PUD	REFI	YES	110,000	110,000	9.1250	2.0000		0.8750	361				72.85%	11/01/91	1
60	CS300	76017968	BLAIN	00	SFR	REFI	YES	80,000	80,000	9.1250	2.0000		0.6250	362				52.98%	10/01/91	1
60	CS300		MARAVAL	00	SFR	REFI	YES	187,500	187,500	9.1250	1.1250		0.1250	361				75.00%	11/01/91	1
60	CF300	87030473	KING	00	SFR	PURCHASE	NO	102,000	102,000	9.1250	2.6250		0.5000	361				77.27%	11/01/91	1

SECTION SUBTOTALS: 8   977,750   977,750   9.1250   1.2666   0.3321   362   68.95%

STATISTICS	OO: 7	%	PURCHASE: 2	%	NUMBER OF RECORDS 8	LTV ABOVE 90%: X
	NOO:	%	REFINANCES: 6	%		
	2ND: 1	%	OTHER: 1			

MORTGAGEFLEX SYSTEMS
WAREHOUSE REPORT

WAREHOUSE BANK - FULL BANK NAME

REPORT DATE 01/15/88
PAGE NUMBER 1

AP #	BORROWER	INVESTOR	COMMIT #	PROD TYPE	STATUS CODE	COMM TYPE	DELIV	ACTIVE	LOAN AMOUNT	WAREHOUSE LOAN AMOUNT	WAREHOUSED DATE	INTEREST RATE	WAREHOUSE RATE	DAILY P&L	FORCASTED P&L FOR 25 DAYS	DAYS IN WAREHOUSE	DAYS REMAINING WAREHOUSE
186765-2	LYNCH	DUMMY INVESTOR	UNASSIGN	P101	60	C	P	Y	200,000	180,000	01/12/88	9.2500	10.0000	-3.69	-92.25	3	297
0	DUMMY	DUMMY INVESTOR	UNASSIGN	P101	3	C	P	Y	87,000	78,300	01/12/88	8.0000	10.0000	-4.29	-107.25	3	297
10400002-7	HERNANDEZ	DUMMY INVESTOR	UNASSIGN	P101	8	C	P	Y	104,000	93,600	01/12/88	10.3750	10.0000	0.96	24.00	3	297
10400011-1	REYAZUDDIN/REYZ	DUMMY INVESTOR	UNASSIGN	P101	2	C	P	Y	90,000	81,000	01/12/88	10.3750	10.0000	0.83	20.75	3	297
10400012-4	ZELLER/TUDIC	DUMMY INVESTOR	UNASSIGN	P101	4	C	P	Y	90,000	81,000	01/12/88	10.3750	10.0000	0.83	20.75	3	297
22600809-6	PAYNE	DUMMY INVESTOR	UNASSIGN	P101	7	C	P	Y	236,650	212,985	01/12/88	10.3750	10.0000	2.18	54.50	3	297
315	SEMIFT	DUMMY INVESTOR	UNASSIGN	P101	1	C	P	Y	176,000	158,400	01/12/88	11.5500	10.0000	6.72	168.00	3	297
512445-9	TAYLOR	DUMMY INVESTOR	UNASSIGN	P101	1	C	P	Y	120,000	108,000	01/12/88	8.9000	10.0000	-3.25	-81.25	3	297
5432	ROB THREE	FNMA	CONN1001	P102	9	C	M	Y	100,300	90,270	01/12/88	11.1250	10.0000	2.78	69.50	3	297
56437129873241	JAMES	FIRST BOSTON	54783295	P102	1	C	M	Y	250,100	225,090	01/12/88	11.0000	10.0000	7.70	192.50	3	297
64532	ROB ONE	FNMA	CONN1001	P101	1	C	M	Y	100,100	90,090	01/12/88	11.0000	10.0000	2.46	61.50	3	297
6543345	ROB TWO	FNMA	CONN1001	P101	3	C	M	Y	100,200	90,180	01/12/88	11.0000	10.0000	2.47	61.75	3	297
67768	JAMES TWO	FNMA	CONN1001	P101	8	C	M	Y	200,200	180,180	01/12/88	11.0000	10.0000	4.93	123.25	3	297
7834778543280 2	JAMES 2	FIRST BOSTON	54783295	P102	1	C	M	Y	250,125	225,112	01/12/88	11.2500	10.0000	7.70	192.50	3	297
8170042	WILLIAMS	DUMMY INVESTOR	UNASSIGN	P101	3	C	P	Y	222,500	200,250	01/12/88	11.0000	10.0000	5.48	137.00	3	297
97560432677864	JAMES 3	FIRST BOSTON	54783295	P102	1	C	M	Y	250,250	225,225	01/12/88	11.2500	10.0000	7.71	192.75	3	297
9098199	REILLY	FIRST BOSTON	GINNIE		60	C		Y	27,250	27,250	08/18/87	8.0000	10.0000	-1.69	-37.25	150	150

* SUBTOTAL: RECORDS PRINTED : 17

	COMMIT	2,577,425	2,319,682				40.03	1,000.75	198	4,902
	UNICOMM	27,250	27,250							

IV

Developments in Mortgage Loan Servicing

Chapter 16

THE SECONDARY MARKET FOR SERVICING RIGHTS

Stephen Z. Hoff
President and CEO
Hamilton, Carter, Smith & Co.

INTRODUCTION

The secondary market for mortgage servicing has changed dramatically since its inception in the early 1980s. Loan servicing is created when a loan is sold, and is recognized as the primary component of value for most mortgage lenders. The servicing process involves the collections, record keeping, remittances, late-fee payments, foreclosure procedures, and other functions necessary to maintain the integrity of the loan until it is fully paid. Once servicing is separated from a loan, it is treated like any other financial asset and may be sold individually or as a part of a portfolio of servicing rights. The principal balance of all single-family mortgages in the United States exceeds $3.8 trillion, and for every mortgage loan, servicing exists or has the potential to be created. The gross amount of new mortgage debt added each year is over $400 billion. The net addition after accounting for prepayment of existing mortgages is $200–$300 billion.

The government agencies, (FNMA, FHLMC, and GNMA) domi-nate the secondary mortgage market. The agencies have established standards that most participants in the mortgage market must meet. By doing so, the agencies have fostered a marketplace for servicing that is dependent on the interchangeability of servicing portfolios among mortgagees. Additionally, the price of servicing has continued to rise since the early 1980s because of a number of changes in the way loans are serviced as well as structural changes in the marketplace. Inflation, for example, has caused a tremendous increase in average loan balances, with a corresponding increase in servicing-fee income. This, coupled with more sophisticated valuation techniques, resulted in a bull market for servicing rights that lasted until 1989, the year the Financial Institutions Reform and Recovery Act (FIRREA) was introduced. Servicing rights traded annually are about $250 billion.

Mortgage servicing rights can be acquired through bulk purchases, on a loan-by-loan basis (sometimes called concurrent transfer), through the normal course of the origination process when loans are sold but servicing is retained, or through the purchase of stock of another company. Sales of servicing support a variety of purposes such as portfolio restructuring, recognizing income and generating cash for operations. No matter what the acquisition technique or the purpose of the sale, the valuation methodology is the same. The evaluator will present value any incremental benefit over the cost to service the portfolio over its expected life. Until 1992, there had been a trend toward more bulk purchases and less origination, although the recent refinance activity has reversed the trend, at least temporarily.

Market growth has tracked the increase in origination volume over the last ten years. For example, in 1982, origination volume was about $100 billion, and by 1992, it had increased to about $750 billion. Over this same time period, the volume of servicing transactions increased to around $250 billion per annum from about $20 billion in 1982. The market for mortgage servicing rights grew as more mortgage bankers and other participants in the mortgage lending arena developed the need to be able to liquefy one of their principal assets, that is, their servicing portfolio. Servicing rights have value to the extent that the right to receive servicing fee income exceeds the servicer's projected loan administration costs.

As servicing costs decreased due to automation, the attainment of scale economies in data-processing applications, and through improvements in cash management techniques, servicers were able to capture more value from their portfolios. As value increased, the number of transactions increased. At the same time, more participants began to realize the advantages of scale economies associated with larger and larger servicing operations. Buyers were willing to pay more and sellers were willing to sell more at a higher price. In 1984, for example, an estimated $80 billion in mortgage servicing rights changed hands. At that time, the price for GNMA servicing exceeded 250 basis points of the unpaid principal balance.

Early on in its evolution, the market was dominated by financial institutions such as banks or thrifts or their mortgage subsidiaries. In the early 1980s, a large mortgage servicer was considered to be one that serviced between $600 million and $1.5 billion worth of loans. The megaservicers in those days, by contrast, were those that had portfolios of between $2 billion and $8.5 billion of unpaid principal balance. Today, the megaservicers are considered to be those who service in excess of $30 billion. By 1986, sales volume had increased to around $100 billion, and more firms were beginning to view both the purchase and sale of servicing rights as a standard part of their operations.

In 1986, we also saw the advent of smaller blocks of servicing being traded, those in the range of $20 to $30 million. The market at this time displayed increased liquidity and increased pricing, especially for current production. The 1980s also saw the production of computerized servicing valuation models, which tended to standardize the pricing process. Toward the end of the decade, more firms became comfortable not only with valuing servicing, but also with buying and selling it. At the end of the decade, the trading in servicing portfolios reached about $250 billion.

The 1980s also saw a rapid growth in the market share of thrifts holding servicing portfolios. Thrift involvement started to decline at the end of the decade because of the savings and loan crisis and its concomitant regulatory changes. The savings and loans were effectively taken out of the market as buyers of servicing rights in 1989, when FIRREA was introduced. This Act restricted the amount of purchased mortgage servicing rights that could be counted toward regulatory capital requirements. The market share for thrifts peaked in 1987 at about 30 percent of all loans serviced, and declined to about 20 percent by 1989. The latest round of regulations regarding restrictions on purchased mortgage servicing is embodied in the Federal Reserve rule issued late in 1992. The Fed allows the inclusion of purchased servicing if the amount does not exceed 50 percent of tier 1 capital. Interestingly, the Fed may view the excessive holding of purchased mortgage servicing rights as an unsafe and unsound practice.

Furthermore, after the passage of FIRREA, many insolvent institutions were taken over by the Resolution Trust Corporation (RTC) and as a consequence, the RTC was responsible for servicing upwards of $200 billion worth of mortgages. Because of these and other regulations impacting depository institutions, fewer thrifts are pursuing the strategic option of growing their servicing portfolios. Many commercial banks, on the other hand, increased their presence in the mortgage industry by stepping up the pace of mortgage originations and/or building large servicing portfolios through acquisition. One consequence of FIRREA and RTC sales activities with respect to loan servicing rights was the entry into the market of outside investors seeking to capture the generous yields associated with owning servicing. During 1990, which was one of the worst years for sellers of servicing in recent memory, yields on high-quality servicing portfolios approached 20 percent. Prices for GNMA portfolios, which two years previously had been sold for 250 basis points, had dropped to 150 basis points. High quality, conventional, conforming product that had commanded prices as high as six times servicing fee had dropped to four times servicing fee during 1990. Outside investors took advantage of this and ended up buying mortgage entities, mostly from the RTC. For sale at the time were servicing platforms with portfolios ranging in size from $500 million to $10 billion in unpaid principal balance.

By 1991, prices had started to recover and during January of 1992 the market saw a 20 percent increase over the previous year's pricing. Supply and demand had a lot to do with the increase in the value of servicing portfolios.

Today, we are looking at a market that has almost totally recovered, with the exception of GNMA servicing and recourse servicing. For example, conventional, conforming, nonrecourse, 30-year, fixed-rate product is selling for close to six times service fee, while GNMA portfolios are selling for around 200 basis points. The fact that GNMA portfolios have not recovered as much as conventional product is a function of the recourse risk associated with the VA's No-Bid policy, which was not evident in the early 1980s when servicing was trading at 250 basis points.

Why has the secondary market for mortgage servicing grown over the last ten years? On a cash basis, the origination business is marginally profitable, but on a value-created basis is quite profitable. Origination creates servicing, which is valuable either as an asset that produces income over the life of the loan, or as a financial asset that be can sold for the present value of its expected cash flows. As stated earlier, to the extent that servicing revenues exceed costs, companies will want to own servicing. As average loan size grows and technological advances make the servicing process less costly, prices will increase.

The real question is, does it make more sense to produce servicing or to buy it? Depending on the level of origination activity, it may be possible to purchase servicing for approximately the same cost associated with its origination. During periods of heavy origination activity, acquiring servicing through production of loans is a more cost-effective option. Those who entered the industry by buying servicing platforms and operations solely as servicing are reevaluating their strategies. Market participants have come to the realization that servicing can no longer be put into portfolios and ignored. It, like other assets, must be managed, especially during periods of rapidly declining interest rates. The growth in the servicing market (see Table 16.1) shows that the annual volume of servicing transfers for GNMA, FNMA, and FHLMC increased from $157 billion to $186 billion between 1991 and 1992, or about 19 percent.

VALUATION

Valuing servicing is part art and part science, since servicing has no explicit principal repayment, no coupon, and no precise term. It is up to the analyst to decide what are the appropriate assumptions to be used in connection with modeling the cash flows.

In simplest terms, the value of a loan servicing portfolio is equal to the present discounted value of the after-tax cash flows generated by a portfolio over its expected life, less operating expenses, and adjusted for prepayments. While this may appear to be a very scientific methodology, the valuation process can evolve into a somewhat subjective process as a result of the assumptions and expectations that a firm has for a particular portfolio. Unlike some fixed-income securities, servicing is a very dynamic asset with many fluctuating variables. As a result, the ultimate determination of the value of a loan servicing portfolio often rests on assumptions made about economic conditions many years hence.

While there are several types of values that can be assigned to a portfolio (i.e., economic value, market value), the fair market value is the most widely used method. It is defined as the price at which a portfolio will change ownership between a willing buyer and a willing seller (neither being compelled to buy or sell the asset, and both having reasonable knowledge of the relevant facts of the transaction). Additionally, the types of representations and warranties that a seller is

Table 16.1   Annual Servicing Volume (in billions)

YEAR	GNMA	FNMA	FHLMC	TOTAL
1990	$38.7	$57.6	N/A	$96.3
1991	$46.6	$62.6	$47.9	$157.1
1992	$54.4	$81.3	$50.6	$186.3

willing and able to offer has a significant effect on the value of a portfolio. That is to say, if a seller is unable to provide representations and warranties that reflect industry standards (or close approximations thereof), the market value of the portfolio will more than likely decrease.

The value of servicing rights is a function of the actual characteristics of a particular portfolio (i.e., unpaid principal balance, weighted average coupon, weighted average service fee, etc.) and certain forecasted variables (i.e., payoff rate, future delinquency, and foreclosure figures, etc.) and the impact that these components have on one another over time. To a large degree, the value depends on a firm's ability to maximize income through the best use of its resources and through an accurate reflection and projection of a firm's operating costs. In other words, beauty is in the eyes of the beholder, and the market value of any portfolio is the highest price any particular buyer is willing to pay at any given time.

Valuation Methodology

The first step in the assessment of a portfolio's value is the stratification of a portfolio into homogeneous segments. This exercise provides the groundwork from which to proceed with the remainder of the valuation process. Once a portfolio is segmented into homogeneous groups, it is easy to see its effect on value. For example, a portfolio of 10,000 loans with a weighted average coupon of 8.25 percent is valued on the basis of a single calculation, using the averages of the different segments. The result is a price of 1.11 percent, using a 10 percent pretax discount rate, a unit servicing cost of $50 per loan, and payoff assumption based on the aggregate note rate. The same portfolio, when segmented by note rate, the average of which equals the aggregate characteristics, has a value of 1.16 percent, or a difference of about 4.5 percent.

Industry standards, per se, do not exist for portfolio stratification but some of the more typical subsets are investor, coupon, loan type, geographics, and distribution original term. Additionally, segmenting loans by remittance cycle is necessary in order to obtain meaningful results. For example, if FHLMC ARC (accelerated remittance) were not separated and valued differently from FHLMC regular remittance, float on principal and interest would be overestimated, as would the overall value of the portfolio.

A carefully stratified portfolio is the basis from which to assess the effect of other components on value. The essential components of a valuation include projecting income, expenses, and prepayments; then, the after-tax cash flows are discounted to arrive at the net present value.

Components of Income

The most important elements of income in a servicing valuation are service fee, principal and interest float, escrow earnings, and ancillary or other income. The relative importance of these elements changes over time due to the changing characteristics of the portfolio.

Service Fee The service fee is usually the major contributor to a portfolio's value. It represents the difference between the weighted average coupon and the investor yield less any guarantee fee charged by the investor. Single-family service fees typically range from 0.25 percent to 0.44 percent, depending on the investor and the loan type. Early in a portfolio's life, the service fees contribute greatly to value because they are directly related to the unpaid principal balance. As the principal balances decline, so does the service fee income. Additionally, change occurs through the prepayment of higher-coupon loans, which often carry higher service fees. Accurately reflecting the runoff and the loss of income associated with these loans is essential to a valuation. When portfolios are traded, the bids are often expressed as a multiple of the service fee. This clearly illustrates the importance of the service fee on the value of a portfolio. The multiple is loosely interpreted by market participants as the number of years that the buyer needs to derive income from the portfolio before his or her purchase price is recouped.

P & I Interest Float and Interest Earnings on Escrow The float earned on principal and interest (P&I), received each month, depends to a great extent on the number of days that the servicer has availability of those funds for investment purposes and the size of the balances. The number of "float days" may range from one to twenty. Although the number of float days appears to be static, the actual float can be reduced as a result of slow payments or delinquent payments. A servicer can be further penalized by late payments or prepayments if the servicer is obligated to advance the uncollected principal and/or interest to the investor. Factoring in the loss of interest income is important to the servicing valuation.

Along with the principal and interest portion of the payment, a mortgagor is more often than not required to contribute to an account established for taxes and insurance (T&I). The value of the funds held by the servicer will vary depending on the frequency of tax payments and the average balance of the account, as well as the expected annual return on balances. While T&I balances often are assumed to have a longer float period, and since escrow balances usually grow as a portfolio ages because of tax increases, T&I balances can continue to contribute to portfolio value as all other income components appear to be declining. A loss of value occurs when interest on escrows is required to be paid to the mortgagor. Currently, interest on escrow is regulated by the individual states (see Table 16.2). However, federal legislation has been proposed that would require the payment of a fixed amount of interest to all mortgagors. If the legislation is passed, the value of the T&I interest component will decrease and to the extent that a servicer derives a great deal of value from escrows, the passage of a national interest-on-escrow law would have a material adverse impact on the value of servicing. For example, the impact on the hypothetical portfolio described in Table 16.3 is a 25 percent deterioration in value.

Ancillary and Other Income This category of income refers to late fees, assumption fees, optional insurance fees, and prepayment penalties. Of these, late charges are the most significant, and contribute approximately 5 percent of the income on an average GNMA portfolio, for example. This component can contribute significantly to value if pursued. In other words, late fees, as well as optional insurance, can add

Table 16.2   States Requiring Interest on Escrow

State	Interest Rate
California	2%
Connecticut	4% on loans before 10/1/85, 5.25% on loans after 10/1/85
Iowa	Passbook savings rate
Maine	3%
Maryland	Greater of passbook savings rate or 3%
Massachusetts	Determined by mortgagee annually
Minnesota	5%
New Hampshire	5%
New York	2% (Set annually by the Banking Board)
Oregon	4.5%
Rhode Island	4%
Utah	5.25%
Vermont	5% or, for institutions that offer savings accounts, the savings account rate
Wisconsin	5.25%

Table 16.3   Hypothetical Portfolio (Base Case)

BALANCE	$1 billion	SERVICE FEE	0.25%
NUMBER OF LOANS	10,000	SVC. COST/LOAN	$50 per annum
MORTGAGE TYPE	Conventional	AVERAGE ESCROW	1.00%
AVERAGE LOAN	$100,000	NO INTEREST ON ESCROW PAID	
NOTE RATE	8.25%	DELINQUENCIES	3.00%
ORIGINAL TERM	360	FORECLOSURES	0.75%
REMAINING TERM	336	AMORTIZATION	12-year SYD

value if the servicer makes an effort to either collect what is due or to cross sell other financial products to mortgagors. It is important to keep in mind, however, that income earned through late fees does not replace the income lost as a result of lost float on P&I or T&I advances. Also, the benefit of late-fee income can be partially offset by the increased cost to service delinquent accounts.

Components of Expense

The elements of income will not be realized to their fullest extent if expenses are not kept in check. That is to say, the income earned from service fees, float, and ancillary fees can be quickly eroded if the costs related to servicing the portfolio are not controlled. As a portfolio ages, service fee income is reduced. Therefore, if the expenses are not reduced proportionately or if economies of scale are not achieved, the market value of a portfolio could well exceed its economic value to the holder. By this we mean that the unit cost used by a potential acquirer of a portfolio would be less than the actual cost of the present owner. Therefore, all other things being equal, the portfolio would be of greater value to the potential buyer.

Servicing Costs The servicing cost essentially reflects the direct unit cost associated with servicing a loan, excluding amortization and fore-closure expense. Historic servicing costs have been made available and appear to be relatively good indicators of what it costs to service a loan.

Currently, the figures range from $60 to $80 per loan per year for a conventional fixed-rate loan and $75 to $95 for an adjustable-rate loan (ARM) although some servicers report that it costs them no more to service an ARM than a fixed-rate loan. Bidders on servicing may use unit costs less than these numbers, which would reflect their perception of scale economies attainable through acquisition, with the concomitant reduction in excess capacity that may exist at the time of the acquisition. Commercial and multifamily loan servicing costs range between $750 and $1000 and (depending on the investor's servicing requirements) could be in excess of $1,000 per loan. The unit cost used in the valuation should be adjusted for the impact of inflation. The aggregate single-family unit cost is distributed across the functional areas as follows: Customer service, 25 percent; collections and foreclosures (excluding REO losses), 25 percent; payment processing and billing, 20 percent; administration, 15 percent; data processing, 12 percent; and document filing and record retention, 3 percent.

To the extent that a purchaser's overall portfolio changes with respect to loan type, increased delinquencies, or geographic diversification as a result of an acquisition, he or she will very likely experience an increase in costs related to servicing. For example, it costs about ten times as much to service a loan that is ninety days delinquent as it does to service a current loan. These sometimes not so subtle changes, if ignored, can add to a servicer's expenses. The ability to recognize the factors that lead to increased expenses, as well as remaining mindful of the fact that almost every aspect of servicing requires some type of expenditure, is the key to maintaining costs and effectively forecasting expenses over the long term. The prospect of increased servicing costs over time looms large as the national and state governments promulgate legislation that will not only increase actual costs associated with servicing loans, but will also impose additional costs associated with compliance.

Foreclosure Costs Foreclosure costs are driven by foreclosure rates, which in turn are driven by defaults. Default activity, in turn, is closely related to the amount of equity a borrower has in a house. If the equity in the house drops below its market value, there is a strong incentive to mail in the keys to the investor. As a rule, default rates are tied to the age of the loan. For example, default rates on conventional loans reach their peak in years three and four. Foreclosure expenses are directly proportional to the foreclosure percentage and are directly related to who bears the exposure in the event of default. For instance, loans sold "with recourse" require that the servicer retain the collateral risk and loans sold on a nonrecourse basis transfer all credit risk to the investor. These two types of portfolios should be valued separately, utilizing an arbitrage pricing methodology for the recourse segment or a substantial increase in the foreclosure cost estimate for the recourse loans. Another illustration of foreclosure cost variance occurs with loans that have a higher frequency of default. FHA and VA loans, largely as a result of less equity contributed by the borrower, often default at a higher rate than conventional loans. This higher frequency and the servicer's exposure to VA No-Bids puts these two product types in a higher foreclosure cost category. The cost assumption also increases as a result of higher administrative expenses associated with FHA and VA loan defaults.

Foreclosure costs are part and parcel of servicing and are not likely to be avoided. Most servicers have the ability to forecast foreclosures to a certain extent, and if foreclosure efforts are well managed, foreclosure losses can be kept to a minimum.

Other Costs Loan setup costs, amortization expense, and interest on escrows are examples of some of the other expenses incurred by a servicer. If economies of scale are achieved, these expenses can be absorbed with little effect on the servicer's bottom line. They, too, require oversight and management in order to keep them in check. Setup costs usually vary between $10 and $15 a loan. Interest on escrow is discussed in a later section.

Amortization The more accelerated the amortization, all other things being equal, the higher will be the net present value of the portfolio. FASB Technical Bulletin 87-3 provides, among other things, guidance on accounting for mortgage servicing rights. While amortization is a noncash expense, it does have an effect on the economic value of the portfolio. The amortization expense is a function of the length of the amortization period and the amortization method that is used (i.e., Sum of the Year's Digit, Straight Line, etc.). Standardization of the duration and method of amortization is currently being proposed in Congress. Suffice it to say that the 14-year straight-line amortization being proposed in Congress has no relation to the economic life of most servicing assets.

Computing the Net Present Value

Once the income and expense elements have been forecasted, the after-tax cash flows are computed by adding the amortization expense to the net after-tax income. The after-tax cash flows are then discounted at a desired yield to arrive at the net present value or purchase price. The purchase price for servicing is usually quoted as a percentage of the unpaid principal balance.

Discount rate Any discussion of discount rates should begin by saying that servicing yields are, to a large degree, a function of supply and demand. For example, the number of portfolios on the market is at a much more manageable level than at the height of RTC activity in 1990 and 1991. As a result, yields have declined somewhat and prices have increased. The appropriate discount rate to use for the present value calculation is subjective, but is effectively the yield one needs to obtain from the investment. The discount rate can be a function of a firm's hurdle rate or marginal cost of capital plus a spread, or it can be based on a risk-adjusted spread over the Treasury yield curve. Often, a number of discount rates are used in order to model multiple future scenarios.

Presumably, the more "vanilla" a portfolio is, the lower the risk associated with the loans and the lower the desired yield. As a portfolio becomes more complex, the required rate of return will increase to reflect the added amount of perceived risk associated with the underlying loans. The realization that yields are market driven and should be changed to reflect what the market requires at a given point in time is vitally important. It is interesting to note that loans with higher servicing fees usually have a higher discount rate applied to their cash flows than those with lower servicing fees. For loans with identical characteristics except for the service fee, there is no rational explanation why the risk of the higher-service-fee loan is greater (and therefore requires a higher discount rate) than the loan with a lower service fee. The tendency of the market to value higher-service-fee portfolios at lower price multiples is referred to as compression. Participants in the secondary servicing market have a strong preference for portfolios with low service fees and manifest this preference in their choice of discount rate.

Prepayments Mortgage loan prepayment estimates are fundamental to a servicing portfolio analysis. The rate of prepayment has a profound effect on the value of servicing rights, as evidenced by the refinance wave of 1992. Lower interest rates create an incentive to refinance. Recent research by the Federal Home Loan Mortgage Corporation indicates, for example, that if interest rates decline by 100 basis points five years after a pool of conventional fixed-rate mortgages is originated, prepayments on those mortgages with at least 15 percent equity will increase from the normal rate of about 12 percent to 19 percent. An additional 100 basis point decline causes prepayment rates to go over 30 percent. Other research indicates that there is a strong relationship between prepayments and equity in the property. Notwithstanding periods of falling interest rates, there has been shown to be a direct relationship between equity buildup and prepayments; as one increases so does the other.

There are many other variables available for the explanation and prediction of prepayment rates. Demographics, loan type, geographic location of the loan, economic conditions, and the age of the loan are all factors that affect prepayments. Even attributes specific to the borrower—financial condition, mobility, and interest-rate sensitivity— have important implications for prepayment rates. While many borrowers are likely to refinance in a period of falling interest rates, differing degrees of interest-rate sensitivity among individuals will cause other borrowers to choose *not* to prepay—or, at least, to be slow in doing it. The estimation of prepayment rate is not an exact science and may never be; however, for the evaluator of servicing rights it is key to the valuation process.

Today, the Public Securities Association (PSA) Standard Prepayment Model is probably the most widely used. It assumes 6 percent of a given portfolio per year will prepay each year after the third year. Expressed as a multiple, 100 percent PSA equates to 6 percent payoff, 200 percent PSA is 12 percent, and so on. The estimated prepayment is based on a loan's interest rate relative to the expected level of interest rates over the life of the loan. Prepayments can be modeled on a static basis, using scenario analysis, or applying the power of option-adjusted spread technology. Obviously, the greater the number of interest paths that can be incorporated into the analysis, the more useful the output of the model will be.

Valuation of ARM-Servicing Portfolios The valuation of ARM portfolios often results in cash flow values of 50 to 70 percent of the value of a comparable fixed-rate package. The reason for this lies in the fact that three of the four primary determinants of a portfolio's cash flow stream are significantly inferior with ARMs relative to fixed-rate product. ARMs are typically subject to higher prepayment rates, are costlier to service, and suffer higher delinquency/foreclosure rates. These disadvantages are not offset by any concessions in the fourth major factor— servicing fees.

There are a number of theories to explain the rapid payoff characteristics of ARMs. First, a flat or inverted yield curve would cause fully indexed ARM rates to approach or exceed long-term rates. Since mortgagors seem to have a strong preference for fixed-rate financing, this would cause borrowers to refinance into fixed-rate mortgages. Secondly, ARM indices, because they are averages, tend to lag rate movements when the yield curve shifts downward. When long-term rates fall quickly, ARM borrowers find it possible to refinance into fixed-rate mortgages at a lower rate than what they would experience at the current fully indexed rate. Third, ARM borrowers are often more mobile. Many home purchasers who do not expect to remain in a house for more than two or three years find it more cost effective to borrow at an adjustable rate, especially if there is a teaser involved. Lastly, under certain circumstances, borrowers may find it advantageous to pay off fully indexed ARMs and refinance into other adjustable-rate loans with attractive teaser rates even if they have no plans to move.

Higher unit servicing costs are associated with ARMs, especially those with negative amortization and short adjustment intervals and the relatively few that have adjustable servicing fees. Today, some servicers estimate that ARMs are no more costly to service than fixed-rate products, due to the enhancement of their systems to accommodate ARM requirements. The majority of servicers, however, still feel that unit servicing costs are higher for ARMs than for a comparable fixed-rate loan. Many secondary servicing market participants estimate the difference to be on the order of $15 per loan. Since many ARMs are newer and have high average balances, the added cost has had a relatively minimal impact on the present value of the servicing.

Additional factors that affect the valuation of ARM servicing are adjustable servicing fees and convertibility. If the servicing fee fluctuates over time, this must be taken into account when modeling the cash flows. It is possible to overcompensate for this added uncertainty, which results in lower values for portfolios with adjustable servicing fees. Also, if an ARM has a convertibility option, and a servicer deems the probability of conversion to be high, he or she would presumably modify the payoff assumption to reflect those currently being used for fixed-rate mortgages.

Prices for ARM servicing are considerably more volatile than those for fixed-rate products. ARM prices are extremely sensitive to anticipated prepayment rates, which are in turn greatly affected by the interest rate environment. The fact that the ARM market is thinner than the fixed-rate market also adds to its price volatility. As with fixed-rate loans, ARM prices tend to strengthen when buyers anticipate relatively little run-off and when the yield curve is expected to remain positively (normally) sloped. On the other hand, abrupt interest rate declines or an inverted yield curve bring higher short-term rates (upon which the ARM rates are indexed) than long-term rates (which are closely related to fixed-rate mortgage interest rates) and lead to a high level of refinancing of ARMs. Buyers then adjust by increasing their prepayment rate expectations, often to three or four times PSA or more. The result is a drop in the value they place on ARM portfolios.

Multifamily Servicing Valuation Multifamily servicing valuation follows the same methodology as fixed and ARM servicing, but there are a few differences. Because multifamily portfolios are made up of fewer and larger loans, it is customary to value each loan separately. Unlike a single-family portfolio, the behavior of one loan can significantly alter the performance of a multifamily portfolio. For instance, while multifamily loans prepay for the same reasons that single-family loans prepay, the rate at which they prepay can vary significantly from project to project, depending on the type of loan. For example, an FHLMC Plan B loan carries a five-year lock-out period during which the mortgagor cannot prepay. This provides a guarantee to the mortgagee that the loan will be in existence for at least that long.

A large number of multifamily loans are originated with government assistance under certain sections of the National Housing Act. The section of the Act, therefore, is a determining factor in estimating the life of the portfolio. For example, loans made under Section 232 may carry an interest rate subsidy, depending on which state the property is located in. Since the mortgagor is indifferent to fluctuations in interest rates, this type of loan will have unique payoff characteristics. The loan will probably be refinanced when it becomes time to rehab the building, however. The advent of Wall Street's interest in commercial and multifamily loan securitization has made modeling prepayments even more difficult. Multi-tranche, LIBOR-based structures have materially changed traditional notions about the prepayment behavior of multifamily loans.

Service fees are often lower on multifamily loans, which leads to relatively more benefit from other income, most notably interest on escrows and reserves for replacement. More experienced multifamily servicers gain from other ancillary income sources as well.

Costs to service multifamily loans are considerably higher than the costs associated with single-family loans. This is largely a result of the number of activities involved in multifamily servicing and the labor-intensive nature of the activities, such as the review of financials and annual property inspections. In recent years, the costs have increased even more as investors, in particular, have further expanded their servicing requirements. With the increase in expenses as a result of the new requirements, the valuation process is further complicated based on the uncertainty of future increases in costs. To exacerbate the already increased costs to service multifamily loans, lenders who had entered the coinsurance program have experienced losses that have threatened their servicing portfolios, and in some cases their entire businesses.

Option-Adjusted Spread Analysis   Option-adjusted spread (OAS) analysis can be a valuable complement to static and scenario analysis, since servicing cash flows are strongly affected by changes in interest rates. OAS analysis can be used to assess the cost to the investor of variations in servicing cash flows caused by changes in interest rates. The OAS calculation involves valuing the portfolio over a large number of randomly generated interest rate paths. The effects of interest rate variation on cash flows are then factored into the analysis. OAS provides a measure of how much impact interest rate variation and resulting changes in prepayments are likely to have on the value of the portfolio.

Another way of thinking of OAS is the expected spread over Treasury yield curve after adjusting for the prepayment risk inherent in the asset. An OAS model simulates a set of future interest rate paths. Usually, 200-500 paths are used to obtain good convergence in the model. Each interest rate path will have its associated cash-flow path. The entire set of cash-flow paths represents the current expected cash flows to be received from the portfolio. These cash flows are then valued using a standard discounting method. Unfortunately, most OAS models do not allow users to measure the impact of varying interest rates on default and reinvestment risk. The OAS model, in essence, values the servicing and determines the expected price sensitivity of the current servicing asset, as well as indicating the amount of imbedded prepayment risk and the expected rate of return over a range of interest and prepayment rate scenarios.

As a practical matter, when the output from a static cash flow model and an OAS model are compared, the OAS model usually results in a higher price. This is because OAS is unbiased in its measurement of the impact of prepayment risk on expected investment returns. In other words, it assigns as likely a probability that interest rates will rise as that interest rates will fall. In the static scenario case, there is always a predisposition on the part of the user to overestimate the likelihood of interest rates falling and underestimate the likelihood of interest rates rising. An easy way to interpret the output of an OAS model is to think of it as the amount by which the IRR should be reduced to obtain a yield that has been adjusted for the adverse impact of interest rate variation.

PRICE SENSITIVITY

The principal variables that impact the value of a servicing portfolio are payoff speed, discount rate, and cost to service a loan. Foreclosure cost, foreclosure rate, and rate of earnings on escrow are also key variables. Compounding the issue of trying to figure out the sensitivity of a servicing portfolio to changes in payoff speeds is the fact that servicing rights have large negative convexities. That is, they lose more during periods of falling interest rates than they gain when interest rates rise. This asymmetry, as well as price differences based on changes in other variables, is indicated in Table 16.4.

While the value of servicing rights may be largely driven by supply and demand, the intrinsic value is derived from the actual portfolio characteristics and the forecast of future economic events. For example, if the analyst foresees interest rates rising in the future, he or she will use a slower prepayment assumption which, *ceteris paribus*, will result in a higher value for the portfolio. A forecast of higher interest rates will also impact the relative amount of income derived from interest on escrow and impound accounts. The higher the expected level of interest rates, the greater will be the benefit of float. During periods of extremely high rates, the cash management function becomes of critical importance to the manager of servicing assets. To the extent that

Table 16.4   The Impact on Pricing of Change in Key Valuation Variables

Scenario	Prices (% of UPB)
Base Case	1.11
14-Year Straight Line Amortization	1.05
1% Decline in Interest Rates	.84
1% Increase in Interest Rates	1.30
$250/Loan Decrease in Foreclosure Cost	1.12
$250/Loan Increase in Foreclosure Cost	1.10
$5/Loan Increase in Ancillary Income	1.13
1% Decrease Interest on Earnings	1.05
1% Increase Interest on Earnings	1.17
50% Reduction in Average T&I	.99
50% Increase in Average T&I	1.22
$5/Loan Decrease in Unit Cost	1.14
$5/Loan Increase in Unit Cost	1.08
1% Decrease in Discount Rate	1.15
1% Increase in Discount Rate	1.07

the servicer is able to accelerate remittances and lag outflows, the benefit of float can be maximized. Linear programming models are often utilized to optimize both the "remoteness" of the disbursement facility and the centralized lockbox. An increase of 1 percent in the interest rate paid on escrows increases the value of the hypothetical portfolio by about 5 percent.

Since most of the relationships among the variables is nonlinear, it is extremely important to be cognizant of the effect that each has on the other. Keeping abreast of current market assumptions, as well as utilizing first-hand experience with one's own portfolio, is fundamental to portfolio valuation. Taking into consideration that more than 33 percent of the typical portfolio's cash flows are realized in the first three years of its life, it is evident that an understanding of the impact of changes in certain key variables on price is essential to the successful valuation of servicing.

The factors that influence value range from whether or not a portfolio is recourse or nonrecourse to whether one is discounting cash flows on a monthly or a yearly basis. Since the relationship among the variables is nonlinear, some of the results obtained when valuing a portfolio may be counterintuitive. For example, very old portfolios, those with 15 or more years of seasoning, produce a higher present value when the discount rate is increased. Normally, increasing the discount rate decreases the present value; but since older portfolios have a larger number of periods of negative cash flow, increasing the discount rate decreases the impact of the later years' negative cash flows on the present value. Consequently, the higher the discount rate used to present value the portfolio, the higher will be the value.

As stated earlier, the prepayment forecast is extremely important in valuing servicing because the major servicing income components are tied to either the balances outstanding or the number of loans remaining in the portfolio. Since no one can predict the course of future interest rates with any degree of certainty, it is important to use a valuation methodology that incorporates as many interest rate scenarios as possible. The OAS technology discussed in the previous section is a good way to do this. Other factors influencing price are the amount of ancillary income, how the portfolio is amortized, the loan quality of the underlying collateral, economic conditions in the geographic area where the loans are located, the type of loan product, the purpose of the loan when it's originated (i.e., owner-occupied, investor-owned, refinance, etc.), the property type and the loan-to-value ratio.

The treatment of late fees and foreclosure costs, for instance, can also have a significant impact on the value of loan servicing. As the number of delinquent loans increases, ancillary income increases (assuming that the mortgagors who are late are paying their late charge) and as ancillary income increases, portfolio value will increase. One has to keep in mind, however, that late-fee income is offset partially by lost float income and by interest expense on any principal and interest advances that may be required. Additionally, a higher delinquency rate usually leads to higher foreclosures, which increases costs because a default subjects the servicer to lost interest and substantial administrative expense. In other words, the results from a valuation model must be tempered by common sense and interpreted in light of past experience.

A factor that is often overlooked by investors in servicing is reinvestment risk. Because as much as one third of a portfolio's value is returned to the investor in the first few years of its life and because users of static cash flow models usually, if not always, assume that monies are reinvested at the discount rate used in the valuation, one must consider the possibility of reinvesting at a yield lower than the original discount rate. Under this scenario, the effective return on investment will be lower than the expected return. Yields on servicing are still at a substantial spread above other investments of similar risk. If one is unable to redeploy assets into other servicing investments at a comparable yield, then the expected rate of return may be materially overstated.

THE MARKET TODAY

Currently, we are in an environment of declining interest rates, which has accelerated payoffs on fixed-rate mortgages. At the same time, a steepening positively sloped yield curve has decelerated payoffs on adjustable-rate mortgages. Soft real estate markets in many parts of the country have resulted in increased foreclosures, which increase the cost to servicers, especially for VA and recourse loans. The extreme imbalance between supply and demand created by the RTC's sales activities has been largely offset by new buyers of servicing attracted to the market by high yields.

Faced with a falling interest rate environment, the question is always asked, "Are servicing prices going higher or are they going lower?" The answer is that prices are going both ways. Since the key element in determining value is the prepayment assumption, many buyers of portfolios during periods of declining interest rates are either reluctant to bid at all, or factor higher prepayment assumptions into their price. This is especially true for portfolios with above-market interest rates. Current coupon portfolios, however, are commanding prices that are approaching levels not seen since 1987 and 1988.

There has been a trend over the last ten years for manufacturers of servicing rights (whether they be banks, thrifts, or mortgage banks) to focus more intently on their most valuable asset. Previously, management did not have the accounting systems that enable them to take servicing value into consideration in their production programs. Today, originators are focusing their efforts on loan products that will command the highest servicing premiums. Clearly, the market provides a strong incentive to concentrate on higher premium product, especially in light of the fact that the cost to originate a loan is the same no matter what the value of the servicing.

According to a recent survey, more than 40 percent of mortgage companies treat servicing as a tradable commodity. The same companies customarily sell servicing released or alternatively retain and then sell the servicing. By contrast, only 16 percent of thrifts are flexible enough to actively make the decision between holding servicing in portfolio or selling servicing released. Although servicing is the primary economic asset of the mortgage business, only 28 percent of the firms in the survey have implemented the use of servicing valuation software.

OUTLOOK

We anticipate that the trend toward a higher awareness of the value of the industry's primary asset will continue. As the market continues to mature, it will become more efficient. Plans are already in the works to deliver portfolios, provide for their valuation, and auction on an interactive basis through at least one of the national electronic mortgage information services. There is talk of someday securitizing loan servicing portfolios. Market practitioners will continue to explore and develop vehicles that will allow the investment in the interest-only component of the servicing stream, thus opening the market to an even larger audience of investors. Methods of valuation will continue to be upgraded and we will see more market participants utilizing OAS technology as they grow in their sophistication.

Advances in technology in connection with the actual servicing of the loans augurs well for increases in servicing prices. For example, it is estimated that the utilization of electronic imaging can cut approximately $15 per loan, per year, from the unit cost of loan servicing. For a large servicer whose unit cost is $60 per loan, this represents a reduction in cost of 25 percent. All other things being equal, a reduction in servicing costs of this magnitude will have a significant positive impact on value, especially for seasoned product.

The consolidation of servicing into fewer and fewer institutions will continue (see Table 16.5). The megaservicers today are servicing

Table 16.5 Top Ten Mortgage Servicers in Combined Servicing
Aggregate Portfolio Size 1988 Through 1992
(in millions)

Rank	1988	1989	1990	1991	1992
1	$45,600	$54,800	$66,100	$69,100	$64,600
2	$29,032	$34,346	$52,300	$56,000	$60,590
3	$24,676	$26,999	$35,585	$38,026	$42,484
4	$23,509	$26,376	$32,201	$35,741	$40,033
5	$19,204	$21,380	$27,242	$32,015	$34,118
6	$18,333	$17,466	$23,753	$29,211	$32,659
7	$15,511	$16,248	$23,740	$26,943	$32,273
8	$14,993	$13,857	$18,967	$22,390	$31,352
9	$13,738	$13,852	$18,688	$21,844	$30,027
10	$13,375	$13,723	$17,879	$21,034	$29,959
TOTAL	$217,971	$239,097	$316,455	$352,304	$398,095

Source: American Banker

portfolios of $30 billion or more. Some firms have stated goals of reaching $100 billion in servicing by the end of the decade. It is difficult at this time to assess the impact of such vast scale on unit costs but it will almost certainly be positive. Additionally, there are pending legislative and regulatory issues that will impact not only the market but also the price of servicing in the future.

For example, a bill currently in Congress would require that purchased mortgage servicing rights (PMSRs) be amortized over 14 years, using the straight line method. Enactment of the legislation would cause a 5 percent decrease in the price of the hypothetical portfolio described in Table 16.3. Another piece of pending legislation relates to interest on escrows and escrow accounting. The bill, which is essentially a national interest-on-escrow law, would require that interest be paid at the current passbook savings rate as defined by the U.S. Department of Housing and Urban Development (HUD). Although it is likely that enactment of the law would probably save the average consumer about $35 a year, it would also cause a drop in the value of the aforementioned portfolio of about 25 percent. Moreover, the escrow administration fee that the servicer currently charges the mortgagor (i.e., the interest on escrow) would be passed back to the consumer in another form along with the additional cost of compliance.

FASB 65 is, and has been, the primary accounting guidance regarding mortgage servicing rights. Among other things, it classifies servicing as an intangible asset and it allows purchased mortgage servicing rights to be capitalized, although it does not allow originated rights to be. The Mortgage Bankers Association (MBA) has petitioned the Federal Accounting Standards Board (FASB) to change mortgage servicing rights from an intangible to a tangible asset and to allow mortgage bankers to capitalize originated mortgage servicing. If the FASB makes the changes requested by MBA, expect to see a change in the supply and demand for servicing, which will probably have a positive impact in pricing of 5 to 10 percent of value over time.

The secondary market for mortgage servicing rights falls somewhere between that of mortgage-backed securities and mortgage derivative products such as IOs and POs. If servicing could be traded as a commodity (which it clearly is not) the spread between the bid and the ask would be relatively large. The market has experienced tremendous growth over the last ten years, and it will continue to grow throughout this decade. Absent any unforeseen legislative developments, participants will be afforded an even more efficient market in which to unlock the value created through the loan origination process. It remains to be seen whether or not nonregulated mortgage lenders and servicers will be able to escape the overregulation that has crippled the thrift industry. The American consumer has been the biggest beneficiary of what is the most vibrant market for housing finance in the world. The U.S. mortgage market is the child of an enlightened legislative and regulatory environment. We hope those in government keep this in mind as they face the challenges ahead. It would be a shame if regulation turned the beneficiaries into victims.

Chapter 17

THE ANALYSIS OF RISK

Hunter W. Wolcott
Chairman,
Reserve Financial Management Corp.
President & CEO,
RF/Spectrum Decision Science Corp.

THE NEED FOR RISK MANAGEMENT SYSTEMS

"To risk" means to expose to chance of loss. Known or accurately predicted losses are not risks: they are a calculated cost of doing business. In servicing, some risks begin with the choice made by mortgage lenders to retain servicing instead of opting for the risk-free choice of selling it.

For instance, prepayment risk stems from the chance that prepayment forecasts will not turn out to be fully on the mark. Similarly, default risk arises from the possibility that foreclosure probability or default severity will be worse than anticipated. Risk, by itself, is neither good nor bad. Lenders must assume some degree of risk, because a risk-free rate of return will not compensate for the costs of doing business and the value, of the capital. Lenders who survive and prosper will be those who get the best assistance from sophisticated management tools designed to help price loans and risks most effectively.

Portions of this article are excerpted from "Calculating Risks" by Hunter W. Wolcott, *Mortgage Banking*, May 1991, and "Managing a Slippery Asset" by Hunter W. Wolcott, *Mortgage Banking*, April 1993. Those portions reprinted by permission of *Mortgage Banking* magazine.

One such portfolio management system that has been created to help mortgage bankers is the RF/Spectrum™ Decision Support System, developed and offered by RF/Spectrum Decision Science Corp.

For six years, clients of RF/Spectrum have been assisted in making many types of management decisions. Here are some examples of the types of decisions and information that companies have used the system for:

♦ Decisions on selling servicing to meet accounting needs for income and to achieve the reduction of prepayment risk.

♦ Measurement of performance, condition, composition, and value of potential purchases.

♦ Evaluation of servicing department operating performance for such items as delinquency progression, borrower relationship retention, advances, and other analyses that are not otherwise immediately apparent.

♦ Pricing of new retail and wholesale production.

♦ Executive compensation decisions (often used to carry out a top-management bonus system that is based upon the change in the total value of the firm, including off-balance-sheet servicing items).

♦ Servicing hedging decisions. The system can evaluate whether a given hedging proposal is worth as much, or more, than it costs.

♦ Loan-level prepayment behavioral modeling and management. This feature allows users to correctly model the prepayment probability of every loan across multiple scenarios, the factors that predict prepayment, and defensive actions to retain the borrower relationship.

♦ Managing default risk with RF/Spectrum's unique loan-level Default Risk Subsystem (DRS™). DRS is used by lenders for buying and selling loans, evaluating merger candidates, setting and maintaining residential loan loss reserves, and in pricing servicing, especially types with recourse risk.

In mid-1992, this system was ported from the IBM mainframe environment and became available to end-users in a powerful desktop version operating under MS-DOS.

The role of a decision support system is to provide the insights, analysis, and guidance to take faster and better actions. The mortgage industry has many talented risk management specialists in secondary marketing, pipeline management, and hedging. But these tasks are highly challenging, and most specialized systems can handle only a few loans at a time.

The size and complexity of mortgage servicing portfolios, however, are beyond small systems' abilities. The sheer volume of data, lack of a central source, and the complexity of the decisions to be made requires large-scale technology to satisfy executives who require immediate actions.

RF/Spectrum is designed to analyze large portfolios by incorporating hundreds of pieces of information about each loan. RF/Spectrum considers dozens of key elements affecting demographic, behavioral, and real estate trends. An expert system within RF/Spectrum computes how these elements interact to help the lender evaluate risk. This chapter shows in detail how default, prepayment, and production-pricing probabilities can be forecast using a large-scale decision support system.

TYPE OF RISKS

All risks can be divided into two categories. Systematic risks are common to all mortgage assets. They are associated with broad economic trends or financial market conditions, such as the health of the national market and the movement of interest rates. Therefore, they cannot be diversified away. For example, falling mortgage rates hurt servicing values of existing loans by increasing prepayment expectations and shortening the expected lives of servicing assets.

Nonsystematic risks, by contrast, are specific to individual assets and can be reduced by intelligent diversification, or can be eliminated surgically, one loan at a time. Examples of nonsystematic risks are those produced by damaging regional housing market conditions, such as the fast prepays of California 1987 loans or the high defaults of Texas 1981 originations. Another example of nonsystematic risks would be those associated with higher loan- to-value ratios, a proven link to defaults.

An obvious example of nonsystematic risk control would be the underwriting of a prospective borrower. Although this process occurs just once in a loan's lifetime, the default risk is ongoing. Default risk is constantly shifting in response to changes in the borrowers' economic affairs or the condition of the real estate markets.

Mortgage risk management involves several components. First, it requires an identification and understanding of each risk in servicing or asset lending and how these risks interact to produce losses. In mortgage lending, these risks center in two areas: the performance of the real estate and the choices made by the borrower.

Second, it requires discovering the exact degree to which those factors are present in a given portfolio. This requires making a detailed analysis of portfolio composition and condition, sometimes integrating information from outside the servicing system, such as data from the origination system.

Third, it involves pricing risks and quantifying their true effect under various scenarios of the future. Risk-pricing is at the heart of risk management, and it requires the highest skills and best analytic tools.

Fourth, risk management requires acting to avoid, reduce, or transfer assets that do not provide sound, risk-adjusted rates of return. Only those assets that can meet the risk-adjusted return test should be retained. Risk-reducing actions include servicing released and bulk servicing sales, regional pooling of loans to increase flexibility to react to subsequent events, nonrecourse securitization, pool insurance, and hedging. Of course, each of these steps carries a cost. That cost must be weighed against the benefits achieved.

During the 1970s, mortgage products in the secondary market were simple, and ongoing housing price growth was an unquestioned assumption. Mortgage performance decisions were based on large, nationwide, mostly homogeneous pools of "benchmark" loans. Examples are FHA Sec 203(b) loans or the 30-year conventional fixed-rate loans in the private mortgage insurance companies' data bases. These benchmark portfolios closely resembled actual portfolios in many ways.

Recent years have brought three developments that demolished much of the simplicity of that earlier business environment. First, there was an amazing proliferation of mortgage product types, with adjustable-rate loans (ARMs), balloons, convertibles, 15-year products and many more. By the early 1990s these new product types accounted for more than 50 percent of all originations, relegating the "benchmark" 30-year, fixed-rate, fully amortizing loan to minority status. Portfolios today no longer resemble any benchmark group of loans against which mortgage bankers can gauge performance.

Second, loan quality risks increased. Underwriting standards were relaxed, while a sharply increased percentage of borrowers resorted to protection under bankruptcy laws to defend against complying with their mortgage debt obligations. Also, the "nationwide" real estate market vanished, along with the myth of uninterrupted property value increases. Differences appeared between regional markets as first one market, then another took punishing drops in real estate values in what became known as the "rolling recession."

Finally, the efficiency of the primary market for mortgage originations has increased. Innovative investors create new loan types with great speed as rate structures and borrowers' appetites change. The origination process is increasingly automated. That decreases the costs, time, and aggravation involved in refinance. Most lenders offer "no-points" and/or "no-cost" options, allowing borrowers to self-select themselves into classes of faster-reacting mortgage customers. The success of Collateralized Mortgage Obligations (CMOs) means that mortgage money will be priced wherever on the yield curve it is most attractive. That means that a drop in long-term rates is no longer a requirement for a refinance boom: a drop in short-term rates (or a steepening of the yield curve) is more than enough. This increased efficiency in mortgage originations means that borrowers can choose among nearly friction-free choices in managing their mortgage liability structure. This improvement comes at the potential expense of servicing investors, because it makes the imbedded prepayment option "in-the-money" more often.

RISK MANAGEMENT DECISION SUPPORT

Local market conditions are highly diverse, and new risk types evolve rapidly. This has led risk managers to demand loan-level decision support systems that can rapidly evaluate the unique pattern of predictive traits of each loan. "Idiosyncratic" analysis is the new standard for risk management, making older aggregated or cohort-group approaches obsolete.

Decision support systems are integrated structures that analyze, report, and distribute information to support the most advanced problem solving. To be practical, they must be "action-oriented," to provide fast, clear solutions to problems in servicing, production, and asset management. These systems use comprehensive, relational data bases—not merely information gleaned from servicing files—and make reports directly to managers, without programmers or intermediaries. They must also provide a fast, cost-effective alternative to expensive and time-consuming mainframe reporting languages.

Additionally, a good decision support system should provide ease of training for managers and other staff who do not have extensive computer backgrounds. Last, the benefits and cost of a decision support system must be directly measurable and should provide a large multiple of value received versus cost involved.

The RF/Spectrum decision support system reflects those characteristics and can be used to evaluate future prepayment, default, and
pricing risk. It can also track cross-period items such as delinquency
progression and past prepayments.

EVALUATING AND PRICING PREPAYMENT RISK

The value of mortgage servicing is so integral to mortgage banking that
proper valuation is crucial. All servicers face this question: "How do I
value servicing rights and correctly price prepayment risk in the face
of volatility and uncertainty?" Part of the answer is straightforward:
Avoid static-case valuations. Use only multiple-scenario assumption
sets, and the idea of "expected value." Expected value is the probability-
weighted average of several possible scenario valuations.

Prepayments stem from three basic choices made by borrowers:
demographic prepayments stemming mostly from home sales, economic prepayment due to refinance or loan payment-in-full, and default. **The American Housing Survey**[1] (AHS) of the U.S. Census Bureau
reports recent mortgage prepayments over four years, in successive
two-year periods. As the AHS chart in Figure 17.1 shows, each of these
prepayment components is material.

Prepayments from Homeowner Mobility Previous   modeling   techniques have largely relied upon the basic model of the Public Securities
Association (PSA), which describes prepayments as a function of loan
life: prepayments are slow during early months, accelerating toward
an equilibrium rate from age 30 months to maturity. Information derived from the AHS shows that the PSA analysis may be incomplete.

The AHS shows that homeowner mobility (and prepays that result
from home sales) are highest during the first two years following move-
in (see Figure 17.2). The longer a homeowner stays in a home, the more
likely he or she is to remain. Specifically, the AHS shows that of all
homeowners who bought a home in 1987, 15 percent had moved by
1989. (As a comparison, 10 percent of all 1987 homeowners had moved
by the end of that two-year period.) Results from the 1985-1987 survey

---

1.   The American Housing Survey (AHS) is a biannual review conducted by the U.S.
      Bureau of the Census. AHS results from the 1985-1987 period and the 1987-1989
      period are analyzed and tabulated by Michael S. Carliner and David D'Alessandris
      in "Home Owner Mobility and Mortgage Prepayment," *Housing Economics* magazine,
      a publication of the National Association of Home Builders, September 1992. Their
      insightful analysis is quoted by permission. The researchers caution that because
      homeowners that respond to the survey may not understand the terms of their
      mortgage, and may provide inaccurate information about other variables as well,
      these results should only be considered suggestive, not definitive. The AHS does
      not measure partial curtailments, delinquency, or default.

**Figure 17.1   Mortgage Prepayments by Reason American
                 Housing Survey: Two-Year Rates**

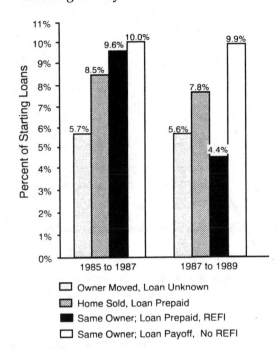

are virtually identical. At face value, the AHS findings suggest an average mortgage life of 6.7 years, far lower than the 14.6 years calculated by prepayments at 100 percent of the PSA model. While some methods in the survey may make broad findings difficult, the PSA model clearly does not sufficiently describe homeowner behavior. Demographic prepayments can be indirectly measured by home sales per capita in local markets. The more active a market is, the higher its home sales per capita will be, and the faster loans will prepay. In submarkets, census demographics accurately pinpoint areas of high homeowners' mobility which is of great value in finding prepayment propensity.

Prepayment by refinance Refinance prepayment is a behavior that requires that the borrower be *willing* and *able* to execute. The borrowers' willingness to refinance requires that there be economic gain, such as equity cash-out, lower rates, or lower payments. The benefits must be in balance with cost in time and money. A drop in long-term rates allows borrowers to refinance a 30-year, fixed-rate loan with a cheaper

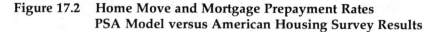

**Figure 17.2   Home Move and Mortgage Prepayment Rates
PSA Model versus American Housing Survey Results**

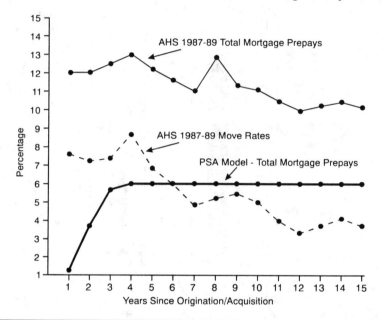

one. Also, a positive shift in the yield curve will encourage refinancing from a 30-year, fixed-rate loan into any of the popular "intermediate" products. Borrowers have many complicated refinance choices. They can get a new one-year adjustable-rate loan, a 15-year, fixed-rate loan, a loan from their stockbroker at the prime rate, or an attractive new convertible product. Refinance choices are also affected by information that only the borrowers have, such as their prospects for continued employment and how long they plan to stay in their home.

But not all borrowers have an equal *ability* to refinance. Home values, and especially the borrowers' adjusted loan-to-value ratio (ALTV) hold the key to gauging that ability (see Figure 17.3). RF/Spectrum has developed the RF Home Equity Index™, an empirical measure of borrowers' equity in all major housing markets. This measure largely explains the regional nature of mortgage prepays. RF/Spectrum's sophisticated algorithms scale prepayments to loan type, interest rates, local and regional housing markets, adjusted loan-to-value ratio, loan type, and several other characteristics. The ATLV-prepayment linkage was first proven by RF/Spectrum Decision Science Corp. in its publication *Predicting & Understanding Regional Mortgage Prepayments, Miami, FL, March 1992.*

Figure 17.3   Prepayment Index: Acutal Observations versus Predicted Values Loans = Conventional FRM Only

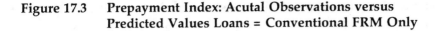

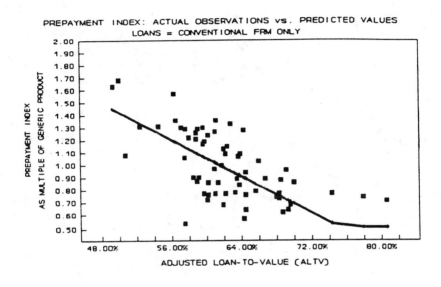

MULTISCENARIO PREPAYMENT ANALYSIS

A static case valuation is one in which the valuation is computed under the assumption that key variables such as market interest rates, prepayment and default patterns will not change over the life of the loan. This approach is the standard for beginning analysis, but its basic premise that interest rates and prepayments never change is wholly unrealistic. Static-case valuations predicting prepayment behavior are misleading because the effect of prepayment risk on servicing is extremely non-linear. That is, declining rates hurt servicing values far more than increasing rates help them. This "negative convexity" is one reason it is crucial to use multiple scenarios of rates, in a pattern that assumes rates go unchanged (the "base" case), higher and lower.

Figure 17.4 shows why this effect occurs. The slope of expected prepayment rates is usually very shallow for loans whose note rates are much higher or lower than "current" coupon. But, loans just at or above current coupon rate (cal. d "cusp" coupons) have very sharply

Figure 17.4   Prepayment Model—Selected Items in Percent PSA

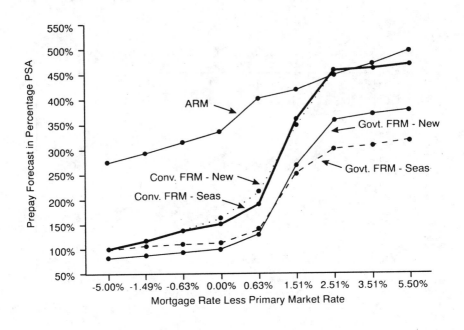

upward sloping prepayment rates. That means that small decreases in interest rates cause a large increase in prepayment expectations for a cusp coupon loan.

Figure 17.5 shows this negative convexity translated into servicing values under seven alternate scenarios: rates unchanged, and up and down 300 basis points in 100 basis point steps. Current coupon loans have prepayment rate projections that are near the lowest they can get. Typically, a new conventional loan will receive a forecast rate of 130 percent to 150 percent PSA, while a government loan might be expected to prepay at 100 percent to 130 percent PSA. Sustained rates below 100 percent PSA are very unusual. But, in a declining rate environment, prepayment rates can soar. Prepays at observed rates over 1,000 percent PSA have occurred several times during the refinance boomlets of the late 1980s and early 1990s. That causes losses of 50 percent or more of servicing values. When rates rise, prepayment expectations for current coupon loans slow a little, and servicing value rises a small amount. In constructing an expected valuation of servicing, the risk manager creates a spread of alternate scenarios, such as those in Figure 17.5. The value that results from each is calculated using a prepayment model such as the one in RF/Spectrum. Then, the probability of each scenario occurring would be computed, using an assumption of interest rate volatility and investment horizon as inputs. The value of each scenario would be multiplied by the likelihood of its occurrence, and the resulting values summed. RF/Spectrum executes this analysis automatically for up to 20 scenarios. Some investors also do option-adjusted spread (OAS) analyses on servicing assets. This prepayment-specific technique is very attractive for interest-only (IO) derivative investments that behave similarly to servicing. But, it is limited in its general usefulness for servicing valuation because so many other factors not correlated with interest rates or prepayments influence servicing values. For example, default probability and severity modeling requires an entirely different kind of scenario analysis, one which is very difficult to combine with the prepayment-only approach of OAS.

Figure 17.5   Servicing Performance under Alternate Interest Rate Scenarios

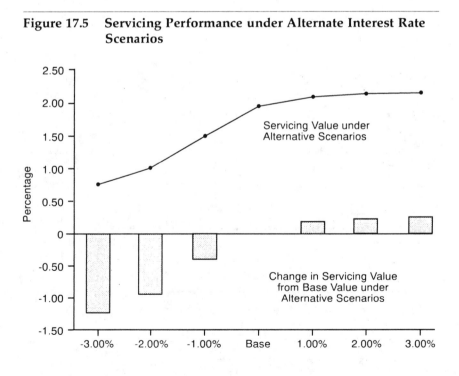

THE IMPACT OF CHANGING REGIONAL
REAL ESTATE MARKETS

Housing prices in some of the nation's most volatile housing markets
have changed directions, with some very important effects on both
prepayments and defaults. Although these changes have been widely
reported, they have not yet been reflected in valuation practices for
loans or servicing.

To illustrate how important these changes will be to the way loans
and servicing are valued, consider the case of Hyper Valley, California,
the nation's only totally homogeneous (and mostly fictitious) community. All the homes in Hyper Valley are the same, and they've had some
amazing changes in value over the past decade. Figure 17.6 shows the
value of homes in Hyper Valley (line, scale right), and the year-to-year
changes in values (bars, scale left). Values grew impressively from
$131,000 in 1982 to a peak over $245,000 in 1989. Then, values slumped
to a December 31, 1992, median price of $211,000. (Readers familiar with

Figure 17.6   Hyper Valley, California

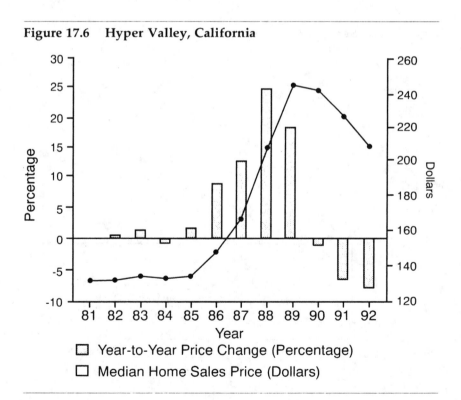

☐ Year-to-Year Price Change (Percentage)
☐ Median Home Sales Price (Dollars)

California values will recognize that this price pattern fits some of the state's largest markets!)

Every home in Hyper Valley is worth $211,000 in December 1992, but the owners' circumstances are quite different. The buyers who paid $131,500 in 1982 are still feeling superior. The buyers who paid $245,000 for homes in 1989 have already lost $34,000 of equity. Those buyers, and their lenders, are becoming nervous. Figure 17.7 shows why.

Naturally, every home in Hyper Valley has a mortgage. But, the prepayment and default performance of the loans depends greatly upon the home price action. All the first mortgages in Hyper Valley were 85 percent original loan-to-value (OLTV) when made, but the alternations of home prices have bent the *real* LTVs all around. When an 85 percent OLTV loan was made in 1982, its beginning balance was only $112,000. By 1989, similar 85 percent OLTV loans had a starting balance $208,000. When these 85 percent OLTVs are adjusted for 1992's home prices, the adjusted LTV (ALTV) ranges from *49 percent* for 1982 loans to *97 percent* for the 1989 crop.

Figure 17.7 Hyper Valley, California

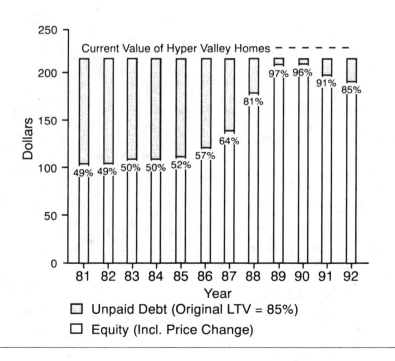

Unpaid Debt (Original LTV = 85%)
Equity (Incl. Price Change)

Obviously, these mortgages will default and prepay in dramatically different ways. The trick is quantifying the correlation between the performance of real estate and the behavior of borrowers. The mortgage insurance companies' studies long ago provided an accurate correlation between ALTV and ultimate rates of foreclosure. Reserve Financial's proprietary research has proven exactly how prepayments are efficiently linked to an ALTV prepayment function as well.

Figure 17.8 shows how these loans can be expected to **prepay** (line; scale right) and **default** (bar; scale left), compared with industry benchmarks. The MI companies' benchmark loan is a 30-year, fixed-rate, fully amortizing conforming loan at an average of 85 percent OLTV (a perfect match to Hyper Valley!). Its foreclosure rate establishes the benchmark. The benchmark prepayment is a nationwide pool of FNMA/FHLMC/ GNMA MBS. An index of 1.5, or 150 percent, means a loan is 1.5 times as likely as the benchmark to default or prepay. *The chart shows that prepayments and defaults vary inversely: rising values = high prepays/low defaults, falling values = low prepays/high defaults.*

Hyper Valley is hypothetical, but the huge changes in home prices, defaults, and prepayments are not. They're real, and are trends that will

Figure 17.8   Hyper Valley, California

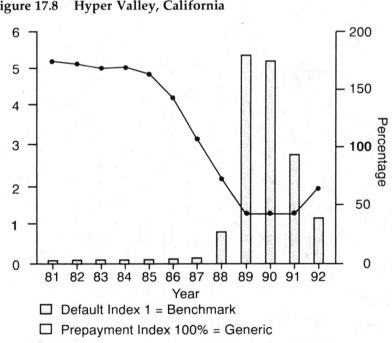

remain in progress for several years. Many of the nation's most important markets are experiencing major reversals in price cycles. Midwest markets and those in many parts of the South are currently going up fast, while the super-hot markets of the far West are coming down. California and Hawaii, the fast-pay champs of 1986–1991, will be the slow-pay markets of 1993 and 1994. They may also be the emerging markets for default loss concerns, eclipsing the New England/Texas scares of the 1980s.

The rolling real estate recession shows no sign of abating. In early 1993, the Cold War "Peace Dividend" is being realized in layoffs by defense contractors and base closures. All these events focus new pressures on highly localized markets. These issues will make residential loan loss issues a principal concern for risk managers. RF/Spectrum allows risk managers to run multiple scenarios that isolate either default issues or interest rate risks for each loan in the portfolio. These are used for setting loan-loss reserves for existing loan or servicing portfolio, or pricing new loan products.

PRICING DEFAULT RISKS

Pricing default risks requires three major components: finding the probability of default, calculating the estimated severity of the loss, and present valuing the future loss stream into an expected loss number.

Estimating Default Probability

Default probability has two major components: real estate values and loan-level risks—the most important of which are loan-to-value ratio (LTV) and its companion, ALTV. Default probability is calculated by RF/Spectrum using default experience from a nationwide benchmark pool of loans, stratified by original LTV. The system then adjusts the benchmark probability to the idiosyncrasies of each individual loan by using 14 different multiplicative default probability indices (DPIs). Some examples of DPIs are:

- ◆ *Housing Markets:* Home price growth is expected to be faster in some regions than others. Strong price growth reduces default probability and vice versa.

- ◆ *Loan-Type DPIs:* Adjustable-rate loans are riskier than fixed-rate loans. Balloons and graduated payment programs also are more default-prone. Faster-amortizing 15-year loans are less risky, and so forth.

♦ *Property type DPIs:* Two-, three-, and four-family homes rely more on rental income than does single-family detached housing. They are considered riskier for that reason. PUD home values can be hurt by a deterioration in the development that is independent of the performance of an individual borrower.

♦ *Loan Purpose DPIs:* Rate/term refinance is less risky than a cash-out refinance.

♦ *Documentation standard:* Low document and "No-doc" loans are deemed far riskier than their fully documented counterparts.

♦ *Loan Status:* RF/Spectrum is, of course, sensitive to the loan's current or delinquent status. A loan already 60 days past due, for instance, is obviously more likely to default than a current loan. But, even loans in foreclosure often reinstate, so status is not a binary issue.

These DPIs are multiplicative: a DPI of 1.5 means that a loan is 150 percent as likely to default as a "benchmark" loan. A DPI less than 1.00 means a loan is less risky than the benchmark. A combination of riskier DPIs (such as a high-LTV, two-family home with a balloon loan in a worsening market) can result in risk-weights 3 to 10 times the benchmark loan.

Estimating Default Severity

The probable loss stemming from a default is independent of the probability of its occurrence. Loss is based upon several factors that need to be calculated separately for each future period (vectored). Borrowers' original equity as a down payment is the starting factor. Next is the gain or loss in home prices from the date of origination to date of default (called historical appreciation). Since prices in most markets are changing continuously, this number needs to be recalculated for each future period (future appreciation). RF/Spectrum does monthly calculations of value and loss. To these numbers must be added interest losses for the expected foreclosure and sale period. This number varies by state due to differences in local law. Then come real estate commissions, property maintenance costs, and so forth. In addition, some observers (especially Moody's Investors Services, Inc.[2]) say that foreclosed properties realize lower prices than the median for their area. This is due to adverse selection factors, loss of competitive position in the market,

---

2.   Rating Residential Mortgage Pass-throughs, Moody's Investors Services, Inc., New York, April 1990.

tenancy damage, etc. This factor is calculated as a deduction from the modeled expected house sale price.

Two different results for default severity must be computed. *Intrinsic loss* is the total loss that is expected to result from a foreclosure, no matter who bears it. It is not necessarily the servicer's share, because it is calculated before giving effect to available mortgage insurance or the recourse status of a loan. This is done to give the truest possible measure of loss potential. Loans that are thought to be insured against default losses may not actually be found to have valid coverage. Alternatively, the MI company may find a defect in origination or servicing voiding a servicer's claim. Also, a servicer may believe a loan to be serviced under a nonrecourse investor contract, only to find that some or all recourse has been retained, or that an investor demands repurchase for some reason. In RF/Spectrum, these factors can be altered across scenarios. RF/Spectrum takes inputs for actual MI coverage, percentage of recourse (zero percent to 100 percent) and creates a *net-loss-to-servicer* forecast. Common uses for these features are estimating the value of pool insurance, calculating loan loss reserves, and in merger and acquisition work, where access to full information may be limited.

Delinquency Progression Behavior

An excellent indicator of delinquency performance is a cross-period analysis called "delinquency progression." It allows reporting and analyses, for instance, of exactly which loans were 30 days past due last month but are 60 days past due this month. By using different strata and extracts of the portfolio, risk managers can learn exactly which characteristics in their operations are predictive of good progression behavior (back to current status) or bad (from current to delinquent or multidelinquent). Table 17.1 shows an example of such a cross-period progression report, done at an overall portfolio level.

The shaded area in this analysis shows that of all loans that were 30 days past due last month, only 36.90 percent were brought current, 44.89 percent stayed 30 days past due, and 16.98 percent progressed to 60 days past due. Detecting and predicting progression from the 30- to 60-day category is considered the best area in which to minimize default losses. RF/Spectrum is the only system that can easily do cross-period analyses for both prepayment and delinquency progression at any ad hoc stratification of a portfolio.

Sophisticated risk managers use progression analyses to provide an early-warning system of emerging trends and problems. Others use it as well to measure the performance of collection staff: those with higher bad progression are in need of help. Other uses can be found in

Table 17.1 RF/Spectrum Delinquency Progression Report

For:
Cutoff Date:

Sample Mortgage
08/31/199x

Status Last Month	# Loans	Curr Status C Pct	Curr Status CB Pct	Curr Status CF Pct	Curr Status D 01 Pct	Curr Status D 02 Pct	Curr Status D 03 Pct	Curr Status D 04 Pct	Curr Status DB Pct	Curr Status DF Pct	Curr Status PAID Pct	Curr Status FCLD Pct
C	29,187	96.10	0.04	0.00	3.16	0.03	0.00	0.00	0.00	0.00	0.65	0.00
CB	99	13.13	73.74	0.00	2.02	0.00	0.00	0.00	11.11	0.00	0.00	0.00
D 01	1,702	36.90	0.06	0.00	44.89	16.98	0.35	0.00	0.29	0.00	0.53	0.00
D 02	383	22.98	0.26	0.00	30.03	12.53	31.59	0.26	1.04	0.00	1.31	0.00
D 03	126	18.25	0.00	0.00	12.70	13.49	3.17	27.78	0.79	22.22	1.59	0.00
D 04	69	4.35	0.00	0.00	1.45	4.35	0.00	53.62	2.90	33.33	0.00	0.00
DB01	51	1.96	25.49	0.00	1.96	1.96	0.00	0.00	68.63	0.00	0.00	0.00
DB02	26	0.00	11.54	0.00	0.00	3.85	0.00	0.00	84.62	0.00	0.00	0.00
DB03	19	0.00	5.26	0.00	5.26	0.00	0.00	5.26	84.21	0.00	0.00	0.00
DB04	144	0.00	0.00	0.00	0.00	0.00	0.00	4.86	87.50	7.64	0.00	0.00
DF02	1	0.00	0.00	0.00	0.00	0.00	100.00	0.00	0.00	0.00	0.00	0.00
DF04	182	3.85	0.00	3.30	0.55	0.00	0.00	0.55	7.14	82.42	2.20	0.00
**	31,992	90.06	0.33	0.02	5.71	1.15	0.42	0.26	0.74	0.66	0.66	0.00

major lenders with an active wholesale department who use this analysis to measure the quality of acquired loans by seller or branch.

SUMMARY

Participating in active secondary markets for loans and servicing requires an instantaneous pricing of known risks. Better risk pricing requires a complete catalog of what those risks are, which are present in a given segment of loans, and how they interact to affect price. High volatility has become a permanent feature of both interest rate and real estate markets. That means risk pricing now requires a multiscenario approach that weighs the possibility of change against the price effect it would create. The size of major portfolios, the complexity of the risks that interact, and the speed of the marketplace requires the use of sophisticated decision support systems such as RF/Spectrum. Increasingly, regulators, investors, and creditors of mortgage bankers are challenging them to show improvements in risk measurement and risk control. Managers who master the use of tools such as these will find it easier to avoid those risks that can be avoided, and to price those that cannot.

Chapter 18

MAXIMIZING RETURNS ON SERVICING PORTFOLIOS

Mary Bruce Batte
Managing Director
Mortgage Dynamics, Inc.

INTRODUCTION

The talk of the 1990s is all about servicing returns. But even with all the heady buzz about double-digit servicing returns, many operational obstacles can stand in the way of servicers actually banking those much-touted profits.

Due diligence firms observe many operational flaws in servicing shops that cost money and prevent companies from maximizing returns on their portfolios. In many instances, the flaws are correctable once they receive recognition from top management and once critical servicing personnel receive training and systems support to do the increasingly complex job of servicing.

A review of 80 servicing operations performed by a nationwide management consulting firm identified the aspects of servicing that suffer the most from an under-investment in staff training and some of the other commonplace problems that hurt servicing profitability. The reviews were conducted by Mortgage Dynamics, Inc. (MDI), a McLean, Virginia-based management consulting firm.

Reprinted by permission of *Mortgage Banking*, a publication of the Mortgage Bankers Association of America.

Most of the reviews were conducted for clients who were buying servicing rights, mortgage servicing operations, or entire companies. Approximately 20 were performed for clients seeking to improve servicing profitability and upgrade the quality of their servicing operations. In some cases, companies were using the review results to prepare for substantial servicing portfolio expansion.

The key conclusion MDI has drawn from the reviews is that substantial opportunities exist for servicers to lower their costs over time through investments that will boost their operational quality and efficiency. In most cases, the means of doing this are through investments to modernize the servicing plant and equipment and through investments in upgrading servicing staff. In addition, management changes and reorganizations will be required in many organizations.

Huge amounts of money are being invested in purchases of servicing these days, and the payback on those investments rides on the validity of many pricing assumptions. One critical pricing assumption that mortgage bankers have substantial control over is their cost of servicing. Given the impact of servicing cost on achieving value and MDI's finding that most bidders underestimate their servicing cost, lenders have an incentive to spend considerable time on this issue. Accordingly, MDI's findings suggest that mortgage servicers need to dig down into the inner workings of their servicing operations and identify the factors that are costing them more than they need to. This chapter identifies some of the more common operational flaws that can be fixed.

OBSTACLES FOR MANAGEMENT

Although the group of servicing operations reviewed included many of the largest and best-known companies, fewer than a dozen could be described as achieving a high level of investor compliance and servicing efficiency. When the review was done simply for a client buying servicing rights, the review did not cover the profitability of the operation. However, in nearly every review, conditions were observed that, if corrected, would have improved the quality and/or profitability of the operation.

The MDI reviews covered a wide spectrum of operations where the portfolio size ranged from less than $100 million to close to $20 billion. The median portfolio had an outstanding principal balance of more than $1 billion. MDI considers the group of 80 operations it reviewed as providing a good cross section of the mortgage servicing industry. The actual operations examined ranged from highly profitable firms buying and selling servicing to several currently under RTC supervision. Most of the firms were mortgage banking subsidiaries of financial institutions, but the group included several independent mortgage banking firms as well.

The operational shortcomings most commonly observed in all but a handful of companies included far less than optimum use of computer systems, many serious investor compliance violations, and inefficient work-flow patterns.

These barriers to achieving top servicing profitability were noteworthy because of their apparent prevalence in a time when cost consciousness in the mortgage business has become the new religion. But even more surprising was the fact that in an estimated 75 percent of the companies, senior management was not aware of the extent of the servicing problems, MDI found.

What accounts for these sleeping problems being left to quietly erode the value of the mortgage industry's most precious asset? In our view there are several reasons why senior management was not fully aware of the extent of the servicing operational problems in the majority of the companies we reviewed. Those reasons are: generally poor communication between management and the servicing division; the prevalence of a corporate culture that discourages staff from bringing operational problems down in the trenches to light; and internal budgetary pressure that makes those suggesting additional expenditures out of step with corporate objectives—even if the added costs promise to pay for themselves over time.

On the issue of poor internal communication between top management and servicing department staff, some important points need to be made. Management's impression of servicing is often blurred because it doesn't look beyond the current profitability. Senior management is not being made aware of the full scope of costly technical problems down in the servicing area and the risks they pose. Similarly, the technicians are not being educated to the components of value in servicing so they can make decisions that will be in line with management's financial goals.

On the second obstacle that prevents these problems in servicing shops from being brought to light—the lack of incentives for staff to expose them—there needs to be a change in corporate culture that rewards such efforts. The prevailing attitude among servicing managers in many servicing operations MDI reviewed is "circle the wagons and we'll solve the problems ourselves." Senior managers may point to audits of their operations done for Freddie Mac, Fannie Mae, GNMA, or HUD, as evidence that they have a clean shop, without considering that these audits are brief and have little to do with profitability or efficiency. Agency audits were examined, when available, for the 80 reviews MDI conducted. Rarely did the agency audits uncover all of the out-of-compliance conditions found during the MDI review. The problem is that most servicing operations have few resources to direct toward uncovering problems, tackling them, and clearing away backlogs. None of the organizations reviewed had servicing problem-identification programs in place that would serve to encourage employees to bring problems to light.

Corporate audit programs, in most cases, were counterproductive in two respects. First, the auditors were not viewed by the servicing technicians as having the level of detailed knowledge about servicing operations and investor requirements needed to identify out-of-compliance conditions or to make meaningful suggestions to improve efficiency and profitability. Second, the audit process was viewed as "we versus they" and not as a forum for identifying problems and moving the organization ahead.

In only two operations, MDI found that internal compliance audits made meaningful contributions toward identifying and solving problems. In the rest of the servicing organizations that underwent such audits, serious compliance violations were not identified, while tremendous time and effort were spent on conditions that have little to do with value or compliance.

Identifying problems and areas for improvement in the context of strategic planning has been effective in a number of organizations MDI has worked with. Such projects have been designed and structured as task forces made up of members of the servicing operation and inside or outside resources knowledgeable in servicing, mortgage finance, and management.

The "fear factor" must be substantially reduced by focusing on how to improve the organization rather than on placing blame for things that have gone wrong. A task force effort can play an important role in identifying and prioritizing problems that pose the greatest risk and identifying operations improvements that will improve profitability.

The final internal obstacle that works against top management being able to identify and fix servicing operational problems is the current industrywide squeeze on corporate expenses. The emphasis on cutting costs in the short run makes it difficult for a servicing manager to break out of the fold and suggest spending money to improve future productivity and profits. The tendency is to look at cutting staff instead of investing in upgrading staff, and training and systems enhancements to improve the quality and efficiency of the operation. The task force approach to identifying servicing problems can be an excellent means of building support for investments in the servicing operation.

Specific examples of the kinds of problems MDI found will help to illustrate the exact nature of the operational flaws that are hampering servicers from being as profitable as possible. We've selected prevalent problems that fall into three major categories: quality of staff, poor systems selection and utilization, and investor reporting.

QUALITY OF STAFF

The most serious overall problems MDI found centered on poorly trained personnel. The prevalence of this condition was not a reflection of the work ethic of the staff in any way. In most of the servicing operations reviewed, the staff appeared to be diligent, yet several conditions were still widespread.

Overall, servicing employees did not seem to understand how what they were doing fit into the overall corporate picture—or into the servicing operation. They also lacked an understanding of exactly what creates servicing profitability. Many did not understand how their function related to other servicing functions and, therefore, did not communicate on their common problems. One example of this was an investor reporting department that could not balance its GNMA II ARM and GPM pools. They suspected they were not using their system properly—and they were right. But an additional problem related to improper adjustments of the underlying loans—an issue they had not explored with their Special Loans division.

MDI also found a serious lack of knowledge about major investor servicing requirements and, particularly, changes found in quarterly amendments to the investors' Seller/Servicer Guides. A surprising number of employees interviewed did not know where the guides were kept in their organizations and did not receive information about updates. In more than half of the organizations reviewed, the Seller/Servicer Guides had not been updated with the most recent changes.

In another operation with both Freddie Mac ARC (accelerated remittance cycle) and non-ARC servicing, MDI found an employee who "simplified" operations by remitting all principal and interest payments to Freddie Mac according to the ARC remittance schedule. This "simplification" cost roughly two weeks of float on the principal and interest (P&I) payments on several hundred million dollars of loans that were non-ARC. In this case, the lost float income amounted to approximately $150,000 per year.

Very few servicing organizations reviewed by MDI had adequate policies and procedures manuals (a requirement of the major secondary market agencies) that reflected changes made by the agencies in the past year. Many of the manuals contained policies or procedures that were in violation of current investor requirements. Even in those organizations that had manuals, staff use of them appeared minimal. In many cases, the procedures that staff said they were following were not the ones specified in the manual.

When questioned by MDI about conditions in their areas that were not in compliance with investor requirements, more than half of the servicing employees and many of the supervisors were not aware that the conditions did not meet investor standards.

To many senior managers, most of the jobs in a servicing operation appear to be clerical. In reality, the technical requirements Freddie Mac, Fannie Mae, and GNMA have imposed, as well as those imposed by state and federal laws, have created the need for people who can understand and perform complex tasks.

Errors made by servicing employees can result in penalties for late payments or reports to investors, denial of mortgage insurance claims, government penalties for late payment of taxes, responsibility for covering hazard losses due to failure to pay hazard insurance premiums and repurchases of mortgages that have not been serviced properly. Noncompliance with investor requirements can even result in having servicing pulled by the investor and can expose the servicer to lawsuits.

Equally important, however, is that poorly trained employees impede the ability of the servicer to generate income from the portfolio. In one servicing operation MDI reviewed, the computer had been programmed to apply the late fee charge only to the amount of principal and interest payment instead of the entire monthly payment (PITI). The condition had existed for several years without anyone noticing it.

The MBA Cost Study assessing industry performance in 1988 showed that personnel costs accounted for about 40 percent of the direct expenses tied to servicing for the average servicer. MBA's studies have also found that the average servicer spends less than 15 cents per loan to train its staff. With constantly changing servicing requirements, an undertrained staff and, typically, a high staff-turnover rate, it is no wonder that many servicing operations function continuously in a state of semi-chaos. Actions that can reduce personnel costs will have substantial cost-saving impact. Furthermore, it is critical that job categories in servicing properly reflect the levels of skill needed and that pay levels promote retention of capable employees. The final goal should be upgrading personnel so each can handle a greater number of loans.

POOR SYSTEMS SELECTION AND USAGE

The second most serious systemic problem in the servicing operations reviewed by MDI concerns the servicing computer system. There are still many operations that have inadequate servicing systems, most of which were generated in-house or as part of a "banking" software system—where mortgages were an afterthought. However, these organizations share common problems with servicing shops that have state-of-the-art systems.

In the majority of operations reviewed, staff members were not fully aware of the capabilities of their servicing computer software. As a result, they were either misusing the system or underutilizing it. In many cases, employees were going to great lengths to circumvent the system.

In many cases, information about system enhancements was not being distributed to employees. Systems manuals were not being updated on a timely basis. In several reviews, we found that systems enhancement letters, a critical part of enhancement installation and use, had never been printed off the system. In several of these servicing operations, serious problems directly resulted, and costly corrective action is now needed. As a result, efficiency was being sacrificed, and in many instances, the company was being shortchanged. Out-of-compliance situations were being created in many cases.

In one review, MDI monitored the use of computer-generated reports each day during the week and found that reports that should form the basis of the staff's daily work were not picked up for several days. Many were not examined at all. Also, many servicing operations were not using audit reports produced by their servicing systems to check their work. Instead they were addressing errors only as customers brought them to their attention.

Even where Computer Power, Inc. (CPI), a large service bureau, was used, MDI found that 50 percent of the staffs did not know what their systems could do.

In at least half the organizations reviewed, systems enhancements—many of which reflect changes in investor requirements or labor-saving methods—were not being installed on a timely basis. In many organizations that did install the enhancements promptly, installations were handled incorrectly and/or there was insufficient training to maximize the benefit of the enhancement.

MDI found serious data quality problems stemming from a variety of conditions. The conditions include failure to clean up data prior to conversions, poorly planned and executed systems conversions, improper loan setups and ongoing misuse of the servicing system. These conditions have created a number of problems for the servicers reviewed, including:

♦ *Incorrect ARM and GPM adjustments*—Overall, the error rate MDI found has been in excess of 20 percent in the operations it reviewed. In one recent review of more than 2,000 loans, ARM undercharges were twice as prevalent as overcharges to the borrower. In a surprising number of cases, the correct index value was selected, but the allocation of the monthly payment between principal and interest was wrong. That suggests improper loan setup or circumvention of the system.

♦ *Incorrect administration of buydown subsidies*

♦ *Inability to pay mortgage insurance premiums by tape*

♦ *The need for costly manual adjustments* to routine reports to investors on a monthly basis

♦ *Errors related to tax payments*—In one organization, there were 20,000 systems errors related to the payment of taxes, and as a result, the servicer had incurred substantial tax penalties.

Most servicing systems have tests that are generally run to determine the quality of data for a conversion. These reports can be used by servicer subscribers to determine the condition of their data for ongoing operations improvement. Under CPI's system, for example, the Master File Verification Report can identify problem areas within servicing by verifying the loan-level data contained in a loan master file. These errors can then be classified to identify ones that, if corrected, would enhance efficiency and accuracy. Some of the errors can be corrected with proper installation of enhancements and workstations, while nothing can be done or should be done about other categories. These reports must be used with caution if they have not been updated to reflect all enhancements made in the software.

For ARM, GPM, and buydown loans, MDI recommends that beyond correcting problems that appear through data verification reports, servicers should sample their portfolios for setup errors. If errors are found, verification of setup data should be performed when the loan's next adjustment date occurs. In addition, a sample verification of all adjustments should be performed going back to the original loan setup.

Nowhere were data and systems problems more serious than in investor reporting. In several instances, the conversions had been a total failure due to incorrect definitions and insufficient preconversion testing.

The 80 reviews also brought to light the shortcomings of many servicing systems. Many small- to medium-sized operations still have either home-grown servicing systems or a universal package of software that provides all routine data processing activities. In many cases the servicing system is not updated on a timely basis to accommodate recent changes in investor reporting requirements or to handle new ARM programs. There frequently are problems in performing routine servicing operations efficiently, such as processing loan payoffs or assumptions or calculating principal and interest advances. Even if a new system costs an extra $1.00 to $3.00 per loan, per year to service, MDI has found it may save $5.00 or more per loan, per year in personnel costs.

When substantial staff time is required to work around the shortcomings of the computer system, the cost of servicing goes up significantly. We have found that manual processing of ARM adjustments can add between $30.00 to $110.00 per year, per loan, in servicing costs, depending on the extent of the system inadequacy and the complexity of the ARM product.

MDI recommends that servicers review all ongoing servicing functions to determine whether any that are handled manually could be automated. We often find employees performing tasks manually that their systems can handle. Lacking sufficient information about their system, they tend to "override" the system and perform the tasks manually. Typically, spending money for staff training on an adequate computer system and servicing functions training will pay off greatly in the future.

INVESTOR REPORTING

Investor reporting was the most poorly administered function in more than two thirds of the companies reviewed. The training and systems problems discussed above were even more evident in the investor reporting departments of the companies reviewed.

Typically, these departments were behind in their reconciliations and were not up-to-date on investor requirements. For example, in recent months, few of the companies reviewed were in compliance with Freddie Mac's new custodial account requirements. Another common problem is failure to review and reconcile previous months' reports to investors with the reports received from investors.

In one operation, 55 percent of the GNMA GPM pools and 30 percent of the ARM pools had errors that had continued for two years. There was no plan in place to correct the problem, and senior management was unaware of the extent of the problem.

An $8 million over-remittance to Fannie Mae was found in one operation reviewed by MDI last summer. The remittances involved "excess" taxes and insurance (T&I) funds for fixed-rate loans sold before 1971 that were serviced at 0.50 percent of unpaid principal balance. The remittances were supposed to be based only on those loans affected, but the servicer based them on the entire Actual/Actual portfolio and remitted the total escrow balance shown on the monthly trial balance rather than escrow receipts. The servicer had no idea this was occurring even though the custodial bank account was overdrawn by millions of dollars.

Delinquent loans were not being liquidated from Fannie Mae MBS pools on the 120th day of delinquency in several organizations, resulting in unnecessary payment to Fannie Mae of scheduled principal and interest. MDI also found that funds due from Fannie Mae when such loans were liquidated were not requested in a timely manner, resulting in corporate advances for lengthy periods of time. In the case of two multifamily loans, Freddie Mac granted foreclosure request, but no one notified investor reporting personnel, and they continued to advance interest to Freddie Mac in the amount of $50,000.

In one operation, Fannie Mae Actual/Actual remittances to the agency were consistently sent in late because the servicer's system failed to generate the reports needed by investor reporting personnel on a timely basis.

In some companies, errors in balances "sold" to GNMA as shown on mortgage loan schedules were noted as well in servicing fee rates and pass-through rates in the system, resulting in miscalculation of remittances to security holders. This also produced errors in booking servicer's income. The servicer had to contact security holders to recover the amounts over-remitted.

In one operation, poor communication resulted in two sets of checks being sent to GNMA security holders for the same month.

Remittance mistakes that are not caught can lead to major long-term problems. One servicing operation reviewed had been paying the investor more than the investor was entitled to. The mistake was not caught because the original error was made with the first remittance many years ago. When the thrift servicer suspected a problem, it did not reconcile accounts back far enough to find the problem. Over a number of years it was found that the excess payments amounted to more than $300,000. This turned out to be a tremendous financial drain on the small association, and correcting the problem was time-consuming and expensive. The investor was only willing to settle by transferring some loans in the securities pools to the servicer.

Investor reporting has been especially troublesome in the RTC-controlled operations MDI has reviewed. This stems from the prevalence of staff turnover in these operations and the difficulty of finding qualified investor reporting personnel to work in organizations facing uncertain futures. MDI has found true disaster areas in investor reporting in some RTC shops it reviewed. Correcting these problems prior to transfer is imperative to minimize the damage to the acquiring organization.

FOCUSING AHEAD

In order to maximize earnings on servicing, senior management must change its focus. The American automobile industry was faced with a similar challenge and has been struggling with this issue for the past 10 years. Top management in mortgage servicing must focus now on modernizing their manufacturing plant so the "car" not only looks great on paper, but also "performs."

In the automobile industry, the trend has been toward upgrading staff in critical areas of the manufacturing process, recognizing the need to move to higher technical skill levels, instilling pride in workmanship, and placing greater responsibility on such workers to make decisions.

Similarly, the most successful servicing operations of the 1990s will reflect dramatic change in their corporate culture, with emphasis on knowledgeable, trained technicians and further labor-saving technology.

V

Shaping Mortgage Banking Operations for Success

Chapter 19

AUTOMATING MORTGAGE BANKING OPERATIONS

Jeffery F. Butler
Managing Director, Chief Information Officer
Countrywide Funding Corp.

"Technology is steamrollering its way throughout the mortgage banking industry. If you're not on the steamroller, you're destined to be imbedded in the pavement."
—*Angelo R. Mozilo*
Vice Chairman and Executive Vice President

"It was the best of times, it was the worst of times . . . ."
—*Charles Dickens*

INTRODUCTION

The purpose of this chapter is not to provide a blueprint of how to deploy the technologies that already exist, but to convey the opportunities that any company, large or small, can take advantage of right now. These technologies are not pipe dreams. They are tools that will enhance productivity within any company that is willing to brave new worlds.

When Joseph Benevides, Jr., wrote the first chapter on "Automating Mortgage Banking Operations" five years ago, his focus was on why you should automate various functions within the operations. Mr. Benevides correctly pointed out the methodologies required to justify the expense and effort required to automate the origination function. He also pointed out the advantages of deploying such a system with the inherent dos and don'ts thrown in for good measure.

But now, it's five years later. To automate or not to automate is no longer the question. The question now is: How quickly can we successfully bring these systems and tools into our shop? Can we utilize these tools to provide better customer service and thereby gain market share before someone else does?

A few short years ago, our business was a very straightforward one. Many of the processes that were done 20 years ago were still being accomplished in the same fashion. Origination and closing documents, delivery, and many other related forms were typed. The only place automation helped was in loan administration, and that had not changed dramatically in the last half decade.

The questions facing our CEOs were: Should we invest in the future of the company by applying current technologies and create the basic infrastructure to build on; or, do we maintain the status quo and watch the business slowly slip away to competitors who have made the monetary and human investment in these technologies?

Today the justification of automation is no longer just basic survival! The justification for automating is gaining the competitive advantage and widening it over time. You must provide better pricing and support to your new applicants by applying new technologies. You must enhance the marketing and delivery of the new loans into the secondary market by incorporating new tools into your existing systems. You must provide the ultimate in customer service to your portfolio by initiating state-of-the-art technologies in loan administration. The desired result should be a loyal customer who thinks only of you when looking for a home loan.

Now, we have a CFO and a COO's dilemma. How do you pay for the investment in the necessary tools to provide the technological advantage needed to succeed? How do you re-engineer the processes to get the most out of the new technology tools and systems? How do you convince people that change is not only good for them, but will actually make them better and more productive employees because of it?

Now that you have convinced your employees that technology will help them to be more productive, you may have just planted the seeds of corporate self-destruction. With the advent of personal computing tied in with client serving, the single largest threat to any corporation is the creation of islands of information. These islands only serve to defeat the free flow of information and the sharing of ideas among the various departments within the organization. Data and programs are maintained within these small groups or even on an individual basis. Often, data and programs are replicated between many of these islands, thereby costing more for storage and making the results very suspect.

So, we have a CIO's dilemma. How do you bring it all together and still maintain the freedom and flexibility desired by the clients while providing the data security and reliability mandated by management? How do you tie in mainframe, mini- and micro-computers into a single cohesive system that will allow people to share information and ideas simply and seamlessly?

OPTIONS GALORE

Centralized versus Decentralized Processing

Every company is different and so is its related culture. And the culture of the company will determine the way in which it does business. Some companies feel more comfortable with centralizing the processing of its loan applications. Large processing center(s) are utilized to gain economies of scale not only in space but in human resources. By reducing the number of centers, scarce skills (i.e., underwriters) are more easily managed. Decentralized processing provides for smaller facilities, which could take the form of a strip-center style of branch, a satellite (one-person) executive-type office, or even a mobile satellite (one person with no physical base) who uses a laptop computer to take and process loan applications.

Each method can be very effective, depending on the needs of the corporate culture. Both methods have advantages and disadvantages that must be weighed prior to making a decision. It must be pointed out that there is no wrong answer here; unless, that is, you choose one that is counter to the culture of your company.

The term "rightsizing" is being bandied about in the technology industry. However, "rightsizing" has as much to do with what platform you process on as it does with choosing the method of how you perform the process. The idea in "rightsizing" is to do what fits best within the framework of your existing culture.

Service Bureau versus In-House Processing

The same corporate culture that determined centralized versus decentralized processing will more than likely determine whether a company will choose a service-bureau style of processing or an in-house style.

Needless to say, there is much to be said about both options. Each option having its good, bad, and ugly points. First, let's discuss service bureaus.

The Good. Service bureaus represent a processing style that generally eliminates the need for internal systems and programming support personnel. All the major service bureaus in business today provide complete support services, which include operations staff, programmers, and both business and systems analysts. They also provide backup and disaster recovery services. In addition, the service bureaus have created user groups to establish system enhancements and prioritize their implementation.

The Bad. Generally, the same users group that determines priority could mean that your priorities may not be high on everyone else's list. Consequently, the system changes you desire may not get done in your time frame. Even if you're willing to pay separately for these enhancements, most services will not make changes to the core system and thereby create multiple versions of their base environment.

The Ugly. If you like to be in control of your destiny, then a service bureau may not be for you. In addition, the cost of using a service bureau could be as expensive as an in-house solution. Service bureaus also have problems providing fast, unilateral service to create a competitive advantage for your company. That alone could cause problems for fast-moving, aggressive companies.

Next, we will examine in-house processing.

The Good. It is yours to do with as you see fit. You control the priority, the timeliness, and the method of how the process is completed. You can bring new products to market faster, create new efficiencies in your work flows, and have a better chance of controlling your costs. If your culture is control, then in-house processing is for you.

The Bad. Be prepared to spend a fair amount of money on equipment and staff to support in-house systems. You are now responsible for operating and maintaining the hardware and software, handling the physical facility security as well as data-security issues, dealing with vendors, keeping up on the latest technologies, and providing your own backup and disaster recovery systems. All of these require a huge amount of time and energy to sustain. No easy task by anyone's standard.

The Ugly. If you think hiring and maintaining non-data-processing people is difficult, wait until you try your hand at this. First of all, the good people already have jobs. To bring qualified people on board, you are generally going to have to pay up. And if you don't like that idea, you can always bring on younger college graduates and take a year or so to teach them your business and systems before they become fully productive. If you're patient, the wait can be very rewarding.

Hardware Platforms

If you have read any type of computer systems magazine or article recently, the two biggest words are "rightsizing" and "downsizing." Basically, all these words mean is to do what's right for you and your company based upon its philosophy and culture. The mainframe and mini-computer zealots are rallying around the big iron, saying that nothing will ever take the place of these huge transaction processing giants. And that may be true.

However, you also have the PC/Client Server zealots who are predicting the second coming in the form of a desktop computer tied to various and sundry types of network servers. So much horsepower for so very little dollars. And that is true! Yet somewhere in between may be the right answer for most companies, if there is any right answer.

Regardless of whether you have in-house systems or are using a service bureau, there are billions of lines of code written to deal with mortgage banking applications. These legacy systems, whether written for a mainframe or a mini, have had huge sums of money invested in them. The chance of rewriting them to be used in a PC/Client Server environment in the short term is negligible. However, over time, as PCs and client serving become more reliable and robust, some transformation will take place.

We must remember, these legacy systems are all mission critical to your business. Consequently, no one in their right mind would risk job and company on platforms that have not totally matured yet.

A glaring exception to this concept is that of application processing. Almost every system being built today is being built on a PC/Client Server platform. Why? First, the cost of developing systems is much less expensive. Second, development time is faster, maintenance is easier, and client training is greatly simplified. And last, the cost of the hardware is getting cheaper by the day.

One additional platform should be mentioned here—a platform that has not gained significant recognition in the mortgage banking industry. That platform is the UNIX-based systems using a RISC type of operating architecture. These systems have the horsepower to handle large transactions processing demands as well as provide the graphical user-friendliness that people demand. Over time, these systems will bridge the gap between both extremes and will provide the ability to build applications that will enrich employee productivity.

Presentation Base—GUI versus Character

Legacy systems, by their very nature, are all character-based. Mainframe and mini-computers were never designed for a graphical user interface environment.

Although character-based presentations served us well for many decades, most users now prefer the graphical presentation. The main reason is that it is easier to use, more intuitive, and just simply more fun. In addition, statistics show that people trained using a graphical-based presentation generally grade higher than those trained in a character-based environment.

Probably the most popular graphical presentation base is Microsoft's Windows. Although Windows is technically an operating system, the point-and-click presentation allows the user an easy and intuitive method of performing system and application functions. Other graphical bases are IBM's OS/2 and Macintosh's System 7.

Case Tools—Upper versus Lower Case

In the last several years, case tools have been introduced to the information systems arsenal. These tools are generally placed into two categories, upper case and lower case.

Upper case tools are specifically created to automate the analysis and design of systems. These tools aid in analyzing work flows, data base design, screen and report formats, and both user and system documentation. Generally, the tools are very user-friendly and walk the analyst through the necessary steps to build the desired applications. A few of the better-known PC-based upper case tools are Accelerator, Knowledgeware, and Erwin.

Lower case tools are basically code generators. These tools actually create programs for applications from the information entered into the generator. The programming languages the code generates vary from proprietary-type code to RPG, C, Cobol, and others.

Products combining the attributes of both upper and lower case tools are called I-case, which stands for integrated case tools. These tools combine the analysis and design with the code generation. By having one product that does it all, integration of case tools from two different vendors is eliminated. Depending upon your platform, there are several I-case tools available. Texas Instruments and Synon are two of the most popular on the market today.

Front-end development tools are also available. These 4GL form-based tools generate screen shells quickly and easily. Users can create prototypes of applications in a fraction of the time taken in most other platforms. Changes can be made to the prototype in minutes, thereby providing the users with a fresh look each time alterations are made. The two products most commonly used are Visual Basic and Power Builder.

Today's Technologies—Productivity in Waiting

Unlike any other time in information systems history, we are in a unique position to take advantage of a wide range of technologies that will greatly enhance the productivity of any mortgage banker. Although these technologies are generally known, very few are being fully utilized by our industry. In addition, it is even rarer that any one company utilizes more than just a few of these technologies simultaneously. The following represents the most recognizable of these technologies together with some meaningful insights about their use.

Artificial Intelligence

Probably one of the most widely recognized technologies is artificial intelligence. Although widely recognized by name, it has not been widely implemented. Not only have most companies failed to take advantage of this tool, very few software houses have developed applications built around this tool for resale to the industry.

Artificial intelligence, often referred to as expert systems, comes in several flavors. Each different methodology used to create applications—statistical predictive, rule-based, neural-network, and judgment processing—has its own process to arrive at the desired answer. Consequently, each method has a different type of construction, with inherent goals, strengths, and weaknesses.

Statistical predictive systems simplify analysis of past experience. These systems are built by statisticians and are most commonly applied. The major weakness is lag time in considering current trends or changes in regulations. Basically, examining the past is not always a key to the future.

Rule-based systems automate complex, explicit relationships. These systems are designed by knowledge engineers. Fuzzy-logic methodologies are incorporated into rule-based systems. Unlike Boolean logic, the boundaries of these ranges are not cutoff points where the label applies fully on one side of the cutoff and does not apply at all on the other side of the cutoff. Rule-based systems are flexible, and the rule relationships and values can be altered quickly and easily. These systems are intellectually attractive, yet bear the stigma that people who only follow rules are never perceived as experts.

Neural-network systems basically organize example sets of information into specified logical patterns. These systems are generally specified by engineers and experts together. Their major strength is combining the best features of rules and statistics systems and giving more flexibility in the results. The major weakness is combining the worst features of rules and statistics and presenting the results with dramatically less clarity. In other words, what did it do?

Judgment-processing systems emulate the best human mentor. The system learns from a human expert in the application being written. Generally, many mentors (experts) must be included in the process to build a consensus answer to any problem. The major strength of the system is to allow for the automation of the best human experts. However, the systems are nontraditional and the approach is uncomfortable to theoretical experts.

Artificial intelligence systems, regardless of means or methodology, take the ordered data and move it along to higher levels of organization, whence come orderly, judgment-type decisions. The key factors in any application using A/I are data collection and decision preparation. The basic components of any A/I system are: a source of accurate and formatted data; an engine to manipulate the data and then to prepare a decision about it; and finally, the product of the decision making. This product is essential, as it offers a historical perspective for use by the company.

Expert systems have the potential for being one of the greatest tools available to the mortgage industry in this decade. The number of potential uses is virtually unlimited and are not necessarily related to any one specific area within the business. Production, secondary marketing, marketing, operations, finance, and loan administration can enjoy the fruits of applications developed using artificial intelligence systems.

The most obvious application for this tool is in loan underwriting. The process of underwriting a loan is extremely labor-intensive. There is a massive amount of data that must be examined and analyzed to arrive at a decision. The whole process can be completed by a knowledgeable underwriter in about 30 to 45 minutes. And even then, the results of the analysis can be as varied as the people who did the underwriting. The point is, underwriting is not an exact science. Consequently, a company that employs many underwriters will generally have very little consistency in the results.

With an expert system, the computer will evaluate the data in a matter of seconds and arrive at a consistent answer. The two operative words here are "seconds" and "consistent." The productivity gain experienced when deploying an expert system is extremely high. Underwriters can double or even triple their productivity when an expert system is used. The expert system can approve the less-complicated files and turn over only those that need a more in-depth review, thus saving the very valuable time of the underwriter. As for consistency, it is hard to beat the consistency of a computer.

The major problem now is that expert systems are not readily available in the marketplace. Only a few currently exist at this writing. However, as software houses or even some larger and bolder mortgage companies gain experience in this technology, many, many more systems will be brought to market. Regardless of the genesis of the product, the application itself will be one you most certainly will want to include in your arsenal.

Imaging

Imaging technology has been around for many years. Unfortunately, during the early years, because of the cost of equipment and the fact that most systems available were proprietary, the vast majority of businesses were basically uninterested in deploying imaging as a productivity enhancing tool.

That was then. This is now. Not only has the cost of these systems dropped dramatically, but most systems are built around an open-architecture design. Simply put, we are in a plug and play environment that is most beneficial to the user community.

There are two basic types of image capture, scanning and computer output to laser disk (COLD). Of the two, document scanning is the most widely used method.

Generally, documents are processed using any variation of low- or high-speed scanners. Once scanned, the documents must be indexed to provide the means for future retrieval. Indexing can take many forms, from a simple manual method to utilizing bar codes and intelligent forms recognition software to pick up data from the physical document to electronically index the form.

In addition to manually scanning documents, some companies are utilizing an electronic process to have images imported into their systems. Most systems will now allow for Group 3 or Group 4 electronic fax formats to be directly accepted as an image and, at the same time, to be automatically indexed from various data points on the document. Without a doubt, this enabling technology has far-reaching implications for the mortgage banking industry.

One challenge that the imaging industry must face is how the industry will deal with EDI (electronic data interchange). EDI is a widely accepted method for the movement of common data elements between business partners. Items such as purchase ordering, invoicing, and the payment of invoices are now everyday occurrences. Although the data transmitted through an EDI format can be made to produce a paperlike form, most companies went into EDI technology to speed up the process as well as reduce the amount of paper flow.

The imaging industry must develop a way to envelop these two technologies and provide the processing speed so essential in today's economy as well as provide the visual effects that people are accustomed to. Imaging vendors and EDI vendors must become technological partners to deliver the best solution for all their clients.

COLD imaging represents an enhanced version of COM (computer output to microfiche). In the good old days, data processing would process business reports and, instead of printing them, would take the spool file and back it off to tape. The tape would then be processed using a system that would transfer the electronic paper image to fiche. Depending on the size of the spool file being converted, the number of fiche required could range from one to literally hundreds. In addition, if more than one person or department needed to view the information simultaneously, duplicates would be made. God forbid these fiche should ever get out of order, or worse yet, get lost.

With COLD, these same spool files are transferred to electronic media. While being transferred, the spool file can be programically indexed to enhance the retrieval of the data within seconds. Not only can you retrieve it in seconds, so can anyone else—simultaneously! There is no need to duplicate platters (except for disaster recovery) and the images never get out of order or are lost. Now, the printed report can be viewed from virtually any terminal in a matter of seconds by any number of people.

When people think of imaging, they generally envision the scanning and retrieving of documents—a very simple process to say the least. However, if that is the limit of what you believe imaging to be, then you are not in tune with the real value of imaging.

Work flow! The ability to move documents electronically from person to person, department to department, or even company to company automatically is probably the single most productivity enhancing feature imaging has to offer. Multiple people can view the same document simultaneously. Notations can be made to the document and forwarded to another person completely outside the automated chain for that document. Many, many variations can be implemented. It is all left to the imagination of those developing the applications.

Imaging systems, if properly designed and installed, will help re-engineer the workplace. Ultimately, in a best-case scenario, these systems will also accelerate the creation of a paperless environment that one day must surely come.

Executive Information Systems (EIS)

If you were asked to describe what an executive information system is, what would your response be? Don't feel bad if you can't come up with the right answer—most people have the same problem. It wasn't until recently that EIS became fashionable in many high places. The word is out, and EIS is cropping up everywhere, from executive suites to the boardroom. A demand for information is growing—information that can be accessed accurately, quickly, and in a format that is easy to use.

Executive information systems are, by their very nature, tailored to executive users. The purpose in using such systems is to extract, filter, compress, and track critical data. Key components of the system are as follows:

♦ To provide on-line status access, trend analysis, exception reporting, and drill-down capabilities

♦ To access and integrate a broad range of internal and external data bases

♦ To be user-friendly and require minimal or no training to use

♦ To have the capability to be used directly by executives without intermediaries

♦ To present information in a variety of forms, with graphs, tables, and/or text

From a corporate standpoint, EIS provides faster and easier access to information. It allows executives to monitor their organization's performance and helps them improve the efficiency and effectiveness of all senior executives by enhancing the communications among a multitude of differing groups.

Executives look for features, such as drill-down capabilities; color monitors; accuracy and security of data; and unlimited access to data. The combination of all these items reflects a desire on the part of executives to be self-sufficient. Considering today's fast pace and the demand for instant decisions, self-sufficiency is no longer merely fashionable—it's become a matter of survival.

Over time, EIS will be interfaced with other support systems, including E-mail, imaging, and expert systems. In addition, many industry groups will begin to share data, thereby increasing the value of the information displayed.

Although executive information systems are relatively new to the financial industry at large, they will soon become a primary weapon in any corporate arsenal. The increase in today's competitive environment and the need for more timely information will ultimately lead the mortgage industry to demand the capabilities that only an executive information system can implement. EIS is no longer a fad—it is an effective management tool.

Bar Coding

Virtually everything you buy now has a bar code on it. For consumers, bar coding has become as ho-hum as yesterday's news.

Yet, when we look around the mortgage industry, there is very little use of bar coding technology. Most bar coding applications are being used to track files from workstation to workstation. And in some cases, even our custodians use bar coding to track the custodial files and documents in and out of their possession.

Although tracking the files through the workplace and beyond is very important, bar coding has many more possibilities, not the least of which is the bar coding of loan documents.

Consider this. Making a very large assumption that your company utilizes laser printers to generate loan documents, why not print your loan number, document type/iteration code, and institution number on the form while printing the document itself? There are several advantages to this. If you monitor receipt of various processing forms, wanding the returned document offers a quick and easy way to know what your outstanding documents are. Now, one could argue that manually recording them would be just as easy; however, the error rate of wanding is virtually zero. What do you think the error rate of manual entry is?

If you image your files after funding, the bar coding of documents will increase your capacity to scan and index documents manyfold over non-bar-coded documents. A real life saver if you do any sort of production volume.

To make a note here, the Mortgage Bankers Association has attempted to establish a de facto document type standard. Together with the coding schema, the MBA has also established the size, shape, and location of the bar code on the vast majority of documents. Although this standard has not been widely accepted as of yet, the hope is that major companies will adopt it and ultimately require their business partners to follow suit. These business partners would include credit agencies, appraisers, title companies, insurance companies, tax authorities, government agencies, and all public and private investors.

There are many others uses for bar coding around the office. From inventory control of equipment to the mailroom (which records not only the incoming express mail packages but the ultimate delivery point using a pen-based system), bar coding will be around in some fashion for a long, long time. It is certainly a proven technology and can be a valuable weapon in your arsenal.

CD-ROM

If you like the idea of "information at your fingertips," as espoused by Microsoft, then you're gonna love those CD-ROMs. As the Joker would say, "Where, oh where did he get all those wonderful toys?"

Well, all those wonderful toys have been on the market for several years. Unfortunately, the main reason they have not been more popular is the gigantic lack of standards by which the applications are run. It is a very sad state of affairs, because this is truly a powerful weapon to have in your arsenal.

There are a host of applications available on CD-ROM disks today. They range from dictionaries to geographic mapping, from magazine articles to system user manuals, from thesauruses to full-motion video encyclopedias.

One of the most intriguing uses of CD-ROMs is the utilization of rewritable disks. Unlike the commercial CD-ROM applications, these disks can be used, erased, and re-used. Consequently, information that is temporary can be stored, used, and then destroyed at intervals relative to the criticalness of the application.

There isn't a company anywhere that doesn't print too much paper. Especially computer reports that are used for a single day and then discarded, only to be regenerated the next day for the cycle to start all over again. The vast majority of reports produced are work lists, daily totals of various activities, and a miscellaneous collection of reports, some of which are no longer being used by the customer who, unfortunately, somehow forgot to tell Information Systems to stop printing the report.

Similar to the COLD imaging applications, which are designed for permanent storage and retrieval, rewritable CD-ROM applications can be used to spool the reports off to disk, index the reports as needed, and maintain them for screen retrieval based on the amount of time your users want to save the information. You can create daily, weekly, and monthly disks, which can be recycled over and over again. Not only have you eliminated the printing of the paper, you have eliminated the distribution of the reports (which is very costly) and provided to your customers a slick, easy way for them to view the information on the reports.

CD-ROM technology is getting cheaper by the day. CD-ROM hardware, coupled with a few PCs and some application software, will not only save you a bunch of money in paper costs, but countless headaches from a customer service standpoint.

Multimedia

If you have been to the recent fall Comdex convention in Las Vegas, you have no doubt noticed the amount of floor space given to multimedia. Although multimedia applications would in no way rival the sheer number of non-multimedia applications, it is undoubtedly gaining ground.

Multimedia applications allow for voice, full-motion video, and user interaction to create a wide array of potential uses, one of which centers on client training.

As the demands for deploying newer technologies and more sophisticated applications increase, employees are in a "Catch-22" mode. They must learn these new technologies and applications, yet they still have a job to do. They must go to class to learn, yet they have no time to go; hence, multimedia training, a.k.a. guided learning centers or computer-based training.

Multimedia training allows the student to learn at his or her own pace. Because the training is interactive, the student can answer questions and go back over areas that are unclear as many times as necessary. This differs from a classroom environment, where students who fall behind the pace either never catch up or tend to hold back the balance of the class while trying to comprehend the subject matter.

Another feature of multimedia training is full-motion video and sound, which tend to hold the attention of students better than previous computer-based training applications. Because it's almost like watching television, the student feels more comfortable and, therefore, generally learns at a more rapid pace.

Most multimedia applications are distributed on CD-ROM and, as previously mentioned, CD-ROM technology is beginning to find strong support in the office environment. Due to this explosion of meaningful business applications, it is only a matter of time until multimedia is on every PC in the office. From "Information At Your Fingertips" to serious training materials, multimedia will be one of the tools every productive office must have.

Groupware—Fad or Fancy?

If your office has only one PC, don't bother to read this section. Groupware wasn't meant for you. For the rest of you who have more and, assuming these PCs are networked, you just might want to read on!

Groupware provides the ability to share data and information with your co-workers—not a unique concept in itself, except that it's all done electronically. And it's all done quickly and efficiently.

By now, everyone has heard of Electronic Mail systems. E-Mail systems come in all flavors and styles. Most are designed around the PC environment; however, some have been built for mainframe and mid-range systems. Regardless, they all have the same purpose—to disseminate information from one person to another or from one person to many people.

E-Mail systems can move textual data by itself or can embed other forms of information into the message being sent. Some of the form types can be spread-sheet data, scanned images, voice response and, someday soon, full-motion video with sound. All these can be cut and pasted into the message being delivered to one or many co-workers. Considering the volume of information that is now disseminated on paper, both within the office and to business partners outside the office, using E-Mail systems to accomplish even a portion of this would astronomically reduce the costs for paper, toner, copying, distribution, and postage.

Another groupware application that is catching on is calendaring. Although we deal with our own calendar for appointments, many of us also deal with attempting to establish group meeting times. Have you ever tried to call a group of people to arrange everyone's schedule? Impossible at best!

Now, help is just a mouse click away. Groupware calendaring systems are now available. Here is a method to review each attendee's calendar quickly and efficiently. Not only can you find where the open times are for each participant, you can even add the meeting time and place to their schedule—automatically. Once the meeting has been added, the system will notify each person invited that an event was added to their calendar and who added it.

Groupware systems are beginning to catch on and costs are inexpensive on a per-machine basis. Basic groupware systems currently deal with E-mail, calendaring, word processing, and spread-sheet applications. However, over time, many new applications will be added. Each company will be able to mix and match the applications best suited to their work environment. These are truly productivity-enhancing tools and almost surely should be added to any company's arsenal.

Video Conferencing

When Dick Tracy used a wrist device to visually and verbally communicate with his colleagues, we all thought that this was pretty "far out." Well, in some ways, it has been far out. About fifty years out! Now, video conferencing has become an everyday way of doing business for many companies.

Just a few short years ago, however, only a few of the Fortune 500 companies could have afforded video conferencing. But that has all changed. Companies of all sizes and shapes are discovering the advantages of video conferencing. Whether companies create their own facilities or rent someone else's, they're finding enormous savings of time and money by utilizing video conferencing.

In the good old days, when groups of people from diverse locations had to come together to share ideas, the only way to accomplish this was via teleconferencing or travel. With teleconferencing, you could not visually share any data from spread sheets or overhead material. Consequently, it lacked the interaction necessary to hold productive meetings. Traveling to these locations was even worse. It was expensive and took valuable people away from their daily tasks.

Now, from desktops or boardrooms, people can join together to discuss important issues, train on new procedures, or announce new products to the production staffs—simply and inexpensively. Personal cameras can sit on top of your PC and can connect you to another person or can connect you to a room full of people. The group can share overhead material, look at spread-sheet data, and even update it from remote locations, none of which can be accomplished over a simple telephone connection.

Video conferencing, unfortunately, is not a mature technology at this writing. The video portion is not exactly full-motion; consequently, the picture is a little jerky if excessive movement takes place. And the cost is still well above $150,000 for a decent system. However, as new compression techniques are applied, the video will become full-motion, similar to our normal television reception. In addition, the cost will be reduced significantly, making it more affordable to almost any size company or individual.

Intelligent Voice Recognition

For those of you who are Star Trek fans, probably one of the funniest scenes was when Scottie and "Bones" were on a mission to find "plastic aluminum" to build a fish tank aboard the spacecraft. After being shown the computer (circa 1989 variety), Scottie picks up the mouse and begins to speak—"Computer, Computer . . ." Obviously, no response! Scottie was confused, because computers of the twenty-fourth century had IVR (intelligent voice recognition).

Today's computers (circa 1993 variety) are beginning to show some similarities to the twenty-fourth-century version. Voice-recognition application is still pretty much a science. However, there are signs that it is becoming an art very quickly. For the most part, these rudimentary applications must still be "taught" the owners' voice patterns for specific words and phrases. Over time, the computers will be less picky about dialect and be able to understand virtually anyone, in a multitude of languages. However, like the twenty-fourth-century counterparts, these computers will have security patterns built in so that certain individuals can apply new programs, do diagnostics, or run restricted programs.

Similar to video conferencing, IVR is a maturing technology. How long it will take to mature is anybody's guess. However, many believe that by the end of this century, IVR applications will be installed in everything from appliances to telephones, from automobile ignition systems to tomorrow's even-more-intelligent workstations.

Voice-Response Units

If you liked the idea of being able to talk to the computer and have it understand your commands, what do you think about it being able to intelligently answer back, verbally? Maybe we should ask "Dave" from the movie "2001, A Space Odyssey." In that movie, "Hal" (the computer) not only heard his verbal commands, but read his lips and took a very unfriendly position with the two astronauts. Hal's response, both verbally and systematically, was certainly predatory in nature.

Currently, voice-response units (VRUs) take the form of canned human speech combined with snippets of data, generally sounded out into numbers or letters, and spoken back to the requester. Certainly not very high-tech, since these systems lack the two major ingredients necessary to fulfill the destiny of the product. The first missing ingredient is the Intelligent Voice Recognition (IVR) component. The second ingredient is the artificial intelligence component to comprehend the request being made and to systematically apply its own rules and logic to answer the request.

When these two issues have been resolved, VRUs, in conjunction with IVRs, will revolutionize the world's workplaces as well as just about every other place. The applications that will be developed from the marriage of these two technologies will be as limitless as the imaginations creating them.

Intelligent Forms Recognition

If you're a big believer that we will always have printed material, then Intelligent Forms Recognition (IFR) applications will be high on your list of productivity-enhancing tools. These tools are already in the marketplace and can be acquired rather inexpensively. There are a host of applications currently being used, but the two that seem to garner the most attention are simple and effective.

The first application allows a printed page of textual information to be scanned. The system then translates the textual information into machine readable characters and stores them on disk. The user can then treat the stored data as if it were manually entered. The application allows the data to be altered and reprinted in the new format or to be displayed on-line. Such an application can save time and money by eliminating the manual entry of legal forms, procedure manuals, and other textual material that is not in a data format.

In addition, the application allows the user to create a hyper-text search environment. By establishing indices within the text, specific material can be found quickly and easily by searching the index component.

The second application involves scanning pre-formatted pages, where the system reads specific areas of the page and, based upon location, translates the characters and deposits them into data fields. Each form must be set up on the system with the data locations identified by quadrant—a time-consuming effort to be sure. However, once the system is set up, manual data entry is eliminated and the job process is enhanced significantly.

Such applications can be used to replace manual entry on insurance policies and due bills, property tax statements, and other similar forms where the placement of data on the form seldom changes. From a production point of view, such applications can read information from 1003s and appraisal forms and translate it into data for future use. This is certainly an easier way of capturing data from business partners than manually entering it.

Again, IFR applications are still maturing and some will soon be able to translate handwriting with zero error rates. When that occurs, IFR applications will blossom like the spring flowers and they will all smell just as sweet.

Intelligent Power Dialers

If you have ever been solicited by phone to "buy something," the chances are good that the folks who called you used a power dialer. Power dialers have long been the marketing tool of choice for direct sales forces. Why? Because your hit ratios are extraordinarily high. And that is how you sell things. Not with busy signals or no answers.

Not too many years ago, the mortgage banking industry figured out the same thing. But instead of trying to sell something, they were trying to collect something—a mortgage payment. Although it took some time to iron out a few operational issues, once management and the collections staffs became accustomed to the process, the application was a huge success. Delinquency ratios improved dramatically because less time was spent on non-productive busies and no answers.

Now, the mortgage banking industry has begun to utilize power dialers to cross-sell insurance products, call borrowers on missing property tax bills, and contact clients who will have forced-orders insurance placed on their properties. Customer service departments can have an automated way to deal with questions left in a voice messaging center awaiting a call back. The applications available through this technology are many. Just add a little creativity and see what grows.

COMMUNICATIONS—THE FUTURE'S KEY

Voice Communications

There are very few business that are as closely tied to the telephone as the mortgage banking industry. Basically stated, no phones mean no business. Virtually every phase of our business is tied to verbally communicating with the customer or business partner.

Until recently, the department responsible for telephone communications was generally *not* related to the Information Systems group. Most companies failed to recognize that the telephone is nothing more than a large, sophisticated computer that can be attached to other devices. Those devices will merge the telephone with voice-messaging units, data-collection units, and voice-response units that utilize a corporation's huge array of data already stored about its customers.

Now, Information Systems groups provide the technical linkage between the telecommunications systems and the computer systems. Whether the telephone systems are in-house or are supplied by the local vendor at their site, the telephone systems must have back-up methodologies and disaster recovery scenarios—not just for the home office facility, but for each branch or center maintained by the corporation.

Telephones have become our lifeline to new business as well as the ongoing support to existing customers. Without that lifeline, our business will eventually die. Each company must work with long-distance and local carriers, hardware suppliers, and maintenance support personnel to ensure maximum availability for incoming and outgoing call processing at all times. Don't become complacent and treat telecommunications as a second-class citizen; it should be first cabin all the way!

Data Communications

Communicating data between business partners has been around for a long time, at least for many industries outside the mortgage banking industry. Now, however, that all seems to be changing with a vengeance. Everywhere you turn, mortgage companies, either through in-house systems or acquired/leased vendor software, are demanding and getting enhanced data communications capabilities built in to their applications that range from loan origination processing to a multitude of customer service support issues.

By tying in credit bureaus, appraisers, title companies, MI companies, depository institutions, employers records and, maybe someday the IRS, virtually every entity that contributes information to process a loan will be captured electronically. The information will be requested from the selected vendor(s) by a simple click of the mouse key. In turn, the data will be returned electronically and automatically "mapped" into the loan processing system's data base. The beauty here is that the information can all be requested and the majority of it received back in a matter of minutes. The results will be more accurate information with virtually no paper involved.

The maturity of information communication systems will be complete when applications can include full-motion video and sound within LAN, MAN, and WAN networks. Currently, these types of applications are partially available. These multimedia-style communications will be central to the IAYF (Information At Your Fingertips) environment being created.

Data communications, today's shining star, will be tomorrow's supernova. Every segment of our business will be tied in electronically to those business partners with whom we share or exchange data. The productivity gains will be monumental for all involved: the mortgage company, business partner, and the customer. Now that's what you call a win, win, win situation.

FUNCTIONAL REALITY—BY THE DIVISION

Originations

In today's environment, there are probably very few mortgage bankers who still type processing documents. The vast array of choices in origination systems currently on the market provide for large productivity gains in processing and document preparation at very low costs. These software packages come in all sizes and shapes, with a wide range of pricing structures to go with them.

Some companies choose to build their own origination systems instead of buying a package. They choose this method because it is their culture to build, plus they feel more comfortable controlling their operational destiny.

Regardless of the means to the end, the end must be to have an automated loan origination system. Without an automated system, it is extremely difficult to compete even today and will be virtually impossible tomorrow. Consider the following scenario.

A potential home buyer calls in and inquires about eligibility and maximum loan amount. Over the phone, you capture some very basic information about names, income, debts, current address, social security number and whether a fixed-rate or an ARM loan is desired. The data is entered directly into the computer system. From that point on, two things happen simultaneously. First, the system takes pieces of the data and dials the credit bureau to obtain an in-file report. Generally, this takes a few minutes.

Meanwhile, the computer is working on the prequalification portion of the caller's inquiry. Based on the information received, the system will provide the maximum loan amount to the caller, with anticipated mortgage payments and closing costs, at various rates and loan programs. While all this is going on, the credit bureau returns the in-file report to the computer and notifies the processor that the credit report is back. With a click of the mouse, the in-file report is displayed on the screen. The processor can validate that the caller will qualify for a lock-and-shop commitment. The caller selects the rates, points, and program and a document is prepared off the laser printer and mailed.

Consider the same scenario, but in this one the processor is at an open house and is completing the same tasks on a laptop computer with a portable printer. Talk about customer service!

The house hunters are happy, as they have virtually assured themselves of financing. The house seller is happy, since he or she does not have to wonder if the buyer will qualify. The realtor/broker is happy, since he or she now has a practically done deal, and the mortgage company is happy, because they just locked in another deal, that is very likely to be approved and closed.

After the house is found, the application must be taken. Here again, the use of automation can add new wrinkles to the process. Applications can be taken over the phone or in person at the mortgage company's office and the data entered directly into the processing system. In addition, with laptop computers and portable printers, the application can be taken in the realtor's or broker's office, at the applicant's current residence or, for that matter, just about anywhere.

The bottom line is that a new layer of flexibility and mobility has been added to the application processing environment. Both ingredients provide better customer service and create a true competitive edge for those companies using these tools.

Now that you have the application, it must be processed. Whether a company uses centralized or decentralized processing is not generally material. However, to be successful in all originations arenas, both approaches must be used. Likewise, based on work loads, the ability to move processing between geographically removed locations is virtually a must. By having multiple types of processing centers (called a Hub and Spoke concept) the interconnectivity between these units can allow for shared workloads.

Look at what happened in the mortgage financing arena in 1992 when the refinance boom went crazy. Companies that couldn't share the workloads easily due to structure or system constraints were unable to accept more business and ultimately lost a great deal of market share to their counterparts that were structurally and systematically capable.

Processing the application, regardless of approach, now becomes the primary focus of all parties involved. The sooner the transaction is a done deal, the happier everyone is. By having a state-of-the-art computerized processing system, a company can gain a true competitive market advantage. A state-of-the-art system should enhance the quality and quantity of packages being processed. Whether the packages are processed by individuals or by teams, a company should expect to produce more loans faster and of better quality than ever before.

Provisions of a State-of-the-Art System

What should a state-of-the-art system provide? Today, the following ingredients should be present:

♦ User-friendly presentation of screens and ease of maneuverability between screens. The preference is a GUI (graphical user interface) presentation with pull-down boxes for easy reference.

♦ Laser printing of all documents, with the MBA's standard bar code identification numbers included. All documents should be grouped and printed based upon predetermined criteria of application phase, state, and product type. The system should automatically provide all the forms necessary plus provide the flexibility to request other forms as desired.

♦ Data communications to all business partners. Provide the ability to electronically order credit reports, appraisals, mortgage insurance, title work and, someday, verifications from a variety of sources. Once ordered, allow for the return receipt of the data elements to be mapped into your data base, eliminating manual input and the chance for human error.

◆ Provide for an underwriting module, which will extract specific pieces of data and process it through an expert system to arrive at a decision. The most flexible underwriting modules will allow a decision to be reached at any stage of processing, thereby eliminating big surprises later. A state-of-the-art underwriting module should arrive at a decision in less than a minute and should either accept or refer to a human underwriter. A "machine" should never turn down a loan. In addition, the ratio of accepts versus refers should ultimately be nearly three to one, or 75 percent accepted to 25 percent referred.

◆ The system should be flexible and must have the capability to react quickly to regulatory changes and also allow for new products to be added in a timely manner. The system should allow for multiple price changes in a day and must be able to capture and update information on the host systems in a timely manner.

Origination systems hold the keys to success in virtually all other areas within the company. Data entered into these systems are passed down to a host of other fully integrated systems. The optimum process would eliminate any rekeying of data from one system to another, thereby providing clean, virtually error-free information.

Secondary Marketing

There probably isn't a more critical, more exacting function in the mortgage banking business than that of secondary marketing operations. Generally, the unit has many responsibilities that are fundamental to the profitability of the business. They include hedging strategies, product pricing, and commitment control. In some companies, they also maintain back office security and "repo" control.

Hedging systems, by their very nature, are fairly complex. Consequently, very few companies have built their own. The larger the origination volume, the more problematic the hedging decisions are. Built into the hedging programs are trade positions, pipeline position, origination volumes, and a company's philosophy about where the market is moving.

Another responsibility, establishing corporate price on the products offered, must be done quickly and correctly. With the degree of difficulty exacerbated by elements of time, market conditions, business volume, and competition, companies have implemented automated pricing systems to accomplish this task.

Pricing systems are equipped to import the market prices (in the form of data files) directly from various market pricing services. Together with market prices, additional pieces of data are also included.

Utilizing all of these ingredients, the process may perform a series of reverse and forward engineering steps to arrive at the actual prices published to the originating entities and business partners.

For many companies, establishing the price is only the beginning of the process. For companies who have far-flung originating units, delivering the prices to their locations can be a big problem. For those companies, specialized data communications systems are available to automatically control the distribution process. The key here is to deliver the prices as quickly as possible, generally within minutes of price setting. Obviously, the more remote origination units there are, the greater the challenge.

One other point must be made with regard to having large numbers of remote originating units. A major part of the pricing model is the matching of the origination volume to the movement of the markets. Some companies have installed Executive Information Systems (EIS) to help track volume. Many of these systems are capable of reporting out volumes every half hour, on-line with drill-down features. Here again, the application of multiple technologies provides companies with vital information to operate their business profitably.

The last major component of secondary marketing is loan delivery and commitment control. The degree of complexity in delivering loans has risen dramatically over the last several years. With he advent of new types of products, new investor requirements, new regulatory requirements and, with production in 1992 at record levels, the ability to process unprecedented loan volumes has put a strain on management and staff alike.

However, new technologies have provided quantum improvements over just a few short years ago. The newest wrinkle has been the introduction of artificially intelligent rule-based systems to automatically earmark loans. These systems are extremely efficient when they are coupled with highly sophisticated pipeline management and inventory control systems. The A/I systems look at loans that are about to fund as well as those in inventory to provide the most advantageous pooling scenario.

The implementation of these types of systems will eliminate much of the labor-intensive process of delivering loans. In addition, we are beginning to see a movement away from our previous paper-based delivery process to an electronic format with virtually all the paper eliminated. We are also beginning to see a movement toward a standardization of the electronic delivery format. Once this is adopted by the agencies and private investors, all parties involved will reap the rewards of greater economies and higher productivity levels.

Operations

Back office systems have generally lagged far behind those of production and loan servicing. The lack of automation in these areas was primarily attributable to manually performed, paper-intensive job functions. However, new technologies are being introduced and some older technologies are being reintroduced to aid in the demanualization of the operations areas.

With the advent of sophisticated loan origination systems and the movement toward laser printers to produce loan documents, there has been a vast improvement in the quality of the loan package. For those companies whose origination systems automatically feed the core systems (secondary marketing, operations, finance, and loan servicing), the correlation between the data and the documentation received has been at or very near 100 percent. Eliminating the manual verification between paper and data has reduced a manual and time-consuming process to virtually zero.

Records management has improved dramatically with the addition of bar-coded files and documents. The ability to track entire files or individual documents from department to department has taken the mystery out of where things are. Even some of the more sophisticated custodian and warehouse banks have taken to bar coding by logging in collateral and custodian files/documents. Also, by linking your document systems to their document systems, you will provide better control and audibility to an extremely important process.

Until recently, the method of retrieving a document from a file was limited. You had two choices. Choice one: pull the physical file and locate the document, or choice two: find the microfilm roll/jacket, then locate the document using a reader. Both choices were time-consuming and extremely expensive. The time to retrieve a document could be measured, at a minimum, in hours and, more than likely, in days. The cost associated with the entire retrieval and delivery process for a single document is estimated at between $10 and $20, not including any vendor storage/retrieval costs.

Today, many mortgage companies, both large and small, are finding that imaging systems are fast becoming the storage medium of choice. Imaging systems range from smaller, department-size to larger, corporate-wide systems that provide maximum benefit from work-flow engineering. Aside from the fact that the cost to implement an imaging system has dropped dramatically over the last few years, the simple fact that loan documents are now laser produced has provided the last meaningful push over the top. By affixing an MBA-standardized bar coding schema, an imaging scanner can read the document, index it automatically, and place it into storage at the rate of thousands of pages an hour.

Ultimately, imaging systems will be fed, not by paper, but by electronic images of the documents directly from the origination systems. These origination systems will include a pen-based attachment that will capture the signature of the borrower(s). Someday, the need to produce the paper initially will be substantially reduced. Remote capture of externally produced documents by electronically formatting their appearance will be commonplace.

Eventually, there will be standards established for all commercially available imaging systems. When that happens, one of the last hurdles will be overcome. Now we move data streams. Soon, we will move data images, voice, and full-motion video. Think how that will affect our relationships with agencies, investors, business partners, and our customers.

Finance

The key to any successful financial area is the ability to integrate huge amounts of data from throughout the company and, ultimately, make sense of it.

In many cases, when systems are being designed, the last functional area that is considered is the financial group. Although they play a major role in just about everything a company does, we seldom consider their needs. Yet, the vast amounts of detail generated by origination systems, secondary marketing, and loan administration is staggering.

Origination systems deal with outgoing funds along with incoming fees and various interest and impound payments. When the loan is ready to fund, the origination system must prepare a "funds request" record to pass on to the treasury department. The request could take the form of a wire, Fed check, or draft. Regardless of form, the linkage to treasury and corporate accounting is imperative. Likewise, the creation of transaction records for "posting" to both the general ledger and to the individual loan record is mandatory.

One additional note. Should the "funds request" take the form of a draft, by establishing a data communications link with your warehouse bank, you can take advantage of "positive pay" systems that honor only the drafts you transmit to the bank every day. All other drafts will be denied, thereby virtually eliminating the opportunity to cash forged drafts.

Financial systems must also be flexible enough to integrate with Executive Information Systems. The ability to create on-line financial statements with drill-down to a more detailed accounting level has widespread desirability. Taken beyond that, the EIS application must also interface with the item-level general ledger postings. The result of this marriage allows management at all levels to be more financially responsible.

A handful of companies have implemented imaging systems in their accounts payable department. Although some applications are simply a retrieval of paid invoices, a few companies have opted for a more robust system. Those companies have implemented a "work flow," rules-based system, which automatically routes imaged invoices prior to payment. The routing is based on a few fields that are indexed by the accounts payable department off of the invoice.

The rules-based matrix then determines the individual(s) that must "sign off" prior to payment and automatically forwards the electronic image of the invoice to each person in succession. To approve the invoice, the individual enters a special password, which affixes his electronic, handwritten signature to the invoice. Should approval not be forthcoming, the invoice can be manually rerouted to any individual with a message asking for clarification.

By adding imaging to the financial systems base, management has the ability to drill-down from the EIS on-line financials to detailed level general ledger postings to actually viewing the paid invoice.

The last major technology that has failed to take hold in the financial services industry is Electronic Data Interchange (EDI), although it is heavily used in the manufacturing arena. Very few mortgage companies and their business partners are prepared to accept and pay invoices from electronic transmissions. Over time, however, the mortgage industry must find more ways to implement EDI applications in order to eliminate the costly paper flow that now takes place.

Loan Administration

The clear winner of all the new technologies is the loan administration area. The ability to service more loans per employee is virtually all due to these emerging technologies. Consider the following changes that have enhanced our operations.

Systems integration has improved the reliability of the information received. The data transferred from the automated origination systems is more accurate and timely than ever before. Much of this is caused by importing electronically exchanged data from strategically important business partners. Credit bureaus, appraisers, title companies, and mortgage insurers are among those that contribute information.

The better the information, the easier it is to service a loan. Eliminated are errors related to special loan type characteristics, such as ARM, GPM, or buydown information. Impound data is correctly calculated at closing, and legal description, parcel number data, and property tax status are all accurate.

Imaging systems provide for many service-related improvements. Customer service can answer inquiries related to loan documents without the need to pull the file or microfiche. Collections staff can review the original loan application when contacting a delinquent mortgagor to get a flavor of what's changed. Even cashiering departments are imaging payment checks that are received with no coupon or billing. By indexing these checks by date and check amount, it is easier to find misposting which, unfortunately, still occurs.

What imaging provides is fast, easy retrieval of information, and that translates to better customer service—service that will ultimately be the key to survival during the balance of this decade.

Artificial intelligence has been talked about for many years. Recently, the discussions have centered on loan underwriting as the application of choice for this technology. However, there is one area that can take advantage of several technologies, including artificial intelligence systems. That area is collections.

By utilizing the ability to interface with your credit bureau of choice, let's say at night, your system transmits a file of delinquent accounts. Before the next business day begins, the credit bureau transmits to you the in-file report on all the accounts submitted. The artificial intelligence systems translate the data received, combine it with data from the original application and review the loan history on the account. From this review, the system determines which people to call the next day, places information about the customer's credit analysis on the screen, and automatically uses an intelligent power-dialing system to make the call. Add imaging to the mix, and the collector has everything in front of him or her to counsel the customer intelligently.

Executive Information Systems have also aided loan administration in ways no one thought possible just a few short years ago. EIS applications have been created to monitor specific activities of vital importance to the company. These applications include cash management, runoff data, telephone activity (ACD monitoring), delinquencies/foreclosures, and a host of operational statistics. What EIS applications add is the ability to see the information on-line and to provide drill-down capabilities.

One such EIS application created at Countrywide is lovingly called the "vegamatic," because it slices and dices the information into literally thousands of views. The system was developed originally for the delinquency and foreclosure areas, but has been expanded to include payoff information. The user can request virtually any combination of categories and the system will, within seconds, return the answer. This feature is extremely important when talking to outside investors, agencies, or reporters.

Currently, this EIS application is being combined with an artificially intelligent front end. The result will be a picture of trends that otherwise would be hard to spot. Eventually, the original application data will be included in the analysis. At that point, the A/I system can truly be used to forecast problem areas before they become a problem.

Certainly, from a communications perspective, loan administration has benefited significantly over the last several years. With improved telephone switches and automatic call distribution (ACD) systems enhancing their features, the loan administration area can instantly monitor the incoming calls. Based on this on-line analysis, managers can add more people to handle the calls or reroute calls to other departments that are not as busy.

Some PBX hardware suppliers have teamed up with computer manufacturers to provide a seamless interface to pass off a call and supply the customer information at the same time. Such a marriage has taken place between Northern Telecom and IBM. The product name is "CALLPATH." When the call is processed by the PBX software, the telephone number of the caller is captured using automatic number identification (ANI). The number is then passed off to a file in the AS/400, which has all the telephone numbers of their customers (home, business, etc.) in it. The numbers are then matched; if a match does occur, the system passes the call to the next available agent and at the same time, presents a base screen of information about the calling customer. If there is no match, the call is also passed and a standard script screen is presented to the agent.

Many medium- and large-sized mortgage companies are utilizing voice response units (VRUs). These units are designed to interface a human script with data from the servicing system. These VRUs are becoming more sophisticated and, in many companies, already handle approximately 20 percent of all incoming calls. When intelligent voice recognition features are added, these systems will be truly interactive and will handle a much larger percentage of calls.

Data communications has been receiving a great deal of added attention lately. Companies are finding that sharing data in this manner helps drive down costs and improves customer service. Many vendors are now willing to put computers and people in their customers' offices to gain efficiencies. Foreclosure attorneys, major insurance companies, title companies, property management services, and a host of others are finding that sharing makes everyone happy (and wealthier). Over time, many taxing authorities who now send out billings by magnetic tape will revert to data communications.

As more investors, agencies, and business partners join the crowd, data standards will emerge. And, as technology improves at the major telecom carriers, the speed of communicating will increase while costs decrease. Eventually, standard communicating speed will be at 56kb with bandwidth on demand available up to T3 fiber-optic configurations, the latter being capable of handling full-motion video for video-conferencing, and movements of large amounts of data, including images and sound.

For most mortgage companies, the loan administration and investor accounting areas print huge amounts of paper reports. Some of the reports are for internal use, while others are sent outside. For those reports that are external, very little can be done until you and those receiving the paper agree on another mutually acceptable format.

Two methods immediately come to mind, one is to send the data that makes up the report and let the receiving entity deal with how they wish to format the information in-house. The second is to transfer the report to a CD-ROM disk and allow the receiving entity the ability to view the report on-line. Obviously, you wouldn't use the second option if the reports were small, but for large reports, such as investor accounting reports, this method would be very appropriate.

For internal reports, there are at least four options available. One is to convert the paper report to an EIS application if the information on the report is basically totals of daily/monthly activity. Delinquency and run-off data are two examples of good EIS applications. A second option would be to convert the report into client server applications. Follow-up type reports such as foreclosure, bankruptcy, and customer service issues are naturals for this application. By building a GUI front end around the data, the manager and clerical staff can massage the information in many ways to keep on top of and balance work loads.

The third option would be to write out the report to a CD-ROM rewritable disk. The report could be viewed on-line and, after a selected period of time, could be written over by newer information. Reports considered for this option are copies of outbound letters and follow-ups sent to customers and business partners. Since most of these are time-sensitive, they can be written over at some point.

The fourth option is to use imaging's COLD application. Here, the printed report is written out to a Write Once-Read Many (WORM) disk, which is permanent in nature. Specific applications would include property tax and insurance disbursements from loan administration and all in-house copies of investor accounting reports. These reports would include all interim and cut-off reports, daily distribution reports, cash and book reconcilement reports, together with a host of other related balancing and research-type reports. The reports are automatically indexed to any search level required, therefore making it easier to look them up on-line.

Loan administration divisions are poised for the future. Many technologies are already in place and many others are just around the corner. However, the key to taking advantage of these technologies centers on the implementation and installation of personal computers on every desk in the corporation. Personal computers provide the basis for productivity gains unheard of just a few short years ago. The old axiom, "a dime a dozen" doesn't quite apply yet to the cost of personal computers, but they are already considered a commodity and, therefore, subject to the realisms of the marketplace.

When personal computers are all attached using networking technologies currently in place, groupware applications such as E-Mail, calendaring, and interactive multimedia systems will inform and educate our employees in a way never thought possible!

AN AWAKENING—UNITED WE STAND

The MBA's Vision—Ultimate Efficiency

Several years ago, the MBA formed a technology committee. One of the committee's goals was to search out new technologies, and inform our industry of the benefits these technologies would bring to the membership. To accomplish this goal, the committee has put together a series of seminars and conferences throughout the year that highlight various technologies. Experts in their respective fields participate and share their experiences and knowledge with the attendees. The main conference is held in March of each year, and currently lasts for two days.

The conference is well-attended by both technical and nontechnical mortgage banking people as well as an ever increasing number of vendors who have systems, products, and services to sell to a technology-starved industry.

Another major part of the committee's goals is to adopt industry-wide standards—standards that relate not only to data, but to the terminology, size, and definition of these data elements. These standards would represent our industry's needs in transmitting data, forms, and images between companies and their business partners. The committee's view is that some day all these standards would be blessed by the ANSI standards group. But until then, our industry will adopt these standards and will continue to use and improve upon them as time goes on.

The last major goal of the committee ties into the standards goal. That goal is to virtually eliminate all the paper between mortgage bankers, agencies, and supporting business partners. By creating data transmission standards for such applications as credit reports, appraisal information, loan delivery, investor reporting, insurance and tax payments, and a host of others, no paper would be generated or exchanged.

Some of these standards have been completed and many are currently being worked on. Over time, the industry will implement these standards and create new ones. The process is a never ending one, just as the technologies that surround them never stop changing.

The New Agencies

During the course of human events, there are times that allow unprecedented changes to take place. This is such a time in the mortgage banking industry. Never before have the agencies been so willing to change the way they carry on their business. Not only are they looking to re-engineer their internal operations, but they are hoping to drastically alter the way their customers do business with them.

Change is the operative word around their offices. *Re-engineering, rethinking,* and *revitalization* are the chosen words. They have created project teams and have given the projects names. They are talking to their competition and working in harmony to achieve these common goals. Yes, they are even talking to their customers to find out what the real world is like out there. What are their business partners (us) doing, and what would we like to see done to simplify everyone's operations?

Currently, there are many joint projects under way. FHLMC, FNMA, and GNMA are part of a group to set standards for electronic loan delivery and loan level investor reporting. By having a single, standard format, the industry would benefit significantly and would put the decision to deliver loans to an investor based solely on price and service. Once these standards have been established, the goal is to spread them to the private investors, thereby making the whole process universal.

Even HUD and VA are becoming more serious about creating common standards with each other and with private mortgage insurers. Data needed to complete claim forms are being studied by all concerned to reach a consensus. Once it is reached, an EDI format to transmit the information to the insurer will be created.

The agencies must be commended! "Partners-in-progress" is a strong theme and must be continued at all costs. The mortgage banking industry is on the threshold of becoming the only real source of home financing funds. As banks and other financial institutions withdraw from the marketplace and become only token players, it is extremely vital that we find the means to provide the best in quality financing at the lowest possible price. Working together and applying the newest of technologies will accomplish those common goals.

Business Partners' Involvement

The last ingredient, but certainly not the least, is the involvement of our business partners in this whole process. The ability to finance home loans quickly and efficiently is tied directly to the ability of the business partner to supply the lender with timely and accurate data. In fact, not only should it be timely and accurate, it should be electronic.

Now, that sounds like a tall order for some business partners who are far from being technologically advanced. Somehow, these folks never got past the idea of a typewriter and paper. Unfortunately, that may be true for some companies as well as industries, but not for all.

Those that are technologically advanced may have to alter their systems to adhere to the standards being established, but that is a small price to pay for the amount of business they will receive. Mortgage companies of all sizes are now finding out that they want their information in a data-stream format, not on paper. The business partners who can meet those demands now will have an inside track not only at getting the business, but keeping it.

Those business partners who cannot meet the requirements will eventually lose business until they, too, can supply the data streams needed by the lender. By then, it may be too late.

The trend has started, and more and more business partners are jumping on board. These services, like all others, will then be put on a level playing field, with price and service being the true determining factors. Technology is a double-edged sword and it cuts both ways. If you don't join, you will surely die, and if you do join, you might just die trying to keep up.

THE HUMAN FACTOR—FEAR AND FASCINATION

Participation and Understanding

When you get the idea that you're going to deploy one of these new technologies, you had better get a grip onto something nailed down. Because the truth of the matter is that for every one person who may think it's a great idea there are at least three or four others who tend to disagree. And that ratio may actually be higher, depending on the degree to which the change directly affects them. There is an old saying, "change is good as long as it affects someone else." No truer words were ever spoken.

Just a few words of advice. Before the project gets too far along, get everyone who will be even remotely affected involved in the discussions. Explain what it is you're trying to accomplish by deploying the new technology and the associated applications. Review all the possibilities of how it will change their jobs and even their roles in the department or company. Talk about how you see the benefits and ask them if they see the same things. Ask them if they have any ideas that could add to the process or, better yet, simplify it even further.

Above all, eliminate any fears that they will lose their jobs when the changes take place. If these fears are not removed, the new application/technology will fail. By involving the people early and often, and by getting their input early and often, you can better the chances that the project will be a huge success.

Re-Engineering versus Paving a Cowpath

So many times, major enhancements to systems or system rewrites are presented to MIS under the guise that the department has undertaken an extensive study to improve operational functionality. Most of the time, this oratory is just so much hogwash. The truth of the matter is, most of the time the requests do little to truly re-engineer the process, but instead simply pave over the existing methodology.

The largest criticism ever laid upon the user community by MIS staffs (whether in-house or service bureau) has been that the user never wants to start with a white piece of paper when examining job functions. The fact is, before you ever think about how a system should work, you had better understand how the job works. Know what the job relationships are with other functional units, what these other groups do that affect your function and, conversely, what you do that affects others downstream of you. All of these issues must be taken into consideration when designing an application.

Once the work flows have been established and the needs clearly defined, then, and only then, can any intelligence be applied toward building a meaningful application. At this critical stage of the process, every need must be examined to determine what technologies would apply to satisfy those requirements. If that process is not done up front, it is very likely that you will not build the best mousetrap.

Paving a cowpath does not solve the major issues confronting the mortgage banking industry. Only re-engineering of work flows and functionalities will eventually bring about the changes we so drastically require. We need all parties to keep an open mind and not only be willing to accept change, but be actively seeking change. We must treat this as a new beginning if we are to accomplish our lofty goals.

JAD and RAD Become JIRAD

If you have ever hired a consulting firm to assist you in developing systems, you have been exposed to various acronyms, SDLC (Systems Development Life Cycle), JAD (Joint Application Development), and RAD (Rapid Application Development). For those of you who have been personally exposed to any of these processes, you have either sworn by it or sworn at it.

With the pace of most companies at break-neck speed, the two methodologies that are gaining popularity are the JAD and RAD variety. JAD is a very good process to say the least, because you bring together both the user community and the MIS analysts and programmers. The other process, RAD, is in fashion because it develops applications rapidly—it is also a very good process.

Unfortunately, with JAD and RAD, the contributing groups do not always remain involved during the entire process of the development. Each group provides its expertise and then passes the project on to the next group. The reason this phenomenon occurs is quite simple—everyone is very busy. People focus in short bursts and then move on to something else.

With JIRAD (Joint Interactive Rapid Application Development) you combine the best of all worlds. You form quality teams for each project, and all the participants meet on a regular basis, which guarantees the interactive approach. These meetings continue through the final and post-implementation review. Each team member is responsible for his or her part of the project and has final approval authority for any piece of the project that affects his or her area. Consequently, it is imperative that quality staff members be assigned to these teams. The better the quality of staff, the faster the project will be completed and implemented.

As the cost of system enhancements and maintenance continue to rise, it is essential that management assign the best and brightest people to these teams. Based upon the premise that companies must re-engineer their work flows and system, anything less would be disastrous.

Training, Then More Training

There is an old axiom that says you can never teach someone too much. Now, more than ever, the axiom applies. Every day, our business is changing! The changes are due to new regulations, agency, or investor requirements, and creative new product lines, which must be sold and serviced. Not only is our business changing rapidly, but so are the technologies we use to operate it.

Consequently, companies must make every effort to train their staffs and management on both fronts. Whether you're a small company or a large company, training will be one of the keys to your success or failure. To be successful, you must follow some very basic principles.

Establish a training department and staff it with qualified people who have taught classes before. Their background isn't as important as their ability to stand up in front of a class and convey the information in an easily understood way. They must exude confidence about the subject matter and be able to answer virtually any question quickly and correctly. Although this sounds rudimentary, it is very difficult to find such people.

Next, establish a curriculum covering the mortgage banking business in general, specialized departmental training, telephone etiquette, and a wide array of computer training in both hardware and software. In a sense, create a college-style atmosphere and actually give credits toward an internal form of certified mortgage banker designation. Class material can be acquired from the Mortgage Bankers Association, created internally to fit your organization's special needs, or purchased from vendors who have put together classes for self-help training and computer-based training.

Whether you hire your own staff, pay vendors to take over these classes, install multimedia guided-learning centers, or use any combination thereof, the key is—do it now! You will not only find you have happier employees, but you will find that your productivity and customer service will improve dramatically. These unmistakable returns will make you wonder why everyone doesn't take training more seriously.

THE FINAL FRONTIER—TOMORROW'S REALITY

Information at Your Fingertips (IAYF)

Over a year ago, Microsoft initiated an idea whose basis was to make people more productive. The monumental premise advanced was to bring people and information together in a simple and user-friendly way. This concept was called Information at Your Fingertips.

In order to pull this concept off, Microsoft made two major assumptions. One, you had a personal computer on your desk and it was attached to a network. Two, you were using Microsoft's Windows operating system along with other Microsoft windows applications. On the surface, it sounded a little self-serving. In reality, however, it was truly a visionary concept.

There are several keys here which must not be overlooked. The cost of PCs is going down rapidly and their power is rising even faster. Network operating systems are becoming more mature, thereby providing the reliability demanded for mission critical applications. Client server architecture is becoming widely accepted as a means to bring the user and the data closer together. Last, but certainly not least, is the simple fact that people like working in a GUI presentation mode. It is user-friendly and very intuitive, regardless of knowledge level.

Earlier in this chapter, differing technologies were discussed. For the most part, virtually everyone required a personal computer on the desktop. For without the personal computer, none of these productivity-enabling technologies would have been created.

The next saga in IAYF's future will be Star Trekian in impact. We have just scratched the surface where people and massive amounts of information are inextricably linked. Every technology of today will mature by unimaginable leaps. Our personal and working world will never be the same.

The 30-Minute Warning

Ponder this if you will: A family sits in front of their TV on a Sunday morning. They have been looking for a new home for several weeks and have not found the right one. While watching the local real estate listing program, they suddenly discover the home of their dreams. They jot down the listing number assigned to each home shown while grabbing the TV's remote control.

They press the "interactive" key on the remote control, which sends a signal to the cable station. The cable station responds with a ready signal on the TV screen. Now, they enter the program code and the listing number of the home they wish to "walk through." The cable station receives the message and immediately runs a full three-dimensional pictograph of the home, its interior and exterior. The view can be rotated to get a full 360-degree look at any portion of the home.

Great! Everybody likes what they see and they all agree this is the home they want to buy. Before everyone goes crazy, however, reality sets in. Can they afford it? Well, let's see! With the simple click of the "option" key on the remote control, a drop-down box appears on the screen. They select the "prequalification" option. Once there, they then select the "loan program" option.

A screen is displayed to enter basic information about the family: income, debts, assets, and liabilities. Information about the subject property is captured from the cable company as are the guidelines for the loan program selected. When all is entered, the information is then "reviewed" to determine eligibility.

The screen flashes back "conditionally approved" and everyone is overjoyed. The screen then asks "Do you wish to make an offer?" "Yes," they all agree as they enter the offer amount.

A few minutes later, the offer is sent to the sellers, who "punch" in their acceptance, the realtors involved are notified, and the deal is done. As the buyers rejoice, they select a lender from a list of prominent companies who participate in the program. At that point, the information they entered initially is transferred to a full application screen. The buyers complete the balance of the data required and "send" it to the lender by selecting the "transmit" option on the screen.

The lender receives the data, maps the information into their formats, and prepares to complete the loan package. Within minutes, the credit report is electronically ordered and returned. Simultaneously, the appraisal is ordered through a national comparable service with interior, exterior, and neighborhood reviews being handled by three-dimensional pictographs and short-range satellites with surface and geological holographs. Verification of employment and deposits are electronically ordered and received through an arm of the IRS.

Within 15 minutes, all the data is received. It is then automatically fed through the artificially intelligent underwriting system and within seconds, the system approves the loan. Instantly, the mortgage insurance carrier is notified and sent the appropriate data, and then returns coverage data. Concurrently, the title company is notified, electronically returns the preliminary title information.

Within 30 minutes, all the data is received and processed. All regulatory statements have been electronically sent, the closing documents are virtually ready to be drawn and the deal is ready to close.

The little scenario is a few years away from being a reality, but much of the process can be done electronically now. The question is, will you be ready to compete when it does? If you're not ready now yet want to be, you had better position yourself quickly and decisively.

"Tomorrow lives in the light of our past"

EPILOGUE

Technology's Rapid Advance

It doesn't take a wizard to figure out that our lives have changed dramatically in recent years. Most of these changes have been due to advancements in technology.

Every day, some new application is announced or some new breakthrough has been made on chip technology. Bigger, better, faster computers are being built that reside on your desk, in your lap, or in the palm of your hand. Applications are becoming more user-friendly and more feature-rich. Information is communicated between computers virtually anytime, anywhere.

That's just today. Tomorrow, the pace of change will quicken even more. Manufacturers and developers will be under even more pressure to build a better mousetrap. What is considered science fiction today will be just science tomorrow.

The Choices Are Yours

Every company must choose its own path. Each must decide how it wants to do business and how the business will be done. Such a simple statement for such a difficult process.

Where in the mass of competition will it place itself? How does it wish to be viewed by the competition, the business partner, and the client? What is the threshold of pain for being a leader in product or process? Can the leadership sustain prolonged growth? Can systems not only sustain the growth, but be capable of being quickly enhanced to add new features, functionality, and products?

As mentioned in this chapter, there are many opportunities to improve the way business is done. But will altering the way business is done also alter the way the company is viewed? The answer is, "without a doubt." Being viewed in a more positive way will undoubtedly bring more business and with more business, it is easier to continually improve the way you do business.

There is little doubt that those companies that utilize technology to improve efficiencies and increase employee productivity will be in a better position to gain a competitive advantage. By providing better customer service and by offering competitive pricing due to lower operational costs, companies will gain market share at the expense of those companies who choose not to utilize technology.

The choices are yours—difficult choices to say the least, but necessary choices nonetheless. The old axiom of "you can pay me now or you can pay me later" has never been truer. However, paying later may prove to be fatal.

Remember—these are the best of times!

"For those who have blazed the trails . . . our eternal debt of thanks,

For those who will brave new tomorrows, a wish for hope, courage and vision"

Chapter 20

TECHNOLOGY IN THE MORTGAGE INDUSTRY

Patricia A. Mikel
Vice President
PMI Mortgage Insurance Co.

INTRODUCTION

A revolution is under way that is radically changing the mortgage industry's real estate lending processes and procedures for the first time in over 50 years. This revolution has the recognizable characteristics of all major historical revolutions that have changed industries and nations. That is, it is being born out of need for change and led by a few who have a vision to improve the system for many. The waves of refinance business that hit the industry in 1992 have shown that much more must be done to provide the necessary customer service and alleviate the "roller-coaster ride" in underwriting departments. Industry surveys conducted in the past two years point especially to the lack of automation within underwriting and quality control departments, regardless of the size of the organization. The tool being used to accomplish change in the mortgage industry is "technology," which comes in many new forms.

From the creation of today's mortgage banking industry in the 1920s until today, the mortgage loan origination process has been virtually the same. Each mortgage finance transaction has begun with a prescribed set of the applicant's personal data and credit documents, followed by an appraisal of the specific property (prepared after physical inspection by a qualified real estate appraiser), an underwriting analysis and decision by an experienced loan underwriter, and loan documents prepared by a qualified loan processor. In the future, and in a very few mortgage banking and mortgage insurance companies across the nation today, these steps are accomplished without stacks of paper moving between the various parties and with little or no human involvement. New methods are saving time and money for all participants.

The use of automation has been growing for several years and today most mortgage origination organizations are equipped with service bureau or on-site mainframes and/or personal computers, operating at least one of many choices of mortgage processing software packages. The capabilities of these software products vary from loan application tracking or "pipeline" software, to full document preparation and management reporting. As examples, for many years mortgage banking firms have been running servicing software packages, either on-site or through a service bureau; both FNMA and FHLMC have provided electronic reporting capabilities for their customers, and some mortgage insurance companies have developed automated risk analysis capabilities and also receive delinquency data via tape or disc. These have all been significant steps in using technology to manage the business of today and in preparing for the future. But they are only a beginning.

Several different types of technology tools exist today to bring the necessary relief to front-line personnel who are dealing with the antiquated methods of the past. The lack of implementation of alternative methods is *not* due to lack of technology-based solutions. For many, the biggest challenge to the use of the new capabilities is slowness in acceptance of change. Yet, from deregulation and its aftermath to the growth of the conventional mortgage-backed securities market, we have proven as an industry that we survive and thrive on change. So, in the same way that we have harnessed the opportunities of the past, we will handle the tool called "technology" and use it to the maximum in our future.

Preparing for change starts with gathering information. Industry publications are full of articles on the subject of the new technologies in the workplace—so many, in fact, with conflicting perspectives and terms, that the subject can be overwhelming and easier to walk away from than confront. Getting comfortable with the vocabulary, understanding the potential value of each tool, and seeing the benefits resulting from the development to date will hopefully help speed comfort levels and move the revolution even faster for the good of everyone involved. To simplify the perceived complexities, let's look at a few examples of different support capabilities being developed and/or used by a few of the "technology pioneers" in the industry.

ARTIFICIAL INTELLIGENCE

"Artificial intelligence" is a term that is used to represent alternative methods of decision making, besides the human mind. There are basically four different methods to automate decision making (see Figure 20.1). Two are "predictive" (statistical and neural networks). Predictive models require a large data base from which patterns can be recognized, based on experience. The other two are referred to as "expert systems" (judgment processing and rule-based systems). Judgment processing software is based on the premise that pragmatic experts make decisions on the basis of intuition, experience, and knowledge. It requires a human expert working directly with the software as a "mentor." Rule-based systems are developed using a human expert who provides information to a "knowledge engineer," who, in turn, uses the skills of a computer programmer.

To get a better perspective on what each method involves, let's look at some actual applications of each type that have been accomplished within the mortgage industry, and/or learn about each of these options in more depth.

STATISTICAL PREDICTIVE

In 1985, PMI Mortgage Insurance Co., a subsidiary of the Allstate Insurance Company, established the strategic goals of (a) automating the mortgage insurance underwriting process, and (b) establishing an electronic "lender network" through which mortgage originators could submit applications for mortgage insurance and receive real-time commitments. It was expected that achieving these goals would provide

Figure 20.1   Technologies to Automate Decision Making

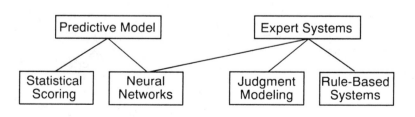

PMI with a competitive market advantage, and would allow human underwriters to spend more time analyzing real estate and economic trends.

In 1986, PMI, in conjunction with the Allstate Planning and Research Center in Menlo Park, California, began development of PMI-AURA^{SM} (Automated Underwriting Risk Analysis), which employs two interactive, statistical predictive models to predict the likelihood of default by a mortgage borrower (see Figure 20.2). The models interact to assign each loan a risk score from 1 to 100, with the higher number representing the higher risk.

Fully implemented in 1987, the initial data base was the actual borrower, credit, and property data from more than 350,000 applications received by PMI for years 1981 through 1986. Through updating, it now exceeds 650,000 sets of data and experience and, as of early 1993, exceeded 1 million profiles. Today, as much as 60 percent of PMI's total daily approved business is approved by the PMIAURA^{SM} system.

The system recognizes regional underwriting requirements down to a specific county level, providing for quick reaction to a local economic change. In addition to the efficiency and consistency of underwriting decisions, one of the major benefits recognized by PMI has been the timely information provided to the underwriting and quality control departments. Daily and monthly tracking reports allow PMI to

---

Figure 20.2   Automated Underwriting Risk Analysis

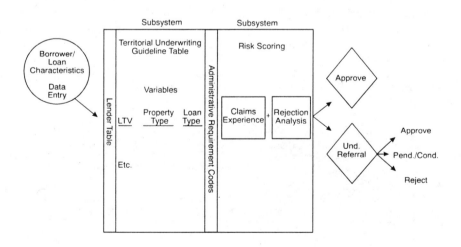

review the quality of its business by loan type, property type, loan purpose, housing/income ratios, etc., by region, customer, underwriter, etc.

Shortly after the implementation of PMIAURA^{SM}, PMI began developing an electronic lender network to provide its mortgage insurance customers with a paperless, optimally efficient mortgage insurance transaction. PMI worked with B.F. Saul Mortgage, a subsidiary of Chevy Chase Bank, to create a prototype of the network, which allows mortgage loan officers to electronically submit applications for mortgage insurance to PMI. Loan officers receive an approval decision on their laptop personal computers within seconds, while "referrals" (applications unacceptable to the PMIAURA^{SM} system), are reviewed by a PMI underwriter within minutes. This prototype Lender Network has been successfully used since June 1990. (See Figure 20.3.)

With the automated underwriting system, PMI's senior underwriters are available to spend more time on highly complex risk decisions. In addition, all underwriting staff have more time to develop client relationships, provide client education, and sharpen their knowledge of their local markets. Peak business periods are handled much more efficiently, and the system allows PMI to achieve its primary goal of giving superior service to its customers because it helps to ensure fast responses and consistent decisions.

Other benefits with the system enhance the productivity of employees and allow underwriters to concentrate on borrower, credit, and appraisal scenarios that warrant closer scrutiny. And, from a portfolio management perspective, the system's quantitative scoring of portfolios allows for improved analyses and reporting.

NEURAL NETWORKS

Neural networks are a new method of information processing. The technology emerged from research scientists' attempts to understand biological information processing. From this biological background, neural networks evolved into an engineering discipline, using new adaptive parallel processing techniques. These techniques produce highly valuable solutions to problems that have stumped computer scientists using more-traditional algorithmic approaches.

They "learn" to perform useful functions through "training." This feature, combined with its biological roots, has prompted advocates of the technology to compare neural networks to the human brain and human learning processes. Neurocomputers "learn" their programs from data that characterized the problem.

Figure 20.3   PMIs Deployed Production Network

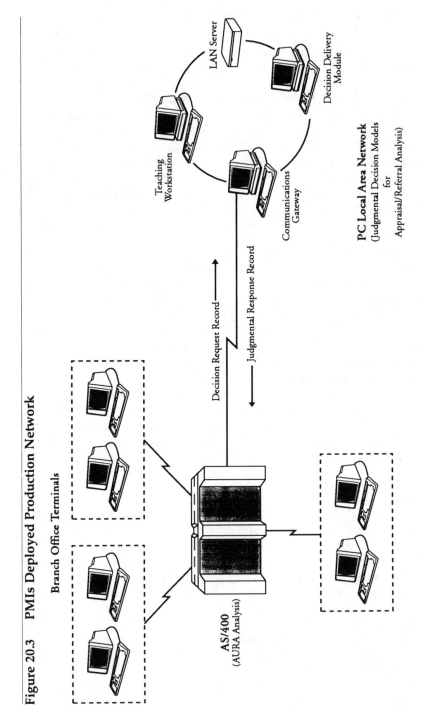

Branch Office Terminals

Decision Request Record

Judgmental Response Record

AS/400
(AURA Analysis)

Teaching
Workstation

LAN Server

Communications
Gateway

Decision Delivery
Module

PC Local Area Network
(Judgmental Decision Models
for
Appraisal/Referral Analysis)

Neural networks are popular because they solve difficult problems without programming. The user identifies a data set that characterizes the problem (for example, a set of hand-written characters with their correct identification) and trains the network to an acceptable level of performance. The result is a solution to a specific, complicated application with little or no programming. The user need not possess any special expertise or sophisticated algorithmic knowledge. The answer emerges from the problem itself.

Their network capabilities are made possible as a result of certain defining characteristics that set neural networks apart from conventional computing technologies. In a traditional computer or expert system, the computer must be programmed with a defined set of instructions. The computer carries out its task by following these instructions. The neurocomputer, however, is repeatedly presented data from which it automatically learns to discern and extract the key relationships underlying the data. Rather than having to be told exactly what to do and how to do it, the neural network can, in effect, teach itself how to accomplish a task.

Building a successful network of this kind requires that the network be trained to reflect the patterns in the data. Training a network involves presenting data records with input and output values. For each record, the inputs are passed to the network's input nodes and the network's outputs are compared to the actual outputs (target values) found in the data. The discrepancy between predicted and actual output values is used to adjust the interconnection weights within the network. Weight adjustments are made after one or several records are presented. Either way, many adjustments must be made to train a model properly. If adjustments are made too quickly, the network may skip over and around the optimum combination of weights. If adjustments are made too slowly, training may take an impractically long time.

In practice, the optimum training regimen typically involves hundreds, or perhaps a few thousand, data records forming a training data set. The entire training set is then presented to the network several hundred or a few thousand times during the training process. When every record in the training set has been presented to the network once, one "epoch" of training has been completed. Generally, many epochs using the same data set are required to complete training. Once fully trained, a properly constructed neural network can capture and represent very complicated nonlinear relationships. Neural networks consistently produce models with accuracy and reliability as good or better than any competing statistical approach. And they do it with greatly reduced demands upon the systems analyst for time, research, and experience.

The most recognized name of a neural network firm active in the mortgage industry is HNC, Inc., of San Diego, California. HNC's Decision Systems division has developed several applications of technology combining neural networks and statistical modeling techniques. Those available in the mortgage industry today include automated loan origination, underwriting, and risk management systems.

NEURAL NETWORK APPLICATION

HNC's Automated Real Estate Analysis System (AREAS™), is a property valuation system that provides multidimensional modeling of a property's location and physical characteristics based upon its relationship to other comparable properties. Key features include: automatically generating a baseline market value for each property, locating the most appropriate comps, analyzing how changes affect value, explaining the factors that contribute to or detract from the property's value, and detecting unusual entries that might contain erroneous or fraudulent data. As a quality-control tool designed specifically for the mortgage banking industry, AREAS enables underwriters to better evaluate appraisal accuracy, and lenders to make better portfolios and risk management decisions. This product is currently available only for California but is planned to expand nationally in 1993.

JUDGMENT PROCESSING

The judgment-processing software is an expert system that is based on inductive technology. The software is based on the premise that pragmatic experts make decisions on the basis of intuition, experience, and knowledge.

In the inductive environment of judgment processing software, the computer assumes the role of apprentice. As it observes the performance of its "mentor," the system creates a dynamic, judgment mode. In other words, the software is able to emulate the decision-making capabilities of a company's best and most experienced people without requesting or generating any explicit logic rules.

Judgment processing software differs from the traditional approach to expert systems in that no knowledge engineering process is required. The knowledge engineering process requires that a technician, usually called a knowledge engineer, interviews and observes the expert in his or her area of expertise. Knowledge engineering can be difficult and time-consuming for the many experts who may be more intuitive than analytical in their decision-making practices.

Under judgment processing, the underwriting decision factors are phrased as a series of questions. In defining the questions, the mentor indicates how individual responses are to be categorized. For example, in mortgage insurance underwriting, certain ratios, such as debt-to-income or loan-to-value (LTV), are calculated to evaluate the application. Whether the LTV is 81 percent or 83 percent is not as relevant to the underwriter as the fact that both are more than 80 percent but less than 85 percent. The "between 80 percent and 85 percent" category is called an "intermediate judgment."

After defining questions, valid responses, and relevant categories, the mentor enters a series of examples and makes a decision or interpretation for each one. The software observes the interpretation and the intermediate judgments associated with each interpretation and stores this information as a situation in a consistent, logical model called the judgment base. As the base develops through the addition of more situations, the system acquires the ability to: identify relevant past experience, compare situations and measure their degree of similarity, predict how the mentor would interpret a particular example, and report, on a scale of 1 to 100, a level of confidence that the mentor would agree with the decision generated.

During this teaching process, the mentor either accepts the system's interpretations or changes them. In either case, this provides a learning experience that enriches the extrapolation abilities of the judgment processor, the component of the software that emulates the decision-making logic of human experts.

After determining which data variables, or decision factors, are required to build a model for decision making, then problems that incorporate all of the decision factors are defined. Forming problems enables complex decision processes to be separated into manageable blocks.

JUDGMENT PROCESSING APPLICATIONS

In 1989, PMI Mortgage Insurance Co. began exploring ways to automate the real estate appraisal process and to convert it from paper to data elements. An expert system was determined to be the best solution. After investigating and evaluting several software providers, Cyberteck-Cogensys Corporation of Dallas was selected. PMI's next step was to assign a mentor to teach the system. The mentor tackled the none-too-simple task of determining which of the myriad data variables (or decision factors) associated with appraisal decision making were required.

After two months, PMI had collected 140 data variables to form a very good appraisal model. However, from feedback generated by the judgment processing software, it was learned that many of the data variables chosen were irrelevant to the decision-making process. During the subsequent development and analysis phase, the software was able to identify which data variables are logically important in making valid appraisal review decisions. Further teaching and testing during the next seven months dramatically improved the appraisal model. The number of data variables thought to be required to underwrite the appraisal was whittled down from 140 to 36. In addition to providing better appraisal decisions, the reduction in the number of data variables also enhanced greatly the model's ease of use.

PMI then took the next step—validating the appraisal model. PMI recognizes how crucial it is to test any system thoroughly and in several different environments. The appraisal model was tested for six weeks, during which time more than 500 real estate appraisals were evaluated. During the validation phase, human underwriters concurrently underwrote the appraisals in order to determine the validity of the automated model's conclusion. Results of the validation were excellent: the system approved 75 percent of the appraisals submitted, and of these, the field underwriter disagreed with only one.

In February 1991, PMI set up a second beta test in Tampa, Florida, a market that differs significantly from the previous test site. During the four-week test, the model evaluated 500 appraisals and approved 68 percent of them. Again only one of the approvals was unacceptable to the field underwriter.

PMI began implementing the appraisal model (PMITERRA^{SM}) throughout its field offices in September 1991. The rollout was conducted slowly and carefully, in keeping with a policy of preventing any potential disruption in service to PMI customers. By March 1992, all 20 field offices were in live production.

PMI's underwriting staff have reported that PMITERRA^{SM} is very easy to use. All that is required is the entry of the 36 data variables and the pressing of a command key. A decision is processed in two to seven seconds.

It is important to note that PMI management made sure to prepare the users for the introduction of the new technology. They had learned during implementation of the PMIAURA^{SM} system that a change in how people work can pose a threat to them, so PMI held sessions and distributed a monthly newsletter that informed the users of how the model would deliver benefits, not jeopardize their jobs.

Today several mortgage banking firms are under way with internal projects of different scopes and purposes using Cybertek Cogensys Judgment Processing software. Firms include ARCS Mortgage, B.F. Saul Mortgage, FBS Mortgage, Firstar Home Mortgage Corp., Great Western Bank, Home Savings of America, Household Financial Network, Metropolitan Financial, Norwest Mortgage, and Wells Fargo Bank.

RULE-BASED SYSTEMS

One of the earliest forms of artificial intelligence or expert systems to be developed were "rule-based," or literally, a series of "If . . . ," "Then . . ." specific steps. The "rules" were those thought processes and action steps the human experts used to make decisions. For example, in an underwriting system, there would likely be rules for ratios of income to debt, and cash reserves to payment. These rules or the results of each of these rules might be combined into an "ability to pay" rule.

Rule-based expert systems are good in translating business policies, procedures, and practical experience into a knowledge data base. Their advantage over judgment systems is that changing requirements is much easier. For example, in a rule-based loan underwriting system, it is much easier to create a new requirement, or "rule," than having to reteach a judgment system through hundreds of new examples.

The problem, or down side, of rule-based expert systems is their extensive knowledge acquisition time. This capture process involves a knowledge engineer working with human experts. The knowledge engineer is a specialist who interviews the expert, takes the information "rules" disclosed, and translates the information into a data base that the expert system understands. It is nearly impossible for the knowledge engineer to meet only once with the human expert and capture *all* the rules they know, partly because the human expert is often not even aware of some thought processes he or she uses. And, no matter how cooperative they are, knowledge does not "pour out," but comes in small chunks over a long period.

RULE-BASED APPLICATION

Countrywide Funding Corp., Pasadena, California, has announced that it expects to roll out a rule-based expert system in 1993, for use in the firm's retail operations. They have selected Inference Corporation of Los Angeles, California, as their case-based-reasoning product vendor. Countrywide's new system, which uses INFERENCE'S ART-IM product, will look at close to 200 pieces of data from the loan application, credit report, and appraisal.

This data will be evaluated against a knowledge base of over 500 rules. An average of 30 percent to 40 percent of all rules will be used to make a decision on any one application. Whenever the system does not approve a file, it will be sent to an underwriter with suggestions for resolving the problem. Countrywide's CEO, Angelo Mozilo, speaking of the system, has said, "This system should help us meet growing demand, despite an increasingly short supply of underwriters."

ELECTRONIC DATA INTERCHANGE (EDI)

Electronic Data Interchange (EDI) is finally making its way into the mortgage banking industry. EDI, the computer-to-computer, or computer application-to-computer application, exchange of business information has been saving companies in other industries millions of dollars by eliminating errors, reducing lead time, lowering inventory costs, improving customer service, and streamlining internal processes. Electronic data interchange is a form of electronic communication that allows trading partners to exchange business transaction information in predefined, structured formats, replacing paper-based exchanges. Historically, EDI has been used by industries to increase efficiency and productivity, reduce costs, shorten critical service windows, and improve customer service and strategic planning. In contrast to the way in which organizations previously exchanged information, the use of EDI has allowed businesses to communicate electronically without specific knowledge of the computer systems at either end. (See Figure 20.4.)

Standardized EDI transactions are used when information is transmitted between two external organizations, known as trading partners. Trading partners can be defined as any external entities that need information from one another to perform a function or complete a task. An organization's use of EDI does not affect its internal processing systems or work flows. In addition, the use of EDI does not dictate the mechanisms used to transmit data between trading partners.

EDI has been used by many industries to reduce costs and improve efficiency. While members of the secondary market have been communicating electronically for many years, they have been doing so without using common, industry-wide standards. The lack of consistent, automated connections between lenders and mortgage insurance companies, credit bureaus, etc., has created the need for rekeying and revalidation of data, which in turn has had a negative impact on costs. Recent efforts of the MBA's technology committee have helped to es-

Figure 20.4   Electronic Data Interface

Without EDI

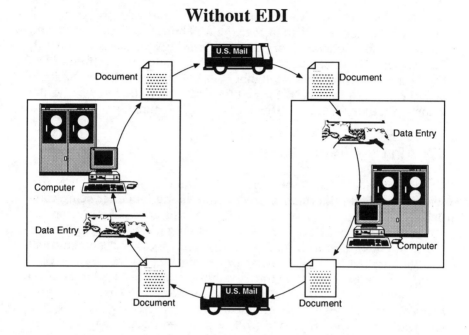

With EDI

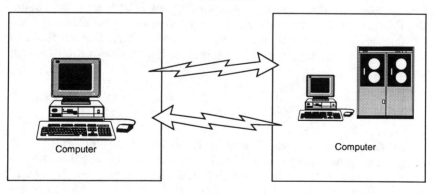

tablish standards for several transactions used within this portion of the industry. The recent commitment of EDI by the Department of Housing and Urban Development also will encourage usage among lenders.

The federal government has recognized and acknowledged that EDI offers numerous advantages to the way business is conducted, and recently issued Federal Information Processing Standards (FIPS) 161, EDI; which adopts the ANSI X12 EDI standards for all electronic processing implemented after September 30, 1991. The American National Standards Institute (ANSI) formed the X12 Committee in 1979 to develop standards for the electronic trading of documents.

EDI APPLICATION

The Department of Housing and Urban Development (HUD) is currently in an EDI pilot phase project with two mortgage servicing companies to electronically receive mortgage insurance claims using the X12 standards. Once HUD has completed the pilot phase, it will begin to expand the program to other trading partners. Other documents will also be targeted for electronic transmission, such as mortgage record change, default status, claim traces, remittance advice, etc. After critical mass has been reached with its trading partners, HUD expects to save between ten and twelve million dollars annually. HUD, with its aggressive trading partner approach, will help the entire mortgage industry begin to realize the benefits of electronic trading.

Packaged Business Solutions, Inc. (PBSI), a San Francisco Bay area consulting company specializing in EDI in the mortgage banking industry, has recently announced its Mortgage EDI Software kit. By using the PC-based software package, a company can economically take advantage of EDI without a large conversion effort. PBSI expects to work with HUD in helping them achieve their EDI goals with their trading partners.

IMAGE PROCESSING

In an attempt to increase their ability to service larger volumes of mortgage, home equity, consumer, and student loans, lending institutions are turning to automation. But studies have revealed that computers automate only 10 percent of the information needed for business operations. The remaining 90 percent originates outside an organization, enters through a company's mail room and is sorted, routed, processed, filed, retrieved, and re-filed in its original paper form.

Today, image processing systems, using advanced optical disk technology, high-resolution workstations, and powerful software, are enabling financial institutions worldwide to automate once elusive information.

Documents enter the system through a scanner, which operates much like a photocopier. Scanners handle various paper sizes and weights, bound documents, double-sided documents, photographs, and jacketed microfiche. Documents can also be entered from remote sites via facsimile or satellite transmission. Incoming documents can be electronically date- and time-stamped. The documents are scanned and indexed, and the digitized images are written to nonerasable optical disks. A single 12-inch optical disk can hold approximately 50,000 8 1/2 x 11-inch document images. Disks are housed in optical storage and retrieval libraries. Any one of the images can be retrieved in seconds and displayed on high-resolution workstations.

The key to full utilization of electronic imaging, however, is software that orchestrates the automatic routing and processing of paper throughout a department or company, while interfacing with various data processing and word processing applications.

Image processing leads to improved management of the volumes of paper required to be processed in a timely manner, since the actual location of the records management center is frequently remote to the service organization requiring the document. Because of the great volume of paper and the storage space required to accommodate such files, there is also the element of rent and staff, besides "missed opportunities" from lost files.

Optical disk technology can eliminate the space needed for departmental filing areas and can also reduce the cost of archival storage, whether on-site or warehoused. Space and staffing requirements for record management facilities can also be dramatically reduced. For example, an optical storage and retrieval library can store approximately 14.4 million pages of images, the equivalent storage capacity of 1,440 five-drawer file cabinets—in the space of just seven five-drawer file cabinets.

IMAGE PROCESSING APPLICATION

A leader in pioneering the concept of work flow management is FileNet Corporation of Costa Mesa, California, applying a work-flow software product that allows an entire work-in-process event to be compressed and streamlined, thereby improving speed of processing, accuracy, and overall efficiencies, resulting in productivity gains that impact the bottom line (see Figure 20.5). Currently, FileNet has over 600 installations.

Figure 20.5   Image Processing Application

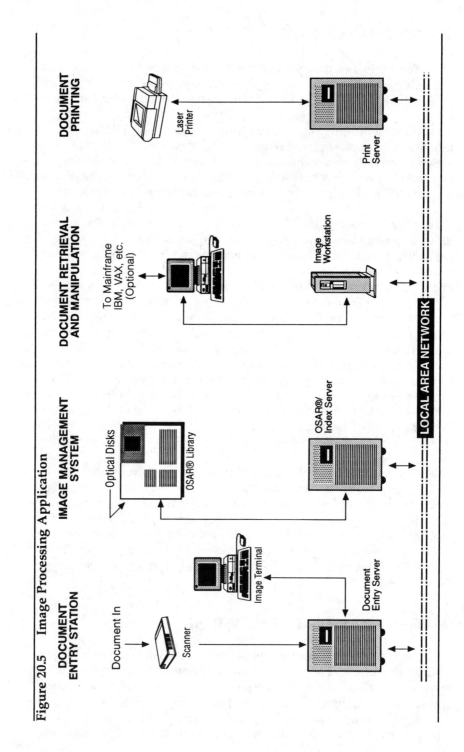

Four years ago, when the image processing industry was in its infancy, Great Western became one of the first financial institutions to invest in optical technology.

As one of the country's leading real estate lenders, Great Western services 441,000 property loans worth more than $42 billion. More than 190 district loan offices in 19 states generate 8,000 loans per month.

All mortgage loans are centrally serviced in Northridge, California, using a FileNet system. Great Western scans a remarkable 35,000 document pages each day. Great Western's document-image processing system is one of the largest in the world, with 1,064 optical disks containing 40 million pages of images.

Image processing is proving its worth in Great Western's customer service department, where response time has been reduced from days to seconds. Previously, to answer customer questions requiring information from a loan file, the customer service employee had to make written request to the microfiche department. It took from three hours to three days to receive the correct microfiche. Now, the customer service representative responds while the customer is still on the line.

IMAGE PROCESSING APPLICATION

Among service providers of mortgages, Lomas Mortgage USA is one of the largest in the United States, with a portfolio exceeding 600,000 loans. Lomas installed a FileNet system in October 1987, and within five months converted 30,000 mortgage files—roughly 1.5 million document-images onto optical disk.

With the FileNet system, Lomas has the ability to transfer mortgages electronically. As an example, in 1988 Lomas purchased 56,000 loans from CitiCorp. Since both financial institutions have installed FileNet document-image processing systems, at CitiCorp, the 200,000 images supporting the loans being sold were written to optical disks by the FileNet system. The disks were then delivered by armed courier to Lomas, where they were imported overnight into the Lomas FileNet system. By the next day, those images were retrievable via the Lomas network.

Between the two companies, well over $150,000 savings in direct labor was attributed to the disk swap. And, since customer service continued uninterrupted during the disk transfer, customer goodwill was maintained.

SUMMARY

The technologies and applications that we have just reviewed will be yesterday's newspaper in a very short time because of the exciting pace of new discoveries and development projects that will benefit mortgage banking. We will see strategic alliances formed among leaders in the industry to shorten the time lines and increase the opportunities for more organizations, especially those of lesser size, to participate in the benefits that technology brings. Certainly the work being done by the MBA's technology committee to develop application standards will greatly expand the list of participants, especially those that will be making use of the capabilities via electronic data interchange.

Yes, a revolution is under way and the momentum is building. The good news about this revolution is that the losses, if any, will be minimal, and the benefits will be tremendous. If you haven't yet become a part of the movement, get started, even in some small way. The rewards will be worth the effort!

Chapter 21

STRATEGIC REENGINEERING OF THE MORTGAGE BANKING BUSINESS

Jan Beaven
Symmetrix, Inc.

Fred Portner
Symmetrix, Inc.

THE NEED TO CHANGE

Change is inherently uncomfortable for most people. We simply are not very adaptable. Enterprises, too, become comfortable with a single competitive environment and resist change. In the tumultuous business climate of the 1990s, however, the successful enterprise must marshal resources to make change within days and weeks, not months and years. It must be able to "turn on a dime."

This chapter deals with strategic Reengineering techniques and approaches that can help make an enterprise fast-moving and adaptable. A key conclusion is that many current organization and management principles are no longer adequate to the challenge. They have produced inward-focused, overspecialized, slow, costly structures that can't quite compete with newer, faster companies that have often thrown out the old structures and started from scratch. Strategic reengineering—the fundamental restructuring of a company to better meet customer needs and be profitable—is a promising approach by which a company radically improves its performance. Mortgage banking, we argue, is an industry positioned for fundamental restructuring, in which there will be big winners and big losers. Strategic reengineering can be a key vehicle for the ambitious company to differentiate itself from the pack.

ADAPTABILITY IN AMERICAN INDUSTRY: FAILURE TO ADAPT HAS SERIOUS CONSEQUENCES

American industry provides poignant examples of companies in dire straits because they failed to be aggressive enough in adapting to changing environments. The U.S. automobile industry is the best known example. The Japanese have achieved a 35 percent share of the American automobile market by applying superior organization, motivation, training, and employee empowerment approaches to produce superior products. Wal-Mart has become the predominant competitor in retailing, again through aligning the organization to get close to the customer, by focusing employees on customer needs, and using enabling technology, thereby unseating Sears, which was unable to adapt its rigid infrastructure to meet the competitive threat. In the relatively new computer industry, IBM has demonstrated that its largely functionalized, bureaucratic organization is not well suited to the new competitive structure of the marketplace. Wang, Digital Equipment Corporation, and Prime Computer are other high-tech examples.

MORTGAGE BANKING: THOSE WHO CAN ADAPT TO DRAMATIC RESTRUCTURING WILL WIN

The mortgage banking industry faces dramatic restructuring. As we enter the twenty-first century, the industry will be transformed from a fragmented, small-firm-dominated industry to a mature business with a combination of several large competitors and a proliferation of very small origination sources. In this new environment, the survivors will be the firms that have strategically reengineered their business practices, organizational structure, and technology to produce these winning characteristics:

- ◆ Customer-driven operations, from stem to stern, throughout the business
- ◆ Lean, integrated, cross-functional structures and employee empowerment to enhance customer service and profitability

♦ Technology used as a crucial strategic weapon to promote and help implement both customer focus and adaptability

WHY CHANGE?

In an industry as large and as fragmented as mortgage banking, the logical question that must be answered is why change radically? Are the threats to economic well-being so pronounced that it is necessary to change to survive? There are at least two reasons: (1) there are enormous productivity gains available because mortgage banking operations lag in using applicable techniques now well established by manufacturers, and (2) distributed technology now is capable of linking operations together in such a dynamic way that the first to do this successfully will achieve substantial strategic, marketing, and technical gains. In short, the industry is positioned for step-function change (that is, dramatic order of improvement) where the winners will demonstrate quantum leaps in performance in all key measures.

It will take a few years to see how restructuring will shake out. What mortgage banking enterprises do in the next two to three years, however, will set in motion competitive forces that laggards will find difficult if not impossible to withstand. In this short time frame, the relative advantage can shift so decidedly to the few firms able to change (because these firms will already have some significant momentum) that it will be difficult for others to catch up.

MAJOR PERFORMANCE GAPS

With the competitive environment shifting, strategic reengineering of the mortgage banking enterprise is imperative for achieving sustainable competitive advantages and bottom-line results. There are several large gaps in mortgage banking between what is possible in terms of customer service, productivity, unit costs, and employee satisfaction and the current practice. In this situation, competitors, either from inside or outside the industry, will seize upon the potential competitive advantage and initiate a share-grabbing strategy that will destabilize the industry. (In fact, a few such conspicuous competitors have emerged.) Major gaps exist in:

♦ *Customer service.* Production and servicing operations are slow and no one "owns" the customer. Fast answers from a single individual, which is characteristic of good performance in other industries, is simply not the focal point of the delivery system in either part of the business.

♦   *Employee satisfaction.* High turnover is an accepted characteristic of the business. However, turnover is a signal that something is inherently wrong, because people will avoid change if possible. Reduced turnover alone would increase productivity, lower unit costs, and improve customer service markedly.

♦   *Productivity.* Production organizations are mired in a low-productivity rut. Retail productivity has changed little over the past ten years, except perhaps to decline as underwriting demands have increased. (See Figure 21.1.) Servicing productivity has improved only incrementally among a few of the larger firms as they refine their use of old technology within highly functionalized, clerical-intensive operations. The potential for breakthrough types of productivity gains in servicing is very large. (See Figure 21.2.)

♦   *Unit costs.* At best, unit costs in both the production and servicing businesses seem to be holding their own, as inflationary and complexity pressures offset whatever scale and technology benefits are realized. (See Figures 21.3 and 21.4.)

Mortgage banking firms that resolve these issues will emerge from the change process as fundamentally different businesses; retail and servicing productivity could double, driving profit up and leaving these organizations the strongest competitors in a consolidated industry. We would contend that the winners will reengineer their entire business using a holistic approach to achieve such results.

MULTIDIMENSIONAL CHANGE: STRATEGIC REENGINEERING

Until recently, change efforts in financial services have been limited to automating existing processes in an attempt to work faster and with fewer people. Mortgage banking executives have become discouraged about this incremental approach, as the magnitude of benefits gained has not matched frequently anticipated results, particularly when compared to the level of investment. Strategic reengineering does not take this incremental approach. By contrast, reengineering focuses on making major improvements by starting with a "clean slate" and determin-

Figure 21.1   Retail Production Productivity

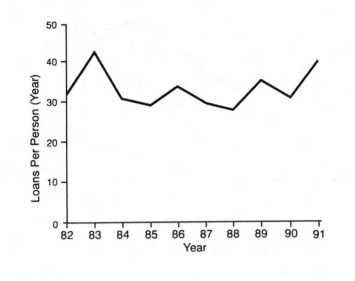

Figure 21.2   Servicing Productivity

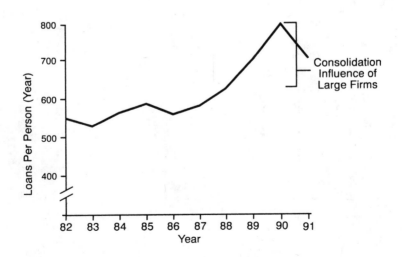

Figure 21.3   Retail Production Unit Cost

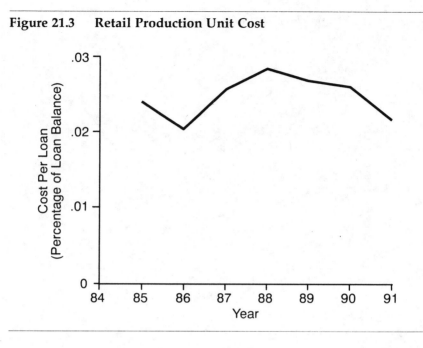

Figure 21.4   Servicing Unit Cost

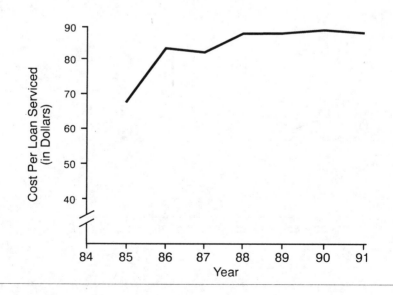

ing the best solutions for becoming world-class competitors. It includes redefining corporate culture, changing processes across functions, and altering jobs and information systems, all driven by a deeper understanding of customer needs. Such initiatives require the commitment of senior management and generally are led by a senior-level team with expertise in business practices, marketing, technology, and training and organizational development.

The challenge for today's enterprise is not to automate existing practices, but to take a reengineering approach to the entire business. Breakthroughs are selected to produce step-function change. The Japanese have been masters at it, and American firms are starting to achieve dramatic results. While accompanying technological breakthroughs could put business on a new plane, 80 percent of the effort is not in changing technology but in using technology when required to support an integrated change solution. *Reengineer*, don't just automate.

STRATEGIC REENGINEERING: A HOLISTIC APPROACH

A successful reengineering vision results from a multidimensional effort. Reengineering begins with focusing on market conditions and on the customer. A key leverage point is represented by customer needs; activities are considered value-added based on relative customer desirability. For example, if customers indicate that speed in response to their inquiries is a determinant in selecting a mortgage firm, then reengineering initiatives should focus on redesign of organization, business practices, and systems capabilities to meet that need. Business transformation will focus on the following:

♦   Organizational structure—a customer-aligned structure that is inherently adaptive and flexible, eliminating the hand-offs and lack of accountability found in a functionalized organization

♦   Process redesign—simplifying processes to eliminate redundancy, eliminate audits and other non-value-added steps and abolish unnecessary tracking procedures

♦   Technology—particularly the use of technology to redistribute information and to modify work across these same activities

♦   Human resources engineering—an increase in the capacity and flexibility of the work force, where appropriate, through cross-training on dependent skill sets, combining logical functions by individuals, and increasing the level of mastery for individuals

One or two of these initiatives viewed in isolation usually results only in modest gains, if any. The institution then resembles a race car whose engine is running on only 75 to 80 percent of its cylinders. While perhaps only 20 to 25 percent of the engine is malfunctioning, the end result is an engine that can reach only a small fraction of its potential and it never will win the race! It is only full, robust attention to all parts of the reengineering process that provides the dramatic bottom line, and customer satisfaction payoffs will result.

BUSINESS PROCESS REDESIGN: FIRST PRINCIPLES

First, the company must outline strategically how it wants to execute its business—which markets, key customer needs, and competitive advantages it wants to develop and protect—and its control needs. Then, a properly facilitated, cross-functional reengineering team can redesign most mortgage banking processes to fit the strategic thrust. Guided by a reasonably articulated strategy, unshackled from existing corporate policy, and stimulated by exposure to available technologies, an internal redesign team can effectively redesign the critical production or servicing processes. Whenever possible, the following steps should be included in the process redesign effort:

- ◆ *Start with the customer.* Design the process from an external perspective, around delivering what the customer wants or is willing to pay for. Avoid starting with an internal perspective, that is, looking at what is needed internally to perform individual functions.

- ◆ *Quantify potential improvements.* Calculate the cost/benefit of each alternative and brainstorm the implementation plan for each. Treat each alternative as an enterprise-wide initiative, not just a functional improvement.

- ◆ *Single accountability.* Design processes to have single or team accountability and minimize hand-offs. When combined with customer focus/contact, this provides real empowerment for employees to feel ownership for customer results and satisfaction.

♦ *Kill the paper.* Paper is *the* enemy in mortgage banking. Given today's technology, there is no justifiable reason in most cases to rely on paper-driven processes. It stifles productivity and adaptability.

♦ *Do it right the first time.* Errors in data or lack of confidence by succeeding users of information add geometrically to the cost and overall time to complete processes.

♦ *Separate exceptions from the mainstream and design processes for the mainstream.* Why make 100 percent of the customers suffer for the 5 to 10 percent problem cases? Design the work to distinguish early on between the two and build separate processing channels for each.

♦ *Capture source data.* Capture data as early in the process and as completely as possible, even if it takes longer at the outset to do so.

♦ *Build teams whenever possible.* Design operations around teams in which workers broaden their scope and capabilities and back each other up using cross-functional skills. Their jobs become enriched, and they feel more accountable for quality as defined by the customer.

♦ *Create a pilot team.* Develop and test reengineered processes, systems tools, and organizational structure; monitor results, based on quantifiable comparisons; redesign where needed prior to organizational rollout.

♦ *Implement reengineering plan.* Deploy throughout the organization, based on the prototype developed and refined in the pilot process.

♦ *Build in a learning adaptability mechanism.* Include mechanisms for people to continue to learn as they work and for the process to be modified as employees' understanding improves in the rollout phase.

Applying these steps to the entire process should lead to substantially enhanced results when combined with technology and human resource redesign. Typical results of process reengineering might include improved turnaround time for customer-sensitive processes, increased quality and reduced rework, improved skill-set allocations for job functions, and reduced expense ratios for account production and/or servicing.

TECHNOLOGY REDESIGN

Reengineered systems development occurs concurrently with process redesign; new systems are prototyped and tested within the environment of the pilot initiative. So far, the industry has moved only at glacial speed to take advantage of new technology; we believe that eventually three phases of systems development will grow out of the initial reengineering vision and pilot.

As uncomfortable as it may be to traditional mortgage banking executives, a potential model for the future use of technology in mortgage banking is to view the business as one large data base available to people at different workstations who operate on this data, some adding new information, some analyzing the data, and others extracting summary reports or documents.

Simplistically, migration to a full data base-based business structure would require three major levels of change:

1. *Internal data base* A necessary first step is to implement a single data base architecture internally, so that work-flow redesign and organizational rethinking can be accomplished without constraints in access to information. Most competitors currently are concentrating on this first phase.

2. *External integration* Mortgage banking is, of course, not a self-contained business. No mortgage can be produced and sold without some reliance on external vendors, investors, or partners of some kind. The speed and quality of service mortgage lenders and/or services provided critically depends on credit bureaus, appraisers, end investors, insurance companies, taxing agencies, and closing agents, to name a few. Phase 2 in systems reengineering could extend the concept of data base management to include integration into these external constituents. Credit bureau interfaces are already common. Because of the significant cost and customer service leverage afforded by many of these interfaces, development will accelerate as the necessary internal data base "backbone" architecture development matures. *Importantly*, as with Wal-Mart, this includes backward integration into the mortgage bank's clients, for example, realtors and mortgage brokers. Reengineering work flows in production must consider bringing the realtor or broker formally into the process.

3. *Paper Reduction* Phase 3, which in some areas overlaps Phase 2, is actually turning mortgage banking into a true information processing business by eliminating the paper. Simply stated, the whole economic structure of mortgage banking changes radically once paper is removed from the system. Creating and handling paper is a major cost component of the business. The technology is close at hand and the legal issues largely are resolved to permit practical redefinition of the business based upon broad scale elimination of paper. At the very least, there is the opportunity to eliminate paper internally, producing hard copy *only* when external constituents demand it.

Today we are merely tinkering in most cases with the use of technology, partly due to the dearth of sophisticated technological resources in the industry and the lack of understanding and vision of senior management. They simply have not been raised or schooled in technology.

HUMAN RESOURCE MANAGEMENT

As powerful an elixir as technology can be, rethinking human resource management practices and organization can have an even more powerful impact, certainly in terms of return on investment and developmental time.

Traditionally, mortgage banks have been organized functionally: sales, processing, underwriting, and closing on the production side; customer service, tax, insurance, and collections on the servicing side. The focus of the work has been on the functional responsibilities, not on serving the customer. Jobs have been routinized in a production-line-like environment, encouraging (logically) a proliferation of clerical roles as the paper is pushed along (or unfortunately back and forth between jobs in the production line). Individual responsibility has been minimized in favor of control. In the functional model, whatever individual workstation productivity has been gained through technology has subsequently been lost through hand-off inefficiencies, functional myopia, and job boredom. High turnover, the distinctive warning sign of a poor organizational environment, is prevalent in most parts of the business.

Improving the organizational environment so that employees are encouraged, if not required, to take full responsibility for performing for the customer, must be the focus of reengineered organizational change. The central concept around which work will be organized is small, cross-functional, empowered teams. Each component being key:

- ♦ *Small*—The work group must be small enough to have intimacy and to truly function as one team—typically 8 to 10 people is considered an optimal size.

♦ *Cross-functional*—Functionalization must give way to possessing all the skills necessary to serve the customer. Technology in fact makes this very possible by (1) eliminating much of the routine clerical work, and (2) providing learning aids accessible as needed on the computer.

♦ *Empowered*—The desired organization is flat, with fewer layers of managers. Instead, the work groups themselves manage their activities. They are *empowered* to act, set goals, determine priorities, discipline the group, and allocate work.

♦ *Team*—*The* central concept of organizational reengineering is the customer team. Work is to be organized around customer groups, not functions. Hierarchical structures cede to customer-aligned teams. The implications of reorganizing teams, while simple in the concept, actually has very profound effects on the organization, because it fundamentally redefines each individual's identity (team member, not functional specialist).

It has been estimated that merely moving from a functional organization to empowered teams, even in the absence of technological sophistication, can improve productivity and unit costs significantly. Outside mortgage banking, where empowered teams have succeeded, productivity differences are regularly acknowledged to be 20 to 50 percent. In a business where the product is information, not hard goods, the prospect of breakthrough-level performance is both real and necessary.

EMPOWERMENT

At the end of the day, who wins may depend on which organization has developed and retained the most motivated, focused employees. There is no product difference that can be patented in mortgage banking. The cost of capital for all major competitors (except the agencies) is largely the same. Ultimately, technology is accessible to all major competitors. The lone differentiating variable is the relative ability of one firm to motivate and channel the energies of its employees better than the competition. If this is so, how does a mortgage bank organize to maximize the potential of its people?

Some years ago a large money-center bank conducted a blind survey of its operations department staff, to determine what they valued most about their jobs. The overwhelming response from the staff was somewhat surprising, and extremely telling in terms of what human beings value. While the staff had limited education and certainly limited financial security, financial rewards did not head the list. In fact, money was not even named second. Good working conditions were also not the focal point of their concern. By far, the dominant desired work factor was organizational respect and trust. These employees, mostly clerical staff, wanted the organization to express trust in them, to show respect for their skills and ability to think and perform.

Amazing? Not really. Trust is the primary characteristic that has driven Japanese workers' performance for decades. It is also a primary reason why American firms have found it so difficult to achieve substantial productivity progress. American industry, including mortgage companies, traditionally has embraced hierarchical organizational structures with their inherent top-down focus. Providing real respect and trust to rank-and-file employees requires a mindset that is 180 degrees different from a top-down approach. In fact, it requires a bottom-up approach, with the supervisors becoming coaches and facilitators, not principally decision makers.

EMPOWERED TEAMS

Implementing empowered teams in mortgage banking necessarily builds on individual trust. In thinking about building and focusing empowerment, three core principles seem to emerge:

1. *Translate respect into ownership.* Acknowledge the need for trust and respect by designing roles to provide real *ownership* of results, to a point where the employee internalizes this ownership.

2. *Appeal to people's corollary need to help.* Most people have an inherent desire to help. Focusing employees as directly as possible on customers is the most effective way to channel this need productively for the organization.

3. *Build in supportive teamwork.* Capture people's need to be part of something, and to have and feel the support of others by using teams as the basic organizational building block.

Together, these three principles lobby hard for customer-focused teams with real end-result ownership as the central organizing principle for all mortgage banking processes.

If applied diligently and honestly (management must believe deeply in these concepts if they are to work), the influences on traditional organizational structure are far reaching:

♦ The organization structure is flattened. Fewer management layers reduce overhead significantly.

♦ The operating environment is transformed from a hierarchical decision-making driven environment to one of coaching others to make the appropriate decision.

♦ Working relationships among groups internally, and between internal groups and external constituents, are significantly redefined.

♦ Frequently, the mix of employees must change, and they must have the requisite skills to bring about change, including:
  – the switch, through attrition or retraining, from clerical workers to knowledge workers who are innately more inquisitive about their work.
  – the switch from control-oriented supervisors/managers to facilitators, coaches, or teachers.

♦ Finally, the demand for quality MIS escalates, to permit empowered employees to interpret and understand their environment.

As a core element for rethinking the operations of mortgage banking, empowerment is an exciting, fundamentally and professionally satisfying concept. Implementation of empowered teams requires careful management and employee buy-in, as well as training in facilitation, team techniques, and functional cross-training. Reengineering does not involve shortchanging in any respect.

STEP-FUNCTION CHANGE

Traditional managers think, plan, and act incrementally. They attempt to balance investment, short-term performance requirements, resource capacity, and the ability to maintain control as they consider improvement in the business. This methodology served American business relatively well from the 1950s through the 1970s. In the 1980s incrementalism all too often proved inadequate to deal with the massive changes required to stay competitive—witness Sears, IBM, and the auto makers to name a few.

Reengineering mortgage banking in the mid-1990s is not about incrementalism. It is about massive step-function change. It is not about rewriting systems or cross-training people. Continuous incremental improvement is a hallmark of good companies and a primary reason the Japanese have been so difficult to catch. But incremental change applied to a work environment that is fundamentally flawed only means slightly smoothing a bad road to a dead end. The real progress in mortgage banking will be made by those who take "a clean slate" in rethinking and redesigning their operations, then develop careful migration paths to get from here to there, and intensively, doggedly make the change happen.

ENTERPRISE-WIDE SUPPORT FOR CHANGE MANAGEMENT

Management generally is reluctant to spend (or don't perceive themselves able to afford spending) considerable time on reengineering their business. This is a mistake. Top management must be involved and committed throughout the process of defining the goals of change and implementing the tasks to achieve it. Similarly, implementation of change requires buy-in from middle management and line workers. Change is disruptive to comfortable patterns of thinking and to those who see traditional organizational structures disbanding and reforming. Organizational inertia will subvert attempts at change unless top management is visibly involved and committed. The focus and vision of change must be communicated effectively and repeatedly to all levels. Anything less promotes business as usual, with the status of reengineering being relegated to "that interesting project."

VISIONS INTO THE FUTURE—SUCCESSFUL CHANGE MANAGEMENT

Step-function change in mortgage banking in the 1990s is still too new to have produced many examples of successful, radical change. However, enough examples of success in both production and servicing exist to provide both credibility for the concepts and hope for the future.

REENGINEERING OPPORTUNITIES—RETAIL PRODUCTION

The traditional retail branch production system represents perhaps the clearest example of the dual weaknesses of poor organizational structure compounded by substantial underutilization of technology. The traditional retail branch falls well short of acceptable performance in almost all areas:

- Customer service is generally rated as poor or at least very uneven by consumers.

- Unreasonably long processing times and demands for documentation are accepted by competitors as "just the way the business is."

- Unit costs are high, and, moreover, have grown rather than declined over time.

- Mortgage firms have failed to establish much evidence of *institutional* value of the distribution system, as evidenced by the fact that the loan originators, not the mortgage companies, own the client relationships in most cases.

Perhaps most importantly, the structural evidence of an inadequate organizational design is strong—high turnover. Typically, 75 to 90 percent of new loan originators wash out in their first year, and the usual turnover rate for processors exceeds 30 percent. Organizational environments that work long-term cannot do so if high turnover is a part of the equation.

The organizational environment that surrounds the processor is particularly discouraging. The processor more often than not finds himself/herself in the following situation:

- Small unit operation with little ability to adjust to volume

- Significant work flow swings

- Complex products with frequently changing rules

- Early career people with little formal training; limited post-entry training

- Ultimate manager (branch manager) who rarely is operationally oriented

- Little potential career mobility

- Caught between the pressures of the originator and the underwriter

In short, the processor faces a job in which it is difficult to win regularly, and if he or she is successful, there are few significant career opportunities.

In addition to the problems caused by organizational weaknesses, there is the absence of technology that would provide the processor reasonable mastery of his or her activities. Daily work typically is reduced to a succession of "fire fights" on time-critical document processing, rather than controlled management of a case load.

Until recently, the industry seemed to accept the situation as an inherent condition of the business. But the condition need not be accepted. It *is* possible for mortgage bankers to simultaneously, significantly improve quality customer service, speed of processing, and unit costs while providing a progressive environment for their employees. At the same time, it is possible to build institutional value with clients, while gaining greater control over them. The cure lies in the combination of aggressive technological and human resource reengineering.

The few firms that have successfully reengineered their retail operations have done so through a series of straightforward, logical steps, yielding significant results:

♦ Create ownership of the customer by moving sales, processing, and underwriting into small teams, with processing and underwriting physically together. Focus these teams on specific customer groups.

♦ Create a critical mass of operations and operating flexibility by regionalizing the processing/underwriting teams.

♦ Create closeness to the customer by locating the originators very close to the customer and by matching the processing/underwriting teams with specific customer groups.

♦ Change and accelerate the flow of work by redefining the responsibilities of the originator. The originator becomes the *technical* salesperson with responsibility for complete up-front processing.

♦ Support the originator and the processing/underwriting team with smart technology to reduce the mundane work and enhance the staff's role as knowledge workers.

♦ Transform the processing/underwriting team activity—traditionally heavy on processing—into an underwriting-focused activity.

♦ Similarly, recast the processing role into a career-entry credit training role—processing work diminishes, replaced by more quasi-underwriting support. The processor role serves as a natural training ground for either underwriting or technically strong salespeople.

Reorganization produces cost savings which, if invested in technology, enable the recasting of activities. This, in turn, permits redefinition of the processor's role and the creation of a natural, logical career path.

Cross-functional teams, in which ultimately all three principal roles—originator, underwriter, and processor—ultimately share a common background and training, provide significant flexibility. Team-based incentive plans provide the glue that ensures customer service focus and cooperation. At the same time, the team focus reduces the dependency of the client on the originator and strengthens the institution's value to the client.

Functional hierarchies largely disappear, and along with them, the inevitable conflicts: conflicting goals, conflicting pressures, conflicting reward structures.

The end environment creates an often dramatic win-win-win for all major constituents—customers, shareholders, and employees:

♦ Customer identification and responsiveness soars.

♦ Speed of service accelerates.

♦ Unit costs typically drop by 50 to 75 basis points, despite significant investments in technology.

♦ Employee motivation and satisfaction improve dramatically.

Moreover, the resulting operating environment achieves an operating and competitive stability that removes much of the feast-and-famine-driven neurosis that has plagued the industry.

BROKER WHOLESALE

Perhaps nowhere has the magic of empowered teams proved so economically effective as for wholesalers in the broker-based end of the wholesale production business. Wholesalers typically have opted to run large regional buy centers, with large, departmentalized operations for registering, underwriting, drawing documents, and funding loans.

Wholesalers typically have been pleased with the relative cost efficiency of such operations, because the net cost of production usually has been materially less than in comparable retail operations. Broker clients, however, typically have been less pleased with the quality of service because all too often brokers have had to tolerate problems such as ineffective communication on the status of loans, multiple contract points, inability to reach a real person (telephone tag), and inconsistent turnaround time. Yet during the formative years of the business, the market has grown so rapidly that relatively poor service generally has been accepted.

Enter a relative unknown with a different approach—the empowered team organized to serve individual local markets. Countrywide Funding has grown from a relative nonentity to the runaway market leader based on 10- to 15-person branches that act as empowered, cross-trained teams. Countrywide has achieved productivity levels that are approximately double that of the industry (18 to 20 loans per person per month versus 8 to 10 for the industry) and an expense ratio that is approximately 50 to 60 percent that of the industry average.

While most observers would attribute Countrywide's superior efficiency to its technology focus, the major benefits in fact come from the intense focus and hands-on management made possible in the branch teams. Operating and underwriting skills dominate the culture, causing everyone to have a relatively common base of understanding. Significant branch performance incentives ensure that focus on productive work is maintained and that people work together on customer-related issues rather than functional measures of performance.

Some competitors have implemented a slight variation of the Countrywide approach, attempting to combine small team dynamics with scale flexibility. These firms have organized empowered, specific customer group-focused teams within a regional processing center. As with Countrywide, these units combine sales, processing, closing, and underwriting in single teams. Also similar to Countrywide, the teams are self-governing, with significant bottom-line-driven incentives.

In these cases, closeness of *all* functions to the customer, shared goals, and significant financial incentives combine to generate dramatic differences in competitive performance.

REENGINEERING OPPORTUNITIES—SERVICING

Nowhere is traditional organizational theory so pervasively applied as in mortgage servicing. Historically, almost every mortgage service has been organized along strict functional lines—collections, tax and insurance, customer service, payoffs, and so on. Supporting systems architectures have been similarly designed, even to the point of supporting actual paper hand-offs between functional areas. Indeed the entire management process revolved around intensively managing (and relatively independently) each functional specialty.

As one might suspect in such an environment, measures of customer performance became secondary to individual functional performance. As well, optimization of the whole business becomes merely the sum of optimization of individual functions. Unfortunately in a business where the functions are not strictly independent, optimizing overall business performance cannot be achieved by focusing on individual functional performance.

Perhaps more importantly, the routinized, narrow jobs prevalent in functionalized servicing operations do not encourage high sustained performance. The individual jobs tend to become boring over time, and a functional structure impedes full problem solving initiative—"I did my job, now I'll pass it on to someone else." Again, the telltale sign of poor organizational design—high turnover—all too often has been present in the servicing business.

Industry productivity and cost performance has reflected the mature, grind it out, incremental technology gains mentality of servicing managements. Overall servicing operating unit costs historically have shown steady increases despite major advances in available technology. Personnel productivity generally shows some scale effects, but not the magnitude of differences one would expect. Moreover, those gains in productivity that have been realized tend to be small and incremental in nature.

The inevitable conclusion is that servicing managements have not really been focusing on the true high leverage opportunities in their business—managing the interfaces between functions and raising interest and skill levels in their staffs. As it turns out, the majority of the cost in servicing is handling problems or exceptions. A loan that always pays on time, rarely calls in with inquiries, and stays on the books for some years is a very inexpensive loan to service—on the order of 20 percent of the average servicing cost or less, depending on allocation methodologies. The *real* costs are in managing problems—loans that in total typically constitute less than 30 percent of the portfolio. Secondly, dealing with these loans more often than not requires interdepartmental communications or hand-offs. Thirdly, these loans, by their "problem" status, require someone to focus on the customer rather than the particular function. All of which argues for a different form of organizational structure to perform optimally.

While empirical evidence is thin, it appears that reorganizing servicing activities around cross-functional teams promises performance improvement that not only speeds customer problem resolution, but provides breakthroughs in productivity as well.

One such pioneer, a medium-sized thrift-based servicer, managed to turn a troubled situation into stellar performance. Operating functionally, with modest technology capability, the thrift's servicing unit had existed under a reputation for poor service and weak productivity. Dealing with a portfolio of loans that was average in complexity, the servicing unit's productivity averaged about 570 loans per employee prior to the reorganization into empowered teams. Fifteen months after the pilot team was established, the productivity for the initial team had risen to 1,900 loans per person, based on the functions that were handled by the team. Adjusting the team's performance for those activities that remained outside the team, so that productivity could be compared fairly to traditional productivity measures, productivity still approached 1,400 loans per person. (See Figure 21.5.)

Not only did productivity soar, but customer complaints declined to almost zero. As a measure of increased employee satisfaction, turnover in the team was also nil, compared to the overall servicing depart-

Figure 21.5   Results: Effect of Cross-Functional, Empowered Team on Servicing Productivity

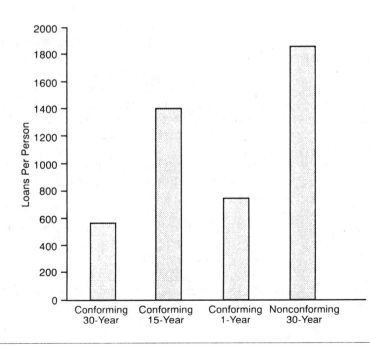

ment experience of 30 percent plus. In the end, shareholders won, customers won, and employees won.

Why the dramatic shift in performance? Part of what makes the value of empowered teams difficult to gauge beforehand is the difficulty in quantifying the productivity lost through multiple handling of problems, poor internal communications, lack of .ownership, or uninspired workers. After the fact, it is easy to quantify the impact, and the reasons reflect very basic human values:

♦ Customer focus—ability to reach out and actually affect someone's life, rather than just process a piece of paper.

♦ Ownership—employees are given full ownership for results.

♦ Trust is expressed—the employee controls his or her own direction.

♦ Challenge—the role is enriched and a method for acquiring skills is implemented.

Also, because these very basic human values are addressed, there is confidence that the performance improvement will be permanent, as long as management reinforces the empowered, cross-functional team concepts.

There is no one right way to organize teams in servicing. Most frequently, the teams are grown over time, beginning with the core customer functions of customer service, setup, taxes, escrow and insurance, and payoffs. Parts of collections can be added as technology permits decentralization of preforeclosure collections. Typically, the pure scale processing parts of functions are centralized, for example, nonexception coupon processing. In these cases, the team handles exception transactions. Foreclosures might be segmented primarily because the customer is different—the customer becomes the investor rather than the borrower. The same is true for investor reporting.

Interestingly, once the roles within servicing are redefined around customers and teams, there is enormous potential to improve work performance through redefining the supporting technology. The technology needs are now defined by the team's needs at their workstations and are centered on customer information as opposed to being defined by discrete processing steps; for example, paying taxes. While there remains, of course, the requirement to actually pay taxes, the technology architecture to support this process in a customer-focused workstation is materially different from the classic functional process.

MANAGING THE TRANSITION

Reengineering a traditional, functionalized hierarchical organization to technology driven, customer focused, lean, integrated structures with empowered employees is not easy. Although the rewards are worth it, the transition inevitably takes considerable time. Because the migration path is necessarily long, getting started properly and addressing the key transitional issues are critical.

Although pages of transitional issues can and should be identified in an actual reengineering effort, four key issues should be thoroughly understood and addressed in planning any reengineering effort:

1. *Develop the need for clear vision of the resulting operation.* It is absolutely essential that a clear vision of the end result be developed and tested in a pilot phase prior to starting and that the vision be *patiently* communicated to all affected employees. The very culture of the organization will be changed. Nothing will be resisted as stiffly by employees as cultural change unless they have had the full opportunity to understand and internalize the changes and the reasons for them.

2. *Educate/condition the staff.* For instance, changing from a traditional hierarchical organization to empowered teams is not, initially, a comfortable move for most employees. *Considerable* front-end investment must be made in training employees to work in teams and to set their own goals rather than look for direction, and for supervisors and managers to change from managers to coaches or facilitators. Rethinking how employees work together is a critical precursor to implementation. An initial pilot team enables proof of concept as well as refinement of the approach before a complete rollout of teams.

3. *Take migration in steps.* Some will argue for the big-bang approach, but this defies logic. In team implementation, for instance, there are at least two basic ways to accomplish controlled migration: (1) Invest the team immediately with all the functions necessary to do the complete job, but retain functional specialties within the team initially, or (2) cross-train all team members in a few functions initially and then gradually expand the team's functional responsibilities.

4. *Pace the speed of migration with the degree of skills gaps that
    initially exists.* Again, in team implementation, gauge care-
    fully the current skills of the staff as well as their ability to
    learn; however, don't be surprised by the capacity of em-
    ployees to learn when given the opportunity for real respon-
    sibility. American industry has consistently underestimated the
    capacity of its employees to perform when asked properly and
    properly motivated.

Change is difficult. It is threatening no matter how sophisticated
or competent employees are. But it is necessary, and even critical. The
challenges are not primarily technological, because they involve the
human side of change. Nowhere is this more poignant than when
suggesting radical organizational change that fundamentally redefines
success for people and how they must work together. Yet proof is
mounting that indicates improvement of this magnitude is well worth
the risk. The evidence is clear regarding long-term effects on traditionally successful firms that are not able or willing to change and adapt.
Despite all the strength exhibited by traditionally dominant firms, even
the IBMs and Sears of the world, ultimately must come face to face with
radical organizational change. And, as history indicates, the longer it is
postponed, the more difficult the change is to accomplish.

Figure 21.6   Potential Targets for Strategic Reengineering of Mortgage Banking Enterprise

Servicing (Loans/Person/Year)

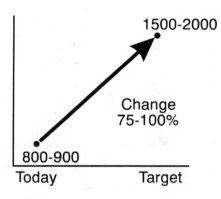

Retail Production (Loans/Person/Year)

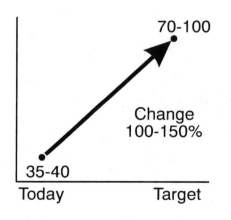

**Figure 21.6   Potential Targets for Strategic Reengineering of
Mortgage Banking Enterprise (continued)**

Wholesale Production (Loans/Person/Year)

Chapter 22

ADVANCING MORTGAGE INFORMATION EXCHANGE: ELECTRONIC DATA INTERCHANGE IN MORTGAGE BANKING

Richard Bryan
Executive Vice President, Operations
Freddie Mac

David Barkley
Director, Operations Industry Support
Freddie Mac

THE MORTGAGE INFORMATION EXCHANGE PROCESS

This chapter looks at the current approach to the exchange of information within the origination, marketing, and servicing facets of the mortgage finance process, and describes a vision of the future that utilizes electronic data interchange (EDI) to assist in the streamlining of the process. EDI is the exchange of information between external parties and their computer systems in predefined, standard electronic formats. Issues relating to the current as well as the future approach to mortgage information exchange are discussed in this chapter.

DATA FLOW OF A TYPICAL LOAN PROCESS

Currently, a mortgage lender typically begins the mortgage process by collecting specific information from the borrower on the loan application. During the next few weeks the lender forwards this data to service

435

Figure 22.1   Current Mortgage Information Exchanges

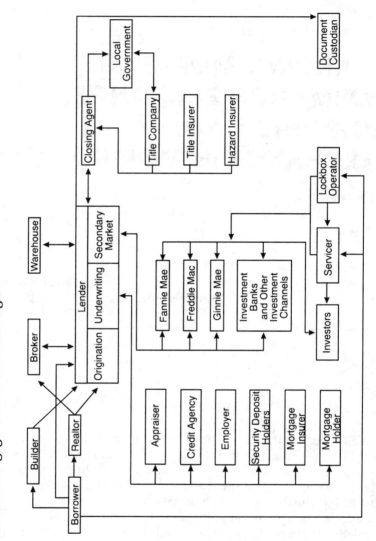

providers for confirmation or updating. Along the way, he or she collects additional details relating to the loan from verifications, credit checks, appraisals, title searches, and interviews.

This information may come from many sources, old files or records, credit histories, or employment portfolios. More and more often this data is being found in a computer somewhere. But even when records have been computerized, the data required to initiate a request for mortgage information is retrieved from its source, printed, and then mailed to a service provider. This service provider may be a credit company, mortgage insurer, appraiser, title company, financial institution, or employer. The service provider completes the request by researching its files. This may be a manual process or it may involve a computer application to complete the request.

Once complete, a response is typically generated from another computer. Today, this response is printed and then mailed back to the requestor. The requestor may enter the new information into its computer system or place the paper document in a file that must be accessed manually whenever one needs to use the data.

Once the loan file is complete, an underwriter sits down and compares all the different sources of information, noting what the borrower wrote down on the application versus what was reported by the borrower's employer, bank, credit report, etc. These are all on separate pieces of paper, and depending on the company, each form might be different. The fields might have various meanings depending on the type of form used or the company supplying the information. If the response has been faxed, the quality of the printing can make the page difficult to read.

Efforts to improve the mortgage origination process occurred in the 1970s, when many of the paper documents were standardized with the help of the secondary mortgage market. But many companies still use their own nomenclature or codes to describe the data that goes into certain fields. For example, there are no set standards for recording names, i.e., last name, first name, etc. Credit reports use different codes, depending on the initiating credit repository to report similar information.

Within servicing processes, computers and automation have played a key role in streamlining internal lender processes. Computerized applications are used to collect and report accounting and default data for internal reporting. But inherent in the process is considerable information transfers to external parties. Renewals and billings of hazard insurance, status of defaults to investors and insurance carriers, and transfers of servicing all require similar information to be exchanged between multiple parties. This becomes extremely complex when each internal system defines the data differently.

When loans are sold into the secondary market, computer applications from Freddie Mac, Fannie Mae, and Ginnie Mae are available to streamline the process, but these applications approach loan delivery and investor reporting in a different way. There is no consistency between what information is collected or how it is defined when reported.

Some companies have begun to reach out to special clients or service providers with customized linkages to improve information flows, but the lack of consistent approaches leads to a tangled web of confused connections.

ISSUES AND BUSINESS IMPLICATIONS OF PREVIOUS/CURRENT SCENARIOS

As computers and computer applications become more prevalent in mortgage banking operations, the amount of mortgage information stored in these computers has increased dramatically. This can lead to internal efficiencies in originating and servicing mortgage products.

But these computing efficiencies tend to be restricted to one's own office. When information needs to be transferred or exchanged between lenders and external service providers—such as mortgage credit agencies, mortgage insurers, appraisers, etc.—the process often reverts back to a paper-intensive flow.

This flow is time-consuming and requires a great deal of re-entering and reprinting similar information. Each time this occurs, there is an opportunity to make mistakes, transpose numbers or letters, or leave off suffixes, etc. During peak periods of business, important pieces of information or simple errors can be missed. Suddenly a lender and borrower are down to the last minute before closing and realize that verifications are missing, the credit report presents problems, or the ratios are off. A last-minute, panic-stricken correction effort ensues.

WASTED TIME AND ENERGY

A great deal of time is wasted sending and receiving information. A number of personnel are required to open mail and manually track and record the status of origination files. This process is slow and fraught with opportunity for oversights and errors. During peak volumes, it is easy to misplace physical pieces of paper that are crucial to a file.

Underwriters must have all of this information to make a well-balanced decision.

Problems do not go away when a loan is closed. Inconsistent and disconnected internal computer systems and their differing applications can make the movement of loan data from an origination system to a servicing system a complicated exercise in translation. Delivery and reporting to a private investor or secondary marketing agency may require a third secondary marketing system and specific interfaces to the software supplied by the investor.

Each time a piece of information is retyped or translated into a new format, there is a chance for errors and omissions. Due to a lack of interconnection between disparate systems, the same information may be stored for a period of time in up to three different internal systems, as well as in numerous credit, mortgage insurance, title, and appraisal data bases. A great deal of energy is expended to resolve issues relating to mismatched or "garbage" data.

These types of errors add even more time to an already lengthy process. The time it takes to originate a loan translates into specific costs for a lender who has borrowed against a line of credit. Extended time to complete the closing process increases a lender's interest rate exposure and general carrying costs.

When considering the overall process from loan application to pay-off, it is overwhelming to realize the number of parties that play a role. For each step—completing the application, ordering the credit report, selling and reporting to an investor, renewing hazard insurance, and escrow maintenance—there are many potential business partners. Any attempt to streamline or automate these exchanges requires relationships with many distinct companies, and each relationship adds to the costs of the process.

Efforts to establish customized relationships and exchanges require considerable resources. Once in place, lenders often hesitate to work with other providers of the same service due to the costs of setting up these exchanges. Sometimes the best business provider for a particular loan product or geographic region may not be the one with which you have established an automated link. But the system costs of adapting to the new provider may outweigh the business-related benefits. Technology works against you.

Escrowed hazard insurance renewals present an especially difficult problem for lenders. The borrower, not the lender, chooses the insurance carrier. The holder of the escrow account must be prepared to maintain business relationships with every company carrying homeowners', fire, flood, earthquake, and forced place insurance. Streamlining this process potentially requires coordination across two industries and hundreds of participants.

The secondary-market process presents a frustrating scenario for the mortgage lender. Each agency requires very similar information, but it is reported and collected in distinct ways. As additional information is requested, it is often defined agency by agency, and rolled out on varying schedules. Such disparities eat up valuable resources and require increased training for staff, leading to more specialized tasks and more difficult staff scheduling issues.

A VISION OF A FUTURE MORTGAGE INFORMATION EXCHANGE PROCESS

As the costs of new technologies and computer applications become more reasonable, and as mortgage banking firms become more comfortable with the benefits that computers, technology, and computer

Figure 22.2   Future Mortgage Information Exchanges

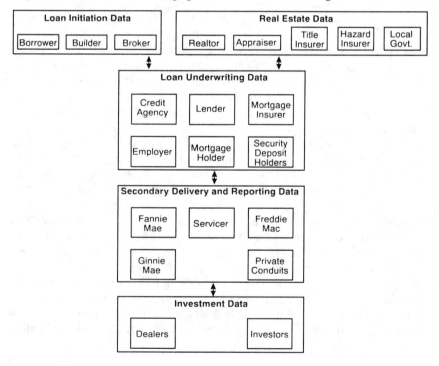

applications can bring to all aspects of the mortgage process, technological solutions present themselves.

According to the MORTECH 92 study of technology use in the
mortgage industry, mortgage companies are adopting newer technologies faster and expanding their reasons for implementing new technologies beyond just cost reduction. Networking personal computers
together, the use of expert systems, and the value of computers in
satisfying customer service needs are all trends cited in the most recent
study. The technologies being considered for implementation take
many forms.

POTENTIAL SOLUTIONS TO CURRENT ISSUES AND PROBLEMS

In the current mortgage life cycle, a great deal of time is spent simply
waiting for the mail to arrive. The widespread use of the facsimile (fax)
machine speeds up the basic flow of information, but the data is still in
a paper form. While a response arrives in seconds, someone still must
manually enter this data into an internal computer application or file
it in a paper file. Errors or misinterpretations may increase due to the
poor quality of some fax copies. Delays or conflicts may occur over the
receipt of data. Although someone faxed it, was it really received, or
was the page upside down, the machine out of paper or temporarily
turned off? What are the advantages of split-second delivery if it takes
three days to happen across the document in the print room?

BAR CODING TECHNOLOGY

Bar coding technology is being promoted in the mortgage industry as
a method for tracking and recording paper documents and files. A
unique bar code is placed on each form and file. The bar code might
define the form, and it might also give specifics about the loan, loan
number, or loan product associated with it. The documents mailed out
to service providers and the responses received are scanned by a bar
code reader to track their progress. This can assist in tracking the receipt
of various documents. Bar codes on physical loan files can be scanned
into a computer to track their location within the office. This is an
improvement compared to current processes that depend on manual
tracking procedures, but the issues relating to paper filing and information access from physical files remain major stumbling blocks. One
is still dependent on the piece of paper to accomplish any tasks. When
this information is stored in a computer file it is more accessible.

Table 22.1 Issues Relating to Mortgage Information Exchange

Customer Business Issues	Benefits from EDI
Paper-and resource-intensive	Electronic, streamlined process; better resource usage
Cumbersome manual processes	Simplified electronic interfaces with multiple trading partners
Delays due to missing/late items	Automated tracking, auditing and reporting systems
Inconsistent and disconnected systems	Simplified internal interfaces; streamlined information access
Information stored in multiple places; errors due to re-entering	Reduced errors; streamlined information access
Costs due to delays (interest rate exposure)	Reduced risks
Varied information sources; many players	Flexibility in arranging business partnerships
Confusion due to differing formats	Simplified training/resource allocation

Thanks to the widespread use of bar codes in the retail industry, this can be an inexpensive approach to document tracking, but printing and applying the bar codes to existing documents can be time-consuming, and benefits disappear if the codes are not legible.

IMAGING TECHNOLOGY

A new technology that takes the piece of paper and re-creates it on the computer screen is known as "imaging." A paper document is scanned into a computer program that can "print" the document on multiple computer screens when requested. This offers a quick and easy method to access a paper file via your computer screen. But typically, this file reflects the paper image without any understanding of the data and data fields on the page. It is simply a faster method for retrieving the piece of paper. In situations where regulations require that the original document be the source, this technology is an improvement to finding a paper file. But in the case of an imaging system, a great deal of money is spent on technology that does not always allow a broader use for the data.

While imaging systems make the document very easy to read, often magnifying it or color-coding certain sections on a form, the process requires massive amounts of storage. Since many imaging systems are storing the entire form in digital format, even the blank spaces, a large amount of memory is required to re-create it. This makes it very costly and difficult to transmit images electronically.

OPTICAL CHARACTER RECOGNITION TECHNOLOGY

Optical character recognition (OCR) is an emerging technology that will blur the distinction between the paper or image, and the data on it. OCR recognizes the characters in certain spaces on a form and can be used to feed a data base with pertinent information. By scanning a page that has previously been defined, typed, or handwritten, data can be fed into a computer system such as an origination or servicing system. Assuming the fields on the page have been "mapped" or translated into data fields within an internal data base, data entry is performed by the computer. This will become extremely helpful when handwritten documents are easily readable and can update internal records with a high level of integrity. Information submitted on predefined paper forms can automatically be fed into a computer for future use. But for the process to work, the layout of the forms and the data fields must be consistent or standard. The computer needs to know in advance which field is where and how to store the information it scans from the form. Once the data is recognized and stored, the original form can be re-created on the screen as well as any additional arrangement of the information that might prove useful.

ARTIFICIAL INTELLIGENCE AND AUTOMATED UNDERWRITING

The use of artificial intelligence in automating the underwriting process can lead to revolutionary changes in the mortgage lending process. In the future, computer systems might review the data that makes up the current loan package collected from the borrower, the appraisal, and the credit report, and make a decision or highlight concerns about making the loan. Simple, or "vanilla," loan packages might receive their initial approval from an automated underwriting system. Loans with questions or more complex scenarios would be reviewed by the underwriting staff. More time would be available for working out acceptable solutions to underwriting issues.

But to work, artificial underwriting systems must know key information about the loan application, the borrower, credit history, and property characteristics. It is very time-consuming and resource-intensive to enter all of this data manually into one's system. It is especially frustrating when one realizes that most of the information is being stored in a computer somewhere else. There is a need to have this information transmitted directly to the system that needs it.

Artificially intelligent applications are only just emerging and offer amazing potential for the future. One issue influencing the acceptance of artificial intelligence is the logical approach to decision making. Proponents of systems based on rules compete with those who support neural networks that are "taught" to make particular decisions based on experience. A clearer understanding of the powers of each of these approaches needs to be outlined.

CENTRAL DATA BASES FOR COMMON INFORMATION

Another possible scenario for the future includes the use of central storage points for mortgage-related information. Electronic files recording historical data on properties and loans might be kept much like credit data on borrowers. Lenders with permission to use this service would simply access the central data base and read or modify the pertinent information.

Such information sharing requires common definitions and values for data items. Standardized data fields are required to make widespread data sharing possible.

ELECTRONIC DATA INTERCHANGE AND STANDARDIZED DATA FORMATS

To achieve the full benefits from many of these emerging or proposed technological concepts requires a standardized approach to information, its definition, format, and usage. The concept of electronic data interchange (EDI) builds on the use of common data elements and code sets to exchange information electronically between computer applications. Information can be exchanged and understood from one computer application to another without delays due to manual intervention and costly customized data interpretation.

Regardless of the computer platform, operating system, or program, mortgage data can be defined and arranged in a common way, and can be transmitted or received in a prearranged format that can easily be understood by computer systems at both ends of the exchange.

Whatever a lender's approach to data storage and definition in their own shop, when it comes time to transfer information to another entity or service provider using EDI, it is arranged into a common format. Formats for the major mortgage information exchanges such as loan application specifics, credit reports, appraisals, mortgage insurance, investor reporting, and loan default status, are being defined using a common set of specific data items and codes. Just as letters are used to build words and words are used to structure sentences, data elements are arranged into data segments, and data segments are arranged into electronic formats reflecting paper forms. One generic format for each information exchange would be available.

Therefore, regardless of the particular company you are working with, you would use the one electronic "order form" for that service. And the resulting report or product you ordered would be returned to you using the electronic report format for that service. Whichever credit company you were working with, you could order and receive all credit reports the same way. When ordering mortgage insurance, all mortgage insurance applications and mortgage insurance payment information would be the same. This greatly simplifies the problems of linking up electronically with many distinct service providers. By building these electronic transactions using a common data language, it becomes much easier to transfer information throughout the various phases of the mortgage process: origination, servicing, and marketing.

APPROACHES TO ELECTRONIC DATA STANDARDS

Typically, electronic data interchange uses a common set of data items and definitions to build transactions that mirror the information currently moved via paper. An EDI transaction can be proprietary, industry specific, or nationally approved.

A proprietary EDI format is a company or trading partner specific electronic format. A trading partner is any company that one does business with electronically. A proprietary EDI format works fine for exchanging information between the two parties, but may be difficult to transfer to other companies or trading partners.

An industry specific EDI format is one that is designed and maintained by a particular industry. These formats may be flat file or tape-oriented formats, or they may be modeled after nationally approved data formats. They are designed and maintained by the particular industry as opposed to being reviewed and approved by a nationally sanctioned standards process.

When using the term "EDI," most people are referring to the nationally approved and maintained standards designed by the American National Standards Institute's EDI Committee, known as Accredited Standards Committee X12. These standards cross all industries and are designed with the greatest degree of flexibility to meet multiple demands. Consensus on the development of the standards is achieved across all participating industries. This can make implementation across industries easier. The mortgage industry depends on the insurance (hazard, title, mortgage), finance, and real estate industries for much of its data. The ANSI X12 Committee offers a common ground for establishing electronic data standards.

The EDI standards developed, approved, and maintained by the ANSI X12 Committee use variable-length fields and are table-driven. This makes them more efficient than a flat, fixed-field format. An X12 format, known as a transaction set, uses groupings of data known as data segments, which consist of data elements.

A data element is the smallest unit in the X12 standards approach. It is a data field that has defined characteristics and valid code values. Data segments are specific arrangements of data elements.

MORTGAGE ORIGINATION EDI USES

By defining the data fields, code values, and information groupings required within the mortgage origination process, technology can be used to great effect in the origination process. The concepts of EDI present an opportunity to streamline the many exchanges of the origination process. Currently many paper-oriented formats are being defined electronically.

Exchanges between credit companies and lenders have already been defined in EDI layouts. Mortgage insurance information and the loan application have also been defined. The data that makes up an appraisal is not far behind. The real estate industry is considering ways to streamline exchanges between realtors, title companies, and recording entities. Financial transaction sets and verifications of employment and income are logical extensions of existing verification and acknowledgment exchanges.

By defining the data that makes up the loan package in common ways, data sources become more accessible to the primary requestor as well as secondary sources. Mortgage insurers can consider requesting their own credit verifications when necessary. Extra data needed to fuel an automated underwriting system can easily be ordered and used.

SECONDARY-MARKET AND SERVICING EDI USES

The servicing side of the mortgage process, though more automated than most phases, can benefit greatly from common information formats. Current transfers of servicing, escrow and insurance renewals, and accounting and default reporting processes are extremely burdensome. Each one is distinct to the agency, insurer, or computer system involved. Considerable industry resources are expended to translate or interpret one collection of data into another.

Currently, under the auspices of the Department of Housing and Urban Development, transaction sets are being defined to automate the mortgage insurance claims process and the status of loan default procedures. Electronic methods for updating servicing records are also in the works. Private mortgage insurance companies, hazard insurance companies, and secondary marketing agencies are tracking the development of these formats and considering their usefulness for existing processes.

Hazard insurance companies are working to adapt existing EDI renewal billing and payment transaction sets for use in renewing escrowed homeowners' insurance. By using a standardized format, the links to multiple insurance companies can be maintained much more easily.

Efforts are under way to standardize data exchanges used in the secondary market. Common data formats for delivering loans into the secondary market, as well as monthly investor reporting and pool processing, are being designed. While the data will be used in different ways by each agency, the definitions of the fields, the valid values, and the possible record layouts will be defined up front to simplify information exchanges with the secondary market.

BENEFITS OF FUTURE SCENARIO

Common formats offer benefits in all phases of the mortgage life cycle. Consistent formats for secondary-mortgage loan delivery and investor reporting allow economies of scale for staffing and resource allocation. Access to information electronically allows faster movement of information, leading to improved loan review and approval cycles and faster closings. More rapid closings reduce a lender's exposure due to interest rate risk or warehouse line carrying costs.

Standardized electronic exchanges to perform common information transfers between trading partners simplifies system resources, maintenance issues, and training requirements. Instead of developing and maintaining customized information transfers between your organization and each individual service company, there is one approach for each type of transaction, credit request, mortgage insurance application, etc.

Just as "Open Systems" signifies simplified interplay between computer systems outside one's own organization, EDI provides a means for the easy transfer of data between computer applications.

REDUCED ERRORS DUE TO ONE-TIME DATA ENTRY

Such computer-to-computer information exchanges streamline the movement of this information and eliminate many of the errors that occur due to re-entering similar data. Assuming some type of communications network (telephone line, value-added network, electronic mail system) is used to transfer the information, data is received in a matter of seconds, overcoming the problems of the mail service. And with EDI, the data is already available for entry into your computer system without effort. This is more beneficial than a hard-copy-oriented solution.

EASY ACCESS TO INFORMATION ELECTRONICALLY

Once the information required to complete or update a loan file is being received electronically, the computer system can offer tracking and editing services. Reports can be generated to note which loan applications are missing credit reports, appraisals, or verifications. As information arrives, it can be edited to make sure any credit items with bad ratings are brought to the attention of the loan processor immediately. Outstanding balances or property comparables could be checked to make sure certain ratios or ranges have not been violated.

For those companies contemplating using automated underwriting systems in the origination process, these electronic exchanges offer the data necessary to easily fuel these systems. Customer service can be enhanced by allowing the computer system to process the vanilla loans while the underwriters and loan processing staff focus on the more complex applications.

ISSUES AND BUSINESS IMPLICATIONS OF FUTURE SCENARIO

Any new approach to business carries with it costs and implications that must be weighed against the benefits. While the benefit from a streamlined electronic flow of information offers great appeal, the industry has a major commitment in existing hardware and software. What impact will this new approach have on this? How does a lender protect its current investment in hardware and software?

Electronic data interchange typically uses a modular approach to data transmission. To reduce the impact on current internal environments, EDI is often implemented using an EDI translation module. The EDI translation module is a software application that uses the data from one's internal system in its current proprietary format, and "maps" or translates it into the approved data format for the particular function, i.e., loan delivery, credit report order, escrow payment, etc.

The EDI translation software or module maintains the tables that define the many different data elements and their valid codes. These are typically "standard" and agreed to across the industry, though they can also be customized to include values agreed upon by only two trading partners. This translation module can also be designed to maintain various versions of the same transaction set, the most current as well as several previous iterations. This allows more flexibility when trying to migrate from an older to a more current version of an electronic format. Depending on the particular company you are doing business with, the EDI software can track the version of a transaction set in use by your trading partner and know to use that particular version when transmitting to them. Migration from one version to a more up-to-date format becomes much simpler.

Table 22.2   Issues and Implications Relating to Future Mortgage Information Exchange

Issues	Implications	Potential Solutions
Protect current investment in computer hardware and software	Avoid high up-front costs to change business practices	Use of modular EDI translation software
Need for intergrated, easy-to-maintain approach	Flexibility that allows for unforeseen changes in business environment	Nationally approved and maintained electronic data standards consisting of adaptable table-driven codes and formats
Cost of new communications and EDI infrastructure	Cost of updating systems versus benefits gained from improved electronic information access	Flexible implementation schedules reflecting individual corporate needs
Easy computer access versus security and privacy concerns	Potential for unauthorized access to classified data	Nationally approved address and security procedures
Inappropriate manipulation of electronic data	Difficulty in detecting fradulent changes to information	Nationally maintained electronic encryption, audit, and control procedures and trading partner agreements
Regulatory requirements for original documents, wet signatures	Regulations impacting business adversely impede technological advances	Obtain comfort level with electronic documents, thereby reducing dependence on paper documents

EDI translation software also maintains a communications piece. Here, your computer system keeps an electronic address log detailing the best way to electronically communicate with each of your trading partners. Some may be on electronic mail networks or value-added networks that supply EDI edit-checking services. Others may simply want you to dial directly into their computer system and deliver the information. This is all defined and maintained outside your current computer program to minimize the impact of programming changes.

NEED FOR AN INTEGRATED, EASY-TO-MAINTAIN APPROACH

While benefits can be gained from defining a common format for each type of information exchange within the mortgage industry, there is a need to coordinate across these exchanges as well. It makes little sense for the lenders and mortgage insurance companies to agree to one code list for "loan type" while the secondary market defines the same data element a different way when it lays out its transaction sets. There is a need for a consistent, table-driven approach to data elements, their definitions, and valid values.

The ANSI X12 approach to electronic data interchange offers this type of common data definition methodology. Data elements are defined across all transactions and then used to build data groupings and data transaction sets that perform certain functions. Where possible, existing data elements, data segments, and data transaction sets are used to perform similar functions. When an existing transaction does not meet a need, then a new one is designed, using existing building blocks wherever possible.

This allows a lender to use one common set of data elements and a table of values to build all the data exchanges within the mortgage life cycle.

COSTS VERSUS BENEFITS OF EXPANDED INFORMATION ACCESS

Although a standardized EDI approach limits the impact on existing internal applications, to gain the benefits of EDI requires an investment in EDI translation software and some type of communications connection. There are still up-front programming and implementation costs. These costs must be weighed against the benefits perceived by the mortgage lender from expanded access to electronic mortgage information. Mortgage lenders interested in benefiting from advancements such as automated underwriting may see immediate advantages from this type of access. Companies planning computer system improvements or modifications can determine the best time to integrate the concepts of EDI into their business processes. Balancing benefits versus the costs of reengineering their system's import and export capabilities will determine a break-even point for each company.

Service bureaus and mortgage software companies can benefit from economies of scale brought on by modifying their programs once and then being able to offer EDI services to all of their customers, regardless of size or sophistication. Small lenders benefit by receiving electronic linkages with service providers that have traditionally been available only to larger, more technically adept lenders. Service bureaus and software companies benefit by needing to make only one electronic interface available for each type of service. This simplifies their development and maintenance efforts.

SECURITY AND AUDIT ISSUES

While the goal of EDI is to achieve easy access to mortgage information and to allow computer-to-computer data exchange, this scenario presents a new set of issues and business implications. When personal information about credit, employment, race, and gender are available at the touch of a button, security measures become critical. Access to computers and authority to request and review certain types of information must be administered with care and in compliance with existing regulations. Audit trails to track the status of information received electronically and controls to determine the consistency and accuracy of the data become critical.

Nationally approved and maintained methods for electronic addressing and security procedures exist today. They need to be reviewed in light of the needs of the mortgage industry and adapted to meet these needs. Other industries utilizing electronic data interchange have developed these tools to meet similar business concerns.

Methods of data encryption and audit and transaction control procedures also exist to track and interpret the status of electronic exchanges of information. Control procedures to verify that the data sent is what is being used at a later date is important to avoid any hint of data manipulation or fraud.

Trading partner agreements are used to define responsibility for data validity in an exchange, and can clarify which version of an electronic document is to be considered the "authentic or correct" one in cases of disagreements. In the case of a lender and a credit company, the credit company may allow a lender to receive a credit report in an electronic fashion, but if the data is changed in any way, the record of the electronic credit report stored on the credit company's system may be defined as the original. Once the data enters the lender's shop, he or she is responsible for maintaining its integrity. Issues such as these must be resolved fairly before electronic exchanges can become commonplace.

Another issue affecting the acceptance of any future scenario utilizing expanded technology is existing regulatory requirements on acceptable documents and procedures. Current regulations often call for specific documents containing particular legal language and "wet" signatures easily available for review by all interested parties. The industry must become more comfortable with electronic exchanges in lieu of paper documents and then persuade regulators that the improved flow of information transmitted electronically outweighs the originally perceived benefits from paper forms and wet signatures. Our processes need to be reviewed to see where legal agreements can be made that allow for the use of equally binding electronic "documents" instead.

CONCLUSION

The mortgage finance industry and related real estate and insurance industries have come to recognize the need to improve the way information is moved between the participants in a mortgage-related transaction. Existing and emerging technologies offer many exciting possibilities for streamlining and reengineering current approaches to business.

One of the most important pieces needed to make a seamless mortgage exchange possible is the standardization of mortgage information. Through the efforts of the Mortgage Bankers Association of America, the American National Standards Institute's Electronic Data Interchange Committee, and other industry groups, EDI standards for mortgage finance are well on their way to being finalized. Once in place these data formats open the way for many important technological opportunities.

Chapter 23

MORTGAGE LOAN UNDERWRITING

Gordon Steinbach
Executive Vice President
Mortgage Guaranty Insurance Company

THE CHANGING NATURE OF MORTGAGE FINANCE RISK

The nature of risk in mortgage finance has dramatically changed over the past decade. New economic forces have emerged to reshape the basic character and operating structure of the nation's lending and housing markets. Deflation, deregulation, and intense nationwide competition for deposits and mortgage loans have replaced the inflationary, heavily regulated lending markets previously dominated by local depository institutions. Mortgage lenders, investors, and insurers operating in today's lending environment clearly face considerably more risk than they did just a few years ago.

Just look at these facts:

♦ Delinquent loans are near peak levels. Despite recent declines, the percent of loans past due for 90 days or more has more than doubled since 1979.

♦ Real estate owned on the books of the nation's thrifts now exceeds $20 billion, a level that is over 11 times higher than in 1979.

♦ Property values in energy markets have declined 30 percent
   or more from their peak levels.

♦ Mortgage insurers incurred over $3 billion in direct losses
   between 1983 and 1986. The record of $1.2 billion in direct
   losses incurred in 1986 was a fivefold increase over the 1982
   loss level.

Inflation-related increases in home prices and personal income
can no longer be taken for granted. In fact, slow income growth now is
more often the rule than the exception, and the direction of home prices
is even less predictable than income growth. Adjustable-rate mortgage
instruments have become an accepted alternative to the traditional
fixed-rate loan. Aggressive new entrants to the mortgage finance industry and large nationwide lending institutions offer fierce competition
to local portfolio lenders. Finally, the growing influence of a global
economy now creates additional economic uncertainty and subjects the
nation's housing markets to unpredictable fluctuations.

Though the risks associated with the modern lending environment are clearly greater and more complex, they can be managed
effectively if they are fully understood. The key to understanding and
managing these risks comes through recognizing that the mortgage
loan, by the very nature of the mortgage contract, represents a long-term
risk—risk affected by fluctuations in borrower credit, regional economic
disruptions, overlending and overbuilding, and quality control decisions.

Borrower Credit

Mortgage loans must have sufficient credit quality to withstand the
wide economic fluctuations that occur in today's economic environment. The growing influence of world economic forces on the economic
stability of many of the nation's housing markets adds volatility to this
condition.

For instance, in 1981 and 1982, as a result of the rise in Japanese
imports, the American auto industry experienced huge layoffs that sent
Detroit's unemployment and default rates skyrocketing. During that
same period, Oklahoma City's oil-related economy boomed and its
default rate fell to historic lows. Little more than five years later, the
two markets had experienced significant reversals. Agricultural America and many mining communities have exhibited similar volatility.
These examples illustrate how our nation's housing markets are now
influenced by forces outside our own regional and national sphere.

Regional Economics

Regional economic disruptions can produce localized stress within our housing markets, even during periods of general economic expansion. Because of the new boom and bust nature of many regional economies, especially areas reliant upon a single industry, home prices can both soar and plummet within the lifetime of a typical mortgage. This volatility significantly increases the potential for catastrophic mortgage losses.

Overlending and Overbuilding

Another risk that is prevalent in many regional and local housing markets, typically during times of optimism, is that of overlending and overbuilding. During boom times, under the stimulus of deregulation, financial resources can move quickly to areas of potential profit. Vying for market share, market participants are prone to liberalizing credit standards. Buydowns and other types of liberal mortgage-design techniques are offered to further expand demand by attracting marginal buyers, in effect overselling markets and creating transactions where none should exist. As home sales rise, speculation appears and home prices appreciate, fueling further building. Under these circumstances, loans offered to marginal, often highly leveraged, buyers can perform well. However, as the economy turns downward, the negative implications of increased unemployment, slow income growth, and flat home prices or deflation lead to high levels of default.

An economic depression of the type that occurred in the energy states is a prime case in point. The accompanying deflation in home prices and reduction in borrower equity produced catastrophic default levels. Many borrowers were forced into a selling situation under these conditions, and they found that the balance owed on their loans exceeded the current market value of their houses. In many cases, this led to an unwillingness on the part of borrowers to continue making loan payments. In fact, experience shows that the level of borrower equity is the best indicator of a borrower's level of commitment to avoid default.

Quality Control

When discussing the changed nature of risk, the significant erosion of quality control standards must be considered. This erosion has been caused by competitive pressures within the lending and mortgage insurance industries. A notable example is the trend toward reduced documentation requirements. While these changes reduce loan processing time, they also reduce the likelihood that an underwriter can perform an accurate and thorough review of a borrower's financial condition. Although these loans may prove to be quality assets, there is unquestionably greater inherent risk due to the lack of a thorough credit review. When considering the pitfalls of the past, any sacrifice of proper credit and collateral assessment can be dangerous to the home buyer, lender, and mortgage insurer alike.

The foregoing discussion emphasizes the need to ensure that an adequate level of equity exists at the time of loan origination. An accurate assessment of beginning equity is critical to establishing the continued prospect of equity in a property. The process must begin with a careful and professional appraisal. Second, the loan instrument must be designed to prevent an inordinate degree of equity erosion. Loan instruments featuring potential or scheduled negative amortization can quickly eliminate the modest equity homeowners have established. Third, the integrity of the underwriting process must be preserved to limit the possibility of borrower fraud or misrepresentation regarding credit history and the source of down payment funds.

QUALITY CONTROL IN UNDERWRITING

Quality Control

The need for an effective quality control system as an integral part of the mortgage lending process has become increasingly important in recent years. No longer can the mortgage lender fall back on real estate appreciation and runaway inflation to compensate for incomplete, inaccurate, and generally "sloppy" loan origination procedures.

Investors, guarantors, and insurers alike have all sustained record losses in recent years and, in turn, have set quality control standards for lenders with whom they conduct business.

Significant value is placed on quality by these organizations. A lender's ability to remain profitable and maintain a place in the market by offering a variety of mortgage programs depends greatly on its reputation as a "quality-driven" organization.

Although specific investor requirements for a lender's quality control review vary widely, the general minimum requirement is that 10 percent of all closed loans have a complete document review with all credit documents reverified and review appraisals completed on 10 percent of the loans selected for review (10 percent of 10 percent).

The primary objective of an effective quality control program should be to assure that all investor, regulatory, and corporate guidelines have been met and individual mortgage loans are originated utilizing industry-wide accepted practices and procedures.

Quality control is not merely another word for "watchdog." The results and findings of quality control reviews should be utilized to identify staff training needs, and to provide both positive and negative feedback to members of the staff and management.

In addition, significant trends can quickly be identified, such as increasing concentrations of risk in specific areas, quality of documentation received from outside vendors, profiling of borrowers, and default trends.

The first and most important step in this process is the commitment to quality control by management and the communication of this commitment to all employees.

Each staff member affected by the process should be provided with a quality control manual that outlines the goals and objectives of the process, and the standards and detailed procedures by which they will be met. Training classes, employee communications programs, one-on-one meetings with management, and other similar efforts will assure that each employee thoroughly understands the purposes and the procedures of the system. The process should not end there—updates and changes must regularly be communicated, with additional training when necessary.

It is important that the manager of the quality control area has direct reporting responsibilities to someone other than the production or underwriting supervisor. Reporting of findings should be done in a consistent manner, on a timely basis (generally every 30 days), with a required response time period established for corrective action and/or additional training/counseling.

Quality control review is conducted at various stages of the loan process, including origination, processing, underwriting, and closing. Audits should be conducted on a post-closing basis, and should also include a preclosing review. A document reverification program should also be established to monitor the integrity of documents on which the lender bases loan decisions. Selection of loans for review should be made on a truly random basis.

In addition to a random selection review, a discretionary audit may be conducted of selected loan types, LTVs, defaulted loans, and/or loans originated under alternative document programs. The criteria, content, and regularity may vary widely, depending on the lender's specific needs.

It is particularly important that the quality control process include a system for review of the performance of all originators, processors, underwriters, and appraisers. Suggested areas for review should include, but not necessarily be limited to, the following:

Originator

1. Loan application information is complete.
2. Proper disclosures are made and are accurate.
3. Proper forms are used.
4. Loan terms comply with loan program requested.
5. Mathematical calculations are correct.
6. Borrowers are properly prequalified.
7. Appropriate signatures are obtained.

Processor

1. Appropriate disclosures are made, accurately and within prescribed time period.
2. Supporting documents are ordered on a timely basis.
3. Verifications mailed versus hand-carried.
4. Sufficient verifications are obtained; i.e., two-year employment and credit history.
5. Supplemental information is obtained when necessary as backup for incomplete and/or insufficient verifications.
6. Proper tax returns are obtained when required.
7. Necessary borrower explanations are requested.
8. Sales contract and addendums are in file and are properly executed.
9. All documents are checked for appropriate signature(s).
10. All documents are current when submitted for underwriting.

Underwriter

1. The loan request and collateral comply with loan program parameters.

2. Any and all specific investor underwriting guidelines are met.

3. Appropriate income calculations are made and are sufficiently supported by VOEs, tax returns, paystubs, divorce decrees, court records, etc.

4. There is sufficient verification of funds necessary to close the loan, with specific attention being paid to source of funds.

5. Liabilities are correctly calculated and evaluated.

6. The appraisal is underwritten to ensure that collateral is sufficient to support the terms of the loan request.

7. Appropriate and adequate conditions are placed on the loan approval.

8. Proper underwriting judgment is exercised in making the loan decision, taking into consideration:

a. Guidelines
b. Program parameters
c. Loan profitability to lender/investor

9. The underwriting decision is sufficiently documented.

Appraiser

1. The appraisal report is complete and on the proper form.

2. The report is consistent.

3. There are adequate explanations for any "less than average" ratings and/or comments.

4. Conditions made for deficiencies are noted.

5. All three approaches to value are used; if not, explanations are noted.

6. Appropriate comparables are used; i.e., distance, sale date, closed sales, and other variables fall within acceptable parameters.

7. Comparable adjustments are consistent.

8. Net/gross adjustments are within guidelines or are otherwise adequately explained.

9. Sales/financing concessions are addressed.

10. The appraisal is mathematically correct.

11. The comparables support the appraised market value.

12. Pictures of subject comparables are clear and match the description of subject property.

13. Supplements (i.e., maps, sketches, addendums, 1004B, etc.), when required, are complete and consistent with the appraisal report.

Document Reverification

No one can compensate for the damage caused when an organization bases its loan decisions on inaccurate and unreliable information. Therefore, establishing a regular document reverification program is imperative. The extent of this program will depend on whether reverification is conducted at the preclosing or post-closing stage. A comprehensive reverification program should include both preclosing and post-closing reviews.

Preclosing

A preclosing review can identify problems before it is too late. In addition to reviewing the originator, processor, underwriter, and appraiser, supporting documents should actually be reverified as to the legitimacy of information. Verbal reverification is heavily relied upon to prevent unnecessary closing delays.

Verification of Employment

Contact employers by using phone numbers obtained through the telephone directory rather than those provided by the borrower. Contact the payroll or personnel department at the borrower's place of employment rather than a specific individual. It may not be possible to verify income levels, but employment status can be confirmed in most cases.

Tax Returns

If tax preparers are used, contact them in the same manner as you contact employers.

Verification of Deposits

Depositories will not typically disclose their customers' account status. Therefore, a thorough examination of VODs must be made. Pay specific attention to the date the account was opened and to the comparison between current balance and average balance. When questions arise, review bank statements from at least two consecutive months and pay particular attention to unusually large deposits or several deposits made within a short time period.

Credit Reports

The content and quality of credit reports varies widely. An in-house credit system that can access various bureaus will allow for a second report to be ordered from a different bureau. The information on each report should be similar (allowing for time gaps, etc.). If the reports are dissimilar, test other reports from the same agencies to determine which bureau provides the most accurate information. Any discrepancies, such as new loans opened since the date of the original credit report, must be adequately explained by the borrower.

Appraisals

Beyond a thorough review of the appraisal document itself, there is little that can be done short of an independent review by a second appraiser. A complete appraisal at the preclosing stage is impractical, but at least a value review or desk review can be performed, utilizing an appraiser's knowledge and resources not available to the underwriters, processors, or quality control reviewers.

Post-Closing

A random selection of closed loans should be reverified, as discussed in the preclosing section. At the post-closing stage, however, hard copy versus verbal, standard factual credit reports versus in-file, and complete appraisals versus value reviews can be secured to establish the validity of the loan documents.

In addition to reverification of credit documents, review the actual closing documents. Suggested areas of review are as follows:

♦ Truth-In-Lending
Complete
Calculations are correct
Executed and dated properly

♦ HUD-1
Complete
Calculations are correct
Executed and dated properly
Loan disbursements match

♦ Note, Mortgage/Deed of Trust and Application Riders
Complete and on correct form
Calculations are correct
No typos or white-outs
Executed and dated properly
Names and legal descriptions are correct

♦ Closing Conditions
All conditions of underwriter, appraiser, and/or closing instructions are met

♦ Title Insurance
Amount, names and legal descriptions are correct
Specific waivers are obtained
Conditions for clear title are met

♦ Hazard Insurance
Coverage is sufficient
Names, addresses, and dates are correct
Mortgage clause is correct
Has flood insurance, if applicable

♦ Mortgage Insurance/Guaranty
Conditions are met
Terms are correct
Names and addresses are correct

♦ Affidavits, Escrow/Buydown Agreements, Assignments, etc.
Calculations are correct
Executed and dated properly

♦ Recording
All necessary documents are properly recorded within necessary time frame

Alternative Document Programs

It is critical to institute special procedures to handle the recent proliferation of alternative or limited document programs.

Due to the nature of these programs (limited verification of borrower income, and cash), primary underwriting emphasis is placed on
the borrowers' equity in the property and their willingness to pay the
mortgage obligation. Therefore, the accuracy of the appraisal and the
credit report is imperative. These documents are also the only true,
third-party verifications utilized in making the loan decision. Consequently, value reviews and second credit reports should be considered
standard operating procedure.

As to income and cash verifications, make sure that verbal verifications have been performed, where applicable, and that supporting
documents such as paystubs, W-2s, tax returns, and bank statements
were secured for the appropriate length of time. These documents
should be supplied by the borrower in their *original* form, with lending
personnel providing copies and properly certifying to their accuracy
and validity.

Wholesale Operations

A recent increase in wholesale originations presents an even greater
area of concern. No longer does the investor have direct control over
employees or the procedures used when originating loans.

Before entering into any correspondent relationship, the lender
must carefully scrutinize proposed originators. The review of financial
statements, resumes of key personnel, references, and sample appraisals is of utmost importance, as is a personal visit to the originator's shop
to observe operations.

Preclosing and post-closing audits for wholesale loans should be
accelerated beyond the audits conducted for in-house originations.
Again, pay particular attention to property values, reviewing every
appraisal. Full re-appraisals should be conducted on a greater percentage of closed loans.

On-Site Audits

In addition to regular individual loan review, an on-site review of
branch operations should be performed at least annually. This on-site
review should include interviews of staff members and observation of
office operations. Areas of concentration should include:

1. Determination of proper staffing level

2. Adequate training of staff

3. Accessibility of all company policy manuals, guidelines, regulations, and other tools that employees need

4. Written operational and work-flow procedures are in place and are followed

5. Branch managers are operating according to company administrative policies

6. Random individual file review of loans in process

Putting It All Together

How good is a quality control system? It all depends on the effectiveness of the results and on how these results are reported. Reporting should be brief and simple. Conclusions and recommendations should be reasonable and understandable.

Expect Responses

Management should utilize the results, implement corrective measures and report their actions. Follow-up procedures will ensure that corrective actions were implemented and are effective. Track results indicate improving or declining trends.

MORTGAGE INSTRUMENTS

The key to success for mortgage lending in the 1990s and beyond is profitability over the long term. To remain profitable, mortgage brokers, mortgage bankers, and financial institutions must address the issue of affordable housing and minimize the risks associated with individual loan instruments.

Before continuing with the discussion of individual loan instruments, defining the common terms of the industry is necessary. Most of the following terms have universal definitions, while others are relatively new.

Terms

Accrual Rate—The stated annual interest rate at which the interest is calculated.

Amortization Period—That period of time over which a specific mortgage payment will fully repay a given loan amount at a given interest rate. A loan's amortization period may differ from its term, as in the case of an early ownership mortgage or a balloon mortgage.

Buydown—Funds provided to a lender by the borrower or a third party for the purpose of reducing the borrower's monthly out-of-pocket payments. Buydowns may be permanent and, therefore, reduce the interest rate over the life of the loan, or they may be temporary, therefore reducing the borrower's payments for a short period of time (such as the first three to five years of the loan).

Cap—A limit on the amount by which the payment may increase or decrease, or on the amount by which the interest rate may increase or decrease.

Fully Indexed Accrual Rate—The base index value of an adjustable-rate mortgage plus the highest gross margin during the life of the loan.

Index—The variable reference rate source upon which future interest rate changes are based for an adjustable-rate mortgage. Common indices include one-year Treasury securities, three-year Treasury securities, and the 11th District Cost of Funds.

Initial Payment Rate—The interest rate used to determine the amount of the initial monthly payment.

Loan Term—The time over which the loan amount must be paid in full. The loan may be paid in full either by a balloon payment or through fully amortizing payments.

Margin—An amount added to the index value to determine the accrual rate of a mortgage.

Negative Amortization—The gradual increase in the outstanding balance of a loan; caused by adding unpaid interest to the loan balance. The unpaid interest is a result of monthly payments being less than the amount required to pay the interest on the loan. Negative amortization can be either potential or scheduled. Scheduled negative amortization is negative amortization that is certain to occur. Potential negative amortization is negative amortization that results from a borrower-optional payment cap.

Rate Concession/Discount—A reduction in the accrual rate from the fully indexed accrual rate offered by the lender to the borrower.

Payment Increases—An increase in the borrower's monthly payment, which occurs either due to unscheduled index increases or scheduled payment increases, which occur regardless of fluctuations in the index and are set forth in the mortgage contract. Scheduled payment increases would occur on a graduated payment mortgage or a loan with a temporary buydown.

Instruments

There are five basic elements of a loan that affect the way a loan functions. These include the amortization period, the payment rate, the accrual rate, the mortgage term, and the loan amount. In many instruments, two or more of these elements may be the same. In a fixed-rate, fixed-payment loan, the amortization period and the term are identical, as are the payment rate and the accrual rate.

Over the course of the last decade, lenders have adjusted these elements to create various types of instruments. The goal in such adjustments has been twofold. First, lenders have attempted to create instruments that are affordable to borrowers, permitting them to purchase homes in an environment in which such purchases otherwise might not be possible. Second, lenders have tried to better match their yield on their mortgages to the cost of funds. To better understand how adjustments to the various elements affect the performance of a mortgage loan, we will examine some of the previously mentioned instruments more closely.

Adjustable-Rate Mortgage (ARM)

The adjustable-rate mortgage is an instrument that permits lenders to share the interest rate risk with the borrower. As its name implies, the interest rate on the loan is adjustable over the term of the mortgage. ARMs are typically structured with interest rate and payment adjustments occurring at one-, three-, or five-year intervals. Some instruments provide for interest rates to adjust more frequently than the payment rate.

The interest rate for an adjustable-rate mortgage is determined by taking the index value and adding a predetermined margin amount. The result is known as the Fully Indexed Accrual Rate. The ability of the lender to adjust the interest rate as index values change permits lenders to better match the yield on their lending portfolios to their cost of funds. This ability to adjust the interest rate and the resulting payment, however, presents the borrower with an uncertainty of payment. To help offset this uncertainty for the borrower, interest rate or payment caps have been instituted by many lenders. The payment cap limits the amount by which the payment may be adjusted, whereas an interest rate cap limits the amount by which the interest rate may be adjusted.

Typically, loans with interest rate caps do not have potential for negative amortization.

Many lenders provide for a rate concession or discount in order to make ARMs more attractive to borrowers. In these instances, lenders would originate loans at an initial interest and payment rate below the Fully Indexed Accrual Rate.

Convertible Mortgages/ROLs

Convertible mortgage loans are mortgages that, at the time of origination, contain an option allowing the borrower to change the mortgage instrument's payment or other characteristics.

The most common of these instruments is an adjustable-rate mortgage that allows the borrower the option to convert to a fixed-rate loan at prevailing market interest rates at predetermined periods in the mortgage life. This option is generally offered on a one-time-only basis at the time of normal rate adjustments, and for a maximum specified length of time, such as during the first five years of the loan term.

In order to obtain this feature, borrowers may have to pay a slight premium at the time of origination through either initial rate or loan fees. The borrower does, however, generally incur substantial savings in costs when converting versus the cost of refinancing.

A recent entrant into the convertible loan instrument arena is the Reduction Option Loan.

Typical ROL mortgages allow conventional fixed-rate loan borrowers to reduce the interest rate on their loans one time during the second through fifth years of the loan. Borrowers do, however, have to wait for market rates to fall a set amount (e.g., at least 2 percent) from their original note rate before exercising their option.

Like other convertible loans, the ROL allows borrowers to take advantage of more favorable interest rates on a one-time basis without the expense and inconvenience of refinancing. The lender also benefits by offering these convertible loan instruments.

More stable servicing portfolios are maintained due to the diminished risk of losing servicing fees on loans that are refinanced.

Early Ownership Mortgage (EOM)

The EOM mortgage, otherwise known as a Growing Equity Mortgage (GEM), is an instrument whereby the initial payments are typically structured using a longer amortization payment, such as 30 years, while the loan term itself will be a period of 15 to 20 years. The early payoff of the mortgage is accomplished through scheduled payment increases. As the payments are increased over the term of the loan, more of the payment is applied to principal, resulting in early amortization. The benefit to the borrower of an EOM is the early payoff of the mortgage, thus resulting in reduced interest costs. The benefit to the lender is that its lendable funds are tied up for a shorter period of time. The inherent risk in the early-ownership mortgage is the payment shock experienced by the borrower resulting from continual payment increases.

Elastic ARM

The elastic ARM is an instrument featuring an adjustable interest rate, but a fixed payment for the life of the mortgage. The term of the loan is adjusted to ensure payoff based on the fixed payment and the interest rate in effect at the time. Elastic ARMs are typically originated at shorter initial amortization periods, say, 20 years, and have a maximum term of up to 40 years. In the event that interest rates remain high for a period of time, the payment is adjusted only if it is insufficient to amortize the loan over a period of 40 years or less. This particular instrument allows the lender to match its yield to its cost of funds, while providing the borrower with a fixed-payment loan. However, the extended term may result in increased aggregate interest expense to the borrower.

Fixed-Rate, Fixed-Payment Loan

The fixed-rate, fixed-payment loan has been the mainstay of the mortgage lending industry. As its name implies, the borrower's payment and the interest rate charged by the lender are fixed for the life of the loan. Although this instrument provides payment certainty for the borrower, it shifts the total burden of interest rate fluctuations to the lender. This instrument is particularly popular with borrowers in middle to low interest rate environments. In an attempt to provide affordability to the borrower in the higher interest rate environments, a feature known as a temporary buydown is frequently incorporated. The borrower's initial payment is supplemented by funds provided to the lender by either the borrower or a third party, thus allowing the lender to maintain the necessary yield on the loan. Typically, a loan with a temporary buydown will have scheduled payment increases for a period of one to five years.

Graduated-Payment Mortgage

The graduated-payment mortgage was designed to address the borrower-affordability issue. In structuring a graduated-payment mortgage, the initial payment is discounted to a point below the payment necessary to cover the interest costs in the loan. Payments are typically scheduled to increase for a period of three to five years. During the initial periods of payment increases, while the payment is insufficient to cover interest, the loan negatively amortizes at a scheduled rate. Since the loan has both scheduled payment increases and negative amortization, the instrument is of a high-risk nature. The scheduled payment increases create payment shock, as the borrower is continually faced with increasing payments for the scheduled period. The initial down payment of the borrower is eroded through the negative amortization. This instrument has been proven to be unacceptable to borrowers and lenders alike due to its high-risk nature.

An instrument that is similar to the GPM is the collateral pledge GPM. This instrument, like the GPM, has scheduled payment increases; however, it does not have negative amortization. Under this instrument, the borrower places funds in a collateral pledge savings account, which are used to supplement the mortgage payment. The difference between this instrument and a fixed-rate, fixed-payment loan with a temporary buydown is the fact that the pledged account funds are used to offset the outstanding mortgage balance in the event of default. Again, this is a high-risk instrument, since funds provided by the borrower at the inception of the loan are eroded as the funds from the pledged account are depleted. The risk characteristics of this loan, again, are payment shock through scheduled payment increases and perceived equity erosion of the borrower as his funds are depleted.

Affordability Considerations

As can be seen by the foregoing description of mortgage instruments, the future is limited only by the creativity of those involved in the mortgage industry. The challenge of balancing borrower affordability with the lending community's need to match mortgage yields to its cost of funds will continue to be a key to the success of the industry.

The affordability issue raises two very important risk considerations:

1. How far below the level of market interest rates is it prudent to start a borrower's monthly payment?

2 . How should the reduced monthly payment be brought back to market levels and interest rates? In response to these risk management issues, increases in the borrower's payments must be limited to avoid excessive payment shock. Prescheduled increases as well as unscheduled increases must also be limited. In the past, payment shock has been avoided by limiting the number of payment in-

creases and applying interest rate or payment caps. While it is understandable to allow some reduction in the initial payment rate to address the affordability issue, it is necessary to ensure that the borrower will have the ability and desire to pay any scheduled or unscheduled increases.

The underwriting of the borrower who uses instruments is especially important. In loans featuring potential payment increases, the lender must require the applicant to have above-average credit and adequate cash reserves. The borrower should have exhibited good money management skills in order to cope with future changes in payments and unexpected occurrences, which may strain the borrower's cash flow.

For loans with potential negative amortization, the underwriter must also carefully consider the impact of the negative amortization on the borrower's willingness and intent to repay the loan. If the borrower's equity is eroded through negative amortization, the only offset is the market value increasing at a rate equivalent to or higher than the negative amortization. Once the borrower's equity in the property has been eroded to a point where he or she sees no benefit in staying in the property, the borrower will more than likely walk away, leaving the lender or any other investors with the risk of loss.

During the 1990s, lenders will continue to address the issues of borrower affordability and investor asset/liability management. It is imperative that, if the industry is to succeed, future mortgage instruments have built-in safeguards to protect borrowers from unreasonable payment increases and equity erosion.

All parties concerned in the lending transaction—the originator, the investor, and the mortgage insurance company—must be willing to analyze the risks associated with the loan and the borrower, and make whatever adjustments are necessary to best match the needs of those concerned.

BORROWER INCOME—SOURCE AND STABILITY

When underwriting an applicant for a mortgage loan, the source and stability of the borrower's income is of utmost importance, as it will be relied upon to make the mortgage payments. A good indicator of future income performance is the borrower's past earning history along with the stability of that income.

During the mid- to late-1980s, major employment sectors such as energy and agriculture experienced severe, adverse economic consequences, the magnitude of which greatly affected default and foreclosure rates in certain areas of the country. Pockets of economic decline occurred in the eighties—industrial and manufacturing sector contraction in Ohio and Michigan, hardship in the rural Midwest due to falling agricultural prices, and greatly reduced energy sector activity in western and south central states due to plummeting oil prices. The mortgage lending industry needs to be aware of the possibility of regional economic dislocations and take them into consideration when reviewing mortgage loan applications.

Historically, mortgage lenders have concentrated on income when qualifying borrowers. The nature of the borrower's employment, long-term prospects, and other aspects of the mortgage loan, such as the mortgage instrument, must also be considered. The mortgage industry must do a better job of analyzing the relationships between these variables in order to succeed and remain profitable.

The following section will look at sources of income, and the effects of varying factors as they relate to income stability. When underwriting mortgage loans, the underwriter needs to be aware of the factors that can affect income as well as how investors and lenders will look at these factors in determining whether a borrower is qualified for a loan. When reviewing the sources of income, we will look at wage earners, including salaried and hourly; commission income; self-employment income, including that from sole proprietorships, small and large corporations, and partnerships; part-time income, including second jobs; and other income sources.

Wage Earner

Although there has been an increase in the number of self-employed, entrepreneurial borrowers, the majority of borrowers seen by mortgage lenders today are still wage earners, both salaried and hourly. Individuals that fall within this category are easier to underwrite because of the steady, consistent flow of income. When analyzing borrowers in this category, it is important to ensure that the borrower has established a history of job stability. It is recognized that borrowers will change jobs in order to improve themselves and their growth potential; however, constant job-hopping should be considered a negative.

The underwriter should look at the history of the borrower's past income, along with its potential for growth in the future. When underwriting salaried and wage-earner income, growth will generally be limited to promotions or merit increases. Future disposable income should be adequate to pay any increased mortgage payments, taxes, and insurance that may occur.

During the late 1970s and early 1980s, annual income growth of 7 to 10 percent was not uncommon. In the future, this type of growth pattern may not be realized. Therefore, the underwriter must review the application not only for whether the borrower will qualify today, but also one, two, or three years down the road. This review is particularly critical when the borrower has applied for a loan where the payments may change over time due to potential or scheduled interest rate or payment increases.

The underwriter should consider past and future labor unrest, such as strikes; the nature of the industry, such as agricultural or energy-related fields; and whether the borrower has a marketable skill or profession where obtaining a comparable job is feasible without relocating.

Other factors that may affect the stability of a borrower's income are seasonal-type employment, such as the construction trades in the north, or industries where periodic layoffs may be anticipated.

Some industries pay overtime or bonuses, which may be allowable as income. When analyzing overtime and bonus income, the underwriter must establish a history of such income and the probability of its continuance. If unable to do so, the underwriter should discount all or portions of this income when qualifying the borrower.

Commissions

The next most prevalent source of income that is seen among borrowers is commission income. Commission income may occur in varying employment fields and to varying degrees. Several factors must be considered when analyzing borrowers when all or a portion of their income is derived from commissions. These factors include such offsets to income as expenses that the borrower must pay out of earnings, and the pattern and stability of the commission income.

Commission income falls into three basic categories:

1.   Draws against commissions

2.   Salary plus commissions

3.   Straight commissions

Borrowers who have the ability to make draws against future commissions must demonstrate that the draws received do not exceed reasonable expectations of commissions to be earned. The history of past commission earnings is a good indicator as to future commissions.

Many industries will pay employees a salary plus commissions or incentives based on performance. The commissions and/or incentives will generally be directly related to the performance of the individual. Again, the underwriter must ensure that a consistent pattern of commissions and incentives have been paid in the past.

Fully commissioned borrowers are customarily seen in the direct-selling field, where compensation is based solely on sales made by the borrower. A pattern of stability and consistency with respect to past commissions is the best indicator of future commissions. The underwriter must be careful to ensure that outside influences or unusual circumstances have not occurred that might abnormally inflate commission earnings. Such outside influences might include such things as a large one-time sale or outside economic factors. When analyzing income growth as it relates to a commissioned borrower, the underwriter needs to determine that a consistent growth pattern has occurred.

Frequently, borrowers who earn commissions also have offsets to earnings from expenses incurred in the performance of their job. These expenses may or may not be reimbursed by their employers. When analyzing a borrower's commission income, it is always advisable to obtain copies of the borrower's tax returns, which will indicate expenses the borrower must pay out of earnings.

Self-Employed Borrowers

The most difficult borrowers to underwrite are those who derive all or a portion of their income from self-employment. Self-employed borrowers are those individuals whose earnings are generated through sole proprietorships, corporations in which the borrower has a significant ownership interest, and partnerships.

When analyzing any type of self-employed borrower, emphasis should be placed on the history and stability of past income, the likelihood of its continuance, and the money management expertise of the borrower. Historically, a high percentage of new businesses fail in their first three years. As a result, the default rate among self-employed borrowers is approximately one and a half times greater than that of salaried or wage-earning borrowers.

Personal tax returns and, if applicable, corporate or partnership returns, must be analyzed. Current financial statements, including Income and Expense Statements and Balance Sheets, should be reviewed for the business as well as for the individual. The underwriter should look for trends within the business itself that are indicative of the business' viability and source of income from which the mortgage obligation will be paid.

When reviewing tax returns and income statements, certain non-cash expenses may be added to net profit to determine the cash flow available for debt repayment. These expenses include depreciation and amortization of upfront organizational expenses.

The extent to which these expenses may be included as cash flow depends on individual investor requirements. However, the under-writer must use caution when using this income for qualification. For example, the mortgage industry has historically added back both chattel and real depreciation. In analyzing chattel depreciation, consideration should be given to the type of chattel and its life expectancy versus its depreciable life. If the asset has a limited life expectancy, it is necessary to determine whether or not the business has or can generate adequate reserves for the replacement of the asset.

When determining qualifying income for a self-employed bor-rower, cash flow should be evaluated for a continuous time period, generally at least two years, and averaged accordingly. Judgment should be used by the underwriter when cash flow from one period to the next changes significantly. The reasons for the change must be explained satisfactorily. Due to the volatility of this type of income, the underwriter should apply a conservative approach in evaluating cash flow.

Significant characteristics of the three primary types of self-em-ployment income are as follows:

Sole Proprietorship

A one-person operation in which the business and the owner are the same for financial and tax purposes. The business is completely reliant upon the owner's management skills to survive and the owner is de-pendent on the business's viability to meet his obligations.

Business net profit is reported and taxed as the owner's personal income on federal tax returns.

Partnerships

A general partnership is a business owned by two or more individuals, each sharing a specified portion of profits and/or losses. For purposes of this discussion, general partnerships, as opposed to limited partner-ships, will be considered. Limited partnerships will be discussed in "Other Income."

Each partner's portion of profit and/or loss sharing should be verified through the partnership's tax returns and supporting schedules. The proportionate dollar amount of those profits or losses is reported by the partners on their personal tax returns. The underwriter must consider only the individual partner's share of noncash expense addbacks when determining cash flow.

Corporations

When evaluating income for the self-employed borrower whose business is incorporated, a determination must be made as to the percentage of common-stock ownership of the borrower. A borrower is generally considered self-employed if he or she owns 25 percent or more of the stock and can have a material impact on the operations. Unlike a sole proprietorship or general partnership, corporate net income is not reported on the borrower's personal tax returns.

The applicability of using corporate income in determining borrower cash flow is dependent upon individual investor criteria as to the borrower's common-stock ownership. This criteria generally dictates no less than 25 percent ownership. The underwriter should use only the borrower's portion of net income and appropriate addbacks if the investor criteria allows use of this as income. As a general rule, it is not desirable to recognize all of the retained earnings on an ongoing basis, as their addition to the capital structure of the corporation may be necessary to maintain the business as a viable, ongoing operation.

Sub-Chapter S Corporations

Unlike corporations previously discussed, Sub-Chapter S Corporations are small corporations with a limited number of shareholders.

As in a partnership, each stockholder's portion of profit and/or loss sharing can be verified through the corporation's tax returns and supporting schedules. The proportionate dollar amount of those profits or losses is reported by the stockholder on his personal tax returns. The underwriter must consider only the individual stockholder's share of noncash expense addbacks when determining borrower cash flow.

Part-Time Income/Second Jobs

Over the past decade, there has been an increase in the number of families who are supplementing their primary income with part-time jobs. Before recognizing this income, the underwriter must establish a history of such income and a strong likelihood that it will continue. Second-job income should also be compatible with the borrower's primary job. One example would be a fireman who has a 24-hour-on/48-hour-off shift. When this occurs, full recognition of the second-job income would be permissible, provided that there is a pattern of such income.

Other Income

The final category to be addressed is other income. Other income includes such sources as limited partnerships, interest, dividends, capital gains and losses, child support and alimony, and rental income.

Limited partnership income is recognizable proportionate to the borrower's position within the limited partnership. Additionally, the proportionate share of depreciation and depletion expenses could be added back to the borrower's taxable partnership income or loss, if verified through copies of the borrower's Form 1065, Schedule K1, "Partner Share of Income, Credits, Deductions, etc.," submitted with the borrower's tax returns. In determining a borrower's cash flow income from a limited partnership, deduct capital contributions required of the borrower, where these have been established. Additional documentation, including the partnership returns, agreements, and any other pertinent data, should be required to support the income and contribution obligations.

Interest and dividend income is recognizable, provided there is an established pattern. When qualifying a borrower, the underwriter should consider any reduction in income-earning assets that will be used for the down payment and closing costs paid by the borrower.

For most borrowers, capital gains and losses do not occur on a regular basis; therefore, capital gains, unless there is a significant pattern of such activity, should not be recognized as cash flow income. Likewise, capital losses may be added back to the borrower's qualifying income, unless there is a history of consistent capital losses.

Child support and alimony are recognizable as income, provided there is documentation to support the stable and ongoing nature of such income. In the case of child support, the ages of the dependent children for which child support is received should be considered.

Rental income is recognizable, provided that there is evidence, through past tax returns or lease agreements, indicating the amount of the rent to be received and for what period of time. Generally, the gross rental income should be reduced by 25 percent to allow for maintenance and vacancy expenses. For a borrower who has a history of this source of income, tax returns verifying both the income and expenses may be used in lieu of the 25 percent maintenance and vacancy factor.

In summary, when reviewing a loan application with respect to income, the underwriter should concentrate on the source of the income, the stability of the income, and the growth potential. A weakness in any one of these areas may play a significant part in the underwriting decision.

FINANCE MANAGEMENT—CASH TO CLOSE

One of the most critical factors in analyzing a borrower's ability and willingness to repay the mortgage debt is the determination of their actual investment in the property, and the source of that investment.

Borrowers will be much more likely to maintain their mortgage payments in times of financial strain if the equity at stake is money that they accumulated on their own.

Various investors and insurers have different guidelines for the minimum amount of funds required from the borrower to close the loan. The borrower must have sufficient funds necessary to cover the down payment, closing costs, and prepaid finance charges. Most investors also require that there be sufficient cash available after closing in reserve funds. This amount is typically defined in terms of number of months of Principal, Interest, Taxes and Insurance (PITI) and can vary from zero to three months, depending on loan-to-value and purpose of loan, such as purchase versus refinance.

It is the responsibility of the originating lender to not only verify the existence of sufficient funds but also the source of those funds. In addition to verifying the source of funds and their adequacy to complete the loan transaction, a determination as to the asset management of the borrower should be made. For example, borrowers who have been paying $500 per month in rent and expect to be making a $1,000 per month housing payment should prove that they have the capability to handle such an increase. If, for example, these borrowers had only been able to accumulate a minimal amount of cash and had very little cash left after closing or were relying on a gift or sale of assets for such, their ability to carry the $1,000 per month housing payment, regardless of debt ratios, should be questioned.

Underwriting financial management is an equal mix of judgment and science. The guidelines discussed in this section can be applied in a scientific fashion. However, the underwriter must also apply a reasonability test. Does the amount and type of assets accumulated by this borrower seem appropriate for his age, vocation, location, and background? If not, is the variance adequately explained? Will whatever caused the variance reoccur in the future and adversely impact the borrower? These are all judgments that the underwriter must make.

Various sources of funds and generally accepted means of verifying them are discussed below.

Accumulated Cash

Cash held in checking and/or savings accounts should be verified on standard Verifications of Deposit. Further documentation as to its source should be secured if an account is less than ninety days old or if the current balance is substantially larger than previous monthly averages. Bank statements, copies of passbooks or CDs should be obtained to supplement any incomplete verification forms with special consideration given to large, one-time deposits or numerous deposits made within a short time period.

Earnest Money Deposits

Carefully consider earnest money deposits when calculating sufficient cash to close. It must be determined if the funds have cleared deposit accounts, which can be determined by evaluating previous average balance versus current balance in accounts. In the case of earnest money deposits exceeding 2 percent of the sale price, most investors require separate documentation that the funds have been paid to the seller or the seller's agent.

Preferably, documentation should be accomplished by obtaining copies of both sides of the cancelled earnest money check(s). Verification of the source of the earnest money minimizes potential collusion to inflate the sale price between the borrower/buyer and the seller.

Gifts

When funds obtained from a gift are to be used for closing, a letter from the donor denoting the amount of funds and the fact that repayment is not expected is required. Other information that should be included on this gift letter includes:

1.   Name(s) of donor(s) and recipient(s)

2.   Address and phone of donor(s)

3.   Date funds were or are to be given

4.   Property address

5.   Relationship between recipient and donor

Individual investor/insurer guidelines must be referred to regarding minimum "borrower's own funds" invested in the transaction when a gift is involved. These guidelines may also vary depending on loan-to-value. Typically, funds received as a gift do not provide the same high incentive for a borrower to work through an adverse situation as does equity from other sources.

Documentation should also be obtained to verify that the donor has sufficient funds to donate and, in turn, that the funds *were* transferred to the borrower.

Sale of Physical Assets

If cash to close is being obtained from the sale of personal assets, a signed Bill of Sale and proof of receipt of funds should be obtained.

If the asset to be sold is real estate, an allowance should be made by the lender for the cost of sale. This allowance is generally 10 percent of the listing or selling price.

In all cases involving the sale of an asset, gross proceeds must be reduced by the amount of any liens secured by the particular asset and proof of receipt of net proceeds must be required prior to loan consummation.

If the sale of assets is a transaction between the buyer and seller of the loan collateral, this sale is considered to be an equity trade.

For example, Party A sells a $100,000 home to Party B, who applies for a $90,000 first mortgage.

Party B sells their $20,000 recreational vehicle, on which they have a $10,000 lien, to Party A. The "equity" in the RV has become the down payment on the residence.

Trade equity is acceptable as long as it represents true value, which must be verified by a written appraisal and lien verification on the traded asset. In addition, proof that transfer has taken place should be provided at closing, such as a title transfer or deed.

Sale of Securities

The value of stock held by the borrower may be verified through a current statement from the stockbroker or copies of stock certificates accompanied by a current market quotation. Unless the redemption value of bonds can be determined, their original purchase price should be used in calculating cash to close. In both cases, proof of sale receipt should subsequently be required. Similar to cash deposits, an analysis of the average balance, length of ownership, and the source of funds used to purchase should be made.

IRA and Keogh Funds

Although IRA and Keogh funds are acceptable sources of cash for down payment, consideration must be given only to the net amount after any withdrawal or tax penalties.

Borrowed Funds

Any funds borrowed in order to close a loan transaction *must be secured* by an asset, i.e., auto, life insurance, stocks, etc. Terms of the borrowing must be verified and payments used in calculating debt service ratios. Unsecured borrowings such as signature loans or lines of credit on checking accounts or charge cards are unacceptable, as they are effectively a reduction of the equity.

Bridge or Swing Loans

This type of loan, which allows a purchaser to close a loan on a new property prior to selling another residence, is acceptable as long as:

    A.   The bridge loan is secured by the other residence, and

    B.   The borrower has the financial capability to carry all indebtedness on the other residence.

Terms of the bridge loan must be verified and proof must be provided at the mortgage closing that the proceeds of the bridge loan have been received.

Lot Equity

The value of a lot owned by the borrower on which he or she is constructing a new home is also an acceptable source of equity. The amount of equity is based on the current value, which must be verified by an appraisal if the property was purchased more than two years prior.

Rent Credits

A borrower purchasing a property that he or she previously has been renting may be credited for a portion of rent payments toward down payment under the following circumstances:

    A.   The original lease included an option to purchase.

B.   The appraisal determines fair market rents.

C.   Only that portion exceeding fair market rents may be applied to the down payment.

D.   The borrower may be required, depending upon loan type and investor, to contribute additional cash equity.

Even though a borrower may have excess assets to close a loan, *all* liquid assets should be verified. Accumulation of liquid assets over and above that needed to close indicates a borrower who can withstand unexpected hardships and increased payments resulting from a mode of financing.

Substantial asset reserve is of particular importance when evaluating a self-employed or commissioned borrower whose income may be sporadic. Likewise, an individual who owns rental properties should be expected to have sufficient liquid assets to compensate for short-term loss of income or unexpected expenses as the result of property damage.

CREDIT

Obligation Ratios

The ability of borrowers to make their housing payments without excessive strain is measured by a ratio of the monthly housing payments (Principal, Interest, Taxes, and Insurance) to the monthly gross income. The housing expense ratio for mortgages with a loan-to-value ratio of 90 percent or less is normally not expected to exceed 28 percent unless there are offsetting, favorable factors. On higher LTVs, the housing ratio should be 25 percent or less to add a margin of capability to survive potential adverse changes.

A comparable ratio measures the total monthly obligations, including housing, compared to total gross monthly income. Interestingly, studies have shown that the default incidence is higher when the spread between the housing and the total obligation ratios exceeds eight percentage points. The data suggests that the larger the spread between the two ratios, the higher the risk of default. The total obligation ratio maximums are generally accepted to be 36 percent and 33 percent, respectively, for 90 percent and 95 percent LTVs.

The ratios are easily understood and calculated. They appear to be objective and reliable. All of which may be true; however, an underwriter should be careful not to rely heavily on the ratios. Many other factors must be considered: verifiable net worth, cash assets, property (collateral), credit histoy, earning potential, fixed-payment debt versus variable-payment, etc.

When evaluating the credit history of loan applications, the following liabilities should be included in computing total debt-to-income ratios:

1. Installment debt extending beyond ten months in duration

2. Payments on all revolving debt regardless of balance

3. Reasonable payments on single-payment notes unless the borrower has sufficient liquid assets over and above the amount necessary to repay the note

4. Payment on mortgage loans, stock pledges, or life insurance loans

5. Negative income from investment properties or partnerships

6. Child support and/or alimony payments extending beyond ten months

Even though an installment debt may have only an eight-month remaining term, the impact of this obligation on the borrower's ability to pay the mortgage in its early months should be carefully analyzed.

In addition, the type of short-term installment debt should be scrutinized. For example, if six monthly payments remain on an auto loan secured by a seven-year-old auto, the likelihood of the borrower being obligated long-term for some type of auto loan is very high. This is a similar philosophy to the one used when all revolving debt payment is included regardless of balance—there exists a good possibility of its long-term continuance as an obligation.

Evaluating a Credit Report

The perusal of the credit report for slow or late payments or any other adverse item is of crucial importance and is a key factor in evaluating the borrower's *willingness* to pay and prior regard for debt.

Any adverse item should be fully explained by the applicant and the supporting documentation carefully analyzed to determine its legitimacy. In addition to standard explanations, specific attention should be paid to:

1.   Proof of payoff of judgments or liens

2.   Full explanations and all supporting documents pertaining to bankruptcies, foreclosures, etc.

Dates of delinquencies as shown on the credit report should correlate to debts contained in explanations and supporting documents.

Additionally, all inquiries and undisclosed debt should be explained by borrowers.

Careful consideration should be given to a credit report which indicates that a borrower is consistently restructuring debt, such as paying off a $2,000 balance at XYZ Financial in 4-93 and opening a $6,000 balance at XYZ Financial or ABC Financial in 4-93 with no indication of corresponding additional assets being accumulated.

A pattern of recently paid-off revolving debt or installment debt that appears to have been prepaid indicates that debt may have been restructured for loan qualification purposes.

Contingent liabilities should generally be considered a part of the borrower's overall liabilities unless a sufficient history can be established supporting payment of the debt by the primary debtors. Know your investors' guidelines, as they will vary on this matter. All material debt which is not adequately verified through credit bureaus should be directly verified through the creditor.

Mortgage or Rental History

One of the prime indicators of borrower creditworthiness is a history of previous housing payments. Direct verification from the mortgage servicer or landlord should be obtained covering at least a 12-month period regardless of credit bureau ratings. If this information is not complete or otherwise appears to be insufficient, a mortgage payment history and/or legible copies of the front and back of cancelled checks should be obtained.

APPRAISALS

The reason for appraisal management is to assure the soundness of mortgage loans and real estate investments by adequately identifying the risks involved in the collateral. To perform this function, two distinct subfunctions are required—management operations and the analysis of risk.

The management operations subfunction includes the lender's responsibility to control the selection, guidance, and review of appraisers and appraisals.

The analysis of risk function includes property valuation and risk management. The value of the individual home in the subdivision may be correct; however, the risk of lending in the subdivision may be sufficiently high to preclude an acceptable mortgage risk.

Management Operations

Lenders are responsible for the quality of appraisals. Investors such as the Federal Home Loan Mortgage Corp. (FHLMC), Federal National Mortgage Association (FNMA) and other secondary market investors have buy-back provisions in their loan purchase agreements. If problems with the appraisal are found, the lender may be required to repurchase the loan. Mortgage insurance companies also have exclusionary language in their master policies that cancels the mortgage insurance coverage in the event of misrepresentation.

An efficient management operations program will include: (1) management of the valuation process, (2) establishment of appraiser qualifications, (3) guidelines and procedures, and (4) provisions for quality control.

In managing the process, the appraiser must be allowed flexibility to complete the appraisal assignment without undue influence to establish a predetermined value. In most prudent lending organizations, separate lines (i.e., underwriting and production) of authority exist to avoid undue influence of one discipline over the other.

Effective communications between lender and appraiser will reduce potential delays and overhead costs due to clarification questions. Appraisers should know and understand the expectations of the lender, the business relationship parameters of the lender, and specific investor underwriting criteria.

The lender must feel comfortable with the general level of appraisal expertise. The following is a recommendation of minimum standards to consider for initially qualifying an appraiser. The appraiser should have:

- ◆ Completed a nationally recognized basic appraisal course or equivalent formal appraisal education (such as the curriculum of the Society of Real Estate Appraisers or the American Institute of Real Estate Appraisers).

- ◆ Two years of full-line appraisal experience.

♦ Become a member of a professional appraisal organization.

The objective of these standards is to ensure a minimum level of appraisal education and relevant experience. The membership in a professional appraisal organization is recommended because the appraiser's work (if questionable) can be reviewed by his or her peers. The degree to which the appraisal organization enforces the available disciplinary measures should be considered.

Six appraisal organizations that meet these requirements are:

♦ National Association of Independent Fee Appraisers

♦ American Association of Certified Appraisers

♦ American Society of Farm Managers and Rural Appraisers

♦ American Society of Appraisers

♦ Society of Real Estate Appraisers

♦ American Institute of Real Estate Appraisers

The first step in qualifying an appraiser is to review a resume of his or her education and experience. This data should include appraisals, appraisal fee structure, and the geographic area the appraiser covers. Does the appraiser's current experience relate to the expected assignments? Does he or she have appropriate appraisal training?

If the typical appraisal format is narrative, the sample appraisals should be narrative. Usually, this format is required for commercial properties, large apartment complexes, and unique properties (including expensive residential homes). Most residential appraisals are form-oriented, and sample appraisals should appear on the form most commonly used by the lender.

The appraiser should be able to provide the reader with valid information in a clear, concise format. A poor example of information would be "dampness in the basement." A good example would be "basement dampness is the result of the house being closed up—opening of windows or the use of fans will cure the musty sensation."

Both education and experience should be from quality sources. Core instructional courses should be from approved appraisal organizations or formal institutions of learning. Experience should have been gained from the same market and property type.

The geographic area covered is important in that it defines an area of expertise. The more experienced an appraiser is in a market, the more accurate and useful he or she can be in isolating value and risk issues.

The issue of responsibility should be considered at this point. The author who signs the appraisal is responsible for the quality and accuracy of the report and must be the one approved by the lender.

Responsibility also raises the issue of liability. To reinforce academic training and experience, errors and omissions insurance is available to protect both the appraiser and the lender. It normally does not cover fraudulent activity. Lenders should consider requiring this insurance.

Appraiser interrelationships are also important. Either staff appraisers who are salaried employees of the lender or independent-fee appraisers should be used. These types of appraisers minimize potential conflicts of interest. It is best to establish a policy that precludes those individuals who are not exclusively committed to the appraisal profession.

The items discussed above should be reviewed by the lender's management on an annual basis.

Appraisal Quality Control

A quality control function updates basic information and reviews the quality of the appraiser's work annually. Updating basic information can easily be accomplished by questionnaires distributed through the mail. Reviewing the appraiser's work can be accomplished through in-house reviews and third-party reviews.

The objective of a quality control program is to alert the lender to any variation from the desired appraisal standards. This basic objective should entail five parts:

1. Accurate reporting of property standards

2. Accurate description of intangibles

3. Appropriate use of judgment

4. Supportable value conclusion

5. Appropriate communication to support a risk decision

There are two basic techniques of reviewing appraisals: desk and field reviews.

Desk reviews involve a knowledgeable appraiser reviewing appraisals without the benefit of seeing the site, neighborhood, comparables, or general market. The desk review is usually limited to the data provided by the appraiser. Desk reviews normally address:

- Accuracy of statements

- Consistent flow of information from the front to the back of the form

- The accuracy of mathematical adjustments

- Logical continuity

- Valid value conclusions

In most instances, the desk reviewer will issue reports that indicate if the original appraiser has performed adequately according to the above criteria. Usually, the lack of field exposure results in reports that attempt to quantify the appraiser by mathematical ratings (i.e., in 95 percent of the reviews, the appraiser accurately completed mathematical functions correctly). The point is that desk reviews can be productive in giving a general overview of the appraiser's performance. Desk reviews can be done in-house and at a lower cost than field reviews.

Field reviews involve an appraiser in the local market actually verifying the existence and ratings of the subject property and comparables. The field appraiser can also identify if intangible items, such as traffic ratings, are adequately described. A key advantage to the field review is that it identifies if the comparables are truly similar to the subject and if other comparables are available that would be better value indicators. A common technique used by some appraisers to mislead the reader is to select better comparables in better locations without proper adjustment, and to neglect to report negative-influence items on the property or property location.

The purpose of an appraisal is to establish the market value at a point in time of the property to be mortgaged. One of the most useful and accepted definitions of market value, issued by FNMA, is as follows:

FNMA Definition of Market Value—"The most probable price which a property should bring in a competitive and open market under all conditions requisite to a fair sale, the buyer and seller, each acting prudently, knowledgeably and assuming the price is not affected by undue stimulus. Implicit in this definition is the consummation of a sale as of a specific date and the passing of title from seller to buyer under conditions whereby: (1) buyer and seller are typically motivated; (2) both parties are well informed or well advised, and each is acting in what he considers his own best interest; (3) a reasonable time is allowed for exposure in the open market; (4) payment is made in terms of cash in U.S. dollars or in terms of financial arrangements comparable thereto; and (5) the price represents the normal consideration for the property sold unaffected by special or creative financing or sale concessions[1] granted by anyone associated with the sale."

Why is market value important? It is important because the lender knows that the collateral for the loan, the property, is worth a certain amount, in the event the borrower is unable to repay his debt.

The lender wants to recoup the mortgage amount, foreclosure expenses, and lost interest through the resale of the house. Hopefully, if there is sufficient equity in the house, the borrower will dispose of the home before foreclosure proceedings. This is the best situation for all parties, since the borrower and lender minimize their financial loss. An accurate market value estimate will help both lender and borrower recognize and quantify their situation.

The appraiser's primary assignment is to reflect the value indicators of the market to the specific property at hand. When clients (whether borrowers or lenders) order an appraisal for loan collateral purposes, their objective, beyond current value, is determining the risk of the property declining in value in the future. Through a professional analysis, the appraiser can reveal items that may affect the client's decision to continue with the transaction—items such as infrastructure support and unique property characteristics that are negatively perceived by the marketplace. An example of the former is inadequate police or fire protection; an example of the latter is the lack of complete bathroom facilities.

In this process, the appraiser is a bridge of information between the specific property and the reactions of the marketplace.

The following section will position and explain items that clients review when examining a property for purchase or for lending. Underwriting insight, often gained from properties that have been foreclosed, is provided to assist parties new to the field.

An appraisal is a document used to establish value. While appraisals are reviewed by underwriters to identify areas of collateral risk, the appraisal's primary purpose is to estimate value, not to identify risk. Underwriters who understand that appraisals are not primarily risk-

---

1. Adjustments to the comparables must be made for special or creative financing or sale concessions. No adjustments are necessary for those costs that are normally paid by sellers as a result of tradition or law in a market area; these costs are readily identifiable since the seller pays these costs in virtually all sale transactions. Special or creative financing adjustments can be made to the comparable property by comparisons to financing terms offered by a third-party institutional lender that is not already involved in the property or transaction. Any adjustment should not be calculated on a mechanical, dollar-for-dollar cost of the financing or concession, but the dollar amount of any adjustment should approximate the market's reaction to the financing or concessions based on the appraiser's judgment.

oriented documents will be better able to evaluate appraisals and interact with appraisers.

An appraisal contains information that is either fact (the house is constructed of brick) or judgment (the "appeal to market" is "fair"). Underwriters must use their judgment when evaluating an appraisal.

One of the primary tenets of appraisal theory is to select good comparables so that the appraiser compares "apples with apples and oranges with oranges." Whether or not those comparables are within the one-mile limit is irrelevant to the appraiser who is primarily concerned with selecting the best comparables to reflect value. Consider the following example:

> One comparable was within a mile of the subject property, but the second and third comparables were 1.2 miles away. Certain investors' guidelines require that two comparables be within one mile of the subject property. In this case, the first comparable was within a mile and the other two were just outside that limit. It is appropriate for the underwriter to exercise judgment and accept these comparables if the underwriter thinks that the neighborhoods are similar.

The appraiser must be able to identify the appropriate degree-of-value impact of various features of a property. The identification of this value impact is derived from the appraiser's judgment of market reactions. The appraiser identifies the unique property features of the home and then examines the market for indications of value adjustment. The basic concept of valuation adjustments is "paired sales" or "match paired sales" which isolate the market value of the unique feature.

The appraiser acts as the lender's "eyes and ears" when appraising the property. The lender must feel comfortable that the property is accurately described. It is important to remember that the property is only part of the lending decision, for the lender's risk is also impacted by the borrower's credit and character. A marginal property with an excellent borrower could be an acceptable risk.

Several areas of the appraisal require that the underwriter exercise judgment. For example, a difference between the age of the comparables and the marketing time may not be an indication of a faulty appraisal. If the comparables are one or two months old in an area in which the market time is six months, it may merely indicate a shift in market conditions. Marketing time is the time it takes to sell the house in the neighborhood. The age of the comparable is the date since the property sold, not the time the house was on the market.

Many appraisers will use the subject property as a comparable if the subject property was sold recently to other parties. Using the subject property as a comparable is a perfectly acceptable practice, as long as the sale was an arm's-length transaction and a satisfactory explanation for the recent sale is given. The subject property, after all, is the most ideal comparable because it is identical to the property being appraised.

There are many situations in which it is appropriate for the underwriter to contact the appraiser, including the following:

1. *"Fair" or "poor" ratings that require further clarification.* Some fair and poor ratings are self-explanatory, such as a "poor" rating for "adequacy of public transportation" in a rural area. However, a "fair" or "poor" rating of the "appeal to market" would definitely require further explanation from the appraiser.

2. *Items left blank that require a specific answer in order for the underwriter to make a decision.* For example, the omission of the type of street surface in an urban area may not require a call to the appraiser. However, if the appraiser neglected to fill in an important item such as whether the appraisal is made "as is" or "subject to repairs, alterations, or conditions listed below," the underwriter should call the lender or the appraiser for further information.

3. *Inconsistent adjustments or large adjustments to the market data approach* probably would require further explanation. It should be obvious to the underwriter that large adjustments for the size of the property mean that the subject property is dissimilar to the comparables.

4. *An invalid conclusion or an unclear statement that could have an important effect on the rest of the report* should be explained further by the appraiser. For instance, a statement such as "The roof is in poor condition but has no effect on market value" would require further explanation.

5. *Issues noted but not discussed in the appraisal* may require further clarification, such as "damp basement."

It is important for underwriters to develop a good professional rapport with appraisers. Despite the concern that some appraisers do not adequately appraise the property, most appraisers are skilled and competent professionals. Underwriters should remember that the appraiser completed the appraisal in order to reflect value, not to determine lending risk. The underwriter should ask the appraiser relevant risk questions in a knowledgeable and professional manner. Negative or condescending underwriting attitudes reflect poorly on the lender's reputation.

UNDERWRITING AN APPRAISAL

Appraisal Guidelines

A thorough and accurate appraisal is essential to proper mortgage underwriting. An acceptable appraisal accurately describes the property, explains any deficiencies or variations in the property, displays the best comparable properties that are available, and explains the logic used to arrive at the final value estimate. It provides the information necessary to determine if the property is viable security for the loan and will reasonably remain so.

Several photographs of the property, a page of limiting conditions, and a sketch of the floor plan should accompany the appraisal form. Photographs of the comparables are useful in helping the underwriter accept the appraiser's logic.

Since property values change as market conditions change, an appraisal signifies value as of a certain date. That date identifies the kind of market environment within which the value estimate is valid.

The bottom line of an appraisal is the estimated *market value* of the property. Market value is the most probable price the property would sell for within a reasonable period of time on the open market under normal conditions. In order to calculate this amount, the appraiser focuses on various aspects of the property, such as the neighborhood, the site, and the nature and finish of the home.

Value is important from the borrower's equity perspective. Due to the potential loss of this equity, a property located in a neighborhood or general market area with declining property values represents a higher and possibly unacceptable risk. Items such as extended marketing times and "fair and poor" neighborhood ratings tend to identify properties of higher risk. This value risk results from a smaller market of potential buyers due to the lower desirability of the property.

Other items of risk, which may be accounted for in the valuation of the property, are best illustrated by the physical condition of the property.

The "condition of the improvement" may be poor and the comparable properties used to reflect the market value may also be in poor condition resulting in an accurate value estimate by the appraiser. However, the usefulness of the structure as a living unit may be so marginal that users would be unable to protect their equity or would default on their loan obligations because the house did not support their lifestyle. Examples could be electrical fuses that continually blow because of inadequate electric service, roof leaks that cannot be repaired without extensive cost, and inadequate plumbing.

Underwriting Overview

The emphasis in underwriting property should by placed on factors that affect marketability, including:

- ◆ Comparability of the subject property with surrounding structures

- ◆ Quality of the construction and equipment, such as furnaces and plumbing

- ◆ Characteristics of design which contribute to convenience, livability, and desirability

Lack of functional utility, as characterized by such factors as poor room arrangement, small room sizes, or lack of adequate storage, adversely affect the marketability of the property and should be noted in the appraisal. These factors can be found in both old and new housing.

The property should meet the needs of the occupants. Unique and/or functionally obsolescent properties may, through occupant dissatisfaction, contribute to default.

The following is a review of the key sections of an appraisal.

Front Page of Appraisal

Appraiser/Appraisal Comments The name of the appraiser and appraisal firm must appear legibly on the appraisal.

The following clarifications refer to specific sections of the appraisal, with the numbered comments corresponding to the numbered items on the appraisal form shown in Figure 23.1.

1. Sales concessions should be compared to the sales concessions reported on the sale contract for consistency and market reaction.

2. The client should verify that property rights appraised are the same as the title/property type indicated in the loan documents.

Figure 23.1 Uniform Residential Appraisal Reports

MGIC RESIDENTIAL APPRAISAL REPORT File No

Borrower ___ Census Tract ___ Map Reference
Property Address
City ___ County ___ State ___ Zip Code
Legal Description
Sale Price $ ___ Date of Sale ___ Loan Term ___ yrs ___ Property Rights Appraised ☐ Fee ☐ Leasehold ☐ DeMinimis PUD
Actual Real Estate Taxes $ ___ (yr) Loan charges to be paid by seller $ ___ Other sales concessions
Lender/Client ___ Address
Occupant ___ Appraiser ___ Instructions to Appraiser

NEIGHBORHOOD

Location	☐ Urban ☐ Suburban ☐ Rural		Good Avg. Fair Poor
Built Up	☐ Over 75% ☐ 25% to 75% ☐ Under 25%	Employment Stability	☐☐☐☐
Growth Rate ☐ Fully Dev	☐ Rapid ☐ Steady ☐ Slow	Convenience to Employment	☐☐☐☐
Property Values	☐ Increasing ☐ Stable ☐ Declining	Convenience to Shopping	☐☐☐☐
Demand/Supply	☐ Shortage ☐ In Balance ☐ Over Supply	Convenience to Schools	☐☐☐☐
Marketing Time	☐ Under 3 Mos ☐ 4–6 Mos ☐ Over 6 Mos	Adequacy of Public Transportation	☐☐☐☐

Present Land Use ___ % 1 Family ___ % 2–4 Family ___ % Apts ___ % Condo ___ % Commercial ___ % Industrial ___ % Vacant ___ %
Recreational Facilities ☐☐☐☐
Adequacy of Utilities ☐☐☐☐
Change in Present Land Use ☐ Not Likely ☐ Likely (*) ☐ Taking Place (*)
Property Compatibility ☐☐☐☐
(*) From ___ To ___
Protection from Detrimental Conditions ☐☐☐☐
Predominant Occupancy ☐ Owner ☐ Tenant ___ % Vacant
Police and Fire Protection ☐☐☐☐
Single Family Price Range $ ___ to $ ___ Predominant Value $ ___
General Appearance of Properties ☐☐☐☐
Single Family Age ___ yrs to ___ yrs Predominant Age ___ yrs
Appeal to Market ☐☐☐☐

Note: FHLMC/FNMA do not consider race or the racial composition of the neighborhood to be reliable appraisal factors.
Comments including those factors, favorable or unfavorable, affecting marketability (e.g. public parks, schools, view, noise) ___

SITE

Dimensions ___ * ___ Sq. Ft. or Acres ☐ Corner Lot
Zoning classification ___ Present improvements ☐ do ☐ do not conform to zoning regulations
Highest and best use ☐ Present use ☐ Other (specify)

	Public Other (Describe)	OFF SITE IMPROVEMENTS	Topo	
Elec.	☐	Street Access ☐ Public ☐ Private	Size	
Gas	☐	Surface	Shape	
Water	☐	Maintenance ☐ Public ☐ Private	View	
San Sewer	☐	☐ Storm Sewer ☐ Curb/Gutter	Drainage	

☐ Underground Elect. & Tel ☐ Sidewalk ☐ Street Lights Is the property located in a HUD Identified Special Flood Hazard Area? ☐ No ☐ Yes
Comments (favorable or unfavorable including any apparent adverse easements, encroachments or other adverse conditions) ___

IMPROVEMENTS

☐ Existing ☐ Proposed ☐ Under Constr. No. Units ___ Type (det, duplex, semi/det, etc.) ___ Design (rambler, split level, etc.) ___ Exterior Walls ___
Yrs. Age: Actual ___ Effective ___ to ___ No. Stories ___
Roof Material ___ Gutters & Downspouts ☐ None Window (Type) ___ ☐ Storm Sash ☐ Screens ☐ Combination Insulation ☐ None ☐ Floor ☐ Ceiling ☐ Roof ☐ Walls
☐ Manufactured Housing % Basement ___ ☐ Floor Drain Finished Ceiling ___
Foundation Walls ___ BSMT ☐ Outside Entrance ☐ Sump Pump Finished Walls ___ ☐ Concrete Floor ___ % Finished Finished Floor ___
☐ Slab on Grade ☐ Crawl Space Evidence of ☐ Dampness ☐ Termites ☐ Settlement
Comments ___

ROOM LIST

Room List	Foyer	Living	Dining	Kitchen	Den	Family Rm	Rec. Rm	Bedrooms	No. Baths	Laundry	Other
Basement											
1st Level											
2nd Level											

Finished area above grade contains a total of ___ rooms ___ bedrooms ___ baths Gross Living Area ___ sq. ft. Bsmt Area ___ sq. ft.

INTERIOR FINISH & EQUIPMENT

Kitchen Equipment ☐ Refrigerator ☐ Range/Oven ☐ Disposal ☐ Dishwasher ☐ Fan/Hood ☐ Compactor ☐ Washer ☐ Dryer ☐
HEAT Type ___ Fuel ___ Cond. ___ AIR COND ☐ Central ☐ Other ___ ☐ Adequate ☐ Inadequate

Floors	☐ Hardwood ☐ Carpet Over		Good Avg. Fair Poor
Walls	☐ Drywall ☐ Plaster	Quality of Construction (Materials & Finish)	☐☐☐☐
Trim/Finish	☐ Good ☐ Average ☐ Fair ☐ Poor	Condition of Improvements	☐☐☐☐
Bath Floor	☐ Ceramic	Room sizes and layout	☐☐☐☐
Bath Wainscot	☐ Ceramic	Closets and Storage	☐☐☐☐

Special Features (including energy efficient items) ___
Insulation—adequacy ☐☐☐☐
Plumbing—adequacy and condition ☐☐☐☐
Electrical—adequacy and condition ☐☐☐☐
ATTIC ☐ Yes ☐ No ☐ Stairway ☐ Drop-stair ☐ Scuttle ☐ Floored
Kitchen Cabinets—adequacy and condition ☐☐☐☐
Finished (Describe) ___ ☐ Heated
Compatibility to Neighborhood ☐☐☐☐
CAR STORAGE ☐ Garage ☐ Built-in ☐ Attached ☐ Detached ☐ Car Port
Overall Livability ☐☐☐☐
No. Cars ___ ☐ Adequate ☐ Inadequate Condition ___
Appeal and Marketability ☐☐☐☐
Yrs Est Remaining Economic Life ___ Explain if less than Loan Term

FIREPLACES, PATIOS, POOL, FENCES, etc. (describe) ___

COMMENTS (including functional or physical inadequacies, repairs needed, modernization, etc.) ___

FHLMC Form 70 Rev 7/79 ATTACH DESCRIPTIVE PHOTOGRAPHS OF SUBJECT PROPERTY AND STREET SCENE FNMA Form 1004 Rev. 7/79

Property Values Due to the potential loss of borrower equity, a property located in a neighborhood or general market with declining property values represents a higher risk. The property must support the loan terms.

3.   A box checked slow, declining, or oversupply may indicate problems with market values. The time adjustments in the market data analysis should be zero or negative, and the terms of sale should be reviewed for excessive seller contributions.

Marketing Time/Land Use The marketing time for similar properties should be less than six months. A slow real estate market reduces borrower equity and weakens a borrower's motivation to cure a default.

4.   If marketing time is in excess of six months, there may be problems in either the neighborhood or the community. These problems may be overbuilding, a weak economy, or the lack of mortgage financing. Properties should then exhibit a high degree of market compatibility, livability, and marketability to be an acceptable risk.

5.   If either the land use box labeled "likely" or the box labeled "taking place" is checked, the impact should be considered. Manufacturing or commercial intrusion should be explained. Properties should otherwise be compatible and marketable.

Older homes may be more susceptible to negative land use change and probable declines in marketability and value.

Predominant Value Some underwriters consider a property value at 90 percent or more of the highest property value in the neighborhood to be a high-risk property. These high-risk properties usually suffer from overimprovements and longer marketing times. Valuations in this high range should be thoroughly explained by the appraiser.

6.   The subject property's value and age should be within the ranges indicated. These high-risk properties must have appraiser explanations and be examined for overimprove-

ments and longer marketing times. Valuations in this high range should be explained by the appraiser.

Neighborhood Rating/Site Considerations Unexplained or unacceptable explanations of fair and poor neighborhood ratings indicate factors that may weaken the borrower's commitment to the property. This may negatively affect the insurability of the loan.

7. Fair and poor ratings indicate neighborhood deficiencies in comparison to other competing neighborhoods, and are caution flags. Fair and poor ratings for "general appearance of properties" and "appeal to market" raise concerns regarding property value stability. The materiality of such ratings depends on property value trends, demand/supply, marketing time, and property conditions. To accurately reflect value, comparables should be taken from the same or similar neighborhoods.

8. The appraiser should comment in this section on items affecting the property's marketability, value, or the stability of the neighborhood, particularly if there are fair or poor ratings.

9. The property should be zoned residential. Highest and best use should be the present use. Nonresidential zoning may indicate nonharmonious, adverse influences requiring explanation.

10. Present improvements should conform to zoning regulations, if they exist.

11. All utilities should be identified as to source or type.

12. Private road maintenance is to be identified. Further explanation may be necessary when the appraiser comments that the condition or adequacy is not normal or typical.

13. Any drainage problem or the existence of a flood hazard condition should be questioned. The existence of such conditions or major problems may require physical correction or flood hazard insurance.

14. In this section, the appraiser should comment on any adverse site conditions that may affect the value or market-

ability of the property. These include such influences as noise, odors, floods, easements, encroachments, or views.

Improvements

15. The subject property should be in an age range consistent with the neighborhood. Where the effective age is less than the actual age, generally, no major repairs or physical inadequacies should be present.

16. Manufactured housing is the generic term applied to all living units constructed off site and assembled in segments on site. Two key construction codes are used to measure the quality standards of the house.

A Specification Code is a construction process that assembles and builds a unit to specific standards required by a housing code. Each component must be of the identified quality and type. For example, all walls are of 2 × 4, kiln-dried studding. Purchasers of these units should know that the units equal or exceed the requirements established by the local building code authority.

A Performance Code is a process of building which permits architectural and engineering flexibility. This flexibility allows wide usage of materials. For example, using 1 × 2s as wall studs spaced closer than 2 × 4 studding, as long as the wall meets certain pressure and usage tests. These *mobile home units* are part of the 1974 Mobile Home Quality Standards Act and may or may not meet the construction standards for site-built housing of the local building code authority.

17. The appraiser's comments should be consistent with and/or support the observations indicated, and identify any unique property characteristics. Use of addenda is strongly suggested.

18. The room list data should suggest that the property is adequate to meet the borrower's and all dependents' housing needs.

Interior Finish and Equipment

19. An inadequate heating system may be unacceptable, especially if the property is located in a cold weather state. The borrower's ability to pay high heating costs should be considered.

20. Fair or poor ratings in this section can affect borrower motivation and cause default. Fair and poor ratings should be thoroughly explained as they indicate property deficiencies. No, or unsatisfactory, explanations may be reason for denial.

21. The remaining economic life should be longer than the loan amortization. An economic life less than 30 years generally indicates structural and/or condition problems.

22. Any amenities such as swimming pools, etc., should be listed here.

Structural Problems The presence of incurable structural problems is a cause for concern. Curable structural problems should be reviewed thoroughly.

23. In this section, the appraiser should identify any modernization or repairs which affect the appraised value. Any functional or physical inadequacies should be explained. Appraiser comments identifying painting or minor repairs usually do not affect loan risk. Comments identifying major needed repairs, or structural problems that affect value or the borrower's use or enjoyment of the property, should be considered as risk factors. The underwriter should determine if the deficiencies are to be cured before closing, escrowed, or if they are acceptable as is. Does the borrower have assets to make needed repairs? These questions should be documented in the file, noting the date, participants, and comments. The underwriter is responsible for determining if the property supports the loan terms and is adequate collateral for the loan amount.

Back Page of Appraisal

Cost Approach The following clarifications refer to specific sections of the back page of the appraisal. The numbered comments correspond to the numbered items on the appraisal form shown in Figure 23.2.

1. A building sketch is usually attached to the appraisal. The room layout, dimensions, measurements, and square footage listed in this section should match the data in the Room List Section, and the market approach. The cost approach value, the reconciled value, and the appraisal's credibility should be questioned if substantial discrepancies exist and they are not commented on.

2. The appraiser should comment on any functional or external obsolescence used to determine depreciation. These comments should match the comments under the Interior Finish and Equipment section. Use of addenda is strongly suggested.

3. Properties with condition or repair comments should have depreciation adjustment in this space.

Land Value The proportion of land value to the value of the residence must be in line with other values in the neighborhood. Any property with a land value higher than the area norm is considered a higher risk. This may negatively affect the insurability of the loan due to the excess land or underimprovement of the property.

4. Generally, the land value should not exceed the norm for the market, usually 25 percent to 33 percent. Higher land value ratios are acceptable in certain markets if explained by the appraiser.

Comparables Normally, a minimum of three comparables for the market value analysis is required.

5. Fewer than three comparables usually indicate a scarce market. More than three comparables may be provided by the appraiser to substantiate his logic.

Source of Comparables—The lender or developer may supply one of the three comparables.

Figure 23.2   Uniform Residential Appraisal Report—Back Page

VALUATION SECTION

Purpose of Appraisal is to estimate Market Value as defined in Certification & Statement of Limiting Conditions (FHLMC Form 439/FNMA Form 1004B). If submitted for FNMA, the appraiser must attach (1) sketch or map showing location of subject, street names, distance from nearest intersection, and any detrimental conditions and (2) exterior building sketch of improvements showing dimensions

COST APPROACH

Measurements	No. Stories	Sq. Ft.
x	x	=
x	x	=
x	x	= **1** =
x	x	=
x	x	=
x	x	=

Total Gross Living Area (List in Market Data Analysis below)

Comment on functional and economic obsolescence:

ESTIMATED REPRODUCTION COST – NEW – OF IMPROVEMENTS:

Dwelling _____ Sq. Ft. @ $ _____ = $ _____
_____ Sq. Ft. @ $ _____ = _____
Extras _____ = _____
Special Energy Efficient Items _____ = _____
Porches, Patios, etc. _____ = _____
Garage/Car Port _____ Sq. Ft. @ $ _____ = _____
Site Improvements (driveway, landscaping, etc.) = _____
Total Estimated Cost New . . . . = $ _____

	Physical	Functional	Economic
Less Depreciation $ **3**	$	$ **2**	= $ ( )

Depreciated value of improvements . . . . . = $ _____
ESTIMATED LAND VALUE . . . . = $ **4**
(If leasehold, show only leasehold value)

INDICATED VALUE BY COST APPROACH . . . $ _____

MARKET DATA ANALYSIS

The undersigned has recited three recent sales of properties most similar and proximate to subject and has considered these in the market analysis. The description includes a dollar adjustment, reflecting market reaction to those items of significant variation between the subject and comparable properties. If a significant item in the comparable property is superior to, or more favorable than, the subject property, a minus (-) adjustment is made, thus reducing the indicated value of subject; if a significant item in the comparable is inferior to, or less favorable than, the subject property, a plus (+) adjustment is made, thus increasing the indicated value of the subject.

ITEM	Subject Property	COMPARABLE NO. 1		COMPARABLE NO. 2		COMPARABLE NO. 3	
Address				**5**			
Proximity to Subj.				**7**			
Sales Price	$	$		$		$	
Price/Living area	$	$		$		$	
Data Source				**6**			
Date of Sale and Time Adjustment	DESCRIPTION	DESCRIPTION **9**	+(-)$ Adjustment	DESCRIPTION	+(-)$ Adjustment	DESCRIPTION	+(-)$ Adjustment
Location							
Site/View							
Design and Appeal							
Quality of Const.							
Age							
Condition							
Living Area Room Count and Total Gross Living Area	Total B-rms Baths Sq.Ft.	Total B-rms Baths Sq.Ft.	**10**	Total B-rms Baths Sq.Ft.	**10**	Total B-rms Baths Sq.Ft.	**10**
Basement & Bsmt. Finished Rooms							
Functional Utility							
Air Conditioning							
Garage/Car Port							
Porches, Patio, Pools, etc.							
Special Energy Efficient Items							
Other (e.g. fireplaces, kitchen equip., remodeling)	**8**						
Sales or Financing Concessions							
Net Adj. (Total)		☐ Plus; ☐ Minus $		☐ Plus; ☐ Minus $		☐ Plus; ☐ Minus $	
Indicated Value of Subject		$		$		$	

Comments on Market Data ___**11**___

INDICATED VALUE BY MARKET DATA APPROACH . . . . $ _____
INDICATED VALUE BY INCOME APPROACH (If applicable) Economic Market Rent $ ___**12**___ /Mo. x Gross Rent Multiplier _____ = $ _____

This appraisal is made ☐ "as is" ☐ subject to the repairs, alterations, or conditions listed below ☐ completion per plans and specifications.

Comments and Conditions of Appraisal: ___**13**___

Final Reconciliation: ___**14**___

Construction Warranty ☐ Yes ☐ No   Name of Warranty Program _____   Warranty Coverage Expires _____

This appraisal is based upon the above requirements, the certification, contingent and limiting conditions, and Market Value definition that are stated in
☐ FHLMC Form 439 (Rev. 10/78)/FNMA Form 1004B (Rev. 10/78) filed with client _____ 19 ___ ☐ attached.

I ESTIMATE THE MARKET VALUE, AS DEFINED, OF SUBJECT PROPERTY AS OF ___**16**___ 19 ___ to be $ _____

Appraiser(s) ___**15**___ Review Appraiser (If applicable) _____
☐ Did   ☐ Did Not Physically Inspect Property

FHLMC Form 70 Rev. 7/79   Form #71-9525 (2/88)   REVERSE   FNMA Form 1004 Rev. 7/79

6.   The source of comparables must be from valid, reliable information sources. Normally, only one of the three comparables should be provided by the lender or developer from their own files, unless justified by the appraiser.

Lender's staff appraisers may use "in-house" comparables as long as they verify the actual terms of the transaction.

Comparable Sales versus Listing—At least two of the comparables must be closed sales, rather than open listings, accepted offers, or contracts. Listings, offers, and contracts may not accurately reflect market value because the details of the transaction could change prior to closing.

In most markets, three closed sales should be used. Additional listings, offers, and contracts are acceptable to validate a value trend if they are fully explained.

Listings must be used with caution, since there may not be a "meeting of minds" between buyer and seller. They are an absolute maximum value indicator in the market. They cannot substitute for credible, arm's-length, closed sales.

Location of Comparables—Except for rural locations at least two comparables should be located within one mile of the appraised property or be fully explained. This one-mile range normally encompasses the neighborhood of the property.

7.   Normally, the one-mile range encompasses the neighborhood of the property. However, if similar homes from *similar neighborhoods* beyond the one-mile guideline are the best comparables available, they are acceptable if justified by the appraiser.

At times, older comparables with appropriate time adjustments within the neighborhood are preferred to comparables beyond the neighborhood that require a location adjustment.

Personal Property Furniture, fixtures, and other personal property should be included in the market value of a property. Chattel is normally ineligible for mortgage proceeds unless secured by a chattel mortgage and Uniform Commercial Code filing.

8. Items such as these are often found in resort and second-home markets as part of a package sale. The value of these items must be subtracted from the sale price, and should not be included in the appraised value. A separate addendum should be developed by the appraiser to clarify the personal property value(s).

Sales and Financing Concessions

9. A *sales concession* is usually a chattel item, such as a car or boat, that is included by the seller to consummate the transaction.

The value of sales concessions must be deducted from the sale price and the appraised value, if included.

A *financing concession* is an interest rate buydown or payment supplement provided by the seller. Appraisers must adjust for seller-paid contributions and subsidies. The maximum allowable financing concession should be within the lender's seller contribution limits. These guideline limits should also apply to land contract and contract for deed transactions. The appraisal should reflect real market conditions and adjust for creative financing on the comparables and the subject.

Adjustments The size of the adjustments indicates the extent of differences between the comparables and the subject property. These differences must be minimal for the comparables to serve their purpose.

Generally, total net adjustments for one of the three comparables may exceed 25 percent of the sale price. Only one comparable may have net line adjustments greater than 10 percent of the sale price. One-directional adjustments should be clearly justified in the appraisal report.

10. The size of the adjustments indicates the extent of differences between the comparables and the subject property. Large differences must be adequately explained for the comparables to serve their purpose.

One-directional adjustments—The appraised value may be inflated when all of the comparables are significantly superior or inferior to the subject property. The appraiser makes many "consistent" adjustments to mask the fact that the comparables are invalid. When all of the adjustments are positive, or all are negative, the valuation is questionable.

The goal is to use properties similar to the subject. Large adjustments begin to question that similarity. However, large, valid differences may exist in the properties while still retaining good comparability. An example would be where the comparable is identical to the subject except that the comparable sits on five acres of land and the subject rests on a half-acre lot. If the value of the four and one-half acres could be appropriately determined, this comparable would present a valid comparison even though the "site/view" line adjustment exceeds 10 percent of the sale price.

11.   The appraiser comments on the subject's and/or the comparables' marketability, and justifies the use of the comparables by explaining the logic used in their selection.

Income Approach

12.   This approach is most effective in appraising income property and is generally not used for single-family residences.

Final Value

13.   The value conclusion may be correct on an "as is" appraisal, but the property may not be suitable for borrower use and enjoyment, and may be, therefore, an unacceptable property for mortgage purposes. The underwriter should confirm and document in the file (date, participants' comments) the completion of major "subject to" conditions.

14.   In reconciliation, the appraiser states which valuation approach was relied upon most heavily, and the rationale for the value conclusion.

15.   The appraisal must be dated and legibly signed by the appraiser.

16.   Does the appraisal reasonably support the final value, or are questions of misrepresentation or overvaluation suspected? In such cases, the underwriter should speak with the appraiser or obtain a second appraisal.

Certification of Appraisal

Appraisals for existing properties that are older than 6 months, and for new constructions that are older than 12 months, should be recertified for current value. This adjustment is necessary to monitor the market valuation movements and the borrower's current equity position.

Condo/PUD Form

Although different appraisal forms are used for condominium and PUD units, appraisal guidelines are essentially the same for both. There are, however, some special considerations for the appraisal of condominium and PUD units.

The underwriter should pay particular attention to the "Project Improvements" section of the Condo/PUD form. This special section describes the project as a whole and should be scrutinized for fair and poor ratings. In the case of a condominium or PUD unit, the rating of the subject unit is more detailed than the rating of a single-family residence. Parking and storage facilities must be reviewed to ensure the marketability of the unit and the project.

This section is a general review of client concerns when reviewing an appraisal. It gives the client the ability to check the appraiser's logic through consistency of information, and to identify risks or aspects of the property that may need additional evaluation.

The following part isolates unique general classes of property and gives some specific items that are useful in review.

Unique Properties

Existing Construction For loans on existing construction, the neighborhood should be characterized as having broad market appeal and good marketability. The subject property should be comparable in value to others in the neighborhood.

New Construction For new construction in areas where marketability has not been established, it is necessary that the appraisal provide pertinent information concerning the distance to schools, shopping, and churches, and the availability of transportation, recreation, water, sewer, gas, electricity, drainage, and any other factors affecting marketability.

Such areas will generally be subdivisions on the leading edge of metropolitan expansion. In the event of a market value turndown, these properties may not have sufficient market appeal to maintain value. The comparables should be from similar neighborhoods.

Older Homes Older homes should have a remaining economic life longer than the proposed amortization period. Particular attention should be given to possible problem areas such as neglected maintenance or obsolete fixtures. If problems are found to exist, restoration, repair, or replacement should be a condition of sale. Otherwise, the buyer should have sufficient resources to correct the problems. The lender should establish an escrow for such restoration, where applicable. A certificate of code compliance may also be required.

Older homes may be subject to changing neighborhood land use (i.e., commercial and/or industrial). The marketability and value of these homes may decline if the transitional land use lowers the enjoyment or appeal of the property.

Rural Properties Valuation should be based on residential use, rather than agricultural or other income-producing use, and, generally, the land and outbuildings should represent a reasonable proportion of the total value of the property, including improvements.

Rural properties need close scrutiny for marketability. Often, single industries or agricultural production are the mainstay of the economy. The shutdown or a substantial decrease in these industries will usually lower property values and significantly extend marketing times. Therefore, only the most typical and stable properties in rural areas should be insured.

Rural properties must be:

♦ Highly marketable

♦ Accessible from public highways

♦ Sufficiently distant from any undesirable influence of adjacent property that would adversely affect marketability

♦ Primarily for residential, rather than income-producing, use

Leasehold Estate (Ground Rent) Residential improvements on leasehold interests must be legal security for a mortgage, according to state statutes or governing local law. Leasehold interests must also be the equivalent of a first lien.

Generally, the leases should extend, or be automatically renewable, for a period of ten years beyond the mortgage term. The lease should also allow the lessee's interest to be freely assignable without the lessor's consent. Additionally, the lease must be subordinated to the mortgage, or the lessee's interest must be assigned to the lender at closing with the assignment to take effect upon foreclosure of the loan. Payment of the ground rent should be included in the borrower's monthly housing expense, and used for computing the house payment and debt ratios.

How to Rate Markets for Risk

Underwriters carefully evaluate the risks of individual loans but must look beyond the traditional loan risks of collateral and credit to consider the risks associated with the market. Market analysis has become increasingly important to risk management plans, which coordinate the evaluation of individual loan risks.

The rating of a particular market's risk is based on several objective standards.

1. Lenders' experience of claims/defaults

2. Market knowledge of building and sale activity

3. Economic activity (i.e., industrial employment)

4. Trend projections for the market

The risk rating is a composite of prior and projected lender loss histories of the market and an analysis of the economic base of the community. A low-risk rating indicates that the market is anticipated to outperform the lender's national experience, a medium-risk rating indicates that the market's performance will be consistent with the lender's national experience, and a high-risk rating is evidence that a market can be expected to perform worse than the client's national average on an ongoing basis.

The loss experience is reviewed with other factors such as prior market knowledge, economic ratings by data resources, and various other economic data.

Market analysts meet with realtors, appraisers, Chambers of Commerce, and other relevant parties. An important part of these visits is a personal inspection of the market to observe market activity and claim properties.

Market analysts also review submarkets within the geographic area, such as concentrations of single-family homes and condominiums, as well as economic submarkets.

A review of the industrial and employment bases of an area is also an important factor in the analysis of a market. Market analysts look for diversity in the economy. This diversity will provide stability in a market that is unavailable in areas dependent upon one employer or industry for a large portion of employment opportunities.

Market analysts review several criteria in each market, including housing stock, construction starts, economic trends, MLS data, employment and unemployment statistics, and retail sales information. Market analysts also seek to answer such questions as:

♦ What are HUD, FNMA, and FHLMC offering in the city?

♦ Are builders advertising concessions?

♦ Do the "For Sale by Owner" ads contain anxious wording such as "Price reduced" or "$2,000 cash if you assume my condo mortgage"?

♦ Is there any unusual activity in the local market?

♦ Who are the developers: local builders, or national tract builders who may be known risks?

The goal of market analysis is to identify both adverse and positive risk situations. Approaches to managing adverse risk may include the modification of underwriting guidelines, such as the special handling of condominium projects in the area. Positive risk situations may create intensified marketing efforts in the area.

Such guideline changes minimize unprofitable loans, and help the lender serve its customers while maintaining reasonable and prudent controls over the risks it assumes.

Chapter 24

LOSS MANAGEMENT TECHNIQUES

Cam Melchiorre
Vice President, Defaults and Claims Manager
Commonwealth Mortgage Assurance Company

PART ONE: FORECLOSURE COMBAT

INTRODUCTION

Geoffrey Chaucer, the great English author, once said: "There are three things that drive a man out of his house, that is to say, smoke, the dropping of rain and wicked wives." Had Chaucer witnessed the decline of the Southwest real estate market in the early- to mid-1980s, he would have added equity erosion and oil industry-related unemployment to his list. Those factors—as well as rampant overbuilding fueled by excessive speculation—have resulted in record losses for lenders, investors, borrowers, and government and private mortgage insurers.

When markets soften, lenders discover that loan-to-value (LTV) ratios calculated when the loan was originated no longer hold up. In a *National Mortgage News* article, a senior Fannie Mae official commented on Fannie Mae's move away from low documentation loans. The official

Reprinted by permission of *Mortgage Banking*, a publication of the Mortgage Bankers Association of America.

509

said, "If we have to foreclose on an 80-percent LTV loan, we lose money—we even lose some money on 75-percent LTV loans." It is painfully clear that the market cannot absorb the inventory of distressed real estate. Losses increase exponentially and, in some cases, institutions fail. Philadelphia-based Commonwealth Mortgage Assurance Company (CMAC), responding to similar conditions in the oil patch states of Texas, Oklahoma, Louisiana, and Colorado, created a loss mitigation department in 1985. Its mandate was to prevent or at least mitigate losses due to residential mortgage foreclosures. CMAC's effort in this area has evolved into a loss-management function that benefits the insured lender's bottom line, as well as the mortgage servicer's cost-per-loan ratio. In the process, a costly, labor-intensive servicing problem has been converted into a source of continuing fee income. Finally, many foreclosure alternatives put together by CMAC's loan workout specialists have preserved the homes and credit ratings of thousands of distressed homeowners.

LOSS MANAGEMENT OPERATIONS

Lamar Kelly, Jr., director, asset and real estate management division of the Resolution Trust Corporation (RTC), spoke at a 1991 seminar on the issue of preforeclosure loss reduction efforts for the RTC's troubled real estate portfolio. "Our preference by far is to restructure and negotiate existing credits or proposed foreclosures," he said. "Quite simply, the bottom line on that is an economic analysis. If the economic justification is then to restructure, as opposed to assuming the costs inherent in foreclosure, then our people should be restructuring."

Other service industries—private health insurance, for example—have realized the economic benefits of a preventive approach. For example, to battle the high cost of unnecessary surgery, many health insurers and large employers require precertification prior to employee surgical procedures.

Specialized companies review hospital bills for insurers and employers to make sure that costs match services rendered. While quality of care remains paramount, financial factors warrant an aggressive approach simply to guarantee that the insurer, employer, and employee are getting what they pay for. The major objective is to obtain the best solution for all those concerned.

Likewise, loan workouts on the residential mortgages make sound financial sense, particularly when the residential mortgage foreclosure is the sole source of loss expense, as is the case with government and private mortgage insurers. Yet, while many espouse the theory, few implement it to the degree possible to realize significant results.

General Accounting Office (GAO) studies of the FHA and VA pointed to the lack of effective loss management as a contributing cause of losses in those two government home loans programs. In response to these losses, the government insurers have tightened underwriting guidelines and in the case of the FHA single-family program, increased premiums. These changes mean these programs will be less accessible for borrowers and, as a result, have been met with dismay from real estate brokers, builders, lenders, and prospective first-time home buyers. Neither mortgage insurance pricing adjustments nor changes in qualifying criteria are without merit when losses suggest they are required. Yet, a measured approach to preforeclosure loss mitigation will provide immediate as well as long-term benefits to the balance sheets of these government home loans programs. Furthermore, there is a great social utility and business soundness to a loss management operation that systematically mitigates losses due to residential foreclosures.

While the VA and FHA have regulations promoting foreclosure alternatives, they lack operations specifically dedicated to active loss mitigation. From the point of view of a mortgage insurer, active loss mitigation means affirmative action to contact the borrower to avoid or lessen the economic consequences of foreclosure. It's important to note that while borrower contact may be made independently of the primary mortgage servicer, no foreclosure alternatives should be agreed to without the consent of the primary mortgage servicer and investor.

The VA and FHA have a "reactive" loan workout perspective that relies entirely on the primary mortgage servicer to find foreclosure alternatives—a viewpoint once embraced by many private mortgage insurers. The fundamental weakness in this approach is that with each type of mortgage insurance (VA, FHA, or private), there exists a "risk differential" to the investor/owner of the loan and the mortgage servicer.

When the mortgage insurer (FHA, VA, or private) reimburses the investor for nearly all elements of exposure—foreclosure costs and attorney fees, taxes, insurance, maintenance repairs, utilities, principal and accrued interest—the investor's need to expend resources to mitigate loss is significantly reduced. Add to this the increasing procedural requirements being thrust on servicers who have only servicing fee income as their motivation, and it is clear that the investors and mortgage servicers have little incentive to develop a potent loan workout unit. CMAC recognized these economic realities early and developed a loan workout department to step in and fill this gap in the default servicing cycle.

MORTGAGE INSURER AS WORKOUT SPECIALIST

CMAC's default department—the company's residential loan workout operation—uses trained specialists to handle defaulted loans that are selected according to their likelihood of producing a loss. Most conventional loans reported in default (45 to 75 days delinquent) reinstate on their own or as a result of mortgage loan collector prompting. In light of this, CMAC developed a mechanism to ferret out, for special servicing efforts, the remaining defaults that were likely to go to a sheriff sale. A rolling loss severity index was created to assist in determining the cases requiring exceptional effort. By taking into account the origination date and the location of the property, it can be readily determined if the property is in a declining market and if it was purchased when prices were skyrocketing. Also, the current interest rate, original loan-to-value ratio, property type, and the existence of negative amortization influence the selection process. Finally, the nature of the ownership—primary residence or investment—is among this list of loan characteristics that help set the sights of the specialist. The system must be arranged so that the loan workout specialists can focus their attention on cases that will produce a bottom line loss if a sheriff sale does occur.

An example would be a loan reported in default on a property located in Roxboro, Massachusetts. If the mortgage servicer's comments appearing on the notice of default indicate that the borrower could not be reached, the loan workout specialist would review other aspects of the case to determine the degree of involvement required. In this example, the loan was originated in 1988 for $100,000 on a two-bedroom condominium with a 90-percent LTV. Because the property is located in a recognizably soft market, the workout specialist can safely assume that this case needs more than the normal collection approach. In this case, foreclosure will result in a claim payment for the mortgage insurer and probably a loss for the insured lender.

Special efforts to locate the borrower would be undertaken immediately. If attempts to contact the borrower at home and at work failed, skip tracing would begin within a week of the initial attempts to contact the homeowner. This strategy has helped CMAC maintain a borrower contact ratio of 90 to 95 percent. The aggressive and persistent effort needed to reduce losses in these cases requires the deployment of a special loan workout force. Asking collectors to perform this additional function is unrealistic in today's delinquent mortgage servicing environment.

TROUBLE IN THE TRENCHES

Delinquent mortgage loan collectors servicing 30- to 90-day accounts must make as many dunning calls as practical in a given time frame. Even with improved technology in the form of automatic dialing systems, the focus is on volume of collection calls. In addition, the yardstick used to measure the collector's performance is the month-end delinquency ratio. While this is certainly a valid and meaningful measurement, it places more importance on the quantity of dunning efforts and leaves little time to formulate and implement loan workouts on the more serious cases that are among the 30- to 90-day delinquent accounts. When a servicer submits a claim for mortgage insurance, the entire default and foreclosure activity record must be included. By reviewing thousands of these files over five years, CMAC has examined the variances in default servicing performance among the different servicers for loans on properties located in nearly every state. The types of institutions represented in these files range from large mortgage banks with hundreds of billions of dollars in mortgage servicing and legions of employees, to small "mom and pop" thrifts with a dozen defaults and one servicing employee. The one constant in many of these files is called "opportunity fallout." Often, a review of the collection activity record reveals that the mortgage loan collector, who is in the first line of defense, failed to recognize a viable workout opportunity on a loan that will surely produce a loss if foreclosure and real estate-owned (REO) sale does occur.

The following case illustrates this recurring problem of opportunity fallout. On July 1, 1989, a collector phoned a delinquent borrower whose two-bedroom townhouse in Phoenix was 60 days away from being sold at a sheriff sale. The collector's notes from his conversation with the borrower produced a familiar story. The property was purchased in February 1987 for $100,000, with a 10 percent down payment. In August 1988, due to a forced relocation, the property was listed for $110,000. No purchase offers were made until April 1989, and that offer was for $100,000. The mortgage balance was $97,000, and with closing costs, there wouldn't be enough net proceeds from the sale to retire the debt. Not only that, there was an $8,000 second lien for a swimming pool. The property was still listed on July 1, 1989, almost a year after it was first placed on the market and the seller keeps getting offers, but now they're coming in between $90,000 and $100,000. The collector responded by recommending a repayment plan, even though the borrower had relocated to Indianapolis. The next entry on the record showed that the case was referred to the foreclosure attorney on August 18, 1990. Finally, a sheriff sale took place on October 2, 1990. Because of continued equity erosion, the lender suffered a loss even after the claim payment.

The opportunity to mitigate loss in this case was through a controlled preforeclosure sale. When the borrower notified the collector on July 1, 1989, the "offers were coming in on the property," a loan workout specialist should have begun to manage the case and quarterback the borrower, the real estate broker, the purchaser and the second lienholder through the closing of the preforeclosure sale. In many cases, borrowers are more than willing to bring cash to settlement or sign a promissory note for the shortage if the net proceeds are not sufficient to satisfy the mortgage. In cases where second liens exist, a loan workout specialist can educate the lienholder as to the value of the security interest relative to the equity in the property. It is easy to reach a compromise with a subordinate secured party if the realities of the situation are communicated effectively. It is likely that a loss would have occurred even with a preforeclosure sale, but to a much lesser degree than after foreclosure and REO sale.

The collector is not the fall guy in this scenario because the effort needed to see the presale through is not within his character. The collector's purpose is to prompt borrowers to pay earlier than they otherwise may have without some outside encouragement, and to establish short-term repayment plans for borrowers with temporary economic problems. If the mortgage servicer had loan workout specialists at hand, however, and the collector was trained to "recognize" a case that needs intensive care, the case could have been transferred from the collection area to that of the loan workout person.

Exacerbating this problem is the trend of investors, quasi-government agencies (Freddie Mac and Fannie Mae) and government and private mortgage insurers to ask servicers to comply with an increasing menu of loss-prevention procedures and policies. The mortgage servicer has to serve many masters, with different economic interests and default servicing requirements. This growing procedural burden can hamstring the workout efforts of the most motivated and conscientious servicers.

The RTC as of late 1990 had 29,000 homes in inventory—more than half of them in Texas. The agency tried everything to dispose of these properties, from the ill-fated satellite super auction to offering homeowner warranties on sales of the REO.

While there have been improvements in the FHA's REO disposition rate, it still held 39,000 properties as of October 1, 1990, which translates into nearly $1 million a day in holding costs.

Had loan workout specialists been in place to aggressively seek preforeclosure solutions, the REO inventories of both the RTC and FHA could have been reduced significantly. If the emphasis is placed on REO avoidance, REO disposition would be merely an annoyance and not a travesty.

During mortgage servicing field visits conducted over the last five years, CMAC has demonstrated the merits of developing a residential loan workout department where preforeclosure sales, deeds in lieu, assumptions, and modifications could receive the special attention needed for effective loss mitigation. The company also spends considerable time constructing decision matrices for collectors, bankruptcy servicers, and foreclosure processors to help them recognize cases that should be transferred to loan workout personnel. The awareness factor of these front-line people is the linchpin to a successful loss management effort. If the mortgage servicer does not have a loan workout department, CMAC instructs default servicing personnel to spot the troubled loan and notify us so that our specialists can attend to the case without interrupting the normal servicing process.

LOSS MITIGATION DURING FORECLOSURE

No area of default servicing reflects the current procedural quagmire faced by mortgage servicers more than the foreclosure monitoring process. Yet, every effort should be made to mitigate loss because the foreclosure sale is just around the bend. It is during this stage that the investors, government and private insurers, as well as Fannie Mae and Freddie Mac, simultaneously push mortgage servicers to proceed to a sheriff sale quickly while badgering them to engage in loan workout efforts. Moreover, because of lender liability issues and restrictions under various state foreclosure laws, foreclosure processors are loath to initiate any contact with the borrower beyond the mandatory legal notices.

It is standard servicing procedure to cease all borrower contact efforts once a case is sent to counsel for initiation of foreclosure proceedings. But, rather than give up at this point, the loan workout specialist can be working on a parallel line to formulate a preforeclosure plan while the case is proceeding to a sheriff sale. The trick is to strictly limit the criteria for which the foreclosure process may be postponed or cancelled. For instance, if a preforeclosure sale materialized, the settlement date should fall within the pendency of the foreclosure action. The foreclosure sale could be cancelled only if the purchaser was prequalified and had an earnest-money deposit in escrow. The foreclosure alternative must be a mirage.

It is sensible to establish reasonable "state-specific" foreclosure time parameters, because undue delays increase expenses on an already costly proposition. The type of mortgage insurance in place—FHA, VA, conventional—and the state foreclosure laws determine the lender's ultimate economic exposure. Foreclosure transaction costs, such as attorney fees and court costs, and asset expenses, such as property insurance, repair, maintenance and utility bills, make up a significant part of that exposure. Lost opportunity cost or the relative investment value of the property is also a factor. In addition, lender liability should instill caution into all servicers who want to become involved in workouts.

These concerns can be overcome, however, by carving out special procedures for loan workouts on cases at this stage. The economic benefits of foreclosure alternatives far outweigh the cost of implementing them. Plus, if a mechanism is in place to at least accept proposals for consideration, losses can be reduced. But because foreclosure processing is bent toward rapid acquisition of title, the system has become a deflector instead of a receptor of loss mitigation opportunities. For example, many purchase offers are made on properties in the foreclosure process, but because the offers are communicated to the foreclosing attorney, they never reach the mortgage servicer. Worse, if an offer to purchase does reach the servicer's foreclosure department, the latter is not equipped to evaluate the offer and take the necessary steps to obtain the borrower's cooperation. If foreclosure attorneys and processors are trained to recognize cost-saving opportunities, and if a loan workout specialist exists to develop an opportunity, the foreclosure cost nightmare can be much less frightening.

A system can be designed to strike a balance among these seemingly conflicting requirements so that each loan in foreclosure is open to a preforeclosure solution.

CASE ANALYSIS

To make a loss management department's efforts bear fruit, some basic guidelines must be in place to help evaluate each case. Management must develop and periodically update guidelines to assist the loan workout personnel in deriving a realistic strategy for each case. This analytical aid must be flexible enough to allow for creativity, yet structured well enough to comply with legal, investor, and regulatory requirements within the context of residential mortgage loan servicing.

To meet this goal, CMAC developed a default analysis matrix (see Figure 24.1) used to train residential loan workout personnel.

The first section of Figure 24.1 helps the loan workout specialist define the problem by identifying the specific reason for the default, the value of the asset, and the particulars of the borrower's current financial profile.

The second section asks that the analyst consider the three general approaches to every case. Should the borrower retain the asset? Should

Figure 24.1   Loan Workout Matrix

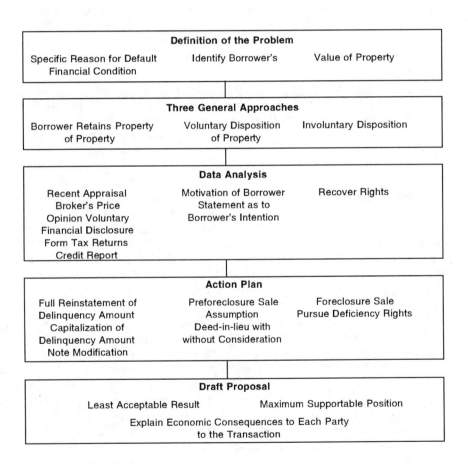

Definition of the Problem		
Specific Reason for Default Financial Condition	Identify Borrower's	Value of Property

Three General Approaches		
Borrower Retains Property of Property	Voluntary Disposition of Property	Involuntary Disposition

Data Analysis		
Recent Appraisal Broker's Price Opinion Voluntary Financial Disclosure Form Tax Returns Credit Report	Motivation of Borrower Statement as to Borrower's Intention	Recover Rights

Action Plan		
Full Reinstatement of Delinquency Amount Capitalization of Delinquency Amount Note Modification	Preforeclosure Sale Assumption Deed-in-lieu with without Consideration	Foreclosure Sale Pursue Deficiency Rights

Draft Proposal	
Least Acceptable Result	Maximum Supportable Position
Explain Economic Consequences to Each Party to the Transaction	

the borrower lose the property through a private preforeclosure sale? Or should the property be recovered through a foreclosure sale?

The third section, titled "Data Analysis," is critical to establishing a viable strategy. Management must set minimal standards regarding acceptable sources of these data. For example, recent tax returns and a completed financial disclosure form may be required before conclusions can be drawn about the borrower's financial ability. Similarly, updated market analyses, as well as an appraisal, may be necessary if the exposure on a particular loan justifies it. Also, the recovery rights against the primary and co-borrower should be identified.

The fourth section requires the analyst to develop a specific strategy. At this point, the traditional foreclosure alternatives—preforeclosure sale, deed in lieu, etc.—must be examined, taking into account the assembled data and all other facts and circumstances of the particular case. It is important to note that foreclosure is a possible, albeit undesirable, course of action.

Once a basic strategy is chosen, a rough proposal should be drafted. Within that proposal the analyst's "maximum supportable position" and "least acceptable result" should be established. The maximum supportable position can be defined as the analyst's most favorable economic stance, having the most objective support. While having the borrower whose loan is in foreclosure reinstated to a current status is the best possible result, it may not be the maximum supportable position—especially if the borrower has relocated and a preforeclosure sale is being considered when the property value is depressed.

In determining the "least acceptable result," the analyst must establish a point of last compromise from which retreat is unacceptable. This is not to say that it is the worst economic position. It is somewhere above that level. For example, while a preforeclosure sale creating a "short payoff" may make economic sense, the deal may hinge on the degree of borrower/seller participation in reducing the shortfall at the settlement table. If the borrower's financial profile shows that assets and income are substantial, the "least acceptable position" may be to require the borrower to make up at least 90 percent of the lender's loss from the preforeclosure sale. If the borrower will not move from an offer of 85 percent, the case should be turned back over to foreclosure. The key here for the analyst is to form a link between a specific proposal and the data collected. This way, the conclusions drawn will have a rational relationship to the particular facts of the case.

Finally, the proposal should spell out the economic consequences to each interested party—the borrower, investor, and mortgage insurer. This will speed the process of obtaining approvals from those parties, because time is of the essence in most of these cases.

The components of this default analysis guide may be manipulated to address the particular needs of different lending institutions.

MEASURING RESULTS

One of the difficulties in establishing a separate loan workout department is how to measure its effectiveness. The delinquency ratio of those loans assigned to that department would not suffice, because loan workouts usually have some loss expense. A more appropriate analysis would be to project the bottom line loss on a case if foreclosure and REO sale took place. Once this figure is determined, the actual loss could be subtracted from it and the specific loss avoided will result. One large Midwest lender estimated that an average of $17,000 was lost on every REO sale, even when there was conventional mortgage insurance.

Because VA "no-bids" are still prevalent, as are the costs associated with FHA-insured loans, the cost effectiveness of loss management operation can be easily justified. An even more precise measurement would be to compare the loss avoided by the loan workout department to the department's operational costs. This ratio would be most telling. CMAC's monthly default department ratio is averaging at 21 percent under such a comparison.

We believe that if lenders were to allocate the resources to set up, train, and maintain loan workout departments using the guidelines presented here, they too could produce exceptional results.

PART TWO: BATTLING THE BANKRUPTCY BOOM

Competition between banking institutions is as much a part of the United States' financial history as it is a part of today's marketplace. In fact, what may be the most bizarre example of admittedly extreme competition occurred during the infancy of the banking industry in this country.

In 1804, the Bank of New York, established by Alexander Hamilton, and the Bank of Manhattan, founded by his political nemesis, Aaron Burr, were struggling for preeminence in the fledgling New York financial market. This battle of the banks fueled the personal enmity between Burr and Hamilton until they settled their differences permanently with pistols at 15 paces. The duel left Hamilton slain. The pistols are enshrined in the offices of Chase Manhattan Bank in New York as mute evidence of the incident.

Much later in this country's financial development, during the early 1980s, with deregulation as a catalyst, S&Ls began to duel other institutions for market share. But this time, the weapons of choice were lenient lending policies instead of pistols. While not as personally lethal as the method chosen by Hamilton and Burr, the results may be deemed just as deadly in the final analysis—several hundred failed thrifts already serve as a stark reminder of the damage caused.

These liberal lending practices also have spawned record bankruptcy filings as a byproduct. At a press conference last year sponsored by the American Bankruptcy Institute, Professor Elizabeth Warren of the University of Pennsylvania commented that the increase in the number of consumer bankruptcies is due largely to a hefty increase in personal debt. According to the Federal Reserve Board, personal debt rose from $1.3 trillion in 1980 to about $4 trillion in 1990. The most dramatic increases occurred between 1983 and 1988. At the end of 1990, total debt (home mortgage plus consumer debt) as a percentage of disposable personal income reached nearly 84 percent, compared to 62 percent in 1983.

So, it comes as virtually no surprise that this lending lunacy has joined with a national recession and regional depressions to create an unprecedented bankruptcy explosion—with no end in sight.

SKYROCKETING NUMBERS

The American Bankruptcy Institute reported that nearly 90 percent of the 782,960 bankruptcies filed in 1990 came from debt-ridden consumers. This figure more than doubled since 1985. Between 1989 and 1990, personal bankruptcies rose 16.4 percent. The projections for 1991 and 1992 are even bleaker, with some experts predicting that nearly one million Americans will file for bankruptcy during 1992.

Bankruptcy filings occurred with particular intensity in the Northeast, where the recession was most severe. Between December 1989 and December 1990, the sharpest increase in filings nationwide was in New England and the Middle Atlantic states. New Jersey filings increased 52 percent; Connecticut's were up by 60 percent; Rhode Island filings rose by 80 percent; Massachusetts' jumped by 95 percent; New Hampshire filings climbed by 106 percent; and Vermont's went up by 238 percent.

It appears that nothing short of legislative reform and a major improvement in the economy will be able to stop the alarming growth of consumer bankruptcies.

Consumer bankruptcy filings have been the bane of residential mortgage servicers, as well as government and private mortgage insurers and institutional investors. Even when the number of filings was not startling, the lender responded in a defensive fashion. Little attention was given to measures that could significantly reduce losses. With the tide of bankruptcies rising, mortgage servicers must focus on alternative means to manage these cases.

This chapter will introduce some nontraditional approaches that can curb losses due to bankruptcy filings in the context of residential mortgage servicing. Some measures are preventative, while some are remedial.

THE BANKRUPTCY BRICK WALL

As soon as a homeowner files a bankruptcy petition—either Chapter 13 or Chapter 7—the mortgage servicer must stop all efforts to collect the debt. Collection calls and dunning notices must cease, and the servicer is precluded from recovering the mortgaged property through foreclosure without court approval. Furthermore, once the discharge order is granted, the borrower cannot be pursued in a deficiency judgment action.

Formal studies have not quantified the degree to which bankruptcy filings increase foreclosure losses. However, Philadelphia-based Commonwealth Mortgage Assurance Company (CMAC) analyzed 100 mortgage insurance claims paid during 1991 involving borrowers who had filed for bankruptcy. The actual claim amount paid was compared to the claim amount that would have been paid without the bankruptcy filing. The average increase in a loss amount due to bankruptcy was $9,000.

Because the average mortgage insurance coverage is 22 percent, it can be further deduced that mortgage lenders lost an average of 78 percent, or $7,200 on each case. This is due in part to legal costs and fees. But the major component of the loss emerges from accrued but unpaid interest on the debt. The loss at real estate owned (REO) sale is also much worse, because the added delay in acquiring title extends the erosion of the property value. In some states, court logjams cause a seven- to twelve-month delay in obtaining an order to release the "automatic stay" and to begin or resume foreclosure proceedings—even if the lender's motion to lift the stay of foreclosure is uncontested by the borrower.

CHEAP CHAPTER 7s

In the Chapter 13 or Chapter 11 filing, not much can be done by the mortgage servicer unless the borrower defaults under the bankruptcy plan or on post-petition payments. However, there is an opportunity to avoid the costs associated with bankruptcy and foreclosure in most Chapter 7, no-asset filings. In this type of insolvency action, the borrower has no intention of retaining any assets.

The bankrupt individual has given up on all secured and unsecured obligations. In fact, CMAC's experience has shown that in most cases, the mortgaged property has been vacated, because there is no equity in it.

The traditional mortgage servicing response to a Chapter 7, no-asset filing is to advise counsel to move to lift the automatic stay so that merchantable title can be acquired through foreclosure. In many of these cases, however, a much different, cost-saving approach can be taken.

Once the Chapter 7, no-asset petition is received, the debtor's attorney, whose name and telephone number will be on the petition, should be contacted to determine if his or her client—the homeowner—has any objection to having the property listed for sale. There is usually little resistance to this approach if the borrower has vacated the premises. The listing should be referred to a real estate broker who understands the process and who will determine a realistic "quick sale" price. An appraisal should be obtained to ensure that the borrower has no equity in the property.

Once a sales offer is obtained, the purchase agreement and the appraisal should be sent to the bankruptcy trustee, who, based on our experience, should readily sanction the sale. In every case that CMAC has handled in this manner, the bankruptcy trustee approved the sale, because there was no equity in the property that would result in proceeds to be distributed among secured creditors through a bankruptcy auction.

Mark J. Udren, Esq., of Federman and Phelan, Philadelphia, Pennsylvania, a law firm specializing in bankruptcy and the foreclosure needs of mortgage servicers, employs another cost-saving technique that may be used in conjunction with the private sale of the property as described earlier. When representing the mortgage servicer in Chapter 7, no-asset case, Udren contacts the debtor's attorney to determine whether the borrower wishes to retain the mortgaged property. If the debtor's attorney indicates that his or her client wishes to relinquish the property, Udren prepares a "stipulation in lieu of litigation," which is sent to the debtor's counsel with instructions to forward it to the trustee.

This allows the trustee to release the automatic stay without a hearing. Udren notes that by providing extra copies of the letter along with envelopes from the debtor's counsel to the trustee and return envelopes to him, he usually receives expeditious cooperation. This procedure works nicely with the preforeclosure sale listing. If the property cannot be sold within 90 days, the servicer would be able to proceed to sheriff's sale without delay by virtue of the stipulation in lieu of litigation.

If the property that is part of the bankrupt estate is located in a judicial foreclosure state, the legal fees and costs plus accrued interest could be excessive if counsel must be retained to lift the stay and proceed to sheriff's sale. While assisting bankruptcy trustees in performing their duties, CMAC has avoided an average of $15,000 in claim expense per case and between $45,000 and $50,000 in losses for our insured lender, depending on the type of coverage in each case. If the property is sold privately, as described, another REO sinkhole is avoided.

RECOVERY FROM GUARANTORS

Another measure that can be taken by mortgage servicers to ameliorate losses is recovery from guarantors. Bankruptcy servicing personnel should be trained to closely scrutinize the bankruptcy petition and schedules for opportunities to reduce losses. For instance, if a co-signer did not file a Chapter 13 petition, there may be a potential to recover some portion of the loss from that party once the case is closed or dismissed. In a Chapter 7 or 11 filing, the lender may proceed against the nonfiling co-debtor immediately, regardless of whether the case is dismissed or closed. It is a common lending practice to require guarantors to bolster weak residential mortgage applicants. These guarantors should not be forgotten as a source of restitution if the primary borrower seeks bankruptcy protection.

TALKING THEM DOWN

Early communication with a homeowner caught in the grips of debt may be the most formidable weapon against consumer bankruptcy filings. The social stigma of bankruptcy has diminished in recent times. Borrowers no longer perceive the experience of bankruptcy to be disturbing or the consequences of it to be detrimental. Mortgage servicers should train collectors and other default servicing personnel to combat these perceptions and counsel borrowers against filing for bankruptcy.

Some counseling tips are illustrated in the following script for mortgage servicing employees who are speaking with a homeowner considering bankruptcy. Several approaches may be used in the discussions between the loan counselor and the borrower. One might be as follows:

"Although you may be in dire financial straits right now, we will be more than willing to work with you to avoid a bankruptcy action, which you should consider only as a last resort. However, in order to help you, we will need to have some information concerning your financial profile, such as assets, liabilities, and income, so that we can arrive at an informed decision concerning what specific steps to take."

A second sample approach might be to say:

"While we are not holding ourselves out as bankruptcy lawyers and we encourage you to at least speak with a licensed attorney for technical advice, we can let you know of some of the possible consequences and alternatives to a bankruptcy filing. Some of those consequences are:

♦   If you file a Chapter 13 or 11, your credit report will reflect this for seven years. If you file a Chapter 7, it will stay with your credit rating for 10 years.

♦   Filing for bankruptcy will cost you attorney's fees just to file and, if litigation ensues, those fees could rise.

♦   Not every debt is dischargeable, so if this house payment is causing you the biggest problem, let's work on it before giving up.

♦   A bankruptcy will involve all of your creditors and assets— your financial life will become an "open book" in many of the proceedings.

♦   Because all of your assets except exempt property will be available to pay debts, filing for bankruptcy could prove extremely detrimental to you.

♦   CMAC's experience has shown that if you are cooperative and honest with us, we can formulate a strategy to "slow the bleeding" to a manageable level. Many people have come through tougher situations and rebounded to relative stability within a few years. As a result, now they can again exercise credit options that are a part of everyday life.

♦ Don't prolong the financial recovery time with a premature and ill-advised bankruptcy filing. A bankruptcy filing may adversely affect future loan requests.

♦ A bankruptcy may also affect future employment opportunities or ability to obtain rental housing.

The key for the servicer is to win the psychological war with the homeowner. If an open line of communication can be established with the borrower, it will be easy to procure financial data. Then, a type of complete underwriting analysis can be performed and a realistic, contra-bankruptcy strategy can be prudently implemented.

CRAMDOWN CRISIS

Bankruptcy filings have become even more problematic to lenders since the decision handed down by the 9th U.S. Circuit Court of Appeals in *In Re Holland* (86 F.2d 1182). This case, which is being followed in other jurisdictions, held that a debtor in a Chapter 13 case may avoid a lien on the principal residence to the degree that the claim is greater than the fair market value of the property. (See *In Re Brouse*, 110 B.R. 539 Colorado.) In states with depressed housing markets, this "cramdown rule" actually allows a Chapter 13 debtor to be discharged of his or her unsecured debt at the end of a successful Chapter 13 plan. This generally means that the borrower has made all of the post-petition payments and payments on arrearage to the trustee, as prescribed by the plan, normally between the three- and five-year term.

If a $100,000 mortgage debt secures a property currently worth only $50,000, the lender's lien may be crammed down to $50,000 if the borrower prevails in the cramdown motion. The remaining $50,000 then becomes an unsecured claim, a small portion of which will be paid back under the plan because the mortgage lender must get in line with other unsecured creditors.

Worsening an already onerous situation for mortgage lenders is the cramdown policy adopted by the FHA and VA. Both government mortgage insurers hold that if the borrower's bankruptcy plan is completed—usually in three to five years—and the outstanding balance has been crammed down, and there is a subsequent default, their liability for paying the claim would be based on the reduced principal balance only. The policies of private mortgage insurers have taken on less unanimity as a few companies have opted to cover the crammed down portion, that is, both the unsecured and secured claim amounts of the mortgage. To date, CMAC has the most comprehensive cramdown coverage in the industry. If a default occurs after the successful completion of the reorganization plan, CMAC will permit the lender to include in a proper insurance claim any unpaid cramdown amount, along with interest from the date that the cramdown occurred.

CONSUMER FRAUD AND CONSUMER BANKRUPTCY

Earlier we reviewed the value of examining the homeowner's bankruptcy petitions and schedules in the context of pursuing nonfiling guarantors for loss recovery. However, there is another vital reason to analyze the bankruptcy documents—the possibility of discovering fraud in the origination of the mortgage loan.

In more cases than we would like, a comparison of the homeowner's schedule of debts in the bankruptcy proceedings to the original mortgage loan application reveals debts and obligations that predate the mortgage loan application. Unfortunately, when completing loan applications, many prospective homeowners, by advice or of their own volition, omit significant debt obligations on the residential loan application. Invariably, if it were not for these other obligations being omitted, the borrower would not have qualified for the new mortgage. This practice also becomes an important element of fraud and could cause the dismissal of the bankruptcy petition, or at least prompt the court to deem the mortgage debt nondischargeable. If these material inconsistencies are discovered and then communicated to the debtor's attorney, a more agreeable posture may be taken by the homeowner that could lead to withdrawal of the petition and even a foreclosure alternative.

An article in the March/April 1991 issue of *Credit World* magazine ("The Bankruptcy Jungle" by Harry Gambill, vol. 79, no. 4) describes the revolutionary approach VISA USA has taken to counter the rise in bankruptcy fraud and abuse. That firm's Bankruptcy Recovery Program supports VISA member banks in identifying and challenging fraudulent and abusive filings. Some of the abuses cited in the article include transferring assets shortly before filing for bankruptcy; incurring debts with no expectation of repayment; understating income and overstating expenses and concealing assets. The most interesting aspect of VISA USA's program is the pooling of resources to mount a challenge to the filing. All creditors are notified within ten days of the filing, and participating banks review the debtor's account for red flags of fraud. If fraud is discovered, other program participants with whom the debtor has accounts are notified.

If two or more banks see evidence of possible fraud, the attorney representing the member banks will challenge the petition. If the debtor persists, a civil fraud complaint is prosecuted in the bankruptcy court against the debtor with the costs and recovery being shared pro rata by the member banks.

Residential mortgage servicers could benefit from a similar approach. If a strong case exists, the mortgage insurer should be contacted to determine if the costs of litigation would be claimable.

There is substantial legal basis to challenge the dischargeability of debts obtained by consumer fraud. 11 U.S.C. Sec. 523 (a)(2) states, inter alia:

"A discharge under Sec. 727 1141 or 1328(b) of this title does not discharge an individual debtor from any debt for money, property, services or an extension, renewal or refinancing of credit to the extent obtained by:

A. False pretense, a false representation or actual fraud or other statements representing the debtor's or an insider's financial condition

B. Use of a statement in writing
   1. that is materially false
   2. respecting the debtor's or an insider's financial condition
   3. on which the creditors to whom the debtor is liable for such
      money, property, services, or credit, reasonably relied
   4. that debtor caused to be made or published with intent to deceive, etc."

For practical purposes, there may be evidentiary problems associated with an action under the dischargeable exceptions of the code. Yet, most of the cases we have encountered were obvious attempts by borrowers to enhance residential mortgage loan applications. Furthermore, a Supreme Court case—*Grogan v. Gomer* (No. 84–1144), which was decided unanimously on January 15, 1991—held that the standard of proof for a nondischargeability claim due to fraud by a debtor is that of a "preponderance of the evidence," rather than the more strenuous evidentiary test defined as proof by "clear and convincing evidence."

As stated earlier, collectors, bankruptcy servicers, and workout personnel can use these creditors' rights as leverage in settlement negotiations. Moreover, making delinquent borrowers and/or their attorneys aware of material misrepresentations and the fraud exceptions to dischargeability may cause a rethinking of their threats to file bankruptcy.

HOME LOANS FOR BANKRUPT BORROWERS

CMAC does not provide private mortgage insurance to borrowers who have gone through bankruptcy. In reviewing claims, we found that some bankrupt borrowers had a history of bankruptcy. Therefore, if they filed for bankruptcy once, they are more likely to do it again than more creditworthy borrowers, notwithstanding certain restrictions in the bankruptcy code.

While there are certainly many legitimate bankruptcy filings, there are a large number of debtors who are encouraged by bankruptcy lawyers to take this extreme action. Bankruptcy judges seem sympathetic to those seeking protection under the bankruptcy act. And many borrowers look back on the experience and find that it was far less painful than they had feared.

This coupled with the fact that there seems to be little stigma attached to bankruptcy today, breeds a bad environment for all lenders. Borrowers must understand that once they have declared bankruptcy, it will be harder to borrow money again. The point is that persons who take advantage of bankruptcy should not expect liberal lending terms in the future. This is not to say that people who have gone through bankruptcy should not own a home. These borrowers should accumulate savings for their next home and contribute substantially to the down payment to prove their commitment to the property. Preventing these borrowers from obtaining high-ratio loans may not be a popular position. However, we believe this is a prudent, sound approach to risk management and one that is in the best interest of all involved.

Chapter 25

MORTGAGE LOAN WAREHOUSING

Clay S. Green
Senior Vice President
Coldwell Banker Residential Mortgage Services

INTRODUCTION

In its simplest form, mortgage loan warehousing is the process of temporarily financing funded mortgages prior to their delivery to a permanent investor. Such a facility is necessary because of the limited capital mortgage bankers maintain in relationship to their overall funding needs. While warehousing facilities vary dramatically in their terms and conditions, most are:

♦ *Short term*—Credit-line agreements generally allow loans to be warehoused for a maximum of 90 to 180 days, though actual warehouse time for an individual mortgage is usually much less.

♦ *Revolving lines of credit*—Because fundings increase and decrease in response to general market conditions, and nonsecurity payoffs are difficult to anticipate accurately, warehouse lines must have the capacity to expand and contract.

In a more generic sense, warehouse lending has an expanded definition that includes various other types of short-term lending needs. Many warehouse line agreements, in fact, provide "within-line alloca-

529

tions" that allow a specified portion of the total facility to be used for commercial paper backups, construction financing, foreclosure processing, principal and interest advances on modified pass-through securities, and general working capital needs. "Within-line allocations" are limited only by the imagination of the mortgage banker and its ability to successfully negotiate with its lenders.

Before examining the evolution of warehouse lending and then reviewing the alternative short-term financing vehicles available to mortgage bankers today, there is value in exploring some general borrowing considerations.

CHOOSING A WAREHOUSE BANK

Because of the capital-short nature of the mortgage banking industry, the selection of a warehouse bank is akin to selecting a long-term business partner. The decision should be made carefully and should include, at least, the following considerations:

◆ *Does the lender know the industry well?* Mortgage banking, from a commercial banker's perspective, is often a mystery. Teaching a loan officer the business is a time- and management-intensive endeavor. Teaching an unfamiliar credit committee (not to mention the lending officer's superiors) the business is sometimes impossible. Arguments can be made that dealing with an unknowing lender offers mortgage bankers a negotiating edge. While that may be true, the counter side of the argument is also true: things that should be simply and quickly done are delayed because the lender is uncomfortable due to its lack of industry knowledge.

◆ *Does the lender have a long-term commitment to the industry?* Uncommitted lenders have an uncanny propensity to exit the industry at time when mortgage bankers most need them. There are numerous banks throughout the country that have dealt with the mortgage banking industry through repeated boom and bust cycles. Such banks make the best warehouse lenders. They understand the industry. They are very unlikely to panic and force an early collateral liquidation in a rising interest rate environment.

◆ *Does the lender have a reputation for being reasonable?* For administrative ease and efficiency the flexibility of the lender is critical. Lenders whose actions and comments imply that they know everything there is to know about mortgage banking and mortgage warehousing are sometimes difficult to deal with because they tend to be inflexible. Such inflexibility can kill an otherwise attractive relationship. A mortgage banker will do well to reconsider lenders who display intransigence in early negotiating sessions.

♦ *Is the account officer you will deal with bright, knowledgeable, and well enough regarded within the bank to successfully fight for your company's proposals?* The account officer is the bank. A good account officer can compensate for a bank that is less than first-rate. A poor account officer can make even the best bank difficult to deal with. The account officer is an important link to a successful relationship.

♦ *Is the bank large enough to provide sufficient lines of credit?* Consider legal limits and house lending limits in the selection of a bank. While small banks can participate out portions of a mortgage banker's line to remain comfortably within their house limit, they generally deal with bankers that are of comparable size or smaller. Larger institutions are usually reluctant to deal with small bank as agents for participated credits. As a result, small banks tend to have a limited pool of funds available for warehouse lending.

♦ *How many banks do you want to deal with?* Although a group of banks can be brought into a single credit under a participation agreement or under a master loan agreement, such arrangements are generally difficult to administer. A single bank is usually adequate for the smaller mortgage company with limited borrowing needs. For lines of credit in excess of $8 million to $10 million, however, a mortgage company needs at least two banks to ensure that each provides aggressive pricing and reasonable terms and conditions. Three banks may be one too many. Banks, although solicitous in dealing with customers, are often acrimonious in their relations with each other. Accordingly, it is sometimes awkward to set up smoothly functioning multibank relationships in which one bank acts as the pool custodian. Difficulty frequently arises when two of the lenders must release their collateral to the custodian for pool certification. This difficulty is exacerbated when payoffs are directed to the custodian bank, which must then split the funds and remit them to the other banks. Independent lending agreements also make it administratively difficult to deal with numerous banks. The offsetting advantage offered by such agreements is the opportunity to work one bank against another to obtain concessions on pricing or other conditions for the warehouse line.

♦ *Does the bank provide quality custodial services at a reasonable price?* This should be a key consideration. One major mortgage banker confided in late 1987 that their lender's custodial functions were so chaotic that the bank could not locate thousands of documents that it had signed for, that it therefore could not certify pools, and that it could not positively identify the recipients of millions of dollars of payoffs.

♦ *What documents does the lender require to make advances on warehouse loans?* In most states the only required documents are the note, endorsed in blank, a certified copy of the mortgage or deed of trust, and an unrecorded corporate assignment. If a bank asks for more, it is probably asking for too much. Providing more than these documents raises a mortgage banker's administrative and borrowing costs. Remember that a bank's redundant paperwork has been built into its line pricing.

After a bank has been selected, the mortgage banker is ready to begin the line negotiation process. The lender-mortgage banker relationship is so important to the ongoing success of the mortgage company that pricing should be considered an important, but secondary consideration. The primary issues are the bank's commitment, size, flexibility, and ability to provide a broad spectrum of reasonably priced, efficient services.

KNOW YOUR COSTS, NEEDS, AND ALTERNATIVES

The first prerequisite to successful implementation of a profitable warehouse facility is knowledge. It is surprising how often otherwise sophisticated mortgage bankers approach their warehousing needs and alternatives with little or no preparation. The requisite preparation includes knowing what alternatives beyond standard warehouse lines are available, what variations to existing lines can reduce overall borrowing costs, what competitors are paying (or claim they are paying) for similar facilities, what competing banks are charging for comparable lines, and what one's specific warehousing needs and objectives are. The importance of warehouse line pricing to a mortgage banker's success is put in perspective when one considers that the single largest expense on a normal mortgage banker's profit and loss statement is interest. Interest expense, therefore, is a logical place to look for savings. The dollar impact on the profit and loss statement arising from warehouse line cost reductions is easy to calculate. Many mortgage bankers attempt to parlay such savings into even greater returns on equity by extending the length of time loans are held in warehouse. Such a strategy presumes an increase in an already positive spread and often meets with mixed success. If a company normally sells its loans as securities, the monthly drop in the forward or futures market rather closely approximates the positive carry on loans being warehoused. Whole loan deliveries to private investors under standby commitments can sometimes be extended to increase warehouse interest income. In a falling interest rate environment mortgage companies whose corporate policies allow the speculative holding of uncovered funded product in warehouse can increase their warehouse interest income by extending the carry period. However, such falling interest rate periods generally result in higher-than-normal production, requiring higher-than-normal warehouse lines, a situation that encourages rapid rather than delayed shipments of product to permanent investors. While the delaying strategy has some merit in certain markets, it is important to remember that a mortgage banker's primary business focus is to make, sell, and service loans. A prudent mortgage banker cannot ignore interest costs or savings opportunities, but he must remain firmly focused on the primary business objectives.

A corollary to knowledge of one's costs and alternatives is fully understanding and reviewing the monthly statements provided by the warehouse bank. The statement should be checked to ensure its mathematical integrity. Daily and average outstanding balances should also be checked for accuracy, as should the application dates of investor payoffs. Trust account statements need to be reconciled on a monthly basis. It is surprising how few mortgage banks religiously reconcile these statements. Such lapses are particularly noteworthy given the fiduciary responsibilities the mortgage company has for such funds. While statement reconciliations are important and should be performed as a matter of course, an even more important analysis is almost never performed except in the most perfunctory way: bank adjustments to impound balances and the application of an earnings credit to the resultant balances. The key elements that should be tracked and reviewed are float, reserve requirements, activity fees, and the earnings allowance factor used to convert free collected balances to an earnings credit. Although there is no simple way to estimate float other than through the use of historical comparisons, those comparisons offer a benchmark against which monthly statement float should be compared.

Any significant variations should be carefully examined. Reserve requirements, on the other hand, are relatively easy to check, as are activity fees. It should be remembered, however, that the vast majority of statement errors occur in the calculation of activity fees. Because of this it is important to carefully review these charges on a monthly basis.

The only real unknown in converting impound balances to an earnings equivalent is the earnings allowance formula. Conscientious mortgage bankers regularly review this calculation with their loan officers, who probably do not understand its derivation. If they do, they are probably precluded by bank policy from divulging it. There is a reason banks don't share this information with their customers, which will be more fully discussed in the following sections. Although understanding the derivation of the conversion factor will not markedly increase the value ascribed to balances, it offers a far superior method of estimating spendable balance equivalents than the blind faith usually applied to the conversion.

NEGOTIATE THE BEST TERMS POSSIBLE

The second prerequisite to an attractively priced warehouse facility is to negotiate for the best terms possible. Industry intelligence gathering is crucial to aggressive negotiations. Intensive courses are offered that teach successful negotiation techniques. While it is not the purpose of this chapter to explore those techniques in detail, a short digression may be helpful. Negotiate initial lines, line modifications, and renewals in your company's, not the bank's, offices. And negotiate them at your convenience rather than at your lending officer's convenience. Schedule meetings with out-of-town lenders on the last day of their trip as close to their departure time as possible. Tired, preoccupied negotiators are likely to give up an extra eighth rather than miss their cross-country flight. The aphorism that you should always leave something on the table for your negotiating adversary may not be applicable to bankers. When you negotiate with your banks, it is very likely that something has been carefully secured off the table long before the negotiations begin.

Along the continuum of negotiating strategies there are two extremes. The first is meekly accepting the proffered pricing. The other is arguing every term and condition and insisting that no matter where the lender starts, the ending price must be lower. The most consistently successful strategy lies somewhere between the extremes. Clearly, your negotiating strategy is influenced by your relationship with the lender, as well as by your mortgage company's capitalization and profitability.

A thinly capitalized start-up operation is going to be more solicitous and less aggressive than an established, successful company.

Both ends of the negotiating continuum present problems. If there are negotiating absolutes, one would be: never accept the first offer. The other end of the continuum is more problematic. Some borrowers feel that a negotiating session cannot be concluded without achieving a concession. Such victories are sometimes pyrrhic; bankers catch on quickly and, like car dealers, will simply start the negotiation at an artificially inflated level. One major West Coast banker approaches negotiating sessions with his must-have-a-concession customers in exactly this manner. He takes great delight in compromising to a reduced number that is almost always higher than what he would otherwise demand.

One essential aspect of any bank negotiation is to recognize that banks very infrequently volunteer pricing reductions. Accordingly, the first thing one must do is ask for a concession. In most cases it also makes sense to ask for something more than one is willing to settle for. And humor sometimes helps. A highly regarded industry negotiator maintains that he came of age as a negotiator quite by accident. He had facetiously asked his sophisticated money center banker for a clearly outrageous concession and held his laugh long enough to be stunned by the banker's acceptance of his proposal. The worst thing you risk in requesting a pricing or condition adjustment is a denial. A series of denials usually result in a concession since even bankers want to be perceived as reasonable.

A final comment: never lie to or mislead your banker. Keep him informed of business developments, particularly negative ones. A surprised banker, especially one who as a result of the surprise has been embarrassed in front of his peers or superiors, is not a strong ally. In a crisis period the assistance and support of one's banker might very well be the difference between corporate success and failure. An informed banker can become a valuable resource in devising and selling problem-solving strategies to the bank.

UTILIZATION OF IMPOUND BALANCES

Historically, mortgage bankers have first utilized their excess balances to offset activity fees. In addition, many have obtained accommodations with their line banks. For example, in return for a predetermined dollar amount of excess balances, some banks will cover the cost of certain services for which the mortgage banker would otherwise be charged. Such services include but are not limited to cash management/lock box expenses; trustee and custodial fees on GNMA and FNMA securities; trust department expenses for corporate trust services; and outside vendor fees. The payment of outside vendor fees for excess balances has come under increasing criticism and has been discontinued by the major money center warehouse lenders. While many savings and loans and smaller commercial banks continue to pay outside vendor fees, it is likely that even these lenders will someday discontinue the practice.

While it is axiomatic that some value is better than none, the trading of balances for bank fees is usually a one-sided transaction. When banks apply an earnings equivalent to impound balances to convert these balances to spendable dollars, the derivation of the earnings equivalent is made in accordance with an arcane, inexplicable formula that few within or without the banking industry fully understand. The conversion incorporates a markup that is equivalent to the bid-offer spread of a securities transaction. Two parts of this transaction are remarkable: first, few mortgage bankers understand the formula; second, the markup is almost unconscionable. The post-markup bank-determined dollar equivalents are then applied to fees for services that have already been priced to include a fair market profit. Accordingly, the financial institution receives not only its standard service fee markup (which it certainly is entitled to), but also a markup for the conversion of balances to earnings equivalents. Shrewd mortgage bankers generally try to avoid paying twice for the same service.

In the absence of precise mathematical models to quantify the multiple markups, a simple exercise can help put the lost dollars in perspective. Take a recent bank statement and determine the dollar cost of all account activity fees and all services that are now being paid for in balance equivalents. Take the total dollar amount of balances currently being used to pay for fees and services and charge yourself 1 1/2 percent to 2 percent to borrow them back. Use the borrowed-back balances to pay down bank lines. Determine gross savings by multiplying the warehouse borrowing rate times the dollar amount of borrowed-back balances used to pay down warehouse borrowings. Subtract from the gross savings the cost of borrowing back the balances. Compare the result to the dollar cost of fees and services currently being paid for with balances. The difference represents the multiple markups generated by the "black box" conversion formula. Most borrowers who try this exercise are more than surprised by the dollars that have regularly been left on the table.

Another common use that mortgage bankers make of their excess balances is to buy down their borrowing costs. While many buy-down arrangements offer the mortgage company an attractive borrowing rate, they are usually extraordinarily costly because of the inherent bias in the conversion formula. Historically, rate balance buy-downs were offered to mortgage companies only after the larger institutions began to demand value for their excess balances. Such a demand created an economic loss to the banks, which had previously enjoyed the full economic benefit of those balances. The various formulae that evolved to convert excess balances to rate buy-downs were heavily skewed in the banks' favor. Value was given to the mortgage companies, but significant value was also retained by the banks. Over the years, the formulae applied to the conversion of excess balances to rate buy-down equivalents have moved more to the borrowers' favor. However, until the formulae are clearly understood and fairly negotiated, the banks will retain a more than appropriate share of the economic benefit. Accordingly, while rate balance buy-downs offer a valuable use for excess balances, there are better ways to capture the benefits of excess balances.

A balance utilization strategy that is growing in popularity is the creation of a marketable securities facility. In some interest rate environments, marketable securities lines offer a more attractive use of excess balances than does the trade of such balances for the lender's payment of fees and services. Even the returns on aggressive buy-down programs are sometimes less attractive than those available through marketable securities lines. The process starts by borrowing back the excess balances at the 1-1/2 to 2 percent spread discussed above. The borrowed funds are then invested in predetermined categories of marketable securities, which can range from T-bills to commercial paper. The securities are held by the lender as collateral for the loan and the mortgage company picks up the spread between the 1-1/2 percent to 2 percent it pays for its borrowings and the return it receives on its investments. When short-term rates are relatively high, the strategy offers a very attractive use for excess balances.

A point should be made regarding the strategies discussed above. Impound balances belong to a multitude of mortgagors and cannot be directly converted to the benefit of the trustee. By leaving the trust balances on deposit with the warehouse bank and borrowing back an equivalent dollar amount, you are actually borrowing new dollars from your warehouse lender and can invest those funds any way you and your lender jointly determine is prudent. The trust balances remain on deposit with the commercial bank in trust for the benefit of the individual mortgagors or permanent investors.

The key elements in maximizing the available return on impound balances include:

◆ Reducing float on clearing items

◆ Reducing the reserve requirements on deposit balances

◆ Choosing the right use for excess balances

The traditional approach to reducing float on clearing items is to utilize a commercial bank's lock box services. Such services can be set up on a regional or national scale, depending on the geographic needs of the mortgage banker. Cash management specialists can present compelling statistical data to demonstrate the relative float reduction advantages inherent in their system vis-a-vis others. Many users have discovered, however, that the promised time savings exceed actual experience. As a consequence, some large users have established internal cash management systems using a mail address assigned a unique zip code, messengers to collect deliveries throughout the day, mail opening machines, and early morning part-time clerks to code and process payments. Collection float is reduced by maintaining deposit relationships with banks that have a dominant share of the deposit market. Each day checks are sorted, bundled, and deposited in mortgage company accounts in the banks on which the mortgagor has drawn his check, thus assuring immediately available funds. At the end of each day deposits are swept out of clearing banks into the appropriate master accounts. Such systems can be relatively simple and inexpensive to operate or they can be highly complex with multiple locations. Whatever the complexity, mortgage bankers have found that internal cash management systems sometimes offer a more timely collection of funds at a lower cost than competing bank systems. As mortgage companies work to maximize their available balances, an internal lock box system is an alternative that should be carefully explored.

The reduction of reserve requirements is a strategy that is often overlooked. Those who have found a way to do it have experienced a sometimes significant advantage over their less aggressive competitors. Reduction techniques run from the mundane to the truly creative. Most commercial banks are willing to explore the reserve requirement advantages of maintaining impound balances in zero percent certificates of deposit. The difficulty, of course, in such an arrangement is account management. CDs are usually established for specific amounts and predetermined periods, making it difficult to effectively or efficiently manage the normal increases and decreases in impound balances. The problems are not insurmountable, but they do create account management problems that require careful and regular cooperation between the commercial banks and the mortgage company.

A more attractive alternative is the placement of trust balances in commercial money market demand deposit accounts. Such accounts require the same 3 percent reserves as zero percent CDs, but create few of the operational difficulties associated with the latter instrument. Money market accounts severely limit the number of checks that can be drawn each month, but have no such limits on deposits or wire transfers to other demand deposit accounts.

A more creative approach to the use of impound balances utilized by a major west-coast mortgage company was adopted more or less intact from the Wall Street securities community. The strategy should not be confused with the illegal transaction that recently led to significant legal problems for a major New York dealer. The mortgage bank attacked the reserve requirement issue by creating a legal kite. The transaction was legal because the banks involved were fully aware of its existence, they were fully collateralized, and they had arranged backup lines of credit to retire the outstanding check in the event the transaction was terminated. In addition, legal opinions were obtained by counsel for the banks and for the mortgage company. The mortgage company's auditors (a top-tier accounting firm) also documented the transaction and signed off on it each year in the firm's audited statement. The benefit from a reserve requirement perspective was that the funds were considered "funds in collection" and required no reserve at all. In addition, the mortgage company obtained immediate and full access to the impound balances. In its simplest form the transaction worked as follows:

- On day one, the mortgage company deposited in Bank A a $60 million check drawn on Bank A. Bank B wired funds to the mortgage company.

- On day two, the mortgage company deposited in Bank B a $60 million check drawn on Bank A. Bank B wired funds to Bank A to cover the previous day's check, which was presented on day two for payment.

- On day three and everyday thereafter, the day-two transaction was repeated.

- To terminate the transaction, the mortgage company would cease delivering the check to Bank B and in lieu of Bank B's wire to Bank A, would deposit good funds into its Bank A account.

While the transaction described above may not be duplicable and may push the effort to reduce reserve requirements beyond where it should be pushed, it demonstrates the creativity and sophistication that can be brought to the balance utilization equation. The mortgage company coupled its utilization efforts with a prohibition against using balances to offset fees or to pay for services. All fees and services were paid in cash, leaving the full complement of impound balances for use in the reserve reduction effort.

There clearly is no right use for excess balances. There are uses, however, that capture greater value than others. Using balances to pay for activity and service fees is not one of the better uses. Balances can be utilized to reduce borrowing costs through formula buydowns. They can be reborrowed for a fee or spread and used to reduce warehouse line outstandings, or they can be directly invested. The key element of balance utilization is creativity and the continuous exploration of alternative uses.

An additional benefit of borrowing back impound balances is that it simplifies the borrowing relationship between the mortgage banker and its lender. By removing the incomprehensible conversion factor utilized to determine spendable equivalents and formula buydowns, it is far easier for the mortgage banker to determine what its true borrowing costs are. The borrowing back of balances also makes it easier to compare the alternative pricing arrangements offered by various warehouse lenders.

SHORT-TERM BANK LINES OF CREDIT

Because the majority of warehouse credit is provided by commercial banks and savings and loan associations, an examination of such facilities is a logical place to begin an evaluation of short-term financing alternatives. Fifteen years ago, bank-provided warehouse lines were strikingly similar. They provided a warehousing capacity for FHA/VA product and not much else. Many banks considered conventional loans too risky to be acceptable collateral. Mortgages could be held in warehouse for 90 to 180 days. Working capital facilities were almost unheard of. Allocations for foreclosed products were relatively rare. And few had considered utilizing borrowed funds to make GNMA advances. Most lenders required fully documented loan packages which made the administration of lines extremely cumbersome and expensive. Virtually all warehouse lenders priced off of their prime rate using either a multiple of prime or a prime-plus arrangement. Balances were typically required to compensate the lender for the committed line as well as for its utilization. A fairly common structure required balances to average 10 percent of the commitment amount plus 10 percent of the average outstandings. During this period mortgage bankers were surprisingly passive in their bank relationships. It was not at all unusual to see large mortgage companies maintain greater deposit balances than their average outstandings under a line. Surplus balances were simply relinquished to the banks.

Today's warehouse lines are far more complex and diverse than their mid-1970s counterparts and reflect the industry's wants and needs to a much greater extent. They are also more aggressively priced, reflecting not only the growing sophistication of mortgage bankers, but also the proliferation of alternative financing vehicles. In addition, new providers of credit (including well-capitalized, liquid mortgage companies and surviving savings and loans) have also entered the market. When some savings and loans began aggressively entering the arena, it appeared that start-up and small mortgage companies would be the primary beneficiaries. Large commercial banks have traditionally shunned the small end of the market, perceiving the risk to be greater and the reward, though higher, not commensurate with the increased risk. Savings and loans, attempting to gain a foothold in the industry, started by soliciting the relatively small mortgage companies. They nevertheless progressively increased their capitalization and minimum line requirements to the point that their requirements are very similar to those of commercial banks. In their defense, it is as costly, administratively, to manage a $1 million warehouse line as it is to manage a $10 million line. The risk is greater; and the return, though higher is not high enough to make the proposition attractive. An extra 0.5 percent on $1 million pales in comparison to the aggregate returns available on a $10 million line. Still, the entry of such lenders has forced existing lenders to become more aggressive and accommodative. This trend has been exacerbated by major mortgage companies that use the proceeds of their own commercial paper to provide lines to their competitors at prices that commercial banks find incomprehensible.

The minimum requirements for warehouse lines vary with the relative level of aggregate demand for such lines. During the 1986–87 boom market, warehouse lenders had a surfeit of commitments and outstandings and consequently tightened up their minimum requirements. By late 1987 those requirements had once again loosened. On average, banks are looking for mortgage companies with a net worth in the neighborhood of $1 million, a servicing portfolio of $100 million, and a minimum line requirement of $1.5 million to $10 million. Some money-center banks will extend credit only to those mortgage companies with line needs of $100 million and more. The alternatives for mortgage companies falling below the traditional minimums are few. If they can find a senior bank official to intercede, they should. The most probable source is a small bank or savings and loan just getting into the business or one that can be persuaded that it should get into the business.

Those trying to either convince a small bank or savings and loan to become a loan warehouser, or attempting to induce a large bank to adjust its minimum line size requirements, should argue that the small end of the market is the true growth area of the industry. Institutions restricting their lines to only the largest and most profitable mortgage companies will ultimately put themselves out of business as their most creditworthy borrowers move to more attractively priced alternative financing vehicles. Sometimes recalcitrant lenders will listen and make exceptions to their standard policy.

There are no standard warehouse lines today. Most good banks are flexible enough to meet their customers' short-term borrowing needs. Today's lines provide for funding and holding all types of residential and commercial properties prior to their delivery to permanent investors. Portions of the line can be utilized to fund construction loans the mortgage company is extending to its builder clients. Portions can be used to repurchase loans from mortgage-backed pools prior to and during the foreclosure process. Working capital needs, and principal and interest advances to modified pass-through noteholders, for example, are often met from borrowing allocations within a short-term warehousing facility. Even backup lines to support commercial paper issuances are sometimes included within the umbrella of a comprehensive warehouse line of credit. The commercial paper rating agencies are not terribly fond of such arrangements, but will concede to them if the mortgage company is well capitalized and the proper controls are in place. Each separate allocation is generally priced independently of the others to reflect the inherent differences in risk. Documentation requirements also reflect the various uses of the line.

Whereas it was once easy to compare the cost of lines offered by competing warehouse lenders, that comparison is now more complicated. Different lenders may evaluate comparable risk in a potential borrower, but structure significantly different pricing mechanisms. For example, three major lenders offered the following pricing alternatives to the same borrower:

- ♦ Bank A—Prime + ¼, with a 25 basis point commitment fee on the unused commitment. A balance pricing arrangement called for prime, 5 percent balances on the commitment amount, and the same 25 basis point commitment fee on the unused portion of the line.

♦ Bank B—The weekly average Fed Funds rate plus 175 basis points, with a 25 basis point commitment fee on the unused portion of the line.

♦ Bank C—175 basis points over a variety of borrower-selected indices (including an internal cost of funds index) with a 25 basis point commitment fee on the total line. The third alternative included the opportunity to fund against a daily floating index or for longer periods of time on a matched basis.

It is difficult to evaluate at a glance which is the more attractive pricing and which, over time, will provide the more aggressive rates. Alternative A is fairly clear-cut. The second bank's proposal is also relatively simple because it uses an easily tracked index. The third proposal is harder to evaluate because the primary index, the bank's internal cost of funds, is not a publicly reported number nor is it independent, in the sense that it cannot be artificially manipulated. Critics have argued for years that prime is also an artificially manipulated number, so the risk of relying on an internally derived, nonverifiable number may not be as great as it first appears. To compare the three alternatives, various indices need to be tracked against each other over time to gauge their relative sensitivity to changing market conditions. In a declining interest environment, which is more likely to move with general interest rates: prime, or the weekly average Fed Funds rate? The same comparisons need to be made to each of the available indices offered by Bank C. And, of course, the exercise should be performed using periods of stable, rising, and declining interest rates. The commitment fee on the unused portion of the line can become very expensive during periods of minimal utilization. If such periods are expected to be lengthy, it is sometimes wise to reduce the company's line size. Except in very rare circumstances, banks will be willing to increase the facility as needs once again grow. To guard against being crowded out of critical line expansions in a hot market, mortgage companies should anticipate their requirements and provide their lenders with reasonable lead time.

Because the various indices offered by Bank C perform differently in different interest environments, they offer mortgage bankers tremendous flexibility in hedging their warehouse borrowings against interest rate fluctuations. If you perceive rates are declining, you may choose to move into the shortest maturity index available. If rates are rising, you can stretch out to a longer-term index. Such flexibility comes at a price: the line must be much more intensively managed than a more traditional warehouse line. Matched fundings must be coordinated with investor deliveries and payoffs. Many of the same challenges arise that face the issuers of commercial paper. The mortgage banker must ask: Is it more cost-effective to shorten maturities and increase administrative expenses? How many different indices can be effectively managed at the same time? So long as the bank considers cash acceptable collateral to secure its advances, no major crisis will arise from poorly anticipated investor payoffs. Such lapses, however, are expensive.

GESTATION REPOS

The gestation repo is a variation on the standard warehouse line and is offered by numerous securities dealers and, surprisingly, by a number of banks. The gestation period, the time from a mortgaged-backed security pool's certification by the custodian until the actual security certificate is issued, is perceived by many to be a period of decreased lender risk in comparison to the risks of warehousing whole loans. In response to this decreased risk, some dealers are willing to assume the warehouse bank's position at reduced rates for the 14- to 21-day gestation period. Since it nearly always makes sense to reduce borrowing costs, gestation repos constitute a financing vehicle that should be explored.

Gestation repos make the most sense when provided by the dealer that contracted the ultimate sale. They also make sense if provided by the mortgage banker's warehouse lender. To attempt to transfer the collateral rights of an as yet unformed security to another broker-dealer or to an outside commercial bank sometimes creates administrative and operational headaches that may outweigh the cost savings. Those cost savings can be sizeable but are relative to the underlying cost of the mortgage banker's warehouse line. Gestation repos are usually priced to provide a yield slightly greater than that required on a standard securities repo. Some banks are aggressively offering gestation repo facilities, no doubt as a means of securing more lucrative ongoing relationships. Many banks, on the other hand, find the concept incongruous, arguing that the risk does not decrease during the gestation period but rather increases because the bank gives up its collateral interest in the underlying mortgages, thus making its secured line unsecured. Gestation repos are available. If they offer a mortgage banker a workable alternative, they should be evaluated for inclusion in the mortgage banker's bag of financing options.

REPURCHASE AGREEMENTS

Repurchase agreements provide a cost-effective method of holding mortgage-backed securities prior to their sale to investors. Most warehouse lenders allow traditional warehouse lines to be collateralized with mortgage-backed securities as well as with individual mortgages. Generally, such arrangements ignore the increased liquidity of the securitized collateral and apply the same warehouse pricing used for whole loans. Securities dealers willingly repo securities for 30 to 180 days at a sizeable cost advantage to most warehouse facilities. Repurchase agreements are relatively simple to initiate and involve the delivery of the security to the dealer with an agreement to repurchase it at a specified date. Upon receipt of the security, the dealer wires the haircut proceeds to the mortgage company, which in turn pays down its warehouse outstandings.

The process is not terribly complex if it is initiated with the dealer through which ultimate disposition of the security has been arranged. In such cases, the repurchase can be done simultaneously with the sale to the investor. When one is repoing with the dealer handling the security's ultimate sale, the haircut should approach very closely the discount on sale. When a security is repoed with a dealer other than the one arranging ultimate disposition, the process becomes more complex because the security must be repurchased and redelivered to the second dealer. Depending on the time frame involved, such redelivery may necessitate a temporary rewarehousing to provide funds to honor the repurchase commitment.

Securities put on repo are usually those that have already been sold or are being held in portfolio on an investment basis. Unsold securities being held for sale can be repoed, but the cost benefits may not outweigh the complexities created in the securities sale. Such repurchase arrangements would probably be entered into for very short periods of time to ensure marketing flexibility and the capacity to respond quickly to changing market conditions.

While repurchase agreements can reduce warehousing costs, they are simply one additional instrument in an array of financing alternatives. They will never be a primary source of funding one's warehouse, but used judiciously in concert with other instruments and financing techniques can have a sizeable impact on financing costs.

COMMERCIAL PAPER ALTERNATIVES

Commercial paper, the financing alternative of choice for major mortgage companies, takes a number of different forms. The least attractive form involves the issuance of documented discount notes (DDNs). While DDNs are technically differentiated from traditional commercial paper issuances because of their attached letters of credit, they are similar enough to be grouped with the other forms. The next rung on an ascending ladder of sophistication and general attractiveness is commercial paper backed by direct- or indirect-pay letters of credit. A derivative of letter of credit backed programs, surety bond backed commercial paper is ranked above traditional letter of credit programs because of the potential cost savings. The next level is mortgage backed notes and collateral trust notes. The highest and most attractive level is unsecured commercial paper. Unsecured paper is restricted to only the largest, most creditworthy mortgage companies, or to those that are subsidiaries of major corporations. In the latter case, the parent may simply issue its own paper and downstream the proceeds to the subsidiary.

Commercial paper is generally considered to be a more attractive financing alternative than bank lines for a number of reasons:

♦ It is almost always less expensive than a bank-provided warehouse line.

♦ It does not require compensating balances, allowing mortgage companies to directly capture the value of those balances. (See Utilization of Impound Balances.)

♦ The commercial paper market is massive, allowing a mortgage company to utilize a single source for its entire warehousing needs. Few banks by themselves can provide $250 million to $300 million warehouse lines; the commercial paper market can absorb such needs with little notice. Part of the single-source advantage is that it allows the use of a single collateral agent with uniform documentation requirements. Such administrative advantages help to offset the administrative disadvantages outlined below.

While the price advantage of commercial paper provides a compelling argument for its use, there are disadvantages that prospective issuers should carefully consider:

♦ With all commercial paper derivatives, other than documented discount notes and other letter of credit based programs, the upfront costs of establishing a program can be enormous. Those costs relate primarily to the legal issues involving the fiduciary responsibilities of the collateral custodian and the trustee, as well as the affirmative obligations and responsibilities of the issuer. Opinions must also be obtained on behalf of the issuing agent and the rating agencies. The process can become extraordinarily complex, time-consuming, and expensive. Startup expenses can easily mount to the $500,000 to $750,000 range. One major mortgage company exploring its commercial paper opportunities found itself in simultaneous negotiations with twelve different entities, each represented by one or more attorneys.

♦ Administrative costs are generally higher than those of comparable bank lines because issuances are of various maturities and must be carefully planned, monitored, and coordinated with the sale and disposition of the underlying asset. Large commercial paper outstandings generally require daily redemptions and issuances, a process that must be managed by well-trained, relatively senior financial staffers.

♦ Commercial paper is a less reliable financing mechanism in turbulent markets than the bank lines it generally replaces. On occasions, the commercial paper market has dried up, forcing issuers to rely on corporate liquidity and backup lines to fund maturing paper. While such a contraction has not occurred during the past few years, the risk is nevertheless there. It is because of this risk that many argue that mortgage bankers should always maintain active bank relationships. The issue is probably moot. Commercial paper issuers in all but the most unusual programs maintain ongoing bank relationships in the form of letters of credit or commercial paper backup lines. If the commercial paper market dries up, for any reason, redemptions will be made through a preexistent bank facility. Banks are anxious to increase their penetration among the largest mortgage companies. If these companies are crowded out of the commercial paper market, they will be quickly embraced by commercial banks. If commitment availability forces anyone out of commercial banks during a period of extreme financial turbulence, it will more likely be the small mortgage companies than the large ones.

♦ Commercial paper issuers can be forced out of the market by exogenous factors beyond their control. Many issuers of mortgage-backed notes and collateral trust notes were forced out of the market in late 1979 and early 1980 when the rating agencies downgraded the ratings of virtually all mortgage banks. The proximate cause of the downgrading, significant speculative losses by a commercial paper issuer, had no bearing whatsoever on the quality of other issuers. The rating agencies, nervous by nature, felt otherwise and by their action pushed most mortgage bankers back into their commercial bank line relationships.

♦ After an institution issues commercial paper, it must remain in the market. Commercial paper purchasers are creatures of habit. Once they purchase a particular issuer's paper, they generally continue to buy it. The challenge, of course, is inducing the first purchase. Buyers are usually enticed by slightly higher rates. Accordingly, it is relatively more expensive to start a new program than it is to maintain it after purchasers have become comfortable with the paper. An issuer that goes out of the market loses its traditional buyers and to re-enter must usually convince a whole set of new buyers of the attractiveness of its paper.

♦ Commercial paper programs are constrained in scope by the governing documents and by the influence on those agreements by the rating agencies. The rating agencies' primary concerns are the timely redemption of maturing paper and the protection of the noteholder, particularly in the case of default. Accordingly, the agencies exert an inordinate influence in defining what is acceptable collateral. The definition is typically far more restrictive than what commercial banks are willing to include in their collateral base, thus affording mortgage bankers less flexibility than they are accustomed to. The agencies usually restrict acceptable collateral to current government and conventional first mortgage loans on one- to four-family properties. Nonconforming product and conforming adjustable-rate loans and their graduated payment variants are excluded from the acceptable collateral base.

DOCUMENTED DISCOUNT NOTES

Documented discount notes (DDNs) share many of the characteristics of commercial paper, but offer the smaller mortgage companies an opportunity to approach commercial paper yields without the substantial legal, rating, and issuance expenses associated with traditional commercial paper. A mortgage banker wanting to access this market must start by finding a commercial bank, usually a regional, that will create and issue the notes. Notes up to the amount of the eligible collateral, which usually consist of warehoused loans, are created by the bank. While DDNs are secured by mortgage loans in warehouse, they are issued in concert with the issuing bank's letters of credit. The purchasers of the notes look to the issuing bank and its letters of credit for repayment. The bank, in turn, is willing to issue the letters of credit because it is collateralized by the unencumbered mortgages it is holding in the mortgage company's warehouse facility. Proceeds of the paper are used to pay down warehouse borrowings. When the notes mature, they can be paid off by the proceeds of investor purchases of the underlying collateral, by corporate cash, or they may simply be rolled over by selling additional DDNs and using the proceeds of the new notes to redeem maturing notes.

Beyond the fact that DDNs do not require a rating by the rating agencies (although such a rating would enhance liquidity and price), the primary differences between commercial paper and DDNs are in their issuance and sale. DDNs, in contrast to commercial paper, are issued by and are the corporate responsibility of the bank rather than of the mortgage company. They are usually sold by the bank rather than by an independent dealer. This can be costly because even a major regional bank's access to buyers is usually limited. Accordingly, DDNs are usually marketed on a regional rather than a national basis. In addition, the selling institution's primary customers are usually looking for higher yields than are investors in Standard & Poors A-1, and Moodys P-1 rated commercial paper sold by Wall Street investment bankers. Accordingly, the DDN market is less liquid and more costly than the commercial paper market. Nevertheless, the savings over a standard warehouse line can be substantial, although this may not always be the case. One major regional bank prices paper to the mortgage company not at the issuance price but at half the difference between the issuance rate and the warehouse rate. If, for example, a mortgage banker were paying 9 percent for its warehouse borrowings, and DDNs were issued at 7.25 percent, the bank would charge the mortgage bank 8.125 percent for its outstanding DDNs. While that is 7/8 percent less expensive than the warehouse line, it represents a rather sizeable issuance fee and is one of the reasons DDNs are less attractive than letter of credit backed commercial paper.

As with most commercial paper transactions, DDNs are issued at a discount. The only significant impact of a discount issuance is that in establishing maturity dates the mortgage banker must carefully consider not only the discount, but also the selling expenses. Issuance costs are fixed whether the paper is sold for one day or forty five. Since such costs are added to the total discount to arrive at an all-in borrowing cost, issuance costs can have a significant impact on shorter-term maturities. For example, if it costs $600 in selling expenses to issue $3 million of commercial paper, the effective rate for a one-day issuance at a discount of 6.85 percent would be 14.15 percent. If that same selling expense is added to the 6.98 percent discount required for a forty-five-day transaction, the effective cost is only 7.14 percent. While there are sometimes compelling reasons for very short term issuances, commercial paper generally is not cost-effective versus standard warehouse lines if it is issued for less than four- or five-day periods. Because of these considerations, as well as the need to carefully plan maturities to achieve an acceptable balance between pricing, maturity dates, investor payoffs, and available collateral, the administrative expenses associated with commercial paper are often significantly higher than the administrative costs of comparable warehouse lines. This does not suggest that commercial paper should be ruled out, but rather that it is not always appropriate. As with any short-term borrowing facility, borrowers must carefully evaluate their costs, both direct and indirect, to determine the most attractive alternative.

LETTER OF CREDIT BACKED COMMERCIAL PAPER

The primary differences between a DDN program and a letter of credit backed (LC) commercial paper program are:

- ◆ LC backed programs usually trade at a significant price advantage to DDNs because they are rated, they are traded in a national market, and they are aggressively promoted and sold by an investment banker.

- ◆ LC programs involve an investment banker and an independent issuing, paying, and authenticating agent.

- ◆ LC programs are usually larger than DDN programs.

Under an LC backed program the commercial paper is issued through an investment banker. Each commercial paper note carries with it an irrevocable LC for the amount of the note. Should the issuer default, the noteholder would present the LC to the issuing bank and demand payment. The bank would then seize and sell the mortgage collateral backing the notes to recoup its LC advances. The LCs backing such paper can be submerged or nonsubmerged, indirect or direct. Normal redemption of notes backed by an indirect LC would involve presentation of the note to the paying agent, which would redeem the note from funds placed on deposit by the issuer specifically for that purpose. The indirect LC would be allowed to expire. Paper backed by direct pay LC would be redeemed in a similar manner, except that the paying agent would present the LCs to the issuing bank for payment. The bank would then charge the issuer's redemption account for the funds advanced. From the noteholder's perspective there is little difference between a direct or indirect pay LC. From the issuer's perspective, however, there is a significant difference. Commercial paper backed by indirect LCs, because of bankruptcy law and the issue of preferential payment of trade debt, is limited to a maximum term of 45 days. Under direct pay LC programs the bank becomes the obligor as the issuer of the paper, thus removing the 45-day constraint. Such paper can be issued for up to 270 days.

Since the rating of the commercial paper is a major determinant of its price, and the rating dependent upon the creditworthiness of the bank issuing the LC, the selection of the LC bank should be made very carefully. While domestic banks have traditionally supported LC commercial paper programs, many of those banks are beginning to argue that by using their credit rating to allow others access to the commercial paper market, they are artificially restricting their own access to these markets and are also increasing the cost of that access. There is some merit to their concern. And the argument has led many to reevaluate their willingness to lend their credit rating for the price of a LC. Fortunately, the domestic banks' reticence has been offset by the entry of many well-managed foreign banks with excellent credit ratings whose LCs are sufficient to secure the rating agencies' highest rating. A concomitant benefit of the entry of foreign banks is that they are generally easier to deal with in LC matters than are domestic banks.

A typical LC backed commercial paper transaction would involve the following steps:

- The mortgage banker instructs the investment banker to sell $10 million of commercial paper.

- Concurrently with the instructions to the investment banker, the mortgage company notifies the bank issuing the LCs that $10 million of LCs will be needed for the pending sale.

♦ The investment banker sells the paper and notifies the issuer of the maturities, dollar amount at each maturity, the discount, and the number of notes to be issued.

♦ The issuer checks the details provided by the investment banker and transmits the information to the LC bank.

♦ The LC bank instructs the authenticating agent to cut the notes.

♦ The notes are delivered to the investment banker.

♦ The proceeds of the sale are wired to the issuer for the pay-down of warehouse lines or for the reimbursement of advances previously wired by the mortgage banker for the redemption of maturing notes.

The advantages of LC backed programs over others include the fact that they are relatively easy to arrange. The rating process is rather perfunctory and thus relatively inexpensive because the agencies are issuing their rating primarily on the basis of the strength of the bank issuing the LC. An LC program is reasonably easy to monitor and control versus the administrative complexities of a CTN or MBN program. Because of the creditworthiness of the bank issuing the LC, LC backed issues are usually well received and achieve excellent pricing and market penetration. The cost of establishing such a program is somewhat greater than that of a DDN, but considerably less than for a collateral trust note, mortgage-backed note, or unsecured programs.

The disadvantages of LC backed programs are relatively limited. They include the 45-day limitation on indirect pay programs and the cost of the individual LCs. This cost can vary dramatically from bank to bank, but generally ranges from 12.5 to 50.0 basis points.

Because the noteholder has the right to redeem the paper after the actual maturity date (even though there is no reason to delay the redemption since no interest is paid past maturity) the rating agencies insist that the LC remain valid beyond the actual maturity date. The extension normally runs 15 days. Consequently, the term of the underlying LCs includes not only the days the paper is outstanding, but 15 days beyond maturity. Like the selling costs discussed earlier, the additional 15 days that are added to each maturity make very short term issuances unacceptably expensive.

SURETY BOND BACKED COMMERCIAL PAPER

A variation on LC backed commercial paper, which has been successfully used by a major home builder and at least two mortgage companies, is commercial paper backed by surety bonds. The concept is almost
identical to that of using LCs, but the implementation is somewhat more
difficult and offers an entirely different set of challenges. The primary
advantage over a traditional LC program is cost. A properly structured
surety backed facility derives its cost advantage from the elimination
of the LC fee in combination with the elimination of backup lines of
credit. One major mortgage company that discontinued its very successful LC backed paper in favor of a surety bond program estimated
a first-year reduction in borrowing costs of nearly 30 basis points, and
that savings was realized by a company that had been paying only $\frac{1}{8}$
percent for its letters of credit under the discontinued program.

A surety program, depending on the conditions prescribed by the
rating agencies and the provider of the surety bond, can also offer
operational advantages. Some facilities allow the mortgage company
to hold the mortgage collateral in trust for the commercial paper note
holder and the bonding company. Others require the more traditional
and expensive use of an independent collateral custodian.

Surety backed commercial paper programs are more difficult to
arrange than LC facilities because they are relatively uncommon, thus
requiring the creation, almost from scratch, of all of the program agreements and documents. There is no existing universe of agreements that
can simply be appropriated for a new program. In addition, insurance
companies are generally unfamiliar with mortgage banking and mortgage loan warehousing, making the educational process difficult, expensive, and sometimes impossible. One frustrated mortgage banker,
after completing seemingly endless rounds of negotiations with attorneys who did not understand mortgage banking and had little appreciation for the surety concept, expressed his dismay in a letter to an
attorney providing one of the required opinions. He apologized for the
sloppy drafting of the controlling documents, and then dryly observed
that he would have been embarrassed to sign the agreement had it not
been so loosely drafted that it allowed him to do whatever he wanted.

Just as an LC program relies on the credit rating of the LC bank,
a surety facility rests on the credit rating of the insurance company
providing the surety bond. That simplifies the rating process and in the
case of at least one mortgage company secured an attractive Moodys

rating for the facility. The downside is that the rating can be only as good as the provider of the surety bond. Unfortunately, many of the largest and best domestic insurance companies have shown little interest in writing this business. The relative anonymity of surety programs is due in part to the exit of one of the early and active proponents of the concept. That exit was caused not by an inherent deficiency in existing programs or in the pricing of those programs, but rather by an unrelated credit downgrading of the insurer, which made it impossible to secure acceptable program ratings using the company's surety bond.

The concept has merit. It has worked effectively in the past for mortgage companies and is actively used today by a number of companies engaging in related mortgage banking activities. It is an alternative that should be explored by an aggressive mortgage company looking for more cost-effective ways of meeting short-term borrowing needs. And just as the issuers of LC backed commercial paper have begun looking to foreign banks for their LCs, so should those investigating surety backed paper consider foreign insurance companies as a source for the underlying surety bond.

MBN AND CTN PROGRAMS

Mortgage-backed note (MBN) and collateral trust note (CTN) programs vary significantly from the DDN, LC, and surety programs discussed above. MBNs and CTNs, designations for nearly identical programs, are issued without supporting LCs. To ensure the salability of the notes, as well as the protection of the noteholders, a relatively large number of entities become involved in an MBN program. In addition to the mortgage company, the players include the warehouse bank, which acts as the collateral custodian. The independent trustee exercises a fiduciary responsibility by opining on the compliance of all indenture covenants prior to authorizing the first and subsequent commercial paper issuances. The rating agencies play a significant role in the creation of the MBN indenture, in its review, and in on-going reviews of the corporation's financial performance. The importance of the rating agencies cannot be underestimated. Only their highest rating will allow the MBN issuance to trade at a price advantage to letter of credit backed paper. The other key participants in an MBN transaction include the issuing and paying agent, the investment banker, and, of course, the ultimate investor.

The creditworthiness of the MBN note is provided by the security interest in collateral held by or on behalf of the trustee. The master document supporting the program is the indenture, which defines and restricts eligible collateral; acceptable takeout commitments; overcollateralization, which can run as high as 5 percent; the frequency of collateral valuation (usually weekly); the events making eligible collateral ineligible, which usually include but are not limited to age, default, and expiration of the underlying takeout commitments; the lack of timely insurance or guarantee of government loans. The indenture also defines the conditions precedent to issuance, which include but are not limited to sufficient eligible collateral, sufficient unused lines of credit, minimum net worth, minimum working capital, and minimum liquidity ratios.

Because of the creditworthiness tests and controls, MBN programs are expensive to start and to administer. The indenture is often measured in weight rather than pages, and a multiplicity of attorneys have opined, grudgingly, on each term and condition of the document. To justify the cost of an MBN program, an issuer must consistently maintain a minimum of $200 to $250 million of notes outstanding. As collateral is shipped and paid off, new eligible collateral must be available for substitution. Maturing notes are generally rolled over into new issuances.

MBN programs expanded rapidly during the late 1970s. When a number of mortgage bankers were hammered by speculative losses in 1979, the rating agencies became concerned about the overall quality and safety of all MBN programs. While one speculator that ultimately filed for bankruptcy was an MBN issuer, the indenture was so well constructed and the trustee so well managed that the outstanding notes were retired without delay or incident of any kind. Issuers felt the MBN concept had withstood the harshest test possible. The rating agencies, however, felt otherwise. In late 1979 and early 1980, issuers were notified that their ratings were being downgraded. Issuers were given the opportunity to restructure their programs to reflect changes in bankruptcy law but the highest rating available appeared to be an A-2. Most issuers chose to pursue other financing alternatives, reasoning that the A-2 rating provided an insufficient price advantage to LC-backed programs to justify the program's administrative complexities.

While complex and expensive to set up, the MBN mechanism provided a workable commercial paper alternative for large mortgage companies. Although still in use, MBN programs have lost much of their luster and attractiveness because of the rating issues discussed above and because of the availability of other commercial paper alternatives.

THE MBN TRUST

A variation on the MBN programs, the MBN Trust, was designed to avoid the 45-day maturity limit imposed on LC backed paper and to allow small mortgage bankers to obtain the benefits of the commercial paper market. In such a program, a fiduciary trust is formed to borrow funds through the issuance of its secured commercial paper notes (MBNs). The trust in turn lends the borrowed funds to mortgage bankers participating in the program. The trust receives trust notes from the participating mortgage companies evidencing their debt. Liquidity is ensured by irrevocable purchase commitments from the program participants' major banks. At maturity, the program banks purchase the trust notes from the trust. The trust then utilizes the proceeds to repay maturing notes.

The list of participants and their interaction in an MBN Trust is almost incomprehensible. In addition to all of the participants in a standard MBN program, the MBN Trust involves program banks as well as a multitude of Trust functions (and functionaries), which require daily and weekly reports on every aspect of the program. It is because of these complexities and their associated costs that the MBN Trusts only infrequently provided attractive financing alternatives. The concept was remarkable. It allowed the issuance of paper for up to 90 days. And in theory it allowed even small mortgage companies into the commercial paper market. But the mechanics were cumbersome, and the operating and reporting costs were extraordinarily high. In addition to the normal costs of a commercial paper program, the Trust extracted an override on a participant's relative share of the Trust's total outstanding paper, and in one program even coerced participants to accept unneeded backup lines from the Trust's sponsoring bank.

Because of the costs and operating complexities, most participants retreated to the less arcane LC-backed programs. The MBN Trust concept still has merit. When it is put together properly, it may become an attractive financing alternative. Today it is not.

UNSECURED COMMERCIAL PAPER

Unsecured commercial paper is restricted to only the largest and most creditworthy mortgage bankers. It is a balance sheet instrument in the sense that only well-capitalized, low-leveraged, profitable institutions are able to access the market. Mortgage bankers start at an inherent disadvantage because of their generally high leverage; they compete in this market against well-run, lower-leveraged industrial companies. For unsecured paper to achieve a sizeable cost advantage over its LC-backed counterpart, requires a Standard & Poors A-1 and a Moodys P-1. Through the years, Moodys has been reluctant to rate mortgage companies unless there is a compelling reason to do so. Exceptions have been made in cases where substantial parent companies have instituted convoluted puts in which maturing paper is retired from the proceeds of strictly defined mortgage company assets that are put to the parent. Exceptions have also been made in response to acceptable comfort letters from reputable parents. The process of extracting a P-1 is neither simple nor inexpensive. The rating process can take an inordinate amount of time.

In unsecured commercial paper programs, the commercial paper note itself is not collateralized. Most programs, however, require 100 percent backup lines and many banks require that the backup lines be fully collateralized. The primary benefit of unsecured commercial paper is expense. In comparison to LC programs, the issuer saves the 12.5 to 50 basis point cost of the LC. In addition, with P-1, A-1 ratings, unsecured paper will probably trade through rated LC backed paper by five or more basis points. Straight backup lines can generally be arranged for a fee that is somewhat less than the cost of the warehouse lines that serve an equivalent function for LC programs. Further, there are administrative savings. Issuers required to collateralize their backup lines with mortgages may not have to actually place the collateral with the backup line bank. Maintaining control of the collateral reduces operational expenses and simplifies custodial procedures. Surprisingly, a nonfinancial inducement—that sometimes plays a significant role in a mortgage company's decision to issue unsecured commercial paper—is status. Mortgage bankers able to tap the commercial paper market with unsecured paper achieve an industry prominence reserved for the very few. The disadvantages of unsecured programs are few beyond the initial startup costs. To justify an unsecured program the issuer must always be in the market. Management expenses associated with monitoring outstandings and carefully controlling maturities and redemptions are a small cost for the advantages such programs offer.

CONCLUSION

While the key elements of a successful, cost-effective financing facility are relatively simple, the actual process of reducing costs is frustratingly difficult. It requires a consistent, dedicated effort. There is no place for complacency. Nor can one be dissuaded by those who claim the sought-after changes or cost reduction efforts are impossible. Creativity is a must. Existing facilities should be regularly examined to isolate borrowing allocations that can be more aggressively priced. New financing mechanisms should be carefully explored. Mortgage bankers must continually ask not only for pricing concessions, but for greater administrative efficiencies as well. A mortgage banker's lender and its investment banker should be two of its greatest allies, and both should help it to explore new alternatives.

Interest expense is such a massive component of a mortgage company's overall expenses that it offers an inviting though somewhat elusive target. That target should be kept clearly in sight.

Index